100 KNITS

INTERWEAVE'S ULTIMATE PATTERN COLLECTION

THE EDITORS AT ▦ INTERWEAVE

a content + ecommerce company

fwcommunity.com

interweave.com

22 21 20 19   5 4 3 2

E-mail: enquiries@fwmedia.com | SRN: 18KN04 | ISBN-13: 978-1-63250-647-4

Editorial Director: Kerry Bogert | **Editors:** Kerry Bogert, Jodi Butler, Hayley DeBerard, Maya Elson
Art Direction & Cover Design: Ashlee Wadeson | **Interior Designer:** Pamela Norman | **Beauty Photographers:** Good Folk,
Joe Hancock, Chris Hartlove, Ken Frantz, Harper Point Photography, Donald Scott, Julia Vandenoever, Carmel Zucker

contents

introduction

SINCE THE fall of 1996, Interweave has worked to provide you—our dear reader—with the best knitting patterns we can find to inspire your needles. Our editors work tirelessly to find talented designers, unique techniques, and the next great trend to keep you stitching. We love releasing new publications to the knitting community and watching which projects stand out as your favorites.

In your hands you're holding 100 of the most-loved patterns from recent issues of *Interweave Knits*, *knitscene*, special holiday issues, and Interweave Books. Using your input as knitters to guide our project selections, we chose patterns that had you, and many others, clicking the "like" button over and over again. While you may have stitched a project or two you see in these pages, we're confident you're going to find many more you can't resist casting-on.

We've divided the book into sections based on project types. To start, enjoy browsing simple accessories such as hats and socks. Cowls, scarves, and shawls of varying techniques and difficulty level follow those quicker knits. If you're like so many other Interweave fans, your favorite sections will be the cardigans and pullovers. They're the heftiest chapters with dozens of projects each. In every magazine issue and book of patterns, it was always the cardigans and pullovers

that are loved most. We'll finish with tanks and tees, those lighter projects that keep your needles as entertained in the summer as in the winter.

Along with recent must-knits, we've also included the top 5 most-knitted Interweave patterns of all time in this collection. At the time of this publication, the Dahlia cardigan by Heather Zoppetti has been logged in Ravelry more than 1,500 times, the Lucy hat by Carina Spencer comes in with more than 2,400 projects, and the Central Park Hoodie by Heather Lodinsky has been posted more than 5,200 times. If those aren't impressive enough numbers, the Koolhaus hat by Jared Flood has been knit by more than 9,000 other knitters and Evelyn A. Clark's Swallowtail shawl has more than 12,000 FOs out there.

Whether you're a knitter who can't resist cables, who lusts after lace, or someone who sticks to stockinette, we know you're going to find more patterns in this collection than can be knit in a lifetime. Though, it's certainly worth a try! Cast-on a new knit today; you won't be disappointed.

Kerry Bogart

Knitter and Editorial Director, Books

curie hat

Amy Christoffers

Finished Size

Brim circumference: 17".

Height: 10".

Yarn

Worsted weight (#4 medium).

Shown here: Lang Yarns Donegal (100% wool; 208 yd [190 m]/50 g): #0067 dark brown (MC), #0099 light brown (A), #0064 burgundy (B), and #0011 yellow (C), 1 skein each.

Needles

Size U.S. 4 (3.5 mm): 16" circular (cir) and set of double-pointed (dpn).

Adjust needle size if necessary to obtain the correct gauge.

Notions

Marker (m); tapestry needle.

Gauge

26 sts and 28 rnds = 4" in charted patt.

COLORWORK

47
45
43
41
39
37
35
33
31
29
27
25
23
21
19
17
15
13
11
9
7
5
3
1

20-st dec'd to 4-st rep

	with MC, knit
	with A, knit
	with B, knit
	with C, knit

	with MC, sl 2 as if to k2tog, k1, p2sso–2 sts dec'd
	with B, sl 2 as if to k2tog, k1, p2sso–2 sts dec'd
	pattern repeat

Band

With MC and cir needle, CO 110 sts. Place marker (pm) and join in the rnd.

Work in k1, p1 rib for 3".

Next rnd: [K10, M1] 10 times, k10—120 sts.

Work Rnds 1-48 of Colorwork chart, changing to dpn when necessary—24 sts rem.

Next rnd: [K2tog] 12 times—12 sts rem.

Break yarns and draw tails through rem sts. Pull tight to gather sts and fasten off on WS.

Finishing

Weave in ends.

Block to measurements.

boreal toque

Andrea Rangel

Finished Size

Head circumference: about 20¼ (21, 22)".

Length: about 7½ (7¾, 8¼)".

Toque A shown on woman measures 21" head circumference.

Toque B shown on man measures 22" head circumference.

Yarn

Sock weight (#1 super fine).

Main Color (MC): 130 (140, 150) yds.

Contrast Color (CC): 39 (50, 60) yds.

Shown here: Brooklyn Tweed Loft (100% Targhee-Columbia wool; 275 yd [251 m]/50 g): colors for Toque A: old world (MC), snowbound (CC), 1 skein each; Toque B: pumpernickel (MC), hayloft (CC), 1 skein each.

Needles

Size U.S. 3 (3.25 mm): 16" circular (cir) and set of 4 or 5 double-pointed (dpn).

Size U.S. 5 (3.75 mm): 16" cir.

Adjust needle size if necessary to obtain the correct gauge.

Notions

Markers (m); tapestry needle.

Gauge

25 sts and 36 sts = 4" over St st using smaller needle.

25 sts and 31 sts = 4" over color chart using larger needle.

Notes

▪ Hat is worked in the round from the bottom up with square crown shaping. Many knitters work more tightly in stranded colorwork than in plain stockinette, so I recommend using a needle two sizes larger than the needle used for ribbing and plain stockinette. Be sure to swatch in both plain stockinette and the color chart to see what needle sizes are appropriate for you.

Brim

With smaller cir needle and MC, CO 126 (132, 138) sts. Place marker (pm) for beg of rnd and join for working in rnds, being careful not to twist sts.

Rnd 1: *K3, p3; rep from * around.

Rep last rnd until piece measures ¾ (¾, 1)" from beg.

Knit 1 rnd.

COLOR

		MC
×		CC
		pattern repeat

Body of hat

Change to larger cir needle.

Work Rnds 1–27 of Color chart. Piece measures about 4¼ (4¼, 4½)". Cut CC.

Crown

Change to smaller cir needle. Knit 1 rnd.

Dec rnd: *K19 (31, 67), k2tog; rep from * to end—120 (128, 136) sts rem.

Set-up rnd: *K30 (32, 34), pm; rep from * 2 more times, then work to end.

SHAPE CROWN

> **Note:** *Change to dpn when too few sts rem to work comfortably on cir needle.*

Dec rnd: *K1, k2tog, knit to 3 sts before m, ssk, k1; rep from * to end—8 sts dec'd.

Next rnd: Knit.

Rep last 2 rnds 12 (13, 14) more times—16 sts rem.

Dec rnd: *K2tog, ssk; rep from * to end—8 sts rem.

Cut yarn, leaving a 6" long tail, draw tail through rem sts, and pull tight to close hole.

> **Note:** *Loft is a delicate yarn and may break if pulled too forcefully.*

Finishing

Weave in ends.

Block to measurements.

lucy hat

Carina Spencer

Finished Size

Circumference: 20 (22)".

Hat shown measures 20" circumference.

Yarn

Worsted weight (#3 light).

Shown here: Madelinetosh Tosh Vintage (100% superwash Merino wool; 200 yd [182 m]/115 g): hickory (tan, MC), tart (red, CC), 1 skein each.

Needles

Size U.S. 6 (4 mm): 16" circular (cir) and set of double-pointed (dpn).

Adjust needle size if necessary to obtain the correct gauge.

Notions

Marker (m); tapestry needle.

Gauge

20 sts and 28 rnds = 4" in St st.

Notes

■ This hat is worked seamlessly from the bottom up using short-rows to create an asymmetrical folded brim that is sewn into place during finishing.

■ When working the short-rows in garter stitch, it is not necessary to work your wraps together with the wrapped stitches. The wraps essentially disappear into the garter stitch when left alone.

STITCH GUIDE

**Woven stitch
(even number of sts)**

Rnds 1 and 3: Knit.

Rnd 2: *K1, sl 1 pwise wyf; rep from * to end.

Rnd 4: *Sl 1 pwise wyf, k1; rep from * to end.

Rep Rnds 1–4 for patt.

Brim

With cir needle and MC, CO 100 (110) sts. Place marker (pm) and join in the rnd.

Purl 4 rnds.

Beg working short-rows as foll:

Short-row 1: (RS) K35 (39), wrap next st, turn.

Short-row 2: K10, wrap next st, turn.

Short-row 3: Knit to 2 sts past previously wrapped st (see Notes), wrap next st, turn.

Rep last short-row 23 (27) more times.

Next row: (RS) Knit to end.

Band

Knit 1 rnd, picking up wrap around first st and working it tog with wrapped st. Break MC; change to CC.

Knit 1 rnd.

Purl 1 rnd.

Work 11 rnds in Woven st patt (see Stitch Guide).

Purl 1 rnd.

Break CC; change to MC.

Shape Crown

▌ **Note:** Change to dpn when necessary.

Work in St st until piece measures 5 (5¼)" from CO (take measurement on an area with no short-rows).

Next rnd: K18 (20), k2tog, [pm, k18 (20), k2tog] 4 times — 95 (105) sts rem.

Dec rnd: [Knit to 2 sts before m, k2tog] 5 times — 5 sts dec'd.

Rep Dec rnd every rnd 16 (18) more times — 10 sts rem.

Break yarn and thread the tail through rem sts to secure.

Finishing

Weave in ends and block. Turn brim up on outside of hat and sew it into place invisibly by using a length of MC yarn and working from inside of hat.

Finished Size

Circumference: 20".

Height: 10".

Yarn

Fingering weight
(#1 super fine).

Shown here: Cascade Yarns
Heritage Silk (85% Merino
wool, 15% silk; 437 yd [400
m]/3½ oz [100 g]): #5681
limestone, 1 hank.

Needles

Size U.S. 3 (3.25 mm): 16"
circular (cir) and set of
double-pointed (dpn).

*Adjust needle size if necessary
to obtain the correct gauge.*

Notions

Removable markers (m); cable
needle (cn); tapestry needle.

Gauge

43 sts and 42 rnds = 4" in
Cable patt.

nautilus hat

Grace Akhrem

2/1 RPC

Sl 1 st onto cn, hold in back, k2, p1 from cn.

2/2 RPC

Sl 2 sts onto cn, hold in back, k2, p2 from cn.

Cable pattern (multiple of 6 sts)

Set-up rnd: *P4, k2; rep from
* to end.

Rnd 1: *P2, 2/2 RPC (see Stitch Guide);
rep from * to end.

Rnd 2: *P2, k2, p2; rep from
* to end.

Rnd 3: *2/2 RPC, p2; rep from
* to end.

Rnd 4: K2, *p4, k2; rep from
* to last 4 sts, pm for new beg of rnd and
remove old rnd m.

Rep Rnds 1-4 for patt.

Hat

With cir needle, CO 216 sts. Place marker
(pm) and join in the rnd.

Work in Cable patt (see Stitch Guide) until
piece measures 8¾." from CO, ending
with Rnd 4 of patt.

Shape Crown

▌ **Note:** *Change to dpn when necessary.*

Rnd 1: *P2, 2/2 RPC (see Stitch Guide);
rep from * to end.

Rnd 2: *P2tog, k2, [p4, k2] 2 times, p2;
rep from * to end—204 sts rem.

Rnd 3: *2/1 RPC (see Stitch Guide), [p2,
2/2 RPC] 2 times, p2; rep from * to end.

Rnd 4: *K2, p3, [k2, p2tog, p2] 2 times;
rep from * to last 17 sts, k2, p3, k2, p2tog,
p2, k2, p2tog, pm for new beg of rnd and
remove old rnd m 180 sts rem.

Rnd 5: P1, 2/1 RPC, *p2, 2/1 RPC; rep
from * to last st, p1.

Rnd 6: P1, k2, *p3, k2; rep from * to last 2
sts, p2.

Rnd 7: *K2tog, k1, p2; rep from * to end—
144 sts rem.

Rnd 8: *K2, p2; rep from * to last 4 sts,
k2, p1, pm for new beg of rnd and remove
old rnd m.

Rnd 9: *K2tog, k1, p1; rep from * to last 4
sts, k2tog, k1, pm for new beg of rnd and
remove old rnd m—108 sts rem.

Rnd 10: *2/1 RPC; rep from * to end.

Remove m, k2, pm for new beg of rnd.

Rnd 11: *K3tog, k2tog, k1; rep from * to
end—54 sts rem.

Rnd 12: *K3tog; rep from * to end—18 sts
rem.

Rnd 13: *K2tog; rep from * to end—9 sts
rem.

Break yarn, leaving a 12" tail.

Finishing

Thread tail on tapestry needle, draw
through rem sts 2 times and cinch closed.
Weave in ends. Wet block to shape.

koolhaas hat

Jared Flood

Finished Size

Circumference: 16".

Height: 7 (8)".

Hat shown measures 7" tall.

Yarn

Aran weight (#4 medium).

Shown here: Shokay Yarn Shambala (100% yak;164 yd [150 m]/100 g): cranberry, 1 skein.

Needles

Size U.S. 6 (4 mm): 16" circular (cir).

Size U.S. 8 (5 mm): 16" cir and set of 4 or 5 double-pointed (dpn).

Adjust needle size if necessary to obtain the correct gauge.

Notions

Marker (m); cable needle (cn); tapestry needle.

Gauge

26 sts and 30 rows = 4" in Lattice chart patt on larger needle.

Hat

With smaller cir needle, CO 104 sts. Place marker (pm) and join for working in the rnd.

Next rnd: *K1, p2, k1; rep from * around.

Rep last rnd 9 more times—piece measures about 1¼" from CO. Change to larger cir needle and work Rnds 1–5 of Lattice chart.

> **Note:** *M placement will shift twice in each chart rep, on Rnds 6 and 8.*

On these rnds, work as foll:

Rnd 6: Work in patt to last st of rnd, sl last st to right needle, remove m, sl st back to left needle and replace m—this marks the new beg of rnd for Rnds 7 and 8.

Work Rnd 7 in patt.

Rnd 8: Work in patt to end of rnd, remove m, sl next st and replace m—this marks beg of Rnds 1–5.

Work Rnds 1–8 of chart 4 (5) times total.

Work Rnd 1 once more.

SHAPE CROWN

Work as foll, changing to dpn when necessary:

Rnd 1: *P1, knit next 2 sts through their back loops (k2tbl), p2tog, k2tbl, p1; rep from * around—91 sts rem.

Rnd 2: *P1, 1/1 LC, p1, 1/1 LC, p1; rep from * around.

Rnd 3: *P1, k2tbl, p1, k2tbl, p1; rep from * around.

Rnd 4: *1/1 RPC, sl 1, k2tog, psso, 1/1 LPC; rep from * around—65 sts rem.

Rnd 5: *K1tbl, p1, k1tbl, p1, k1tbl; rep from * to last 5 sts, k1tbl, p1, k1tbl, p1, sl last st, remove m, sl st back to left needle and replace m.

Rnd 6: *Ssk, p1, k1tbl, p1; rep from * around—52 sts rem.

Rnd 7: *K1tbl, p1, k1tbl, p1; rep from * around.

Rnd 8: *K1tbl, p1, ssk; rep from * around, remove m, sl next st, replace m—39 sts rem.

Rnd 9: *P1, ssk; rep from * around, remove m, sl next st, replace m—26 sts rem.

Rnd 10: *Ssk; rep from * around—13 sts rem.

Finishing

Break yarn, leaving a 10" tail. With tail threaded on a tapestry needle, draw tail through all rem sts and pull to gather. Secure tail to WS. Weave in loose ends.

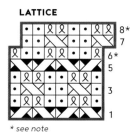

LATTICE

* see note

⌢	knit through back loop (tbl)
•	purl
☐	pattern repeat

1/1 LC: sl 1 st onto cn and hold in front, k1tbl, k1tbl from cn

1/1 RPC: sl 1 st onto cn and hold in back, k1tbl, p1 from cn

1/1 LPC: sl 1 st onto cn and hold in front, p1, k1tbl from cn

deep woods toque

Kiyomi Burgin

Finished Size

Circumference: 18".

Height with brim unfolded: 12".

Yarn

Fingering weight (#1 super fine).

Shown here: Madelinetosh Tosh Merino Light (100% superwash Merino wool; 420 yd [384 m]): whiskey barrel (MC), 1 skein.

Madelinetosh Unicorn Tails (100% superwash Merino wool; 52 yd [48 m]): big sur (CC1), 2 skeins; neon peach (CC2), 1 skein.

Needles

Size U.S. 3 (3.25 mm): 16" circular (cir) and set of double-pointed (dpn).

Size U.S. 2 (2.75 mm): 16" cir.

Adjust needle size if necessary to obtain the correct gauge.

Notions

Marker (m); tapestry needle.

Gauge

33 sts and 34 rnds = 4" in charted patt on larger needle.

Notes

■ This hat is worked in the round from the bottom up.

■ The chart is worked using the stranded method. Always pick up the first color over the second and pick up the second color from under the first; this will prevent tangling.

■ Keep floats loose. For floats longer than 5 stitches, twist yarns together on wrong side of work.

TREE

				▲									57
													55
				▲									53
										+		51
										+		
+				▲					+	+		49
										+		
		+					+		+		47
+				▲					+	+		
		+					+				45
	+						+		+		
+		+				+		+	+		43
	+					+			+		
	+					+		+		41
+								+	+		

12 st to 2 st repeat

MC

+ **CC1**

▲ sl 2 sts as if to k2tog, k1, p2sso–2 sts dec'd

no stitch

pattern repeat

Hat

With smaller cir needle and CC2, CO 144 sts. Place marker and join in the rnd.

Work in k1, p1 rib for 1 rnd.

Break CC2. Join MC. Work in k1, p1 rib until piece measures 5¼ " from CO.

Change to larger cir needle.

Work Rnds 1–58 of Tree chart, changing to dpn when necessary—24 sts rem.

Break CC1.

With MC, knit 1 rnd.

Next rnd: [K1, k2tog] 8 times—16 sts rem.

Break yarn and draw tail through rem sts. Pull tight to gather sts and fasten off/ on WS.

Finishing

Block to measurements. Weave in ends. Fold rib brim in half to RS. With CC2, make 1 pom-pom about 2" in diameter and sew to top of hat.

phyllotaxis hat

Marie Godsey

Finished Size

Circumference: 20".

Height: 9¾".

Yarn

Fingering weight
(#1 super fine).

Shown here: Jade Sapphire
Mongolian Cashmere 4-ply
(100% cashmere; 200 yd
[183 m]/2 oz [55 g]): #174
dinosaur dawn, 1 skein.

Needles

Size U.S. 6 (4 mm): 16" circular
(cir) and set of double-
pointed (dpn).

*Adjust needle size if necessary
to obtain the correct gauge.*

Notions

Marker (m); tapestry needle.

Gauge

21 sts and 34 rnds =
4" in Leaf Lace patt.

CROWN

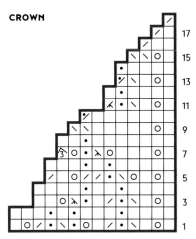

15 st dec'd to 1 st repeat

LEAF LACE

15 st repeat

	knit			k3tog
•	purl			sl 1 kwise, k2tog, psso
o	yo			k3tog tbl
/	k2tog			no stitch
\	ssk			pattern repeat
	p2tog			

Hat

With cir needle, CO 104 sts. Place marker (pm) and join in the rnd.

Work in k1, p1 rib for 16 rnds.

Next rnd: K1, M1, knit to end—105 sts.

Work Rnds 1–10 of Leaf Lace chart 5 times.

Work Rnds 1–18 of Crown chart, changing to dpn when necessary—7 sts rem.

Break yarn, leaving a 12" tail. Thread tail onto tapestry needle and draw through rem sts. Pull tight to gather sts and fasten off on WS.

Finishing

Weave in ends. Block.

brighton hat

Megan Nodecker

Finished Size

Circumference: 18 (20, 22)".

Height: 8¼ (8¾, 9)".

Hat shown measures 20" circumference.

Yarn

Worsted weight (#4 medium).

Shown here: Zealana Kauri Worsted (60% Merino wool, 30% brushtail possum, 10% silk; 94 yd [86 m]/50 g): #K01 natural (MC) and #K14 red tuhi (CC), 1 ball each.

Needles

Sizes U.S. 6 (4 mm): 16" circular (cir).

Size U.S. 7 (4.5 mm): 16" cir and set of double-pointed needle (dpn).

Adjust needle size if necessary to obtain the correct gauge.

Notions

Marker (m); tapestry needle.

Gauge

16 sts and 22 rnds = 4" in St st on larger needle.

Notes

▪ This hat is worked in the round from the brim to the crown. When shaping the crown, change to double-pointed needles when necessary.

Hat

With MC and smaller cir needle, CO 72 (80, 88) sts. Place marker (pm) and join in the rnd.

Work in k1, p1 rib for 1".

Change to larger cir needle.

Work in St st until piece measures 2¾" from CO.

Next rnd: *K1 with CC, k1 with MC; rep from * to end.

Next rnd: *K1 with MC, k1 with CC; rep from * to end.

Rep last 2 rnds until piece measures 5¾ (6, 6¼)" from CO. Break MC and cont with CC only.

Work even for ½".

Next rnd: Knit, dec 0 (2, 4) sts evenly spaced—72 (78, 84) sts rem.

Shape crown

Rnd 1: [K2tog, k8 (9, 10), ssk] 6 times—60 (66, 72) sts rem.

Rnds 2 and 3: Knit.

Rnd 4: [K2tog, k6 (7, 8), ssk] 6 times—48 (54, 60) sts rem.

Rnds 5 and 6: Knit.

Rnd 7: [K2tog, k4 (5, 6), ssk] 6 times—36 (42, 48) sts rem.

Rnd 8: Knit.

Rnd 9: [K2tog, k2 (3, 4), ssk] 6 times—24 (30, 36) sts rem.

Rnd 10: Knit.

Rnd 11: [K2tog, k0 (1, 2), ssk] 6 times—12 (18, 24) sts rem.

SIZE 20" ONLY:

Rnd 12: Knit.

Rnd 13: [K2tog, k1] 6 times—12 sts rem.

SIZE 22" ONLY:

Rnd 12: Knit.

Rnd 13: [K2tog, ssk] 6 times—12 sts rem.

ALL SIZES:

Break yarn, thread tail through rem sts, and fasten off.

Finishing

Weave in ends. Block.

winter waves slouch hat

Melissa LaBarre

Finished Size

Circumference: 20".

Height: 10¾".

Yarn

Worsted weight (#4 medium).

Shown here: Cascade Yarns Longwood (100% superwash extrafine Merino wool; 191 yd [175 m]/100 g): #23 stonewash, 1 ball.

Needles

Size U.S. 7 (4.5 mm): 16" circular (cir) and a set of 4 double pointed (dpn).

Adjust needle size if necessary to obtain the correct gauge.

Notions

Marker (m); tapestry needle.

Gauge

21½ sts and 31 rnds = 4" in Ripple patt worked in rnds.

STITCH GUIDE

Ripple pattern (mult of 12 sts)

Rnds 1 and 2: Purl.

Rnd 3: *K1, [k2tog] 2 times, [yo, k1] 3 times, yo, [ssk] 2 times; rep from *.

Rnd 4: Knit.

Rnd 5: Rep Row 3.

Rnd 6: Knit.

Rep Rnds 1–6 for patt.

Hat

With cir needle and using the long-tail method, CO 84 sts. Place marker (pm) and join for working in rnds, being careful not to twist sts.

Work in k1, p1 rib until piece measures 1" from CO.

Inc rnd: [K1f&b] 4 times, *k3, k1f&b; rep from *—108 sts.

Work Rnds 1–6 of Ripple patt (see Stitch Guide or Ripple Pattern chart) 10 times.

Purl 2 rnds—piece measures 9" from CO.

Shape Top

> **Note:** *Change to dpn when too few sts rem to work comfortably on a cir needle.*

Rnd 1: *K1, [k2tog] 2 times, k3, [ssk] 2 times; rep from *—72 sts rem.

Rnd 2: Knit.

Rnd 3: *K1, k2tog, k3, ssk; rep from *—54 sts rem.

Rnd 4: Knit.

Rnds 5 and 6: Purl.

Rnd 7: *K1, k2tog, k1, ssk; rep from *—36 sts rem.

Rnd 8: Knit.

Rnd 9: *K2tog, ssk; rep from *—18 sts rem.

Rnd 10: Knit.

Rnds 11 and 12: Purl.

Rnd 13: *K2tog, rep from *—9 sts rem.

Cut yarn, leaving an 8" tail. Thread tail on a tapestry needle, draw through rem sts, pull tight to close hole, and secure on WS.

Finishing

Weave in loose ends. Block lightly.

RIPPLE PATTERN

12-st repeat

	knit		k2tog
	purl		ssk
	yo		pattern repeat

city park hat

Thea Colman

Finished Size

Head circumference: 20¼ (21¾)".

Height: 9".

Hat shown measures 20¼" circumference.

Yarn

DK weight (#3 light).

Shown here: Green Mountain Spinnery Sylvan Spirit (50% fine American wool, 50% tencel; 180 yd [165 m]/58 g): #7562 citrine (MC); #7790 sterling (CC), 1 skein each.

Needles

Size U.S. 4 (3.5 mm): 16" circular (cir).

Size U.S. 6 (4 mm): 16" cir and set of double-pointed (dpn).

Adjust needle size if necessary to obtain the correct gauge.

Notions

Marker (m); tapestry needle.

Gauge

22 sts and 29 rnds = 4" in charted patt on larger needle.

Notes

■ This hat is worked in the round from the bottom up.

STITCH GUIDE

S2kp2
Sl 2 sts as if to k2tog, k1, pass 2 sl sts over—2 sts dec'd.

Brim

With CC and smaller needle, CO 120 (128) sts. Place marker and join in the rnd.

Work in k1, p1 rib for 2".

Next rnd: [K13 (14), k2tog] 8 times— 112 (120) sts rem.

Break CC.

Change to larger cir needle and MC.

Work Rnds 1–16 of Lace chart 2 times, then work Rnds 1–12 once more.

Shape Crown

▌ **Note:** Change to dpn when necessary.

Dec rnd: *K1, s2kp2 (see Stitch Guide), p1, s2kp2; rep from * to end—56 (60) sts rem.

Next rnd: *K2, p1, k1; rep from * to end.

Dec rnd: *K1, s2kp2; rep from * to end— 28 (30) sts rem.

Next rnd: Knit.

Dec rnd: ⌊K2tog⌋ 14 (15) times—14 (15) sts rem.

Next rnd: Knit.

Break yarn and draw tail through rem sts. Pull tight to gather sts and fasten off on WS.

Finishing

Weave in ends. Block. With CC, make 3" pompom and attach to top of hat.

LACE

•			•			•	•
O	╱		•		╲	O	•	15
			•				
			•					13
			•				
	O	╱	•	╲	O			11
	•	•	•				
O	╱	•	•	•	╲	O	•	9
	•	•	•				
	╲	O	•	O	╱	•		7
			•					5
			•				
╲	O			O	╱	•		3
•			•			•	•
•	╲	O	•	O	╱	•	•	1

▢	knit	╱		k2tog
•	purl	╲		ssk
O	yo	▢		pattern repeat

cuff-to-cuff socks

Courtney Spainhower

Finished Size

Circumference: About 5¾ (6½, 7, 8)".

Foot length: About 5¾ (7, 7, 7¾)".

To fit: 5-8y (7-10y, Women's U.S. sizes 6-9, Women's U.S. sizes 8-11).

Socks shown measure 5¾" and 8".

Yarn

DK weight (#3 light).

Shown here: Tanis Fiber Arts Yellow Label DK (100% superwash Merino wool; 260 yd [238 m]/115 g): sprout, 1 (1, 1, 2) hanks.

Needles

Size U.S. 6 (4 mm): 2 16" circular (cir) and set of 2 double-pointed (dpn).

Adjust needle size if necessary to obtain the correct gauge.

Notions

Markers (m); waste yarn; tapestry needle.

Gauge

25 sts and 34 rnds = 4" in St st worked in rnds.

Notes

■ These socks are worked by casting on at one cuff, and the first sock is completed cuff-down with a no-wrap short-row heel. The toe is shaped before working scrap yarn (to be removed later). Rejoin yarn and begin second sock starting at the toe. It is completed toe-up with a no-wrap short-row heel. Remove scrap yarn and graft toes closed (see Separating Toes on page 32).

■ For men's U.S. sizes 8½-10 socks, add ½" length to the leg and foot when knitting the women's U.S. sizes 6-9.

■ For men's U.S. sizes 10½-12 socks, add ½" length to the leg and 1" to the foot when knitting the women's U.S. sizes 8-11.

STITCH GUIDE

1×1 Rib (multiple of 2 sts)

Rnd 1: *K1, p1; rep from *.

Rep Rnd 1 for patt.

Elastic Bind-Off

*K2tog tbl, transfer the new stitch from the right needle back to the left needle; repeat from * to end. Break yarn and thread tail through last stitch pulling tight to secure.

First sock

TOP-DOWN LEG

CO 36 (40, 44, 50) sts. Divide sts over 2 cir needles, place marker (pm) for beg of rnd and join to work in the rnd, being careful not to twist sts.

> **Note:** "Needle 1" holds the first 18 (20, 22, 24) sts for the front/instep; "needle 2" holds the last 18 (20, 22, 26) sts for the back/heel.

Work in 1x1 rib until piece measures 1" from CO edge.

Knit 1 rnd.

Est patt: Needle 1: k4 (5, 6, 7), pm, work 10 sts in Woven chart, pm, knit to end of needle 1; needle 2: knit.

Cont working even as est until piece meas 6 (6½, 7, 7½)" from CO edge, ending last rnd after Rnd 3 of Woven chart is worked on needle 1; do not work sts on needle 2.

TOP-DOWN HEEL

Heel is shaped by working no-wrap short-rows back and forth over needle 2 only as foll:

Short-row 1: (RS) Sl 1 st purlwise with yarn in back (pwise wyb), knit to last st, turn so WS is facing; (WS) sl 1 st pwise wyf, purl to last st, turn so RS is facing.

Short-row 2: Sl 1 st pwise wyb, knit to 1 st before gap, turn so WS is facing; (WS) sl 1 st pwise wyf, purl to 1 st before gap, turn so RS is facing.

Rep the last short-row 4 (5, 5, 8) more times.

Next row: (RS) Sl 1 st pwise wyb, knit to end of needle 2, closing gaps as you come to them.

Next rnd: Work across needle 1 in patt and knit to end of needle 2, closing rem gaps as you come to them.

TOP-DOWN FOOT

Cont working even as est until piece meas 4½ (5½, 5½, 6)" from back of heel, or 1¼ (1½, 1½, 1¾)" shorter than desired total length. Remove markers for Woven chart on the last rnd.

WOVEN CHART

		knit
	ⱅ	sl 1 st pwise wyf
		pattern repeat

TOP-DOWN TOE

Set-up rnd: Needle 1: K6 (7, 7, 8), pm, k6 (6, 8, 8), pm, k6 (7, 7, 8); needle 2: k6 (7, 7, 9), pm, k6 (6, 8, 8), pm, k6 (7, 7, 9).

Shape toe

Dec rnd: *Knit to 2 sts before m, ssk, sl m, knit to m, sl m, k2tog, knit to end of needle; rep from * for needle 2—4 sts dec'd.

Next rnd: Knit.

Rep the last 2 rnds 4 (5, 5, 6) more times—16 (16, 20, 22) sts rem.

Break yarn, leaving 8" tail.

Join waste yarn and knit 3 rnds.

Second sock

TOE-UP TOE

Rejoin working yarn, leaving 8" tail.

Knit 2 rnds.

Shape toe

Next rnd: Knit.

Inc rnd: *Knit to m, M1R, sl m, knit to m, sl m, M1L, knit to end of needle; rep from * for needle 2—4 sts inc'd.

Rep the last 2 rnds 4 (5, 5, 6) more times—36 (40, 44, 50) sts.

Remove markers for toe on the last rnd.

TOE-UP FOOT

Est patt: Needle 1: k4 (5, 6, 7), pm, work 10 sts in Woven chart, pm, knit to end of needle 1; needle 2: knit.

Cont working even as est until piece meas 4¼ (5¼, 5¼, 5½)" from beg of toe, or 1½ (1¾, 1¾, 2¼)" less than total desired length, ending last rnd after Row 1 of Woven chart is worked on needle 1; do not work sts on needle 2.

TOE-UP HEEL

Work same as for top-down heel.

TOE-UP LEG

Cont working even as est until piece meas 5 (5½, 6, 6½)" from end of heel shaping. Work in 1x1 rib for 1".

BO all sts using elastic bind-off (see Stitch Guide).

Finishing

Remove waste yarn from between toes and use 8" tail to graft toe sts together (see Separating Toes). Block to measurements. Weave in ends.

SEPARATING TOES

Here's how to cut your sock tube and finish your toes to create a perfect pair. Using sharp scissors, carefully cut across waste yarn along the second round of waste yarn stitches **(Figure 1)**. You now have two separate socks **(Figure 2)**. Remove waste yarn between toes and place sts onto 2 dpn so that top sts are on one needle and bottom sts are on one needle, redistributing as needed so each needle has the same number of sts **(Figure 3)**. Using 8" tail and tapestry needle, graft toe sts together using Kitchener st **(Figure 4)**.

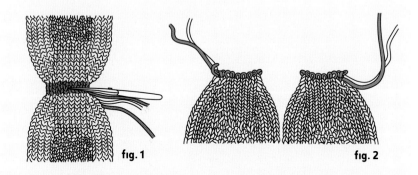

fig. 1   fig. 2

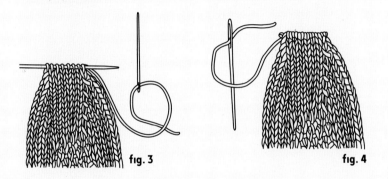

fig. 3   fig. 4

slippery slope socks

General Hogbuffer

12

Finished Size

Foot circumference: About 6¼(7)".

Foot length from back of heel to tip of toe (length is adjustable): 9¼ (9¾)".

Socks shown measure 7" foot circumference.

Yarn

Fingering weight (#1 super fine).

Shown here: Schoppel Wolle Admiral Uni (75% virgin wool, 25% polyamide; 459 yd [420 m]/3½ oz [100g]): #0320 vanille (white; MC), 1 ball.

Schoppel Wolle Crazy Zauberball (75% virgin wool, 25% polyamide; 459 yd [420 m]/3½ oz [100g]): #1702 rich jewels (varigated; CC), 1 ball.

Needles

Size U.S. 1½ (2.5 mm): needles for working in rounds as you prefer.

Adjust needle size if necessary to obtain the correct gauge.

Notions

Markers (m); cable needle (cn); tapestry needle.

Gauge

36 sts and 46 rnds = 4" in St st.

Notes

■ These socks are worked in the round from the cuff down.

■ Slip stitches purlwise with yarn in back, except where indicated otherwise.

Cuff

With MC, CO 72 (80) sts. Place marker (pm) and join in the rnd.

Work in K2, P2 Rib (see Stitch Guide) for 24 rnds.

Leg

Join CC.

Work Rnds 1–56 of Leg chart for your size, working Rnd 11 as foll:

Rnd 11: Work to last st of rnd, work cable using last st of rnd and first st of next rnd, keeping beg-of-rnd m at center of cable. (First st of rnd is also used for cable at beg of Rnd 12.) Break CC

Heel flap

Heel flap is worked with MC back and forth over first 18 (20) sts of rnd and last 18 (20) sts of rnd; rem 36 (40) sts of rnd will be worked later for instep. Remove m.

SIZE 6¼" ONLY:

Next row: (RS) [K2, ssk] 2 times, k3, ssk, k2, ssk, k1, turn—32 heel sts rem.

Next row: (WS) Sl 1, p15, p2tog, p2, p2tog, p3, p2tog, p2, p2tog, p1, turn—28 heel sts rem.

SIZE 7" ONLY:

Next row: (RS) K2, ssk, [k3, ssk] 3 times, k1, turn—36 heel sts rem.

LEG, SIZE 6¼"

Work as given in directions   **36 st repeat**

Chart row numbers (right side): 55, 53, 51, 49, 47, 45, 43, 41, 39, 37, 35, 33, 31, 29, 27, 25, 23, 21, 19, 17, 15, 13, 11*, 9, 7, 5, 3, 1

	MC
×	CC
╱	k2tog with MC
╱	k2tog with CC
╲	ssk with CC
V	sl 1 pwise wyb
V	sl 1 pwise wyb
	no stitch
	pattern repeat

sl 1 st onto cn, hold in back, with CC, k1, k1 from cn

sl 1 st onto cn, hold in front, sl 1 pwise wyb, with MC, k1 from cn

sl 1 st onto cn, hold in front, with MC, k1, k1 from cn

sl 1 st onto cn, hold in back, with CC, k1, sl 1 pwise wyb from cn

Next row: (WS) Sl 1, p17, [p2tog, p3] 3 times, p2tog, p1, turn—32 heel sts rem.

BOTH SIZES:

Row 1: (RS) *Sl 1, k1; rep from * to end.

Row 2: (WS) Sl 1 pwise wyf, purl to end.

Row 3: Sl 2, *k1, sl 1; rep from * to last 2 sts, k2.

Row 4: Sl 1 pwise wyf, purl to end.

Rep last 4 rows 7 (8) more times, then work Rows 1 and 2 once more. Turn heel using short-rows as foll:

Short-row 1: (RS) Sl 1, [sl 1, k1] 7 (8) times, ssk, k1, turn.

Short-row 2: (WS) Sl 1 pwise wyf, p3, p2tog, p1, turn.

Short-row 3: Sl 1, knit to 1 st before gap, ssk, k1, turn.

Short-row 4: Sl 1 pwise wyf, purl to 1 st before gap, p2tog, p1, turn.

Rep last 2 short-rows 4 (5) more times— 16 (18) heels sts rem.

Next row: (RS) K8 (9), pm for new beg of rnd.

Gusset

With RS facing, rejoin CC.

Next rnd: With CC, k8 (9), pick up and knit 18 (20) sts along side of heel flap, work instep sts as foll:

K2, sl 1, pm, k3 (4), sl 1, k4, sl 1, k3 (4), sl 1, k17 (19), pm, k3, pick up and knit 18 (20) sts along side of heel flap, k8 (9)— 88 (98) sts total.

Work Rnds 1-56 of Foot chart for your size, removing all m except beg-of-rnd m after Rnd 24 (26) of chart—56 (64) sts rem.

Next rnd: With MC knit.

Next rnd: With CC knit.

Rep last 2 rnds until foot measures 7½ (7¾)" from back of heel, or 1¾ (2)" less than desired finished length.

Toe

Cont in stripe patt, work as foll:

Next rnd: [K11(13), k2tog, k1, pm, k1, ssk, k11 (13)] 2 times—52 (60) sts rem.

Work 3 rnds even.

Dec rnd: [Knit to 3 sts before m, k2tog, k1, sl m, k1, ssk] 2 times, knit to end—4 sts dec'd.

Rep Dec rnd every 3rd rnd 2 more times, then every other rnd 3 times, then every rnd 3 (5) times—16 sts rem.

Knit to m; break yarn, leaving a 12" tail.

Finishing

With tail threaded on a tapestry needle, graft sts using Kitchener st. Weave in ends. Block lightly.

LEG, SIZE 7"

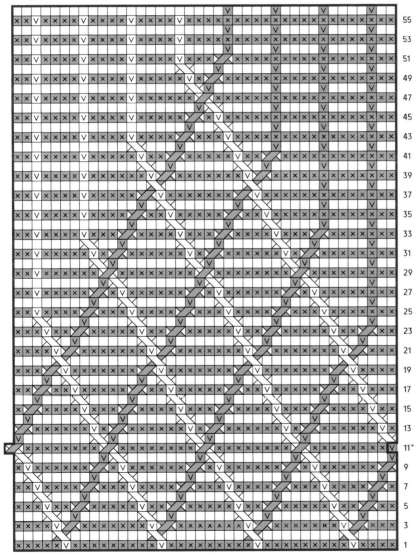

*Work as given in directions

40 st repeat

FOOT, SIZE 6¼"

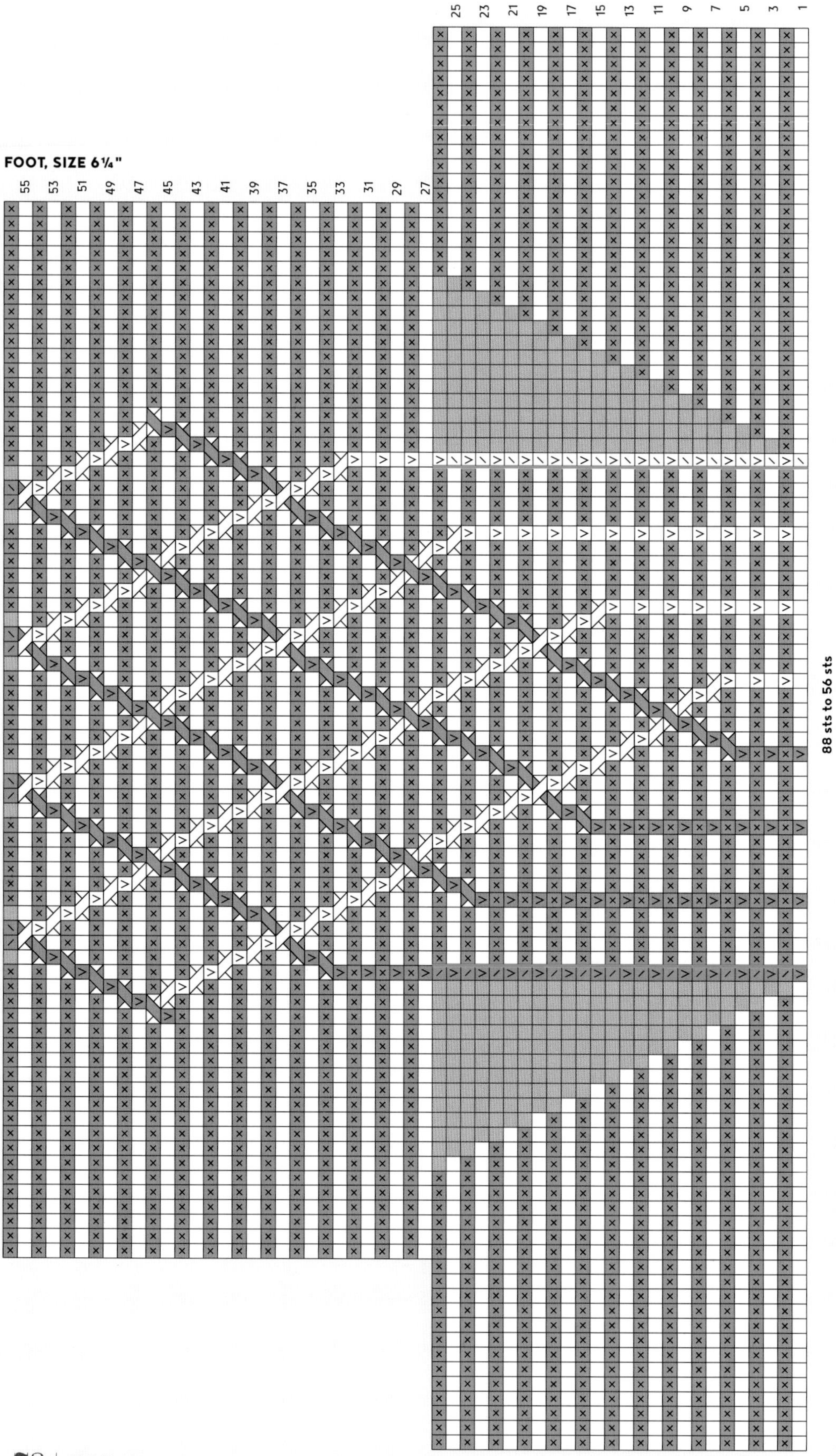

88 sts to 56 sts

☐	MC
✕	CC
╱	k2tog with MC
╱	k2tog with CC
╲	ssk with CC
V	sl 1 pwise wyb
V	sl 1 pwise wyb
☐	no stitch
☐	pattern repeat
⧄⧅	sl 1 st onto cn, hold in front, with MC, k1, k1 from cn
⧄⧅	sl 1 st onto cn, hold in back, with CC, k1, k1 from cn
⧄⧅	sl 1 st onto cn, hold in front, sl 1 pwise wyb, with MC, k1 from cn
⧄⧅	sl 1 st onto cn, hold in back, with CC, k1, sl 1 pwise wyb from cn

FOOT, SIZE 7"

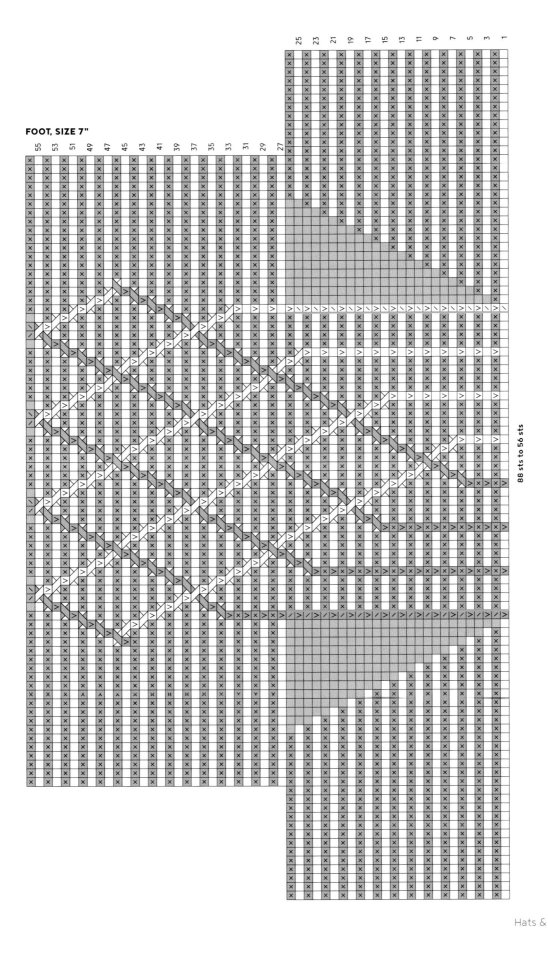

88 sts to 56 sts

u-turn socks

General Hogbuffer

Finished Size

Foot circumference: about 6½ (7, 7½, 8, 8½)".

Foot length from back of heel to tip of toe: 9 (9½, 10, 10½, 11)".

Leg length from top of cuff to base of heel: 10½".

Socks shown measure 7½" foot circumference.

Yarn

Fingering weight (#1 super fine).

Shown here: Schoppel Wolle Zauberball Crazy (75% superwash wool, 25% nylon; 462 yd [422 m]/100 g]): #1507 herbstwind (autumn wind), 1 ball for all sizes.

Needles

Size U.S. 1½ (2.5 mm): two 24" circular (cir) and set of 4 or 5 double-pointed (dpn) or third 24" cir.

Adjust needle size if necessary to obtain the correct gauge.

Notions

Smooth cotton waste yarn in a contrasting color for provisional cast-on; markers (m); tapestry needle.

Gauge

32 sts and 48 rows = 4" in St st worked in rows.

34 sts and 44 rows = 4" in St st worked in rnds.

Notes

■ This project has an unusual construction that does not follow the "standard" sequences for top-down or toe-up socks.

■ The socks shown were knitted using the two ends from the same ball of yarn, changing ends every 4 rows or rounds for the stripes. Not every yarn is packaged to allow easy access to both ends *at the same time*. If you're struggling with tangles, you may want to consider rewinding your yarn into two evenly sized balls; a digital kitchen scale is helpful for this.

■ The two working strands are referred to as color A and color B in the directions, even though they are two ends from the same ball of yarn. If you're using two different colors, decide which will be A or B; you'll need about 50 grams of each color. If you use a self-striping yarn, ignore any instructions for changing colors.

■ It's not necessary to cut the yarn between the stripes unless instructed. Carry the unused color loosely up the side of the work (when working in rows) or inside the tube on the back of the work (when working in rounds) until it's needed again.

Back leg and heel

The center back leg extends from just below the ribbed cuff to the base of the heel.

With waste yarn and using a provisional method, CO 70 sts. Do not join.

Change to A (see Notes).

Set-up rows 1 and 3: (RS) Knit.

Set-up row 2: (WS) P1, p2tog, purl to end-69 sts rem.

Set-up row 4: Purl.

Carefully remove waste yarn from provisional CO and place 69 exposed sts onto second cir needle-one 4-row rectangle of color A between needles. With RS facing, join B to beg of live sts from Set-up Row 4.

Row 1: (RS) With B, use Needle 1 to k46 leg sts, place marker (pm), k23 heel flap sts, pm; with RS still facing, pick up and knit 1 st from selvedge of 4-row rectangle; with Needle 2, pick up and knit 1 st from the same selvedge of 4-row rectangle, pm, k23 heel flap sts, pm, k46 leg sts— 140 sts total; 70 sts each needle; 2 sts at base of U between second and third m.

> **Note:** You now have live stitches around three sides of a narrow rectangle; the fourth side will become the top of the leg. Work back and forth in rows around three sides of the starting rectangle to create a U-shape to form the back of the leg and heel cup. Because you're working around three sides, every four U-shaped rows add two 4-row stripes, 1 stripe on each long side of the starting rectangle.

Cont as foll:

Row 2: (WS) With B, purl.

Row 3: (inc row) With B, k46, slip marker (sl m), k23, sl m, M1, knit to next marker, M1, sl m, k23, sl m, k46—2 sts inc'd at base of U between second and third m; 1 st inc'd each needle.

Row 4: With B, purl—3 stripes between long sides of U; 1 starting rectangle stripe and 1 stripe on each long side of U.

Cont for your size as foll:

SIZES 6½ (7, 7½)" ONLY:

Rows 5-17: Changing colors every 4 rows, rep Rows 3 and 4 six more times, then work RS Row 3 once more—156 sts; 78 sts each needle; 18 sts at base of U between second and third m (9 sts each needle).

Rows 18 and 19: Cont to change colors as est, work even for 2 rows, ending with a RS row.

The 42 rows between the long sides of the U are a 3-row partial stripe and 4 complete stripes on each side of the starting rectangle stripe.

SIZES 8 (8½)" ONLY

Rows 5-20: Changing colors every 4 rows, rep Rows 3 and 4 eight more times—158 sts; 79 sts each needle; 20 sts at base of U between second and third m (10 sts each needle).

Rows 21-23: Cont to change colors as est, work even for 3 rows, ending with a RS row.

The 50 rows between the long sides of the U are a 3-row partial stripe and 5 complete stripes on each side of the starting rectangle stripe.

ALL SIZES

> **Note:** The 46-stitch leg sections at each end of the row will be joined to the front leg panel as it is worked, forming a tube. The front leg joins one back leg stitch at the end of each row. In order for the pieces to join at the correct rate, the stitches in each back leg section are decreased to half the number of front leg rows.

Next row: (WS) Using the color needed to complete the 4-row stripe in progress, purl to first m and **at the same time** dec 14 sts evenly spaced, sl m, purl to last 46 sts, sl m, purl to end and **at the same time** dec 14 sts evenly spaced—128 (128, 128, 130, 130) sts rem; 64 (64, 64, 65, 65) sts each needle; 32 leg sts; 23 heel flap sts; 9 (9, 9, 10, 10) sts at base of U.

The 44 (44, 44, 52, 52) rows between the long sides of the U form 11 (11, 11, 13, 13) complete stripes; 5 (5, 5, 6, 6) complete stripes on each side of the starting rectangle stripe; piece measures about 3¾ (3¾, 3¾, 4¼, 4¼)" between long sides of U.

> **Note:** For joining purposes, the needle holding the stitches at the beginning of RS rows is the left back needle; the needle holding the stitches at the end of RS rows is the right back needle.

Front leg

With dpn or third cir needle and waste yarn, use a provisional method to CO 29 (31, 33, 35, 37) sts. Do not join.

Set-up row: (WS) With B (B, B, A, A), purl across waste-yarn sts. Cut yarn.

> **Note:** The last 4-row stripe completed on the back leg was worked with B (B, B, A, A). To ensure that the 16 planned front leg stripes also end with a stripe in B (B, B, A, A), the first front leg stripe is worked with A (A, A, B, B).

With RS of front sts facing, join A (A, A, B, B). Work front leg sts back and forth in rows, joining to back leg at end of each row as foll:

Row 1: (RS) K1, k2tog, knit to last front st, ssk (last front st tog with first st on left back needle), turn work—28 (30, 32, 34, 36) front sts rem; 1 left back st joined.

Row 2: (WS) Sl 1 purlwise with yarn in front (pwise wyf), purl to last front st, p2tog (last front st tog with first st on right back needle), turn work—1 right back st joined.

Row 3: Sl 1 pwise with yarn in back (wyb), knit to last front st, ssk (last front st tog with next left back st), turn work.

Row 4: Sl 1 pwise wyf, purl to last front st, p2tog (last front st tog with next right back st), turn work.

Changing colors every 4 rows and removing m at end of leg sts when you come to them, rep Rows 3 and 4 thirty more times—64 front leg rows completed; all 32 leg sts on left and right back sts have been joined; 92 (94, 96, 100, 102) sts rem; 28 (30, 32, 34, 36) front sts; 32 (32, 32, 33, 33) sts on each back needle, with 23 heel flap sts and 9 (9, 9, 10, 10) sts at base of U.

Shape gussets

Cut both yarns. Rejoin A (A, A, B, B) with RS facing in center of heel, between the two back cir needles.

Set-up rnd: On Needle 1, k9 (9, 9, 10, 10), remove m, k22, k2tog (last back st tog with front st after it), pm, k13 (14, 15, 16, 17); on Needle 2, k13 (14, 15, 16, 17), ssk (last front st tog with back st after it), pm, k22, remove m, k9 (9, 9, 10, 10)—90 (92, 94, 98, 100) sts rem; 45 (46, 47, 49, 50) sts each needle.

Dec rnd: Knit to 2 sts before first m, k2tog, sl m, knit to second m, sl m, ssk, knit to end—2 sts dec'd; 1 st dec'd each needle.

Changing colors every 4 rnds, rep the dec rnd every rnd 5 more times—78 (80, 82, 86, 88) sts rem; 39 (40, 41, 43, 44) sts each needle.

Changing colors every 4 rnds, [work 1 rnd even, then rep the dec rnd] 11 (10, 9, 9, 8) more times—56 (60, 64, 68, 72) sts rem; 28 (30, 32, 34, 36) sts each needle.

Foot

Changing colors every 4 rnds, work even until the foot measures 7 (7½, 8, 8½, 9)" from center back heel, or about 2" less than desired finished sock foot length.

Toe

Changing colors every 4 rnds, cont as foll:

Rnd 1: [K5 (13, 6, 15, 7), k2tog] 8 (4, 8, 4, 8) times—48 (56, 56, 64, 64) sts rem.

Rnds 2–6: Knit.

Rnd 7: [K4 (5, 5, 6, 6), k2tog] 8 times—40 (48, 48, 56, 56) sts rem.

Rnds 8–11: Knit.

Rnd 12: [K3 (4, 4, 5, 5), k2tog] 8 times—32 (40, 40, 48, 48) sts rem.

Rnds 13–15: Knit.

Rnd 16: [K2 (3, 3, 4, 4), k2tog] 8 times—24 (32, 32, 40, 40) sts rem.

Rnds 17 and 18: Knit.

Rnd 19: [K1 (2, 2, 3, 3), k2tog] 8 times—16 (24, 24, 32, 32) sts rem.

Rnd 20: Knit.

Rnd 21: [K0 (1, 1, 2, 2), k2tog] 8 times—8 (16, 16, 24, 24) sts rem.

Size 6½" is complete; skip to All sizes.

SIZES 7 (7½, 8, 8½)" ONLY

Rnd 22: [K0 (0, 1, 1), k2tog]—8 (8, 16, 16) sts rem.

Sizes 7 (7½)" are complete; skip to All sizes.

SIZES 8 (8½)" ONLY

Rnd 23: *K2tog; rep from *—8 sts rem.

ALL SIZES

K2, then cut yarn, leaving a 12" tail. Arrange sts so that the first and last 2 sts of rnd are on one needle for the sole and the other 4 sts are on another needle for the top of the foot. Thread tail on a tapestry needle and use the Kitchener st to graft rem sts tog.

Cuff

Carefully remove waste yarn from front leg provisional CO and place 28 (30, 32, 34, 36) exposed sts on cir or dpn. With color used for set-up row of front leg, RS facing, and beg at start of back section, pick up and knit 30 (30, 30, 36, 36) sts along back selvedge, then knit across front sts from provisional CO—58 (60, 62,

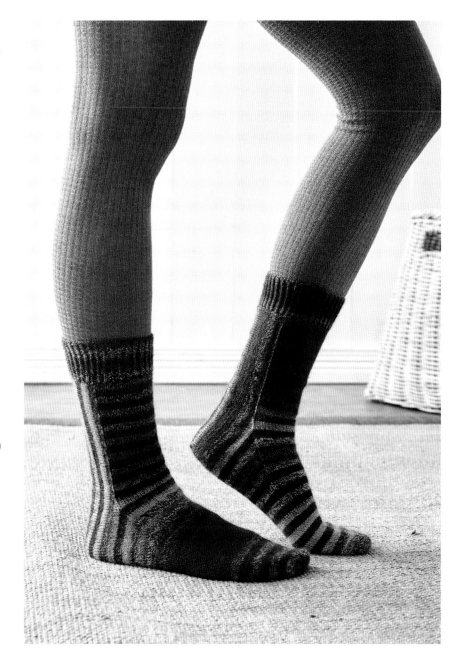

70, 72) sts total. Arrange sts on dpn or two cir needles, pm, and join for working in rnds.

Next rnd: *K1 through back loop (tbl), p1; rep from *.

Rep the last rnd for twisted rib patt until cuff measures 2" from pick-up rnd or desired length. Using Jeny's Surprisingly Stretchy Bind-Off or the Sewn Bind-Off BO all sts. Weave in loose ends. Block as desired.

cleave socks

Hunter Hammersen

Finished Size

Foot circumference: About 6½ (7½, 8½, 9½, 10¼)".

Foot length from back of heel to tip of toe (length is adjustable): 9 (9¼, 9¾, 10, 10½)".

Leg length from top of cuff to start of heel turn: 7¾ (8¼, 8¾, 9, 9½)".

Socks shown measure 7½" foot circumference.

Yarn

Fingering weight (#1 super fine).

Shown here: String Theory Caper Sock (80% Merino wool, 10% cashmere, 10% nylon; 400 yd [365 m]/4 oz [113.5 g]): light teal, 1 (1, 1, 2, 2) skein(s).

Needles

Size U.S. 1 (2.25 mm): needles for working in rounds as you prefer.

Adjust needle size if necessary to obtain the correct gauge.

Notions

Markers (m); cable needle (cn); tapestry needle.

Gauge

34 sts and 40 rnds = 4" in St st worked in rnds, relaxed after blocking.

Notes

■ The cable patterns are different for the right and left socks. The Double-Cable pattern in each leg chart runs along the outside of the leg, then divides at the top of the gusset. One half of the Split cable continues to the bottom of the heel flap; the other half continues along the outside of the foot to the toe.

Left sock

LEG

CO 56 (64, 72, 80, 88) sts. Arrange sts on needles as preferred, place marker (pm), and join for working in rnds, being careful not to twist sts. Rnd begins on inside of leg at start of front-of-leg sts.

Work Rnds 1-8 of Left Leg chart 6 times, ending with Rnd 8—48 chart rnds completed; piece measures 4¾" from CO.

To prepare for heel incs, place two markers (A and B) after the 28th (32nd, 36th, 40th, 44th) st, then place an additional marker after the last st of the rnd, next to the end-of-rnd m (C and D)—2 markers next to each other at the mid-point and end-of-rnd.

HEEL FLAP AND GUSSET

Set-up rnd: Work Rnd 1 of Left Leg chart as est over 28 (32, 36, 40, 44) sts, sl Marker A, M1P, sl Marker B, work Rnd 1 of Left Heel chart over 28 (32, 36, 40, 44) sts, sl Marker C, M1P, sl Marker D—58 (66, 74, 82, 90) sts total; 1 gusset st between each pair of markers.

> **Note:** *The gussets are shaped over the following 30 (34, 38, 42, 46) rounds. For the stitches of the Left Leg chart, continue the est pattern. For the sts of the Left Heel chart, continue in pattern until Rnds 1-8 have been worked 2 (3, 3, 4, 4) times, then work Rnds 9-16 once, then work the stitches as they appear in Rnd 16 (knit the knits and purl the purls) for 7 (3, 7, 3, 7) rnds. Work all gusset stitches in reverse stockinette (purl RS rows; knit WS rows).*

Next rnd: Keeping in patts as set, work to Marker A, sl Marker A, purl to Marker B, sl Marker B, work to Marker C, sl Marker C, purl to Marker D, sl Marker D.

Inc rnd: Keeping in patts as set, work in patt to Marker A, sl Marker A, p1, M1P, purl to Marker B, sl Marker B, work in patt to Marker C, sl Marker C, purl to 1 st before Marker D, M1P, p1, sl Marker D—2 sts inc'd.

Rep the last 2 rnds 14 (16, 18, 20, 22) more times—88 (100, 112, 124, 136) sts total; 16 (18, 20, 22, 24) gusset sts between each pair of markers; heel flap measures about 3 (3½, 4, 4¼, 4¾)" from set-up rnd; piece measures about 7¾ (8¼, 8¾, 9, 9½)" from CO.

Make a note of the last Left Leg chart rnd completed so you can resume working in patt with the correct rnd later.

HEEL TURN

Set-up: Work instep sts in patt to Marker A, sl Marker A, purl to Marker B, sl Marker B, knit to Marker C, then stop.

The heel turn is worked over the 28 (32, 36, 40, 44) back-of-leg sts between Markers B and C. Rearrange the sts as necessary to isolate these sts on a single needle; the rem 60 (68, 76, 84, 92) sts will be worked later for gusset decs and instep.

Work 28 (32, 36, 40, 44) heel sts back and forth in short-rows as foll.

Short-row 1: (WS) Sl 1, p16 (18, 20, 22, 24), p2tog, p1.

Short-row 2: (RS) Sl 1, k7, ssk, k1.

Short-row 3: Sl 1, p8, p2tog, p1.

Short-row 4: Sl 1, k9, ssk, k1.

Short-row 5: Sl 1, p10, p2tog, p1.

Short-row 6: Sl 1, k11, ssk, k1.

Short-row 7: Sl 1, p12, p2tog, p1.

Short-row 8: Sl 1, k13, ssk, k1.

Short-row 9: Sl 1, p14, p2tog, p1.

Short-row 10: Sl 1, k15, ssk, k1.

Size 6½" is complete—18 heel sts rem; 78 sts total.

Skip to Bottom of heel.

LEFT HEEL

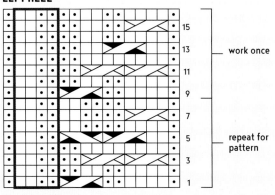

work once

repeat for pattern

4-st rep; work
4 (5, 6, 7, 8)
times

LEFT LEG

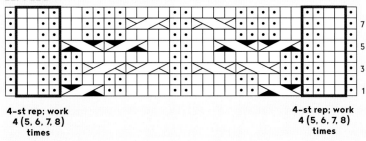

4-st rep; work
4 (5, 6, 7, 8)
times

4-st rep; work
4 (5, 6, 7, 8)
times

LEFT TOE

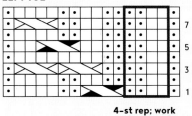

4-st rep; work
4 (5, 6, 7, 8)
times

☐ knit

• purl

☐ pattern repeat

sl 2 sts onto cn and hold in back of work, k2, then k2 from cn

sl 2 sts onto cn and hold in front of work, k2, then k2 from cn

sl 2 sts onto cn and hold in back of work, k2, then p2 from cn

sl 2 sts onto cn and hold in front of work, p2, then k2 from cn

SIZES 7½, (8½, 9½, 10¼)" ONLY

Short-row 11: (WS) Sl 1, p16, p2tog, p1.

Short-row 12: (RS) Sl 1, k17, ssk, k1.

Size 7½" is complete—20 heel sts rem; 88 sts total.

Skip to Bottom of heel.

SIZES 8½ (9½, 10¼)" ONLY

Short-row 13: (WS) Sl 1, p18, p2tog, p1.

Short-row 14: (RS) Sl 1, k19, ssk, k1.

Size 8½" is complete—22 heel sts rem; 98 sts total.

Skip to Bottom of heel.

SIZES 9½ (10¼)" ONLY

Short-row 15: (WS) Sl 1, p20, p2tog, p1.

Short-row 16: (RS) Sl 1, k21, ssk, k1.

Size 9½" is complete-24 heel sts rem; 108 sts total.

Skip to bottom of heel.

SIZE 10¼" ONLY

Short-row 17: (WS) Sl 1, p22, p2tog, p1.

Short-row 18: (RS) Sl 1, k23, ssk, k1.

Size 10¼" is complete—26 sts rem; 118 sts total.

BOTTOM OF HEEL

Remove markers B and C between heel and gusset sts as you come to them to accommodate the decs.

Cont working heel sts in rows, dec 1 gusset st at end of each heel row as foll:

Row 1: (WS) Purl to last heel st, p2tog (1 heel st tog with 1 gusset st)—1 gusset st dec'd.

Row 2: (RS) Knit to last heel st, ssk (1 heel st tog with 1 gusset st)—1 gusset st dec'd.

Rep these 2 rows 10 (11, 12, 13, 14) more times—56 (64, 72, 80, 88) sts rem; 18 (20, 22, 24, 26) heel sts; 5 (6, 7, 8, 9) sts each gusset; 28 (32, 36, 40, 44) instep sts.

Cont working back and forth in rows, inc 1 heel/sole st and dec 1 gusset st every row as foll:

Row 3: (WS) Purl to last sole st, M1P, p2tog (1 heel st tog with 1 gusset st)—no

change to st count; 1 sole st inc'd, 1 gusset st dec'd.

Row 4: (RS) Knit to last sole st, M1, ssk (1 heel st tog with 1 gusset st)—no change to st count; 1 sole st inc'd, 1 gusset st dec'd.

Rep these 2 rows 3 (4, 5, 6, 7) more times, ending with a RS row—still 56 (64, 72, 80, 88) sts; 26 (30, 34, 38, 42) heel sts; 1 st each gusset; 28 (32, 36, 40, 44) instep sts.

Foot

Joining rnd: With RS still facing, p1, sl Marker D, work 28 (32, 36, 40, 44) instep sts in patt, sl Marker A, p1, knit across heel/sole sts to 1 st before Marker D, p1, sl Marker D—28 (32, 36, 40, 44) sts each for instep and sole; rnd begins at Marker D on inner edge of foot, at start of instep sts.

Keeping sole sts in St st with p1 at each side, cont instep patt as set until foot measures 6½ (6½, 6¾, 6¾, 7)" from center back heel, or 2½ (2¾, 3, 3¼, 3½)" less than desired finished sock foot length, ending with Rnd 8 of Left Leg chart. Do not work any partial reps of the leg chart; if ending with Rnd 8 leaves you short of the target length, change to working the instep sts in patt from Left Toe chart, beg with Rnd 1.

Toe

Change to working 28 (32, 36, 40, 44) instep sts in patt from Left Toe chart if you have not already done so. Cont until Rnds 1–8 of toe chart have been worked once, then work the sts as they appear in Rnd 8 of chart until foot measures 8 (8, 8¼, 8, 8¼)" from center back heel, or 1 (1¼, 1½, 2, 2¼)" less than desired finished sock foot length.

Dec rnd: K1, ssk, work sts as they appear to 3 sts before Marker A, k2tog, k1, sl Marker A, p1, ssk, knit to 3 sts before Marker D, k2tog, p1, sl Marker D—4 sts dec'd.

Next rnd: Work sts as they appear to Marker A, sl Marker A, p1, knit to 1 st before Marker D, p1, sl Marker D.

Rep the last 2 rnds 1 (2, 3, 4, 5) more time(s)—48 (52, 56, 60, 64) sts rem.

Rep Dec rnd every rnd 6 (7, 8, 9, 10) times—24 sts rem for all sizes.

RIGHT LEG

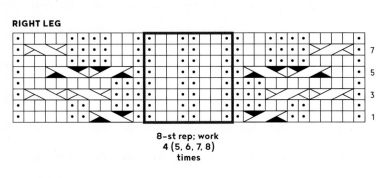

8-st rep; work
**4 (5, 6, 7, 8)
times**

RIGHT TOE

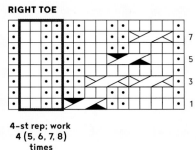

4-st rep; work
**4 (5, 6, 7, 8)
times**

	knit
•	purl
	pattern repeat

sl 2 sts onto cn and hold in back of work, k2, then k2 from cn

sl 2 sts onto cn and hold in front of work, k2, then k2 from cn

sl 2 sts onto cn and hold in back of work, k2, then p2 from cn

sl 2 sts onto cn and hold in front of work, p2, then k2 from cn

Finishing

Removing markers, arrange sts so that 12 top-of-foot sts are on one needle and 12 bottom-of-foot sts are on a second needle. Cut yarn, leaving a 12" tail. Thread tail on a tapestry needle and use the Kitchener st to graft the sts tog. Weave in loose ends. Block lightly.

Right sock

LEG

CO 56 (64, 72, 80, 88) sts. Arrange sts on needles as preferred, pm, and join for working in rnds, being careful not to twist sts. Rnd begins on outside of leg at start of front-of-leg sts.

Work Rnds 1–8 of Right Leg chart 6 times, ending with Rnd 8—48 chart rnds completed; piece measures 4¾" from CO.

Place Markers A, B, C, and D as for left sock—2 markers next to each other at the mid-point and end-of-rnd.

HEEL FLAP AND GUSSET

Set-up rnd: Work Rnd 1 of Right Leg chart as est over 28 (32, 36, 40, 44) sts, sl Marker A, M1P, sl Marker B, work Rnd 1 of Right Heel chart over 28 (32, 36, 40, 44) sts, sl Marker C, M1P, sl Marker D—58 (66, 74, 82, 90) sts total; 1 gusset st between each pair of markers.

> **Note:** The gussets are shaped over 30 (34, 38, 42, 46) rounds in the same manner as the left sock, substituting the charts for the right sock. For the stitches of the Right Leg chart, continue the est pattern. For the sts of the Right Heel chart, continue in pattern until Rnds 1–8 have been worked 2 (3, 3, 4, 4) times, then work Rnds 9–16 once, then work the stitches as they appear in Rnd 16 for 7 (3, 7, 3, 7) rnds. Work all gusset stitches in reverse stockinette.

Complete heel flap and gusset as for left sock—88 (100, 112, 124, 136) sts total; 16 (18, 20, 22, 24) gusset sts between each pair of markers; heel flap measures about 3 (3½, 4, 4¼, 4¾)" from set-up rnd; piece measures about 7¾ (8¼, 8¾, 9, 9½)" from CO.

Make a note of the last Right Leg chart rnd completed so you can resume working in patt with the correct rnd later.

HEEL TURN

Work as for left sock—78 (88, 98, 108, 118) sts total; 18 (20, 22, 24, 26) heel sts.

BOTTOM OF HEEL

Work as for left sock—56 (64, 72, 80, 88) sts rem; 26 (30, 34, 38, 42) heel sts; 1 st each gusset; 28 (32, 36, 40, 44) instep sts.

Foot

Joining rnd: With RS still facing, p1, sl Marker D, work 28 (32, 36, 40, 44) instep sts in patt, sl Marker A, p1, knit across heel/sole sts to 1 st before Marker D, p1, sl Marker D—28 (32, 36, 40, 44) sts each for instep and sole; rnd begins at Marker D on outer edge of foot, at start of instep sts.

Keeping sole sts in St st with p1 at each side, cont instep patt as set until foot measures 6½ (6½, 6¾, 6¾, 7)" from center back heel, or 2½ (2¾, 3, 3¼, 3½)" less than desired total length, ending with Rnd 8 of Right Leg chart. Do not work any partial reps of the leg chart; if ending with Rnd 8 leaves you short of the target length, change to working the instep sts in patt from Right Toe chart, beg with Rnd 1.

Toe

Change to working 28 (32, 36, 40, 44) instep sts in patt from Right Toe chart if you have not already done so. Complete toe as for left sock—24 sts rem for all sizes.

Finishing

Work as for left sock.

RIGHT HEEL

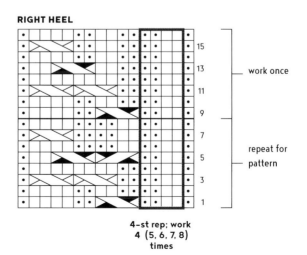

work once

repeat for pattern

4-st rep; work
4 (5, 6, 7, 8)
times

15
13
11
9
7
5
3
1

bandelier
socks

Lisa Shroyer

Finished Size

Foot circumference: 7½".

Foot length from back of heel to tip of toe (length is adjustable): 9¾".

Socks shown measure 7½" foot circumference.

Yarn

Fingering weight (#1 super fine).

Shown here: Brown Sheep Company Nature Spun Fingering (100% wool; 310 yd [283 m]/1¾ oz [50 g]): #720 ash (MC), #142 spiced plum (dark wine; A), #N89 roasted coffee (brown; B), #158 fanciful blue (light blue; C), #101 burnt sienna (rust; D), #135 hurricane seas (purple; E), and #145 salmon (F), 1 ball each.

Needles

Size U.S. 1 (2.25 mm): needles for working in rounds as you prefer.

Adjust needle size if necessary to obtain the correct gauge.

Notions

Marker (m); stitch holder; tapestry needle.

Gauge

28 sts and 32 rnds = 3" in charted patt.

Notes

■ These socks are worked in the round from the cuff down using Priscilla Gibson-Roberts' short-row heel method.

■ The foot's 35-round pattern repeat is shown twice in the 70-round foot chart, with toe decreases worked in pattern in the last 10 rounds. Because of this long repeat, it is difficult to alter the foot length while maintaining the pattern as shown. For a shorter foot, you could work the foot section in solid-color stockinette with MC until it measures 3¾" less than desired length, then work Rounds 36-70 of the foot chart, and then work the last decrease round as instructed in the toe section. If your gauge in solid-color

stockinette is different from your stranded colorwork gauge, you may need to adjust the needle size or the stitch count in the solid-color foot section, and you may also want to work an equal number of plain rounds using MC between the end of the leg chart and the start of the heel so that the patterning of the leg and foot are mirrored above and below the heel.

■ You can lengthen the foot about 1" by working the toe decreases every other round instead of every round. After the chart has been completed, continue in stockinette with MC, decreasing every other round as est until you have the required 26 stitches remaining before grafting the toe.

Backward yo (byo)

Bring yarn over right needle from back to front.

Leg

With MC, CO 74 sts. Place marker (pm) and join in the rnd.

Work in k1, p1 rib for 1¼".

Knit 2 rnds.

Join A and knit 1 rnd.

Work Rnds 1-35 of Leg chart 2 times.

With A, knit 1 rnd.

With MC, knit 2 rnds—piece measures about 8¼" from CO. (See Notes if adjusting leg length.)

Set-up row: (RS) With MC, k2tog, k17, place next 38 sts on holder for instep—35 sts rem for heel.

Heel

Heel is worked back and forth with MC over first 18 sts and last 17 sts of rnd; 38 instep sts will be worked later.

Next row: (WS) P18, remove beg-of-rnd m, p17.

Work first half of heel using short-rows (see Notes) as foll:

LEG

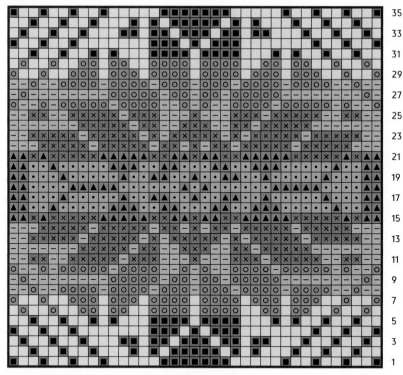

37-st rep

Short-row 1: (RS) Knit to last st, turn—1 st left unworked.

Short-row 2: (WS) Byo (see Stitch Guide), purl to last st, turn—1 st left unworked.

Short-row 3: Yo (from front to back), knit to st/yo pair (1 st with yo after it), turn—3 sts left unworked (st/yo pair, plus 1 st unworked from end of Short-row 1).

Short-row 4: Byo, purl to st/yo pair, turn—3 sts left unworked.

Short-row 5: Yo, knit to st/yo pair, turn.

Short-row 6: Byo, purl to st/yo pair, turn.

Short-rows 7–22: Rep Short-rows 5 and 6 eight times.

Short-row 23: Rep Short-row 5–11 center sts between last two st/yo pairs; 13 total sts between innermost yo's (1 st from pair at each side, plus 11 center sts between the pairs). Do not turn.

Work 2nd half of heel using shortrows as foll:

Short-row 1: (RS) K1 (first st of pair), correct st mount of yo so right leg is in front of needle, k2tog (corrected yo with first st of next pair), turn.

Short-row 2: (WS) Byo, purl to first pair, p1 (first st of pair), ssp (yo tog with first st of foll pair, turn.

Short-row 3: Yo, knit to pair, k1 (first st of pair; 2 foll sts on left needle should be yo's), correct st mount of 2 yo's, k3tog (2 yo's tog with first st of next pair), turn.

Short-row 4: Byo, purl to pair, p1 (first st of pair; 2 foll sts on left needle should be yo's), sssp (2 yo's tog with first st of next pair), turn.

Short-rows 5–22: Rep Short-rows 3 and 4 nine times—all yo's from first half of heel have been consumed; 36 sts total on heel needle: 35 heel sts, plus yo from beg of Row 22.

Joining rnd: Yo, knit to yo at end of heel needle, sl this yo to instep needle, k2tog (yo tog with first st of instep), k6, [k2tog, k9] 2 times, k2tog, k6, k2tog (last instep st tog with yo on heel needle from beg of joining rnd), knit first 18 sts of heel needle again, M1—70 sts: 35 heel/sole sts, 35 instep sts. Sl M1 inc made at end of joining rnd to left needle, pm for beg of rnd, and knit 1 rnd with A. Rnd beg at center of sole.

Foot

Work Rnds 1–60 of Foot chart (see Notes for adjusting foot length)—piece measures about 8" from center back heel.

▢	MC
■	A
⊙	B
−	C
⊠	D
▲	E
•	F
╱	k2tog with color shown
╲	ssk with color shown
▦	no stitch
▢	pattern repeat

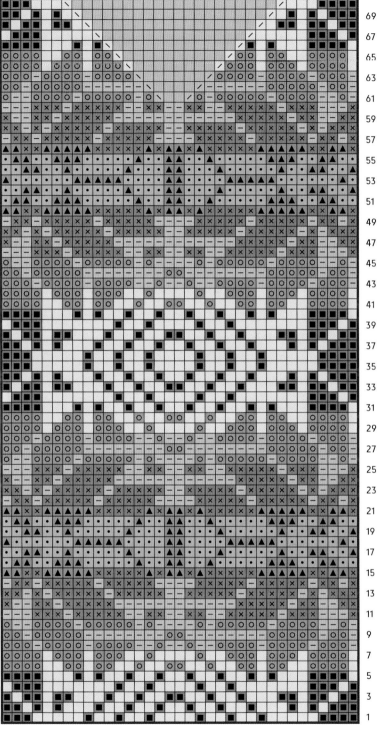

69
67
65
63
61
59
57
55
53
51
49
47
45
43
41
39
37
35
33
31
29
27
25
23
21
19
17
15
13
11
9
7
5
3
1

35-st rep

Toe

Work Rnds 61–70 of chart—30 sts rem.

Next rnd: With MC, *k6, k2tog, ssk, k5;
rep from * once more—26 sts rem: 13 sole
sts and 13 sts for top of toe.

Remove beg-of-rnd m and k7 to end at side
of toe. Graft sts tog, using Kitchener st.

Finishing

Turn socks inside out and weave in ends.
Use MC to close any holes at corners of
heel. Rinse socks in cold water, then use
towel to blot out excess moisture. This
yarn is not superwash, so be careful to
avoid hot water or any agitation. With
socks still inside out, lay flat and cover
with a damp towel. Use an iron on the
hottest setting to press down firmly
on towel over sock; do not make any
sweeping motions, just press. Pay special
attention to areas where you changed
needles working in the rnd because
stranded floats at needle changes tend
to be tight and need a good blocking. Let
air dry. Turn socks right side out and block
again, if needed.

durango socks

Sarah Jordan

Finished Size

Foot circumference:
6½ (7½, 8½)".

*Foot length from back
of heel to tip of toe:* 8½
(9, 9½)".

Socks shown measure 7½"
foot circumference.

Yarn

Fingering weight
(#1 super fine).

Shown here: Brown Sheep
Company Wildfoote Luxury
Sock (75% washable wool,
25% nylon; 215 yd [197 m]/
50 g): #SY45 goldenrod, 2
skeins (see Notes).

Needles

Size U.S. 1 (2.25 mm): needles
for working in rounds as you
prefer.

*Adjust needle size if necessary
to obtain the correct gauge.*

Notions

Markers (m); cable needle
(cn); tapestry needle.

Gauge

32 sts and 44 rnds = 4" in
St st.

Notes

■ These socks are worked from
the cuff down in the round.

■ The largest size socks use all
of two skeins of yarn. Consider
purchasing an extra skein as
insurance.

Cuff

CO 56 (64, 72) sts. Place marker (pm) and join in the rnd.

Next rnd: P1 (0, 1), [k1tbl] 2 (1, 2) time(s), p2, *[k1tbl] 2 times, p2; rep from * to last 3 (1, 3) st(s), [k1tbl] 2 (1, 2) time(s), p1 (0, 1).

Rep last rnd until piece measures 1" from CO.

Leg

Set-up rnd: K28 (32, 36), p5 (7, 9), [(k1tbl) 2 times, p6] 2 times, [k1tbl] 2 times, purl to end.

Next rnd: K28 (32, 36), beg and ending as indicated for your size, work Cable chart over 28 (32, 36) sts.

Cont in patt through Rnd 18 of chart, then work Rnds 1–18 of chart 2 more times— piece measures about 6" from CO.

Heel

> **Note:** Heel flap is worked back and forth over first 28 (32, 36) sts of rnd; last 28 (32, 36) sts will be worked later for instep.

Remove beg-of-rnd m.

Row 1: (RS) [Sl 1 kwise wyb, k1] 14 (16, 18) times, turn.

Row 2: (WS) Sl 1 pwise wyf, p27 (31, 35), turn.

Rep last 2 rows 13 (15, 17) more times.

TURN HEEL

Short-row 1: (RS) Sl 1 kwise wyb, k16 (18, 20), ssk, k1, turn.

Short-row 2 : (WS) Sl 1 pwise wyf, p7, p2tog, p1, turn.

Short-row 3: Sl 1 kwise wyb, knit to 1 st before gap, ssk, k1, turn.

Short-row 4: Sl 1 pwise wyf, purl to 1 st before gap, p2tog, p1, turn.

Rep last 2 short-rows 3 (4, 5) more times—18 (20, 22) heel sts rem.

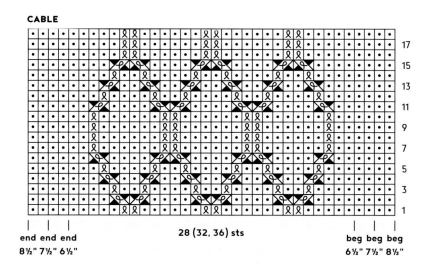

CABLE

17
15
13
11
9
7
5
3
1

end end end
8½" 7½" 6½"

28 (32, 36) sts

beg beg beg
6½" 7½" 8½"

| ℤ | k1tbl |
| · | purl |

sl 1 st onto cn, hold in back, k1tbl, p1 from cn

sl 1 st onto cn, hold in front, p1, k1tbl from cn

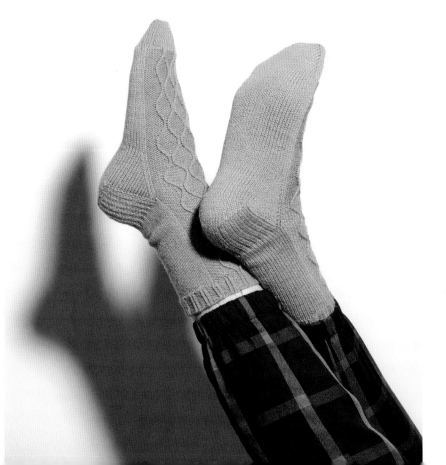

SHAPE GUSSET

Next rnd: K18 (20, 22) heel sts, pick up and knit 15 (17, 19) sts along side of heel flap, pm, work 28 (32, 36) instep sts in patt, pm, pick up and knit 15 (17, 19) sts along side of heel flap, k9 (10, 11) heel sts—76 (86, 96) sts total. Pm and join in the rnd.

Rnd 1: Knit to 3 sts before m, k2tog, k1, sl m, work instep sts in patt, sl m, k1, ssk, knit to end—2 sts dec'd.

Rnd 2: Knit to m, sl m, work instep sts in patt, sl m, knit to end.

Rep last 2 rnds 9 (10, 11) more times—56 (64, 72) sts rem.

Next rnd: Remove beg-of-rnd m, knit to m, sl m, work instep sts in patt (do not finish rnd); this is new beg of rnd.

Foot

Work even until foot measures 6½ (7, 7½)" from back of heel, or 2" less than desired finished length

Toe

Next rnd: Knit.

Dec rnd: *K1, ssk, knit to 3 sts before m, k2tog, k1; rep from * once more—4 sts dec'd.

Rep Dec rnd every other rnd 9 more times—16 (24, 32) sts rem.

Next rnd: Knit.

Break yarn, leaving a 10" tail.

Finishing

With tail threaded on a tapestry needle, graft sts using Kitchener st. Weave in ends. Block.

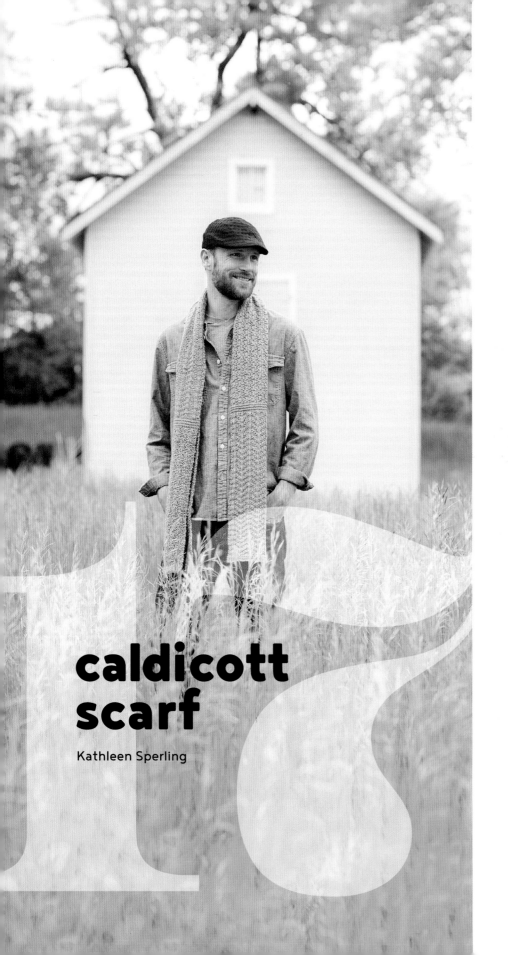

caldicott
scarf

Kathleen Sperling

Finished Size

8" wide and 66" long.

Yarn

Worsted weight (#4 medium).

Shown here: Wisdom Yarns Poems
Silk Solids (75% wool, 25% silk;
109 yd [100 m]/[50 g]): #702
sterling, 4 balls.

Needles

Size U.S. 6 (4 mm).

*Adjust needle size if necessary
to obtain the correct gauge.*

Notions

Tapestry needle.

Gauge

18½ sts and 28 rows = 4" in
charted patts.

Scarf

CO 37 sts.

*Knit 7 rows, ending with a RS row.

Beg with a WS row, work Chart A for 107 rows, ending with a WS row.

Knit 7 rows, ending with a RS row.

Beg with a WS row, work Chart B for 107 rows, ending with a WS row.

Rep from * once more.

Knit 6 rows.

BO all sts.

Finishing

Weave in ends. Block.

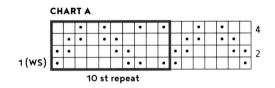

CHART A

10 st repeat

1 (WS)

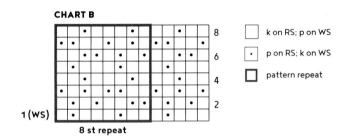

CHART B

8 st repeat

1 (WS)

☐	k on RS; p on WS
·	p on RS; k on WS
☐	pattern repeat

arches scarf

Kyle Kunnecke

Finished Size

59 ¼ " long by 10" wide.

Yarn

Worsted weight (#4 medium).

Shown here: HiKoo Simplinatural (40% baby alpaca, 40% fine Merino wool, 20% mulberry silk; 183 yd [167 m]/100 g): #053 cabernet, 4 skeins.

Needles

Size U.S. 7 (4.5 mm): 16" circular (cir) or straight.

Size U.S. 8 (5 mm): 16" cir or straight.

Adjust needle size if necessary to obtain the correct gauge.

Notions

Stitch markers (m); cable needle (cn); tapestry needle.

Gauge

22½ sts and 25 rows = 4" in chart patt with larger needles, blocked.

Notes

■ Most of the cabling on this scarf is worked on RS rows, leaving the WS rows full of knit and purl stitches. Every once in a while, however, the center cable wraps over itself, which requires cabling on a WS row. Pay careful attention to this cable and remember that it is worked differently than the others.

■ To keep from stretching cabled stitches, choose a cable needle with a diameter equal to or smaller than the project needle size.

1 × 1 Ribbed Cast-On: Make a slipknot, leaving a yarn tail that is 6" long. Insert needle into loop, then snug it up. This first stitch looks like a purl stitch.

Insert RH needle tip as if to knit, yarn over and pull through a loop, then place the new stitch on LH needle tip.

*Insert RH needle tip as if to purl between 2 sts on LH needle tip, yarn over and pull loop through a loop, then place the new stitch on LH needle tip.

Insert RH needle tip as if to knit between first 2 sts on LH needle tip, yarn over and pull through a loop, then place the new stitch on LH needle tip. Repeat from * until the required number of stitches are on LH needle tip; the final stitch is the last loop made.

Seed Stitch Bind-Off: Use a needle one or two sizes smaller than for the project for the bind-off.

P1, move yarn to back, sl st just made to LH needle tip, k2tog-1 st BO.

*Move yarn to front, sl st from RH needle tip to LH needle tip, p2tog-1 st BO. Move yarn to back, sl st from RH needle tip to LH needle tip, k2tog-1 st BO; repeat from * until all sts have been BO.

2/1LPC (2 over 1 left purl cross): Sl 2 sts onto cn and hold in front, p1, k2 from cn.

2/1RPC (2 over 1 right purl cross): Sl 1 st onto cn and hold in back, k2, p1 from cn.

2/2LC WS (2 over 2 left cross on wrong side): Sl 2 sts onto cn and hold in front, p2, p2 from cn.

2/2LPC (2 over 2 left purl cross): Sl 2 sts onto cn and hold in front, p2, k2 from cn.

2/2RPC (2 over 2 right purl cross): Sl 2 sts onto cn and hold in back, k2, p2 from cn.

Scarf

With smaller needles, CO 56 sts using the 1×1 Ribbed Cast-On method (see Stitch Guide).

Row 1: (RS) *K1, p1; rep from *.

Row 2: (WS) *P1, k1; rep from *.

Work 3 more rows in est patt.

Change to larger needles.

Set-up row: (WS) [P1, k1] twice, place marker (pm), [p1, k1] 3 times, p5, [k1, p1] 5 times, k1, p5, [k1, p1] 5 times, k1, p5, [k1, p1] twice, k1, pm, [p1, k1] twice.

BEGIN CHART

Work Rows 1–24 of the Chart A 14 times, slipping markers as you come to them.

Work Rows 1–23 once more. Piece should measure 58¼" from beg.

CHART A

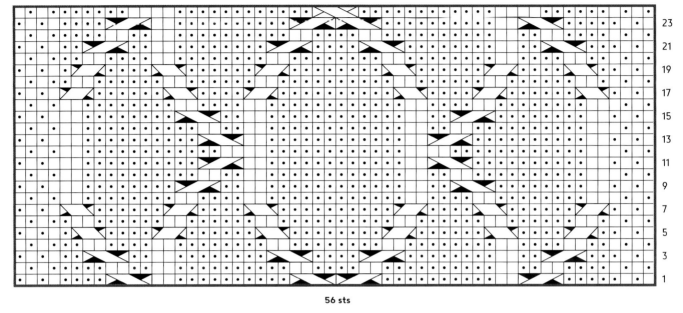

56 sts

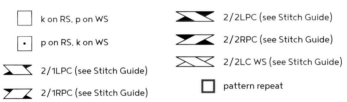

	k on RS, p on WS
	p on RS, k on WS
	2/1LPC (see Stitch Guide)
	2/1RPC (see Stitch Guide)
	2/2LPC (see Stitch Guide)
	2/2RPC (see Stitch Guide)
	2/2LC WS (see Stitch Guide)
	pattern repeat

Next row: (WS) (P1, k1) twice, remove marker, (p1, k1) 3 times, p5, (k1, p1) 5 times, k1, p5, (k1, p1) 5 times, k1, p5, (k1, p1) twice, k1, remove marker, (p1, k1) twice.

Change to smaller needles.

Next row: (RS) *K1, p1; rep from *.

Next row: (WS) *P1, k1; rep from *.

Work 3 more rows in est patt.

BO using Seed st method (see Stitch Guide). Cut yarn, leaving a 6" tail.

Finishing

Weave in all ends, waiting to cut yarn tails until after piece has been blocked.

Soak piece in cool water with a little wool wash. Lift out and gently squeeze to remove water. Lay on a towel and roll up to remove excess water. Unroll, shape, and lay piece flat to dry.

leadville cowl

Annie Watts

Finished Size

Circumference: 25½".

Height: 8½".

Yarn

Bulky weight (#5 bulky).

Shown here: The Fibre Company Tundra (60% baby alpaca, 30% Merino wool, 10% silk; 120 yd [110 m]/3½ oz [100 g]): mink, 3 skeins.

Needles

Size U.S. 9 (5.5 mm): 24" circular (cir).

Size U.S. 10 (6 mm): 24" cir.

Adjust needle size if necessary to obtain the correct gauge.

Notions

Marker (m); cable needle (cn); tapestry needle.

Gauge

17 sts and 22 rnds = 4" in Lattice patt on larger needle.

Notes

■ Cowl is worked in the round and then the cast-on and bind-off edges are sewn together to form a doubled fabric with the ribbing on the inside and the Lattice pattern on the outside.

Cowl

With smaller needle, CO 108 sts. Place marker (pm) and join in the rnd.

Next rnd: K1, *p2, k2; rep from * to last 3 sts, p2, k1.

Rep last rnd until piece measures 2½" from CO.

Change to larger needle and cont in rib patt until piece measures 3½" from CO.

Work Rnds 1–16 of Lattice chart 2 times, working Rnd 11 of chart as foll:

K1, *p1, M1P, p1, k2tog; rep from * to last st, sl last st to right needle, remove m, return slipped st to left needle, k2tog, pm.

Work Rnds 1–9 of chart once more—piece measures about 11" from CO.

Next rnd: K1, *p2, k2; rep from * to last 3 sts, p2, k1.

Cont in rib patt until piece measures 12" from CO. Change to smaller needle and cont in patt until work measures 18" from CO. BO all sts loosely in patt.

Finishing

Weave in ends. Turn cowl inside out. Fold CO edge up and BO edge down and seam them tog. Turn cowl right side out, wash, and lay flat to dry, adjusting cowl so that lattice panel is centered on outside. Laying a tall glass in the center of the cowl to separate the sides will help expedite the drying of the thick layers.

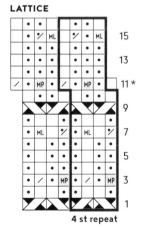

LATTICE

☐	knit
·	purl
╱	k2tog
⟋	p2tog
ML	LLI
MP	M1 pwise
⧄	sl 1 st onto cn, hold in back, k1, p1 from cn
⧅	sl 1 st onto cn, hold in front, p1, k1 from cn
☐	pattern repeat

4 st repeat

* Work as given in directions

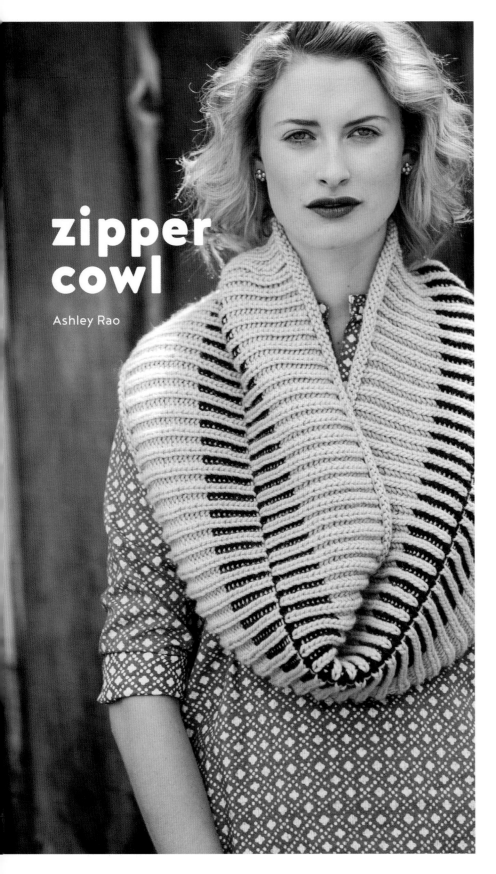

zipper cowl

Ashley Rao

Finished Size

Circumference: 44".

Height: 12¼".

Yarn

Worsted weight (#4 medium).

Shown here: Blue Sky Alpacas Worsted Hand Dyes (50% royal alpaca, 50% Merino wool; 100 yd [91 m]/3½ oz [100 g]): #2015 putty (MC), 4 skeins; #2012 cranberry (CC), 1 skein.

Needles

Size U.S. 7 (4.5 mm): 40" circular (cir).

Size U.S. 9 (5.5 mm): 40" cir.

Adjust needle size if necessary to obtain the correct gauge.

Notions

Marker (m); tapestry needle.

Gauge

12 sts and 36 rnds = 4" in Fisherman's Rib I on smaller needle.

STITCH GUIDE

Knit 1 below (k1B)

Knit into center of st below next st on left needle, drop st from left needle.

Purl 1 below (p1B)

Purl into center of st below next st on left needle, drop st from left needle.

Fisherman's Rib I (even number of sts)

Rnd 1: *P1B (see Stitch Guide), k1; rep from * to end.

Rnd 2: *P1, k1B (see Stitch Guide); rep from * to end.

Rep Rnds 1 and 2 for patt.

Fisherman's Rib II (even number of sts)

Rnd 1: With CC, *p1B, k1; rep from * to end.

Rnd 2: With MC, *p1, k1B; rep from * to end.

Rep Rnds 1 and 2 for patt.

Fisherman's Rib III (even number of sts)

Rnd 1: With MC, *k1B, p1; rep from * to end.

Rnd 2: With CC, *k1, p1B; rep from * to end.

Rep Rnds 1 and 2 for patt.

Fisherman's Rib IV (even number of sts)

Rnd 1: *K1B, p1; rep from * to end.

Rnd 2: *K1, p1B; rep from * to end.

Rep Rnds 1 and 2 for patt.

Cowl

ROLLED EDGE

With MC and larger needle, CO 154 sts. Place marker (pm) and join in the rnd.

Knit 3 rnds. Change to smaller needle.

Dec rnd: *[P1, k1] 2 times, p1, ssk; rep from * around—132 sts rem.

Work Rnds 1 and 2 of Fisherman's Rib I (see Stitch Guide for all patts) 16 times.

Work Rnds 1 and 2 of Fisherman's Rib II 9 times, then work Rnd 1 once more.

Next rnd: With CC, *k1, p1; rep from * to end.

Work Rnds 1 and 2 of Fisherman's Rib III 9 times.

Break CC and cont with MC only.

Work Rnds 1 and 2 of Fisherman's Rib IV 16 times, then work Rnd 1 once more.

Change to larger needle.

ROLLED EDGE

Next rnd: *K5, k1f&b; rep from * around—154 sts.

Knit 3 rnds.

BO all sts.

Finishing

Weave in ends. Block.

blackcomb cowl

Holli Yeoh

Finished Size

58" in circumference and 14" tall.

Yarn

Chunky weight (#5 bulky).

Shown here: Miss Babs K2 (100% Merino wool; 240 yd [219 m]/204 g): blackwatch, 3 skeins.

Needles

Size U.S. 10½ (7 mm): straight.

Adjust needle size if necessary to obtain the correct gauge.

Notions

Spare smaller needle for three-needle BO; tapestry needle.

Gauge

13½ sts and 12 rows = 4" in Double Garter st, blocked.

Notes

■ This cowl is knit in two stages. After the first panel is complete, stitches are picked up along one edge for the second panel.

■ This cowl begins with a double-wrap long-tail CO (see Stitch Guide), which is very similar to the standard long-tail cast-on and requires a familiarity with this method. The yarn is wrapped twice around the needle, creating a Double Wrap for each stitch.

■ The edges are joined by working modified three-needle bind-off with picked up selvedge stitches on the back needle. Alternately, simply bind off and then seam the two ends together.

Double-Wrap Long-Tail CO

Beg with a slipknot on the right needle. Set your yarn and hand position as for the long-tail CO. *Come up through loop on thumb as usual, catch strand around index finger and wrap yarn twice around the needle, go back down through loop on thumb and complete stitch as for long-tail CO; rep from * to desired number of sts. The initial slipknot counts as 1 st and each Double-Wrapped st counts as 1 st.

Double Garter St (odd number of sts)

Row 1: K1 into first wrap of Double-Wrap st, leaving 2nd wrap on left needle, *k2tog (rem wrap of first st with first wrap of next st), wrapping yarn twice around right needle; rep from * to end of row.

Rep Row 1 every row for Double Garter St patt.

Cowl

WORK FIRST PANEL

Using the double-wrap long-tail method (see Stitch Guide), CO 95 sts.

Beg with a WS row, work Double Garter St (see Stitch Guide) until piece measures 14" from CO, ending with a RS row.

Loosely BO as foll:

BO row: (WS) K1, *K2tog (rem wrap of previous st with first wrap of next st), pass first st on right needle over 2nd st and off needle; rep from * to end.

WORK SECOND PANEL

With first half, RS facing, beg in lower right corner, pick up and knit 1 st, then, wrapping yarn twice around the needle, pick up and knit 46 sts along right edge—47 sts; 1 single st, 46 double-wrap sts.

Work Double Garter st until cowl measures 58" from edge of first half, ending with a RS row.

JOIN ENDS

With spare needle, WS of first half facing, and entering st from back to front, pick up but do not knit 47 sts evenly along left edge.

With RS tog and second half in front, join pieces as foll:

Joining row: (WS) K2tog (first wrap of st on front needle with first st on back needle), *k3tog (rem wrap of previous st and first wrap of next st on front needle with next st on back needle), pass first st on right needle over 2nd st and off needle; rep from * to end.

Finishing

Block lightly to measurements. Weave in ends.

atoll cowl

Jenn Emerson

Finished Size

Circumference at top: 19".

Circumference at bottom: 34¾".

Height: 17¾".

Yarn

Lace weight (#0 lace).

Shown here: Jade Sapphire Khata (50% yak, 50% silk; 700 yd [640 m]/100 g): #K3 heavenly lake, 1 skein.

Needles

Size U.S. 5 (3.75 mm): 16" and 24" circular (cir) needles.

Adjust needle size if necessary to obtain the correct gauge.

Notions

Marker (m); tapestry needle.

Gauge

22 sts and 28 rnds = 4" in patt

Notes

■ This cowl is worked in the round from the top down.

■ Change to longer circular needle when necessary.

STITCH GUIDE

Elongated Stitch Band:

Rnd 1: *K1, wrapping yarn 3 times around right needle instead of once; rep from * to end.

Rnd 2: *K1, dropping all 3 wraps as st is removed from left needle; rep from * to end.

Cowl

With shorter cir needle (see Notes), CO 104 sts. Place marker (pm) and join in the rnd.

Purl 1 rnd.

Knit 8 rnds.

Work Rnds 1 and 2 of Elongated St Band (see Stitches).

Knit 7 rnds.

Rep last 9 rnds 2 more times.

Work Rnds 1 and 2 of Elongated St Band.

Knit 5 rnds.

Inc rnd: K2, *M1L, k5; rep from * to last 2 sts, M1L, k2—125 sts. Knit 1 rnd.

Work Rnds 1 and 2 of Elongated St Band.

Knit 7 rnds.

Rep last 9 rnds once more.

Work Rnds 1 and 2 of Elongated St Band.

Knit 6 rnds.

Inc rnd: K2, *M1L, k6; rep from * to last 3 sts, M1L, k3—146 sts.

Work Rnds 1 and 2 of Elongated St Band. Knit 7 rnds.

Work Rnds 1 and 2 of Elongated St Band.

Knit 6 rnds.

Inc rnd: K3, *M1L, k3; rep from * to last 2 sts, M1L, k2—194 sts.

Work Rnds 1 and 2 of Elongated St Band. Knit 7 rnds.

Rep last 9 rnds 3 more times.

BO all sts as foll:

K1, *transfer 1 st from right needle to left needle, k2tog tbl; rep from * to end.

Finishing

Weave in ends. Block to measurements.

snowflake cowl

Jesie Ostermiller

Finished Size

Circumference: 50¼".

Width: 8¾".

Yarn

Fingering weight
(#1 super fine).

Shown here: The Fibre
Company Cumbria Fingering
(60% Merino wool, 30%
brown masham wool, 10%
mohair; 328 yd [300 m]/3½ oz
[100 g]): #48 derwentwater
(dark blue; MC), 3 skeins; #01
scafell pike (gray; CC), 1 skein.

Needles

Size U.S. 3 (3.25 mm):
16" circular (cir).

*Adjust needle size if necessary
to obtain the correct gauge.*

Notions

Marker (m); removable m; size
D/3 (3.25 mm) crochet hook;
waste yarn for provisional
CO and to be used as a stitch
holder; spare size U.S. 3 (3.25
mm) or smaller 16" cir needle
for grafting; tapestry needle.

Gauge

25 sts and 28 rnds = 4" in
charted patt.

Notes

■ This cowl begins with a
crochet chain provisional
cast-on and is worked in the
round to form a long tube; the
ends of the tube are grafted
together using the circular
grafting method.

■ The circular grafting method
(see page 77) is designed
specifically for invisibly joining
two pieces that have been
worked in the round. For the
circular grafting method to
work best, it is important
to start with a provisional
cast-on (such as the crochet
chain provisional method)
that results in a single row of
working yarn stitches.

Cowl

With MC and using the crochet chain provisional method (see Notes), leaving an 8" tail of MC, CO 110 sts. Place marker (pm) and join in the rnd.

*Work Rnds 1–10 of Lice chart 7 times, then work Rnds 1–8 once more.

Work Rnds 1–37 of Snowflakes chart.

With MC, knit 2 rnds.

Rep from * once more.

Work Rnds 1–10 of Lice chart 7 times, then work Rnds 1–8 once more.

Work Rnds 1–37 of Snowflakes chart.

Break yarns, leaving a 2-yd tail of MC for grafting. Place sts on waste yarn holder.

Finishing

Turn tube WS out and weave in ends (except CO and grafting tails), then turn tube RS out. Block.

SNOWFLAKES

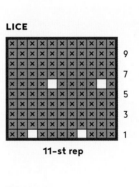

22-st rep

LICE

9
7
5
3
1

11-st rep

⊠ MC

☐ CC

☐ pattern repeat

CIRCULAR GRAFTING

Place CO sts onto spare cir needle as foll:

Undo just enough of waste yarn chain to release CO tail. With CO tail threaded on a tapestry needle, create a temporary loop by drawing tail from front to back through same loop from which it's emerging **(Figure 1)**. Gently pull tail until loop is same size as other CO sts. Place a removable m in row above this newly made st (this st is marked by a dot in the illustration and will come into play at the end of the grafting). Beg with this newly made loop, place CO sts onto spare cir needle, removing chain as you go—110 CO sts on needle.

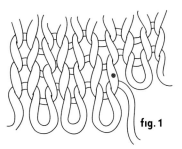

fig. 1

Transfer live sts from waste yarn holder to working needle. Hold the 2 needles tog, needle holding live sts and grafting yarn in front and needle holding CO sts in back, making sure tube isn't twisted. Thread yarn from front needle onto tapestry needle and graft 109 sts in St st—1 st rem to be grafted.

Draw grafting yarn through after last step **(Figure 2)**. Place a removable m in st on each needle (other 2 sts marked by dots in illustration) and remove sts from needles. Remove CO tail from st marked with removable m at beg of grafting.

fig. 2

Graft last st in St st **(Figure 3)** by drawing yarn through sts as foll:

Step 1: Pwise (from WS to RS) through st from front needle.

Step 2: Pwise (from RS to WS) through st from back needle.

Step 3: Kwise (from WS to RS) through marked st from beg of grafting.

Step 4: Kwise (from RS to WS) through st from front needle.

To weave in ends, twist tails once around each other, then take each tail to opposite side of gap and run tails through to inside of tube, giving each tail a tug to make sure gap is closed.

fig. 3

loveland cowl

Laura Reinbach

Finished Size

Circumference: 23".

Height: 9¼".

Yarn

Fingering weight (#1 super fine).

Shown here: Wonderland Yarns Cheshire Cat (100% superwash Merino wool; 512 yd (468 m)/113 g): #00 white rabbit (MC), 1 skein.

Wonderland Yarns Cheshire Cat Miniskein pack (100% superwash Merino wool; 128 yd (117 m)/28 g per skein; 5 skeins per pack): #14 cats in the coffee (browns; CC1–CC5), 1 set of 5 skeins.

Needles

Size U.S. 3 (3.25 mm): 24" circular (cir).

Adjust needle size if necessary to obtain the correct gauge.

Notions

Marker (m); spare 24" cir needle, same size or smaller than main needle; tapestry needle.

Gauge

27 sts and 36 rnds = 4" in St st.

Notes

■ This cowl is worked in the round, then the ends are grafted together using Kitchener stitch.

■ The chart is worked using the stranded method.

■ Always pick up the first color over the second and pick up the second color from under the first; this will prevent tangling.

■ Keep floats loose. For floats longer than 5 stitches, twist yarns together on wrong side of work.

■ Break yarn at each color change.

■ If necessary, use a larger needle for the charted rounds to maintain gauge.

Cowl

With CC1 and using a provisional method, CO 156 sts. Place marker and join in the rnd.

Knit 6 rnds.

With CC2 (see Notes), knit 7 rnds.

With CC3, knit 7 rnds.

With CC4, knit 7 rnds.

With CC5, knit 13 rnds.

With CC4, knit 7 rnds.

With CC3, knit 7 rnds.

With CC2, knit 7 rnds.

With CC1, knit 7 rnds.

With MC, knit 7 rnds.

Purl 1 rnd for turning ridge.

Work Rnds 1–83 of Colorwork chart.

With MC, purl 1 rnd for turning ridge.

Knit 6 rnds.

Break yarn, leaving a 3½ yd tail for grafting.

Finishing

Place sts on waste yarn holder. Block. Weave in all ends except for grafting tail. Return sts to needle.

Remove waste yarn from provisional CO and place 156 CO sts onto spare cir needle. Fold cowl at turning ridges with WS tog. With tail threaded on a tapestry needle, graft sts using Kitchener st.

COLORWORK

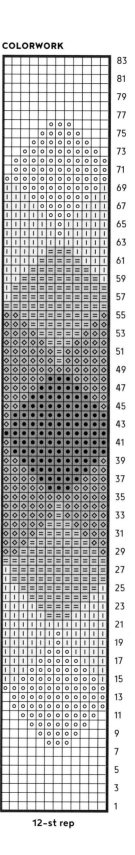

12-st rep

	MC
o	CC1
I	CC2
=	CC3
◇	CC4
●	CC5
	pattern repeat

trapper cowl

Lisa R. Myers

Finished Size

Circumference: 28".

Height: 9".

Yarn

Worsted weight (#4 medium).

Shown here: Manos del Uruguay Maxima (100% extrafine Merino wool; 219 yd [200 m]/3½ oz [100 g]): #M2540 kohl (gray, A) and #M2110 zinnia (red, B), 1 skein each.

Needles

Size U.S. 6 (4 mm): 24" circular (cir).

Adjust needle size if necessary to obtain the correct gauge.

Notions

Marker (m); tapestry needle.

Gauge

30 st-pairs and 25 rnds = 4" in Double Knitting patt.

Notes

■ This cowl is worked in the round using a two-color double-knitting technique. In double knitting, two layers of fabric are created simultaneously. The outer layer is worked with the knit side facing you and reflects the color assignments shown on the chart. The inner layer is worked with the purl side facing you and with the chart colors reversed.

■ Each square on the chart represents a pair of stitches: a knit stitch and a purl stitch. For each square on the chart, knit with the color shown on the chart and purl with the other color.

■ The term "st-pair" refers to a knit/purl pair of stitches.

■ Before knitting a stitch, bring both yarns to the back of the work; before purling a stitch, bring both yarns to the front of the work.

Cowl

With both colors and using the 2-color long-tail method, CO 108 st-pairs (108 knit/purl pairs; see Notes). Remove slipknot. Place marker and join in the rnd.

Work Rnds 1–16 of Plaid chart 3 times, then work Rnds 1–8 once more.

With A, BO all sts as foll:

K1, *k2tog, pass first st over 2nd st; rep from * to end.

Fasten off last st.

Finishing

Weave in ends. Block.

PLAID

| 15 |
| 13 |
| 11 |
| 9 |
| 7 |
| 5 |
| 3 |
| 1 |

12 st-pair repeat

×	with A, k1, with B, p1
●	with B, k1, with A, p1
□	pattern repeat

hoxey cowl

Meghan Huber

Finished Size

Circumference: 22¼".

Height: 9½".

Yarn

Super bulky weight (#6 super bulky).

Shown here: Plymouth Yarn Baby Alpaca Grande (100% baby alpaca; 110 yd [101 m]/3½ oz [100 g]): #100 natural (MC), 1 skein.

Plymouth Yarn Baby Alpaca Grande Hand Dye (100% baby alpaca; 110 yd [101 m]/3½ oz [100 g]): #39 red/green/gray variegated (CC), 1 skein.

Needles

Size U.S. 10 (6 mm): 16" circular (cir).

Adjust needle size if necessary to obtain the correct gauge.

Notions

Marker (m); tapestry needle.

Gauge

13 sts and 15 rnds = 4" in Two-Color Moss st.

Notes

- This cowl is worked in the round from the bottom up.

STITCH GUIDE

Two-color Moss stitch (even number of sts)

Rnd 1: *With CC, k1, with MC, k1; rep from * to end.

Rnd 2: *With CC, p1, with MC, k1; rep from * to end.

Rnd 3: *With MC, k1, with CC, k1; rep from * to end.

Rnd 4: *With MC, k1, with CC, p1; rep from * to end.

Rep Rnds 1-4 for patt.

Cowl

With MC, CO 72 sts. Place marker and join in the rnd.

Purl 1 rnd.

Work in Two-color Moss st (see Stitch Guide) for 32 rnds.

Break CC.

With MC, knit 1 rnd.

Purl 1 rnd.

BO all sts.

Finishing

Weave in ends. Block to measurements.

winter thyme cowl

Moira Engel

Finished Size

Circumference: 43".

Width: 12".

Yarn

DK weight (#3 light).

Shown here: Sweet Fiber Merino wool Twist DK (100% superwash Merino wool; 260 yd [238 m]/4 oz [115 g]): forest, 3 skeins.

Needles

Size U.S. 6 (4 mm): straight and 40" circular (cir).

Adjust needle size if necessary to obtain the correct gauge.

Notions

Marker (m); stitch holder; cable needle (cn); tapestry needle.

Gauge

25 sts and 32 rows = 4" in Bobbles and Waves patt.

Notes

▪ This cowl is worked back and forth starting with a provisional cast-on, and then the ends are grafted together in pattern. The edgings are picked up along the side edges and worked in the round.

STITCH GUIDE

Edging bobble

Knit into front, back and front of next st—3 sts; turn, p3; turn, k3; turn, p3; turn, sl 1, k2tog, psso—returned to 1 st.

Cowl

With straight needles and using the crochet chain provisional method, CO 80 sts, leaving a 6" tail.

Work Rows 3–12 of Bobbles and Waves chart once, then rep Rows 1–12 of chart until piece measures about 43" from CO, ending with Row 12.

Break yarn, leaving a 54" tail for grafting. Place sts on holder.

BOBBLES AND WAVES

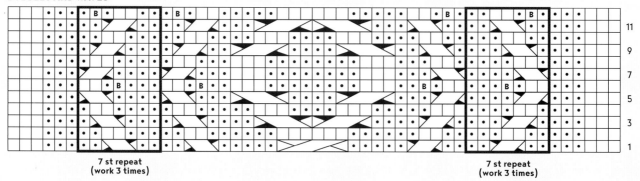

7 st repeat
(work 3 times)

7 st repeat
(work 3 times)

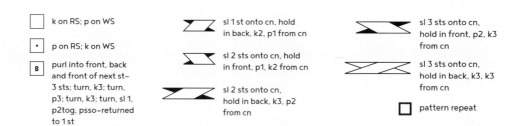

	k on RS; p on WS
	p on RS; k on WS
B	purl into front, back and front of next st– 3 sts; turn, k3; turn, p3; turn, k3; turn, sl 1, p2tog, psso–returned to 1 st

sl 1 st onto cn, hold in back, k2, p1 from cn

sl 2 sts onto cn, hold in front, p1, k2 from cn

sl 2 sts onto cn, hold in back, k3, p2 from cn

sl 3 sts onto cn, hold in front, p2, k3 from cn

sl 3 sts onto cn, hold in back, k3, k3 from cn

pattern repeat

Finishing

Block. Remove waste yarn from provisional CO and place 80 CO sts on needle. With 6" CO tail threaded on a tapestry needle, create an extra st on same needle by wrapping yarn clockwise once around needle and bringing it to WS of work—81 sts.

Return 80 live sts to a 2nd needle and, holding needles parallel with CO sts in back, WS tog, and with grafting tail threaded on a tapestry needle, graft sts in patt, foll grafting chart or written instructions.

> **Note:** In the written instructions, the sequences appear first, followed by the order in which the sequences are worked.

SEQUENCE A (knit st on FN, knit st on BN)

Step 1: Pwise through st on FN, leave.

Step 2: Pwise through st on BN, remove.

Step 3: Kwise through next st on BN, leave.

Step 4: Kwise through st on FN, remove.

SEQUENCE B (purl st on FN, purl st on BN)

Step 1: Kwise through st on FN, leave.

Step 2: Kwise through st on BN, remove.

Step 3: Pwise through next st on BN, leave.

Step 4: Pwise through st on FN, remove.

SEQUENCE C (2/1 RPC on FN; 2 knit sts, 1 purl st on BN)

Rearrange 3 sts on FN as foll: Sl 1 st onto tapestry needle and hold in back, remove next 2 sts from FN temporarily and transfer 1 st from tapestry needle back onto FN, then return 2 live sts to FN.

Work Sequence A 2 times, work Sequence B once.

SEQUENCE D (3/3 RC on FN; 6 knit sts on BN)

Rearrange 6 sts on FN as foll: Sl 3 sts onto tapestry needle and hold in back,

remove next 3 sts from FN temporarily and transfer 3 sts from tapestry needle back onto FN, then return 3 live sts to FN.

Work Sequence A 6 times.

SEQUENCE E (2/1 LPC on FN; 1 purl st, 2 knit sts on BN)

Rearrange 3 sts on FN as foll: Sl 2 sts onto tapestry needle and hold in front, remove next st from FN temporarily and transfer 2 sts from tapestry needle back onto FN, then return live st to FN.

Work Sequence B once, work Sequence A 2 times.

GRAFT IN PATT

Work Sequence A 3 times, work Sequence B 3 times, *work Sequence B 2 times, work Sequence C (over 3 sts on each needle) once, work Sequence B 2 times; rep from * 3 more times, work Sequence B 3 times, work Sequence D (over 6 sts on each needle) once, work Sequence B 3 times, **work Sequence B 2 times, work Sequence E (over 3 sts on each needle) once, work Sequence B 2 times; rep from ** 3 more times, work Sequence B 3 times, work Sequence A 3 times.

EDGING

With cir needle and RS facing, pick up and knit 228 sts evenly around one edge of cowl. Place marker and join in the rnd.

Purl 1 rnd.

BO all sts as foll:

*BO 5 sts pwise, make Edging Bobble (see Stitch Guide) in next st on left needle, then using st rem on right needle after BO, BO bobble pwise; rep from * to end. Fasten off last st. Rep for opposite edge. Weave in ends.

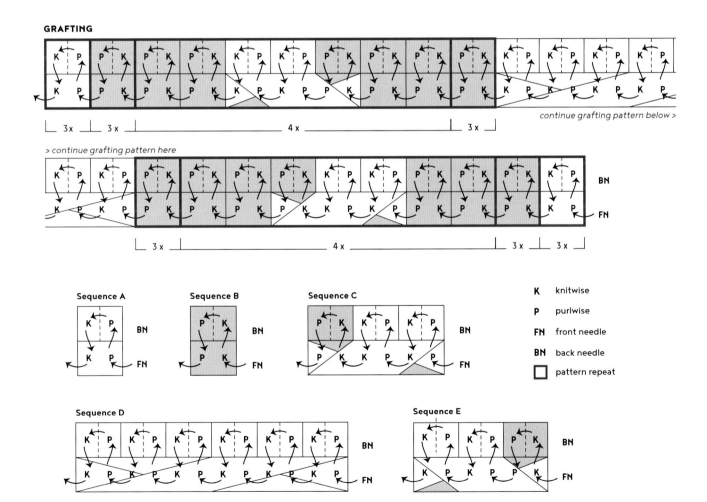

bear lake cowl

Quenna Lee

Finished Size

Circumference: 45".

Depth: 6½".

Yarn

Worsted weight (#4 medium).

Shown here: Cascade Yarns Eco Cloud (70% undyed Merino wool, 30% un-dyed baby alpaca; 164 yd [150 m]/100 g): #1803 fawn, 3 hanks.

Needles

Size U.S. 15 (10 mm): 40" circular (cir).

Adjust needle size if necessary to obtain the correct gauge.

Notions

Marker (m); tapestry needle.

Gauge

11½ sts and 15 rnds = 4" in charted patt.

Notes

▪Work with two strands of yarn held together throughout.

MOCK CABLE

26 st repeat

☐ knit	╱ k2tog
• purl	╲ ssk
○ yo	☐ pattern repeat

Cowl

With 2 strands held tog (see Notes), CO 130 sts.

Place marker m and join in the rnd.

Work Rnds 1–8 of Mock Cable chart 3 times.

BO all sts in patt.

Finishing

Weave in ends. Block to measurements.

Finished Size

Circumference: 40½".

Height: 13½".

Yarn

Bulky weight (#5 bulky).

Shown here: The Fibre Company Tundra (60% baby alpaca, 30% Merino wool, 10% silk; 120 yd [110 m]/100 g): #209 allium, 3 skeins.

Needles

Size U.S. 10 (6 mm): 40" circular (cir).

Adjust needle size if necessary to obtain the correct gauge.

Notions

Markers (m); tapestry needle.

Gauge

13 sts and 22 rnds = 4" in charted patt.

Notes

■ This cowl is worked in the round from the bottom up.

badge cowl

Tanis Gray

NORDIC STAR

22 st repeat

43
41
39
37
35
33
31
29
27
25
23
21
19
17
15
13
11
9
7
5
3
1

☐ knit

• purl

☐ pattern repeat

Cowl

CO 132 sts. Place marker and join in the rnd.

[Knit 1 rnd, purl 1 rnd] 2 times.

Work Rnds 1–44 of Nordic Star chart once, then work Rnds 1–22 of chart once more.

[Knit1 rnd, purl 1 rnd] 2 times.

BO all sts.

Finishing

Weave in ends. Block to measurements.

edora cowl

Yoko Johnston

Finished Size

Circumference: 49".

Width: 16".

Yarn

Laceweight (#0 lace).

Shown here: The Fibre Company Road to China Lace (65% baby alpaca, 15% silk, 10% cashmere, 10% camel; 656 yd [600 m]/100 g): grey pearl, 2 skeins.

Needles

Size U.S. 7 (4.5 mm).

Adjust needle size if necessary to obtain the correct gauge.

Notions

Size G/7 (4.5 mm) crochet hook; stitch holder; waste yarn for provisional CO; tapestry needle.

Gauge

18 sts and 20 rows = 4" in charted patt with two strands held tog, blocked.

Notes

- This cowl is worked back and forth in rows, then the ends are grafted together.

- Work with two strands of yarn held together throughout.

Knot stitch (worked over 3 sts)

With tip of right needle, pass 3rd st on left needle over first and 2nd sts, then work first and 2nd sts as k1tbl, yo, k1tbl.

Bobble fringe

With RS facing and using the backward-loop method, CO 5 sts, turn; work [k1, yo, k1, yo, k1] into first st, turn; k5, turn; sl 2 pwise wyf, p3tog, p2sso, BO 5 sts—1 st rem on right needle (this st counts as first worked st of next WS row and is not included in instructions).

Cowl

With 2 strands of yarn held tog (see Notes) and using the crochet chain provisional method, CO 39 sts.

Next row: (RS) K1, p1, *k1tbl, p1; rep from * to last st, k1.

Next row: (WS) K2, *p1tbl, k1; rep from * to last st, k1.

Rep last 2 rows until piece measures 7" from CO, ending with a WS row.

INC SECTION 1

Row 1: (RS) K1, M1L, p1, work Knot st over 3 sts (see Stitch Guide), *p1, k1tbl; rep from * to last 6 sts, p1, work Knot st over 3 sts, p1, M1R, k1, work Bobble Fringe (see Stitch Guide)—41 sts.

Row 2: (WS) Not counting first st already on right needle, *p1tbl, k1; rep from * to end.

Row 3: K1, M1L, [work Knot st over 3 sts, p1] 2 times, *k1tbl, p1; rep from * to last 8 sts, work Knot st over 3 sts, p1, work Knot st over 3 sts, M1R, k1—43 sts.

Row 4: K2, *p1tbl, k1; rep from * to last st, k1.

Row 5: K1, M1L, p1, k1tbl, p1, [work Knot st over 3 sts, p1] 2 times, *k1tbl, p1; rep from * to last 11 sts, [work Knot st over 3 sts, p1] 2 times, k1tbl, p1, M1R, k1—45 sts.

Row 6: *K1, p1tbl; rep from * to last st, k1.

Row 7: K1, M1L, k1tbl, p1, [work Knot st over 3 sts, p1] 3 times, *k1tbl, p1; rep from * to last 14 sts, [work Knot st over 3 sts, p1] 3 times, k1tbl, M1R, k1—47 sts.

Row 8: K2, *p1tbl, k1; rep from * to last st, k1.

Row 9: K1, M1L, p1, [work Knot st over 3 sts, p1] 4 times, *k1tbl, p1; rep from * to last 17 sts, [work Knot st over 3 sts, p1] 4 times, M1R, k1, work Bobble Fringe—49 sts.

Row 10: *P1tbl, k1; rep from * to end.

Row 11: K1, M1L, [work Knot st over 3 sts, p1] 5 times, [k1tbl, p1] 4 times, [work Knot st over 3 sts, p1] 4 times, work Knot st over 3 sts, M1R, k1—51 sts.

Row 12: K2, *p1tbl, k1; rep from * to last st, k1.

Row 13: K1, M1L, p1, k1tbl, p1, [work Knot st over 3 sts, p1] 5 times, [k1tbl, p1] 2 times, [work Knot st over 3 sts, p1] 5 times, k1tbl, p1, M1R, k1—53 sts.

Row 14: *K1, p1tbl; rep from * to last st, k1.

Row 15: K1, M1L, k1tbl, p1, *work Knot st over 3 sts, p1; rep from * to last 2 sts, k1tbl, M1R, k1—55 sts.

Row 16: K2, *p1tbl, k1; rep from * to last st, k1.

INC SECTION 2

Row 1: (RS) K1, M1L, p1, *work Knot st over 3 sts, p1; rep from * to last st, M1R, k1, work Bobble Fringe—2 sts inc'd.

Row 2: (WS) *P1tbl, k1; rep from * to end.

Row 3: K1, M1L, *work Knot st over 3 sts, p1; rep from * to last 4 sts, work Knot st over 3 sts, M1R, k1—2 sts inc'd.

Row 4: K2, *p1tbl, k1; rep from * to last st, k1.

Row 5: K1, M1L, p1, k1tbl, p1, *work Knot st over 3 sts, p1; rep from * to last 3 sts, k1tbl, p1, M1R, k1—2 sts inc'd.

Row 6: K1, *p1tbl, k1; rep from * to end.

Row 7: K1, M1L, p1, k1tbl, p1, *work Knot st over 3 sts, p1; rep from * to last 2 sts, k1tbl, M1R, k1—2 sts inc'd.

Row 8: K2, *p1tbl, k1; rep from * to last st, k1.

Rep Rows 1-8 three more times, then work Rows 1-4 once more—91 sts.

TWISTED MESH

4-st rep

	k on RS; p on WS
·	p on RS; k on WS
⌿	k1tbl on RS; p1tbl on WS
◆	bobble fringe (see Stitch Guide)
⊡	st on right needle after bobble fringe
☐	pattern repeat
⊂○⊃	knot stitch (see Stitch Guide)

BODY

Work Rows 1-8 of Twisted Mesh chart 11 times, working Bobble Fringe at end of each Row 5 as shown, then work Rows 1 and 2 of chart once more.

DEC SECTION 1

Row 1: (RS) K2tog, *work Knot st over 3 sts, p1; rep from * to last 5 sts, work Knot st over 3 sts, ssk—89 sts rem.

Row 2: (WS) K1, *p1tbl, k1; rep from * to end.

Row 3: K2tog, p1, *work Knot st over 3 sts, p1; rep from * to last 2 sts, ssk, work Bobble Fringe—2 sts dec'd.

Row 4: K1, *p1tbl, k1; rep from * to last st, k1.

Row 5: K2tog, k1tbl, p1, *work Knot st over 3 sts, p1; rep from * to last 3 sts, k1tbl, ssk—2 sts dec'd.

Row 6: K1, *p1tbl, k1; rep from * to end.

Row 7: K2tog, p1, k1tbl, p1, *work Knot st over 3 sts, p1; rep from * to last 4 sts, k1tbl, p1, ssk—2 sts dec'd.

Row 8: K2, *p1tbl, k1; rep from * to last st, k1.

Row 9: K2tog, *work Knot st over 3 sts, p1; rep from * to last 5 sts, work Knot st over 3 sts, ssk—2 sts dec'd.

Row 10: K1, *p1tbl, k1; rep from * to end.

Rep Rows 3–10 three more times, then work Rows 3–6 once more—53 sts rem.

DEC SECTION 2

Row 1: (RS) K2tog, p1, k1tbl, p1, [work Knot st over 3 sts, p1] 5 times, [k1tbl, p1] 2 times, [work Knot st over 3 sts, p1] 5 times, k1tbl, p1, ssk—51 sts rem.

Row 2: K2, *p1tbl, k1; rep from * to last st, k1.

Row 3: K2tog, [work Knot st over 3 sts, p1] 5 times, [k1tbl, p1] 4 times, [work Knot st over 3 sts, p1] 4 times, work Knot st over 3 sts, ssk—49 sts rem.

Row 4: K1, *p1tbl, k1; rep from * to end.

Row 5: K2tog, p1, [work Knot st over 3 sts, p1] 4 times, [k1tbl, p1] 6 times, [work Knot st over 3 sts, p1] 4 times, ssk, work Bobble Fringe—47 sts rem.

Row 6: K1, *p1tbl, k1; rep from * to last st, k1.

Row 7: K2tog, k1tbl, p1, [work Knot st over 3 sts, p1] 3 times, [k1tbl, p1] 8 times, [work Knot st over 3 sts, p1] 3 times, k1tbl, ssk—45 sts rem.

Row 8: K1, *p1tbl, k1; rep from * to end.

Row 9: K2tog, p1, k1tbl, p1, [work Knot st over 3 sts, p1] 2 times, [k1tbl, p1] 10 times, [work Knot st over 3 sts, p1] 2 times, k1tbl, p1, ssk—43 sts rem.

Row 10: K2, *p1tbl, k1; rep from * to last st, k1.

Row 11: K2tog, [work Knot st over 3 sts, p1] 2 times, [k1tbl, p1] 12 times, work Knot st over 3 sts, p1, work Knot st over 3 sts, ssk—41 sts rem.

Row 12: K1, *p1tbl, k1; rep from * to end.

Row 13: K2tog, p1, work Knot st over 3 sts, p1, *k1tbl, p1; rep from * to last 6 sts, work Knot st over 3 sts, p1, ssk, work Bobble Fringe—39 sts rem.

Row 14: K1, *p1tbl, k1; rep from * to last st, k1.

Next row: (RS) K1, p1, *k1tbl, p1; rep from * to last st, k1.

Next row: (WS) K2, *p1tbl, k1; rep from * to last st, k1. Rep last 2 rows until ribbed section measures 7", ending with a RS row.

Next row: (WS) Purl.

Place sts on holder. Break yarn, leaving a 36" tail for grafting.

Finishing

Block piece to 19½" wide at widest point (not including fringe) and 52" long; piece will relax to about 16" wide and 49" long after blocking. Remove waste yarn from provisional CO and place 39 sts onto needle. Place 39 held sts on 2nd needle. Hold needles parallel with WS tog and both needle points facing to the right. Thread grafting tail onto a tapestry needle and graft sts using Kitchener st. Weave in ends.

edmonia shawl

Anne Hanson

Finished Size

Width: 84".

Height: 38".

Yarn

Fingering weight
(#1 super fine).

Shown here: Bare Naked
Wools Stone Soup Fingering
(80% wool [rambouillet,
lincoln, columbia, navajo-
churro], 15% alpaca, 5%
combination of tencel,
bamboo, yak, and silk; 450
yd [411 m]/3.8 oz [108 g]):
granite, 2 skeins (see Notes).

Needles

Size U.S. 7 (4.5 mm): 24"
circular (cir).

*Adjust needle size if necessary
to obtain the correct gauge.*

Notions

Markers (m); tapestry needle.

Gauge

18 sts and 27 rows =
4" in St st.

16 sts and 27 rows =
4" in Eyelet Lace patt.

14 sts and 26 rows = 4" in
Openwork Mesh patt.

Notes

▪ This shawl is worked from
side to side, starting at the
left tip.

▪ The sample used all of
2 skeins of yarn. Cosider
purchasing an extra skein as
insurance.

▪ A circular needle is used
to accommodate the large
number of stitches.

Shawl

CO 6 sts, place marker (pm), CO 1 st, pm, CO 3 sts—10 sts: 3 right border sts, 1 main panel st, 6 left edge sts.

Work Rows 1–36 of Chart A—28 sts: 3 right border sts, 19 main panel sts, 6 left edge sts.

Work Rows 1–12 of Chart B 11 times—94 sts: 3 right border sts, 85 main panel sts, 6 left edge sts.

Work Rows 1–12 of Chart C, working 6-st rep 11 times, and working 1-st rep 3 times—100 sts: 3 right border sts, 91 main panel sts, 6 left edge sts.

Work Rows 1–12 of Chart C once more, working 6-st rep 11 times, and working 1-st rep 9 times—106 sts: 3 right border sts, 97 main panel sts, 6 left edge sts.

Work Rows 1–12 of Chart D, working 6-st rep 11 times, and working 1-st rep 15 times—112 sts: 3 right border sts, 103 main panel sts, 6 left edge sts.

Work Rows 1–12 of Chart E, working 2-st rep 6 times, 6-st rep 11 times, and 1-st rep 12 times—118 sts: 3 right border sts, 109 main panel sts, 6 left edge sts.

Work Rows 1–12 of Chart E once more, working 2-st rep 12 times, 6-st rep 11 times, and 1-st rep 6 times—124 sts: 3 right border sts, 115 main panel sts, 6 left edge sts.

Work Rows 1–12 of Chart F 12 times, working 2-st rep 18 times in first chart rep and inc by 6 times for each foll rep (24 times in 2nd rep, 30 times in 3rd rep, etc, ending with 84 times in 12th rep), and working 6-st rep 11 times in first chart rep and dec by 1 time for each foll rep (10 times in 2nd rep, 9 times in 3rd rep, etc, ending with 0 times in 12th rep)—196 sts: 3 right border sts, 187 main panel sts, 6 left edge sts.

Work Rows 1–12 of Chart G—202 sts: 3 right border sts, 193 main panel sts, 6 left edge sts.

CHART A

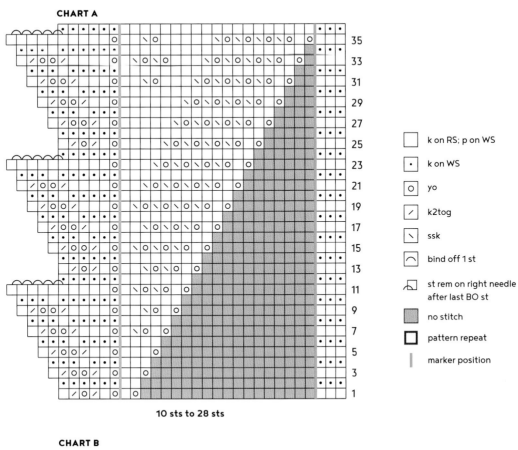

10 sts to 28 sts

☐	k on RS; p on WS
•	k on WS
○	yo
/	k2tog
\	ssk
⌒	bind off 1 st
⌐	st rem on right needle after last BO st
▨	no stitch
▢	pattern repeat
▮	marker position

CHART B

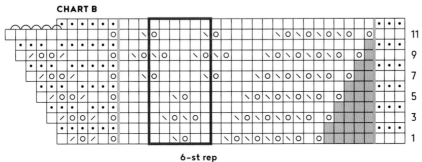

6-st rep

CHART C

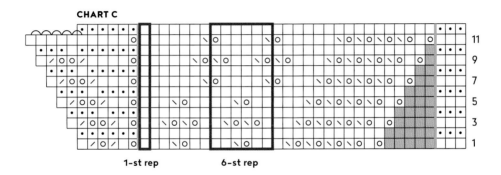

1-st rep   **6-st rep**

CHART D

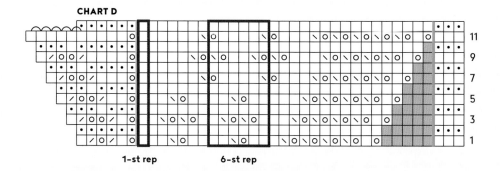

1-st rep   6-st rep

CHART E

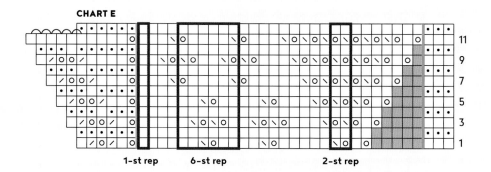

1-st rep   6-st rep   2-st rep

CHART F

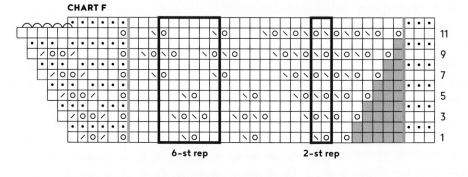

6-st rep   2-st rep

CHART G

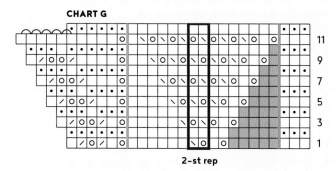

2-st rep

	k on RS; p on WS
•	k on WS
○	yo
╱	k2tog
╲	ssk
⌒	bind off 1 st
	st rem on right needle after last BO st
▨	no stitch
▢	pattern repeat
▏	marker position

CHART H

8-st to 10-st rep

Work Rows 1–24 of Chart H—252 sts: 3 right border sts, 238 main panel sts, 11 left edge sts.

Loosely BO all sts.

Finishing

Weave in ends. Block to measurements. Soak shawl in cool water with wool soap for approximately one hour or until fiber is fully saturated. Stretch and pin piece to finished dimensions (use blocking wires if available) and allow to dry thoroughly in place before unpinning.

hanshi wrap

Beatrice Perron Dahlen

Finished Size

Width: 72¾".

Depth: 12".

Yarn

Fingering weight (#1 super fine).

Shown here: Shibui Knits Staccato (70% superwash Merino wool, 30% silk; 191 yd [175 m]/1¾ oz [50 g]): #2004 ivory (MC), 4 skeins (see Notes); #2001 abyss (CC), 1 skein.

Needles

Size U.S. 4 (3.5 mm): 32" circular (cir).

Adjust needle size if necessary to obtain the correct gauge.

Notions

Tapestry needle.

Gauge

23 sts and 42 rows = 4" in Garter st.

Notes

▪ This wrap is worked on the bias. The contrasting color sections are worked with short-rows.

▪ This wrap used almost all of four skeins of the main color. Consider purchasing an extra skein as insurance.

▪ It may be helpful to mark the right side of the work.

▪ A circular needle is used to accommodate the large number of stitches.

STITCH GUIDE

Bias Pattern

Row 1: (WS) Knit.

Row 2: (RS) K1, M1, knit to last 3 sts, k2tog, k1.

Rep Rows 1 and 2 for patt.

Wrap

With MC and using the long-tail method, CO 360 sts. Do not join.

Work Rows 1 and 2 of Bias patt (see Stitch Guide) 14 times, then work Row 1 once more.

SHORT-ROW SECTION

Short-row 1: (RS) With MC, work 230 sts (inc'd to 231 sts) in patt, *drop but do not break MC, join CC, k100, wrap next st, turn.

Short-row 2: (WS) Knit to last 10 sts of CC section, wrap next st, turn.

Short-row 3: Knit to 10 sts before wrapped st, wrap next st, turn.

Rep Short-row 3 two more times.

Next row: (WS) Knit to end of CC section, wrap next st, turn. Break CC.

With RS facing, pick up MC and work in patt to end of row.

Work Rows 1 and 2 of Bias patt 14 times, then work Row 1 once more.*

SHORT-ROW SECTION

Short-row 1: (RS) With MC, work 130 sts (inc'd to 131 sts) in patt, work from * to * of first short-row section.

SHORT-ROW SECTION

Short-row 1: (RS) With MC, work 30 sts (inc'd to 31 sts) in patt, work from * to * of first short-row section.

Loosely BO all sts.

Finishing

Weave in ends. Block to measurements.

arrowhead stole

Courtney Spainhower

Finished Size

Width: 9¾ (18)".

Length: 51 (116)".

Stole shown is 18" x 116".

Yarn

Fingering weight
(#1 super fine).

Shown here: Shibui Linen
(100% linen; 246 yd [225
m]/1¾ oz [50 g]): 2022
mineral, 3 (5) skeins.

Needles

Size U.S. 5 (3.75 mm): straight.

*Adjust needle size if necessary
to obtain the correct gauge.*

Notions

Markers (m); removable
marker (optional); tapestry
needle.

Gauge

32 sts and 34 rows = 4" in
garter st blocked.

Notes

▪This stole is worked from end
to end. Increase along the
right side for the first point,
work even through the center,
then decrease along the left
side for the second point.

▪It may be helpful to mark the
right side of the work with a
removable marker or safety
pin.

▪After completing tassels,
tying a small knot at the end
of each strand will prevent the
chain ply yarn from unraveling.

Pleat Pattern (multiple of 32 + 15 sts)

Row 1: K15, *p1, k31; rep from * to end of row.

Rep Row 1 every row for Pleat Pattern.

Pleat Increase Pattern

Row 1: (RS) K1 front and back (k1f&b), k14, *p1, k31; rep from * to end of row—1 st inc'd.

Row 2: Work in Pleat Pattern to last st, place marker (pm), k1.

Row 3: K1f&b, (sl m), work in Pleat Pattern to end of row—1 st inc'd.

Rows 4 and 6: Work in Pleat Pattern to m, sl m, p1, knit to end of row.

Row 5: K1f&b, knit to m, sl m, work in Pleat Pattern to end of row—1 st inc'd.

Rows 7–36: Rep Rows 5 and 6—15 sts inc'd.

Row 37: K1f&b, pm, p1, knit to m, sl m, work in Pleat Pattern to end of row—1 st inc'd.

Rows 38 and 40: Rep Row 4.

Row 39: K1f&b, knit to m, sl m, p1, knit to m, sl m, work in Pleat Pattern to end of row—1 st inc'd.

Rows 41-64: Rep Rows 39 and 40, removing m on last row—12 sts inc'd.

Stole

CO 1 st.

Next row: (RS) K1f&b—2 sts.

Knit 1 WS row.

Inc row: (RS) K1f&b, knit to end of row—1 st inc'd.

Cont in garter st (knit every row), rep Inc row every RS row 14 more times—17 sts.

Next row: (WS) K15, p1, knit to end of row.

Rep Inc row—18 sts.

Rep last 2 rows 15 more times—33 sts.

Work 1 WS row.

Inc row: (RS) K1f&b, place marker (pm), p1, knit to end of row—34 sts.

Next row: (WS) K15, p1, knit to end of row.

Inc row: K1f&b, knit to m, slip m (sl m), p1, knit to end of row—1 st inc'd.

Rep last 2 rows 12 more times—47 sts.

Work 1 WS row, removing m.

Work Rows 1-64 of Pleat Increase Pattern (see Stitch Guide) 1 (3) times—79 (143) sts.

Work even in Pleat Pattern until piece measures 33 (83)" from CO, ending with a WS row.

Dec row: (RS) Work in patt to last 2 sts, k2tog—1 st dec'd.

Rep Dec row every RS row 76 (140) more times—2 sts rem.

Next row: K2tog—1 st rem.

Break yarn and fasten off.

Finishing

Weave in ends. Wet block.

MAKE 2 TASSELS

Make two 18" tassels, wrapping yarn 20 times and cinching tassel 1" from top (see Notes).

swallowtail shawl

Evelyn A. Clark

Finished Size

Width across top edge: 49".

Length from bottom center point to top edge: 23".

Yarn

Laceweight (#0 lace).

Shown here: Misti Alpaca Lace (100% baby alpaca; 437 yd [400 m]/ 50 g): #7120 sea mist, 1 ball.

Needles

Size U.S. 4 (3.5 mm).

Adjust needle size if necessary to obtain the correct gauge.

Notions

Marker (m); saftey pin; size E/4 (3.5 mm) crochet hook; waste yarn in contrasting color; rustproof pins for blocking.

Gauge

17½ sts and 17½ rows = 4" in Budding Lace patt after blocking.

Notes

▪ The first and last 2 stitches of every row are worked in garter stitch for top edge border.

▪ The shawl increases 4 stitches every other row until Row 11 of edging.

▪ It is helpful to place a stitch marker after the yarnover and before the center stitch and to place a safety pin along side edge to mark beginning of odd-numbered rows.

▪ The shawl can be made larger by working it with fingering, sport, or worsted-weight yarn on larger needles.

LILY OF THE VALLEY BORDER 1

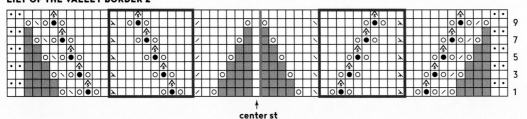

center st

LILY OF THE VALLEY BORDER 2

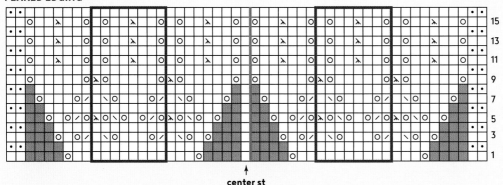

center st

PEAKED EDGING

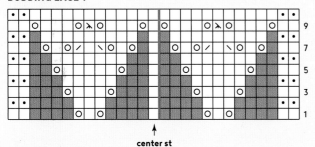

center st

BUDDING LACE 1

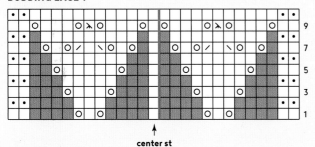

center st

	k on RS; p on WS		●	nupp: (k1, yo, k1, yo, k1) in same st
●	p on RS; K on WS		⬆	p5tog
O	yo			no stitch
╱	k2tog		☐	pattern repeat
╲	ssk		▎	marker position
⋏	sk2p: sl 1 kwise k2tog, psso			

BUDDING LACE 2

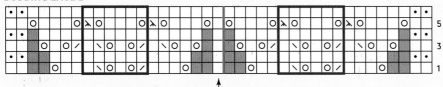

center st

Top border

Beg at center back neck, work crochet chain provisional CO as foll: Using crochet hook and waste yarn, ch 4, fasten off. With shawl yarn and knitting needles, pick up and knit 1 st in each of 2 nubs at back of chain—2 sts.

Rows 1–6: Knit.

Row 7: K2, pick up and knit 1 st in each of 3 garter ridges along side edge; unzip waste yarn chain, putting the 2 exposed sts onto left needle; knit these 2 sts—7 sts.

Work Rows 1–10 of Budding Lace 1 chart—27 sts.

Work Rows 1–6 of Budding Lace 2 chart 14 times total—195 sts.

Work Rows 1–12 of Lily of the Valley Border 1 chart—219 sts.

Work Rows 1–10 of Lily of the Valley Border 2 chart—239 sts.

Work Rows 1–16 of Peaked Edging chart—259 sts.

Next row: (RS) K2, *yo, k7, yo, k1; rep from * to last st, k1—323 sts.

Next row: (WS) Knit.

BO as foll: K2, *return both sts to left needle and k2tog through back loop (tbl), k1; rep from * until all sts have been bound-off.

Finishing

Weave in loose ends—do not trim tails until after blocking.

BLOCKING

Soak shawl for at least 20 minutes. Wrap in towel to remove excess water. Lay flat and smooth into shape. If using blocking wires, run through eyelets along top edge and pin. Pull out points along side edges at each yo, k1, yo and pin. Leave in place until thoroughly dry. Trim yarn ends.

potter's shawl

Jen Lucas

Finished Size

Width: 56".

Depth: 15".

Yarn

Fingering weight
(#1 super fine).

Shown here: Shalimar Yarns
Breathless (75% superwash
Merino wool, 15% cashmere,
10% silk; 420 yd [384 m]/3½
oz [100 g]): crayfish, 2 skeins.

Needles

Size U.S. 5 (3.75 mm): 24"
circular (cir).

*Adjust needle size if necessary
to obtain the correct gauge.*

Notions

Tapestry needle.

Gauge

16 sts and 36 rows = 4" in
Garter st.

Notes

■ Shawl body is worked from
the center neck to the bottom
with increases at each edge.
After the shawl body is
completed, live stitches are
left on the needle and bound
off by working one stitch from
the edging together with one
stitch from the body as the
lace edging is worked.

■ Slip stitches purlwise with
yarn in back.

■ A circular needle is used
to accommodate the large
number of stitches.

■ For the Garter stitch portion
of shawl, it may be helpful
to mark the right side of the
work.

Shawl

CO 6 sts.

Row 1: (WS) K1, k1f&b, k2, k1f&b, k1—8 sts.

Row 2: (RS) [K2, yo, k1, yo] 2 times, k2—12 sts.

Row 3: K3, yo, knit to last 3 sts, yo, k3—2 sts inc'd.

Row 4: K2, yo, knit to last 2 sts, yo, k2—2 sts inc'd.

Row 5: Rep Row 3—2 sts inc'd.

Row 6: K2, yo, k3, M1L, knit to last 5 sts, M1R, k3, yo, k2—4 sts inc'd.

Rep Rows 3-6 twenty-four more times—262 sts.

Next row: (WS) Knit.

Edging

With RS facing and using the knitted method, CO 14 sts onto left needle. Do not turn.

Next row: (RS) K13, ssk (last border st with first body st), turn—1 body st dec'd.

Next row: (WS) Sl 1, k13.

Rep last 2 rows once more—260 body sts rem.

Work Rows 1-12 of Edging chart 43 times—2 body sts rem.

Next row: (RS) K13, ssk—1 body st rem.

Next row: (WS) Sl 1, k13.

Next row: (RS) K13, ssk—14 edging sts rem.

BO all sts kwise on WS.

Finishing

Weave in ends. Block.

EDGING

20 sts

Chart legend:

- ☐ k on RS; p on WS
- • p on RS; k on WS
- ∖ ssk
- ∕ k2tog
- ↓ [(k1, yo) 3 times, k1]
- ↯ into same st–6 sts inc'd sl 1 wyb on WS
- O yo
- ⅄ sl 1, k2tog, psso– 2 sts dec'd
- ▨ no stitch
- ∖ ssk (last st of edging tog with 1 shawl st)

blake shawl

Laura Reinbach

Finished Size

Width: 83".

Height: 21".

Yarn

Fingering weight
(#1 super fine).

Shown here: Brown Sheep
Company Nature Spun
Fingering (100% wool; 310 yd
[283 m]/ 1¾ oz [50 g]): #148
autumn leaves, 4 balls.

Needles

Size U.S. 4 (3.5 mm): 32"
circular (cir).

*Adjust needle size if necessary
to obtain the correct gauge.*

Notions

Tapestry needle.

Gauge

25 sts and 42 rows = 4" in
body patt.

Notes

▪ The triangle shaping occurs
with a yarnover increase at
the beginning of right-side
rows and an ssk decrease at
the beginning and a yarnover
increase at the end of wrong-
side rows.

▪ A circular needle is used
to accommodate the large
number of stitches.

Set-up

CO 4 sts.

Row 1: (RS) K1, p1, yo, p1, k1—5 sts.

Row 2: (WS) [K1, p1] 2 times, k1.

Row 3: K1, p1, yo, k1, p1, k1—6 sts.

Row 4: K1, p4, k1.

Row 5: K1, p1, yo, k2, p1, k1—7 sts.

Row 6: K1, p1, ssk, p1, yo, p1, k1.

Row 7: K1, p1, yo, knit to last 2 sts, p1, k1—1 st inc'd.

Row 8: K1, p1, ssk, purl to last 2 sts, yo, p1, k1.

Rep Rows 7 and 8 six more times—14 sts.

Body

Row 1: (RS) K1, p1, yo, *p1, k1; rep from * to end—1 st inc'd.

Row 2 and all WS rows: K1, p1, ssk, purl to last 2 sts, yo, p1, k1.

Row 3: K1, p1, yo, knit to last 2 sts, p1, k1—1 st inc'd.

Row 5: K1, p1, yo, k6, p1, k5, p1, k1—17 sts.

Row 7: Rep Row 3—18 sts.

Row 9: K1, p1, yo, k2, p1, k7, p1, k3, p1, k1—19 sts.

Row 11: Rep Row 3—20 sts.

Row 13: Rep Row 1—1 st inc'd.

Row 15: Rep Row 3—1 st inc'd.

Row 17: K1, p1, yo, k2, *p1, k7; rep from * to last 2 sts, p1, k1—1 st inc'd.

Row 19: Rep Row 3—1 st inc'd.

Row 21: K1, p1, yo, k6, *p1, k7; rep from * to last 8 sts, p1, k5, p1, k1—1 st inc'd.

Row 23: Rep Row 3—1 st inc'd.

Row 25: Rep Row 1—1 st inc'd.

Row 27: Rep Row 3—1 st inc'd.

Row 29: K1, p1, yo, k6, *p1, k7; rep from * to last 4 sts, [p1, k1] 2 times—1 st inc'd.

Row 31: Rep Row 3—1 st inc'd.

Row 33: Rep Row 17—1 st inc'd.

Row 35: Rep Row 3—1 st inc'd.

Row 37: Rep Row 1—1 st inc'd.

Row 39: Rep Row 3—1 st inc'd.

Row 41: K1, p1, yo, k2, *p1, k7; rep from * to last 6 sts, p1, k3, p1, k1—1 st inc'd.

Row 43: Rep Row 3—1 st inc'd.

Row 45: Rep Row 29—1 st inc'd.

Row 47: Rep Row 3—1 st inc'd.

Row 49: Rep Row 1—1 st inc'd.

Row 51: Rep Row 3—1 st inc'd.

Row 53: Rep Row 21—1 st inc'd.

Row 55: Rep Row 3—1 st inc'd.

Row 57: Rep Row 41—1 st inc'd.

Row 59: Rep Row 3—1 st inc'd.

Row 60: (WS) Rep Row 2.

Rep Rows 13-60 six more times—188 sts.

Work Rows 13-48 once—206 sts.

Seed st border

Row 1: (RS) K1, p1, yo, *p1, k1; rep from * to end—1 st inc'd.

Row 2: K1, p1, ssk, k1, *p1, k1; rep from * to last 2 sts, yo, p1, k1.

Row 3: K1, p1, yo, p1, *k1, p1; rep from * to last 2 sts, p1, k1—1 st inc'd.

Row 4: K1, p1, ssk, *p1, k1; rep from * to last 2 sts, yo, p1, k1.

Rep Rows 1-4 nine more times—226 sts.

Loosely BO all sts in patt.

Finishing

Weave in ends. Block to measurements.

shetland shawl

Rebecca Blair

Finished Size

Width: 20".

Length: 60".

Yarn

Laceweight (#0 lace).

Shown here: Jamieson & Smith Shetland Supreme Lace Weight 1-ply (100% Shetland wool; 436 yd [400 m] 7/8 oz [25 g]): fawn, 2 skeins.

Needles

Size U.S. 4 (3.5 mm).

Adjust needle size if necessary to obtain the correct gauge.

Notions

Markers (m); tapestry needle.

Gauge

22 sts and 33 rows = 4" in Center patt, blocked.

Notes

■ The edging of this shawl is worked first, then stitches are picked up and worked for the center. The shawl is completed with a knitted-on edging.

Shawl

CO 5 sts.

Beg with a WS row, work Rows 1-6 of Bottom Edging chart 24 times, then work Row 1 once more.

BO all sts, but do not fasten off last st. Do not turn.

Next row: (RS) Yo, picking up in each garter ridge, *pick up and knit 1 st, yo, pick up and knit 2 sts; rep from * 23 more times; pick up and knit 1 more st—99 sts total.

Knit 1 WS row.

Next row: (RS) Work Right Edging chart over 10 sts (inc'd to 11), place marker (pm), work Center chart to last 10 sts, pm, work Left Edging chart to end.

Cont to work charts as est through Row 34 of Center chart, then rep Rows 3-34 of Center chart 13 more times, then work Rows 3-29 once more.

Next row: (WS) Work edging in patt to m, sl m, knit to m, sl m, work edging in patt to end.

Rep last row 2 more times.

Next row: (RS) K1, [k2tog, k1] 2 times, [k2tog, k2] 21 times, [k2tog, k1] 2 times, k2tog—73 sts rem.

Using the knitted method, CO 5 sts—78 sts.

Next row: (WS) K4, k2tog (last edging st and first body st), turn.

Work Rows 1-6 of Top Edging chart 24 times, then work Rows 1 and 2 once more—5 sts rem.

BO all sts.

Finishing

Weave in ends. Block to measurements.

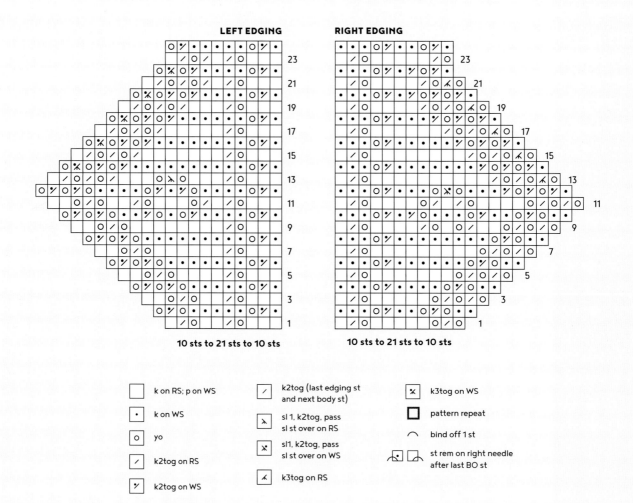

LEFT EDGING   **RIGHT EDGING**

10 sts to 21 sts to 10 sts   10 sts to 21 sts to 10 sts

	k on RS; p on WS
	k on WS
	yo
	k2tog on RS
	k2tog on WS

	k2tog (last edging st and next body st)
	sl 1, k2tog, pass sl st over on RS
	sl1, k2tog, pass sl st over on WS
	k3tog on RS

	k3tog on WS
	pattern repeat
	bind off 1 st
	st rem on right needle after last BO st

TOP EDGING

5 sts to 7 sts to 5 sts

BOTTOM EDGING

1 (WS)

5 sts to 7 sts to 5 sts

CENTER

16-st rep

☐		k on RS; p on WS
•		k on WS
o		yo
╱		k2tog on RS
⅄		k2tog on WS
╱		k2tog (last edging st and next body st)
⋋		sl 1, k2tog, pass sl st over on RS
⋊		sl1, k2tog, pass sl st over on WS
⋌		k3tog on RS
⋇		k3tog on WS
☐		pattern repeat
⌒		bind off 1 st
⌒		st rem on right needle after last BO st

squall line shawl

Romi Hill

Finished Size

Width: 78".

Height: 37".

Yarn

Worsted weight (#4 medium).

Shown here: Malabrigo Yarn Merino wool Worsted (100% Merino wool; 210 yd [192 m]/3½ oz [100 g]): #98 tuareg, 5 skeins.

Needles

Size U.S. 9 (5.5 mm): 32" circular (cir).

Adjust needle size if necessary to obtain the correct gauge.

Notions

Markers (m); cable needle (cn); tapestry needle.

Gauge

16 sts and 21 rows = 4" in charted body motif.

Notes

▪ The body of this triangular shawl is worked back and forth from the bottom up. Stitches are picked up and a small border is worked along the lower two edges, then the edging is knitted on sideways.

▪ A circular needle is used to accommodate the large number of stitches.

STITCH GUIDE

Elastic BO

K1, *k1, transfer 2 sts to left needle, k2tog tbl; rep from * to end.

Body

CO 1 st.

Work Rows 1–20 of Point chart—34 sts.

Work Rows 1–12 of Body chart 11 times—210 sts.

Work Rows 1–12 of Top chart—228 sts.

REV ST ST I-CORD BO

Using the knitted method, CO 5 sts, p3, k2tog tbl, *wyb, return 4 sts to left needle, bring yarn between needles to front, p3, p2tog tbl; rep from * to end—no body sts rem, 4 I-cord sts rem.

Wyb, return 4 sts to left needle, bring yarn between needles to front, p3tog, p1—2 sts rem.

Border

With RS facing and working into loops along selvedge edges, pick up and knit 164 sts along side, place marker (pm), 10 sts along bottom point, pm, and 164 sts along side, then pick up and purl 2 sts in rev St st BO—342 sts total.

Row 1: (WS) [K1tbl] 2 times, purl to last 2 sts, [k1tbl] 2 times.

Row 2: (RS) [K1tbl] 2 times, yo, k1tbl, yo, [k2tog, yo] 81 times, k1tbl, yo, sl m, [k1tbl, yo] 10 times, sl m, k1tbl, [yo, k2tog] 81 times, yo, k1tbl, yo, [k1tbl] 2 times—357 sts.

Row 3: Rep Row 1.

Edging

Using the knitted method, CO 22 sts.

Work Rows 1–10 of Edging chart once, then work Rows 11–22 of chart 58 times, then work Rows 23–29 once—no body sts rem.

With WS facing and using the elastic method (see Stitch Guide), BO all sts.

Finishing

Weave in ends. Block to measurements.

POINT

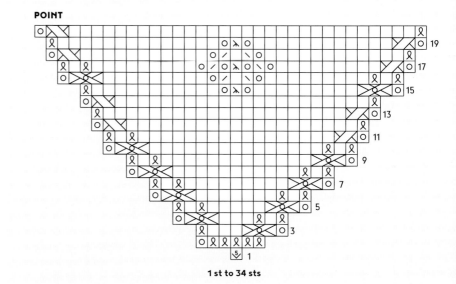

1 st to 34 sts

BODY

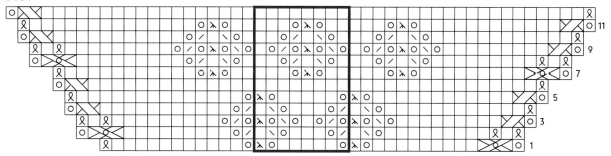

8 st repeat

TOP

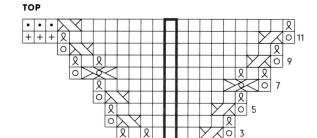

1 st repeat

EDGING

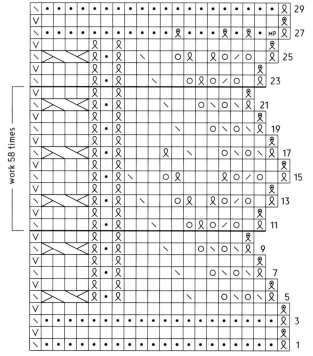

22 sts to 19 sts to 22 sts

	k on RS; p on WS
·	p on RS; k on WS
ᘺ	k1tbl on RS; p1tbl on WS
ᘺ	p1tbl on RS; k1tbl on WS
O	yo
/	k2tog on RS; p2tog on WS
\	ssk on RS; ssp on WS
\	k2tog tbl (last edging st and next body st)
⅄	sl 1, k2tog, psso
V	sl 1 pwise wyf on WS
MP	M1P
⅋	(k1, yo, k1, yo, k1) in same st
+	backward-loop CO
☐	pattern repeat
⧄	on RS: sl 1 st onto cn, hold in back, k1, k1 from cn
⧅	on WS: sl 1 st onto cn, hold in front, p1, p1 from cn
⊠	on RS: sl 1 st onto cn, hold in back, k1, yo, k1 from cn
⊠	on WS: sl 1 st onto cn, hold in front, p1, yo, p1 from cn
⧄	sl 2 sts onto cn, hold in front, k2, k2 from cn

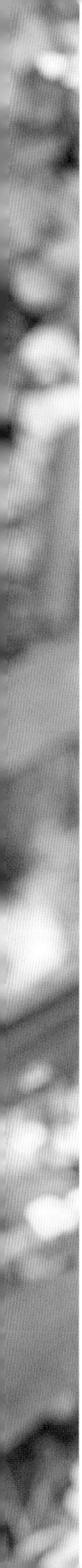

town square shawl

Romi Hill

Finished Size

Width: 84".

Height at center: 35".

Yarn

Laceweight (#0 lace).

Shown here: All for Love of Yarn Brilliance Lace (55% superwash Bluefaced Leicester wool, 45% silk; 875 yd [800 m]/100 g): kiss me pink, 1 skein.

Needles

Main triangle and borders: size U.S. 3 (3.25 mm): 24" or 32" circular (cir).

Cast-on: size U.S. 5 (3.75 mm): 24" or 32" cir.

Adjust needle size if necessary to obtain the correct gauge.

Notions

Markers (m); cable needle (cn); removable markers or coil-less saftey pins; blocking wires; T-pins; tapestry needle.

Gauge

18 sts and 30 rows = 4" in Chart E pattern on smaller needle.

Notes

▪ Short-rows in Charts A and B are used to shape the main triangle. Each right-side row begins and ends with a 2-stitch twist. Each wrong-side row begins by slipping the first stitch of the first twist, and ends by turning before working the second stitch of the last twist. This reduces the number of working stitches in the center section by 2 and shapes the triangle with a little help from a few ordinary decreases along the way. You may find it helpful to mark the turning points with markers that can be removed and replaced at each turn.

▪ If you use markers to set off individual pattern repeats, you'll need to move the markers in the following chart rows to accommodate a double decrease that falls next to an outlined pattern repeat: Rows 7, 9, 11, 19, 21, and 23 of Chart A; Row 3 of Chart C; Rows 1 and 9 of Chart D-2; and Rows 3, 7, 11, and 15 of Chart E.

▪ For perky little nupps, make sure not to pull yarn too tightly. If you have a difficult time keeping the stitches relaxed, add an extra yarnover at the end of the nupp stitches on right-side rows. On the following wrong-side row, drop the extra yarnover to provide extra slack and make it easier to purl the 7 nupp stitches together.

M1P

Insert left needle tip from back to front under the horizontal strand between the needles, then purl the lifted strand—1 st inc'd.

M1

Insert left needle tip from back to front under the horizontal strand between the needles, then knit the lifted strand—1 st inc'd.

Nupp

Very loosely, work ([k1, yo] 3 times, k1) in same st—7 sts made from 1 st. Purl the 7 nupp sts tog on the following row as shown on chart.

T2L

Sl 1 st to cn and hold in front, k1tbl, then k1tbl from cn.

T2R

Sl 1 st to cn and hold in back, k1tbl, then k1tbl from cn.

T2R-dec

Sl 2 sts to cn and hold in back, k1tbl, then k2togtbl from cn—3 sts dec'd to 2 sts.

K2-into-3

K2tog without removing sts from left needle, yo, then work same 2 sts k2tog again, and remove sts from needle—3 sts made from 2 sts.

K3-into-3

K3tog without removing sts from left needle, yo, then work same 3 sts k3tog again, and remove sts from needle—3 sts made from 3 sts.

5-into-1 dec

Sl 2 sts individually knitwise, k3tog, pass 2 slipped sts over—5 sts dec'd to 1 st.

Picot

Use the knitted method to CO 3 sts. K2togtbl, k1tbl last new CO st, pass first st over second st on right needle, k1tbl next shawl st, pass first st over second st on right needle—all new CO sts have been removed; 1 shawl st rem on right needle.

Main triangle

With larger needles, use the knitted method to CO 217 sts.

Change to smaller needles and knit 2 rows—1 garter ridge on RS.

Work Row 1 of Chart A across all sts, working the 8-st repeat box 21 times and ignoring the short-row turn symbol at the end of the chart because the very first Row 1 is worked over all sts—215 sts.

Work Row 2 of Chart A to last st, turn work—1 unworked st at end of short-row.

Work Rows 3–24 of Chart A, working each short-row to turning point indicated on chart, and dec as shown—209 sts total; with RS facing, 186 worked sts between turning gaps (including sl st at start of Row 24) with 12 unworked sts before and 11 unworked sts after them.

Work Rows 1–24 of Chart A, working the 8-st repeat box 17 times, and turning at the end of Row 1 as shown—201 sts total; with RS facing, 154 worked sts between turning gaps (including Row 24 sl st), with 24 unworked sts before and 23 unworked sts after them.

Work Rows 1–24 of Chart A, working the 8-st repeat box 13 times—193 sts total; with RS facing, 122 worked sts between turning gaps (including Row 24 sl st), with 36 unworked sts before and 35 unworked sts after them.

Work Rows 1–24 of Chart A, working the 8-st repeat box 9 times—185 sts total; with RS facing, 90 worked sts between turning gaps (including Row 24 sl st), with 48 unworked sts before and 47 unworked sts after them.

Work Rows 1–24 of Chart A, working the 8-st repeat box 5 times—177 sts total; with RS facing, 58 worked sts between turning gaps (including Row 24 sl st), with 60 unworked sts before and 59 unworked sts after them.

Work Rows 1–24 of Chart A, working the 8-st repeat box 1 time—169 sts total; with RS facing, 26 worked sts between turning gaps (including Row 24 sl st), with 72 unworked sts before and 71 unworked sts after them.

Work Rows 1–20 of Chart B—163 sts total; with RS facing, 1 worked st between turning gaps, with 81 unworked sts both before and after it.

CHART A

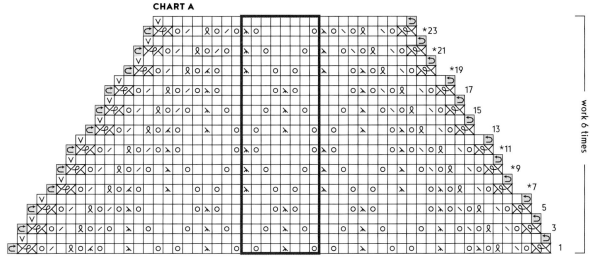

repeat according to instructions

see notes

work 6 times

*23
*21
*19
17
15
13
*11
*9
*7
5
3
1

CHART B

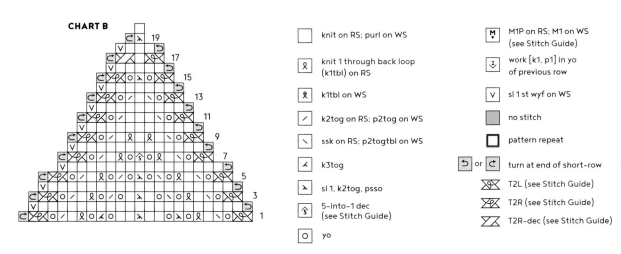

19
17
15
13
11
9
7
5
3
1

	knit on RS; purl on WS		M1P on RS; M1 on WS (see Stitch Guide)
	knit 1 through back loop (k1tbl) on RS		work [k1, p1] in yo of previous row
	k1tbl on WS		sl 1 st wyf on WS
/	k2tog on RS; p2tog on WS		no stitch
\	ssk on RS; p2togtbl on WS		pattern repeat
	k3tog	or	turn at end of short-row
	sl 1, k2tog, psso		T2L (see Stitch Guide)
	5-into-1 dec (see Stitch Guide)		T2R (see Stitch Guide)
o	yo		T2R-dec (see Stitch Guide)

CHART C

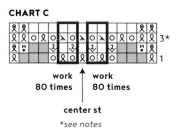

3*

1

work 80 times | work 80 times

center st

see notes

CHART D1

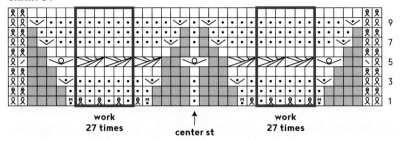

work 27 times

center st

work 27 times

9 7 5 3 1

CHART D2

continue chart D2 below >

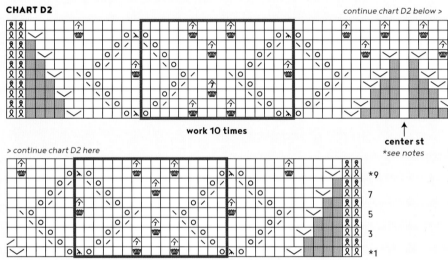

work 10 times

center st
*see notes

> continue chart D2 here

work 10 times

*9 7 5 3 *1

CHART D3

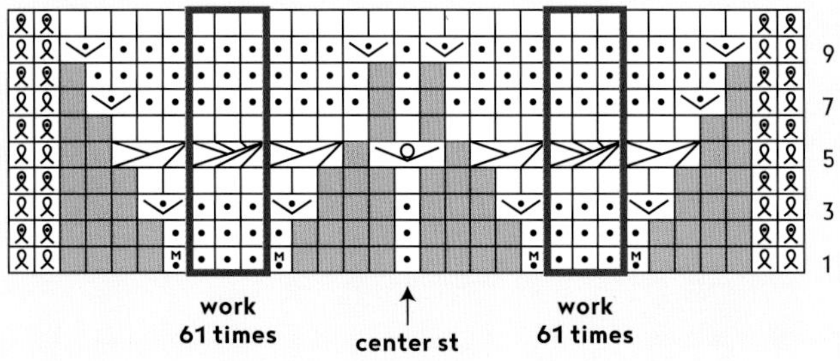

work 61 times

center st

work 61 times

9 7 5 3 1

☐ knit on RS; purl on WS	♛ nupp (see Stitch Guide)
• purl on RS; knit on WS	⤊ p7tog on WS
⟑ knit 1 through back loop (k1tbl) on RS	▨ no stitch
⟑ p1tbl on RS; k1tbl on WS	☐ pattern repeat
╱ k2tog on RS; p2tog on WS	⌄ k1f&b on RS; p1f&b on WS
╲ ssk on RS; p2togtbl on WS	⌄ k1f&b on WS
⤝ k3tog	⬩ work [k1, yo, k1] in same st
⋋ sl 1, k2tog, psso	⟋ k2-into-3 (see Stitch Guide)
○ yo	⟍ k3-into-3 (see Stitch Guide)
M M1P on RS; M1 on WS (see Stitch Guide)	

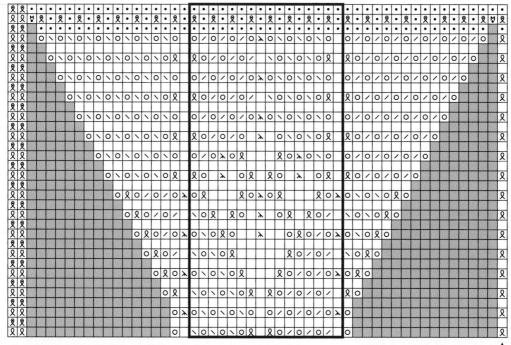

work 12 times

← center st

> continue chart E here

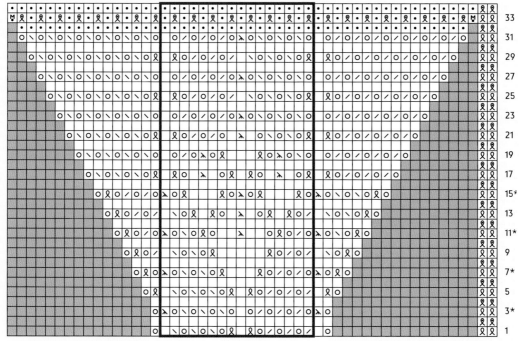

work 12 times   *see notes*

Transition

Cut yarn. Slide sts to beg of left needle tip, and rejoin yarn to all sts, ready to work a RS row.

Work Row 1 of Chart C—325 sts.

Work Row 2 of Chart C—489 sts.

Work Rows 3 and 4 of Chart C—331 sts; 1 center st and 165 sts each side.

Diamond inner border

Work Rows 1-10 of Chart D1—351 sts.

Work Rows 1-10 of Chart D2—371 sts.

Work Rows 1-10 of Chart D3—391 sts; 1 center st and 195 sts each side.

☐	knit on RS; purl on WS
·	purl on RS; knit on WS
ℛ	knit 1 through back loop (k1tbl) on RS
ℛ	p1tbl on RS; k1tbl on WS
╱	k2tog on RS; p2tog on WS
╲	ssk on RS; p2togtbl on WS
⊼	k3tog
⋋	sl 1, k2tog, psso
O	yo
M	M1P on RS; M1 on WS (see Stitch Guide)
⬚	nupp (see Stitch Guide)
⋔	p7tog on WS
▨	no stitch
☐	pattern repeat

Outer border

Work Rows 1-34 of Chart E—455 sts; 1 center st and 227 sts at each side.

Finishing

BO all sts as foll:

[Picot, BO 4 sts, return st on right needle after last BO onto left needle] 56 times—3 sts rem before center st.

Work next 7 sts as picot, k1tbl, pass first st over second st on right needle, k2togtbl, pass first st over second st on right needle, return rem st on right needle (center st) onto left needle, picot, k1tbl, pass first st over second st on right needle, BO 3 sts, return st on right needle onto left needle—224 sts rem.

[Picot, BO 4 sts, return st on right needle to left needle] 55 times—4 sts rem.

Work last 4 sts as picot, BO 3 sts, return st on right needle onto left needle, picot—1 st rem. Fasten off last st. Wash in wool wash. Gently squeeze out water, then roll in towels to remove excess moisture. Insert blocking wires into damp shawl through ends of outer border picots and upper edge diamond points. Place on a flat surface and pin to measurements. Allow to air-dry thoroughly before removing wires and pins. Weave in loose ends.

yorkville wrap

Sachiko Burgin

Finished Size

Width: 18½".

Front length: 32".

Back length: 26¾".

Yarn

Aran weight (#4 medium).

Shown here: Rowan Felted Tweed Aran (50% wool, 25% alpaca, 25% viscose; 95 yd [87 m]/ 50 g): #740 garden, 10 balls.

Needles

Size U.S. 10 (6 mm): 32" circular (cir).

Adjust needle size if necessary to obtain the correct gauge.

Notions

Removable marker (m); stitch holder; tapestry needle.

Gauge

14 sts and 19 rows = 4" in St st.

Notes

■ This shawl is worked back and forth in two separate pieces, which are then joined and worked as one piece.

■ A circular needle is used to accommodate the large number of stitches.

STITCH GUIDE

Sk2p
Sl 1 kwise, k2tog, psso—
2 sts dec'd.

First half

CO 65 sts. Do not join.

Work Rows 1–14 of Chart A 5 times.

Work Rows 1–10 of Chart B once.

Next row: (WS) K2, purl to last 2 sts, k2.

Next row: (RS) Knit. Rep last 2 rows until piece measures 32" from CO, ending with a WS row.

Break yarn and place sts on holder.

Second half

Work as for first half, but do not break yarn.

Joining row: (RS) Knit to last 2 sts, sl last 2 sts kwise, one at a time, to right needle, place 65 sts from first half onto left needle, with RS facing, then k2tog, p2sso, place a removable marker (pm) in single rem st, knit to end—127 sts.

Next row: (WS) K2, purl to last 2 sts, k2.

Dec row: (RS) Knit to 1 st before marked st, sk2p, remove m and replace it in single st, knit to end—2 sts dec'd.

Rep last 2 rows 60 more times—5 sts rem.

Next row: (WS) K2, p1, k2.

Next row: (RS) K1, sk2p, k1—3 sts rem.

Next row: (WS) K3.

Next row: (RS) Sk2p—1 st rem.

Fasten off last st.

Finishing

Weave in ends and block.

CHART A

12 st repeat

Rows numbered 2, 4, 6, 8, 10, 12, 14; 1 (WS)

CHART B

12 st repeat

Rows numbered 2, 4, 6, 8, 10; 1 (WS)

Legend:

□	k on RS; p on WS
•	k on WS
o	yo
∕	k2tog
＼	ssk
人	sk2p (see Stitch Guide)
▢	pattern repeat

waxwing shawl

Susanna IC

Finished Size

Width: 75".

Height: 21½".

Yarn

Fingering weight
(#1 super fine).

Shown here: Manos del
Uruguay Marina (100%
superwash Merino wool; 875
yd [800 m]/3½ oz [100 g]):
#N0026 hueso, 1 skein.

Needles

Size U.S. 7 (4.5 mm): 32"
circular (cir).

Size U.S. 8 (5mm) for BO.

*Adjust needle size if necessary
to obtain the correct gauge.*

Notions

894 size 6 mm Swarovski
rondelle crystals; size U.S. 10
(0.75 mm) steel crochet hook;
tapestry needle; blocking pins.

Gauge

17 sts and 26 rows = 4" in body
patt on smaller needle.

Notes

▪ This crescent shawl begins at
the center top and increases
along the upper edge to its
full width.

▪ A circular needle is used
to accommodate the large
number of stitches.

S2kp2

Sl 2 sts as if to k2tog, k1, pass
2 sl sts over—2 sts dec'd.

> *Note:* In rows where dec is
> placed directly next to patt
> rep border, if you have used
> m for rep you will need to
> move m to form dec.

Place bead

Insert crochet hook through
hole in bead and slide bead
up onto hook. Insert hook
pwise into st on left needle
and transfer st to hook. Slide
bead down hook and onto st.
Transfer st to left needle and
knit it.

Shawl

With smaller needle, CO 7 sts.

Knit 2 rows.

Row 1: (RS) K2, yo, k3, yo, k2—9 sts.

Row 2 and all WS rows: K2, purl to last 2 sts, k2.

Row 3: K2, yo, [place bead (see Stitch Guide), yo] 5 times, k2—15 sts.

Row 5: K2, yo, place bead, yo, k1, yo, k2tog, yo, k3, yo, ssk, yo, k1, yo, place bead, yo, k2—21 sts.

Row 7: K2, yo, place bead, yo, k1, yo, k2tog, yo, *k3, yo, s2kp2 (see Stitch Guide), yo; rep from * to last 9 sts, k3, yo, ssk, yo, k1, yo, place bead, yo, k2—6 sts inc'd.

Row 8: K2, purl to last 2 sts, k2.

Rep last 2 rows 46 more times—303 sts.

Work Rows 1–31 of Border chart—399 sts.

With larger needle, BO all sts as foll:

*K2tog, k1, transfer 2 sts to left needle; rep from * to last 2 sts, k2tog—1 st rem.

Fasten off last st.

Finishing

Weave in ends. Wet-block to measurements.

BORDER

continue border chart below >

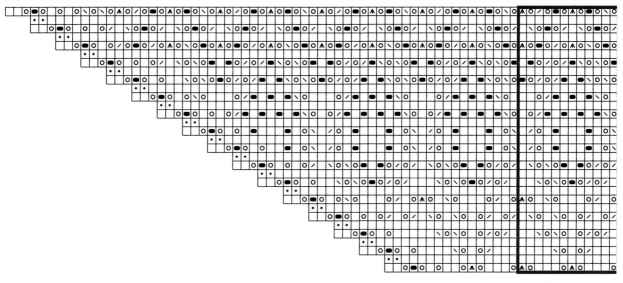

12-st rep

> continue border chart here

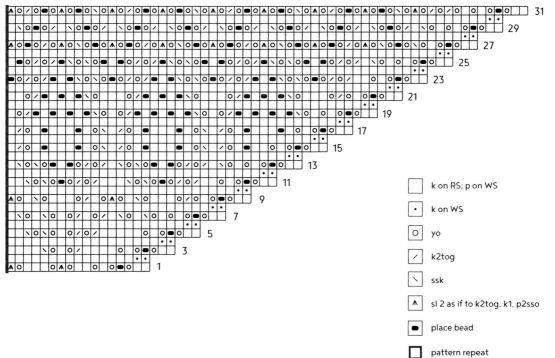

	k on RS; p on WS
•	k on WS
O	yo
╱	k2tog
╲	ssk
⋀	sl 2 as if to k2tog, k1, p2sso
⬛	place bead
▢	pattern repeat

o'kelly's chapel shawl

Shirley Paden

Finished Size

Width: 27¾".

Length: 66¼".

Yarn

DK weight (#3 light).

Shown here: Vijay Fibers Grandioso (100% silk; 328 yd [300 m]/3½ oz [100 g]): sliver/gray, 4 skeins.

Needles

Size U.S. 6 (4 mm).

Size U.S. 7 (4.5mm).

Adjust needle size if necessary to obtain the correct gauge.

Notions

Waste yarn for provisional CO; stitch holder; tapestry needle.

Gauge

18 sts and 22 rows = 4" in charted patt on larger needles.

Notes

■ This shawl is worked in two pieces and grafted together in the center. The edging is worked separately and sewn to each end.

First half

With larger needles and using a provisional method, CO 125 sts.

Work Rows 1–46 of Beads & Trees chart 3 times, then work Rows 1–36 once more.

Break yarn. Place sts on holder.

Second half

With larger needles and using a provisional method, CO 125 sts.

Work Rows 1–46 of Beads & Trees chart 3 times, then work Rows 1–37 once more.

Break yarn, leaving a 3½ yd tail for grafting. Place sts of first half on one needle and sts of 2nd half on the other needle. Hold pieces WS tog, with first half in front and 2nd half in back.

With tail threaded on a tapestry needle, graft sts tog using garter st grafting as foll:

Step 1: Insert tapestry needle pwise into st on front needle, leave st on needle.

Step 2: Insert tapestry needle pwise into st on back needle, leave st on needle.

Step 3: Insert tapestry needle kwise into st on front needle, remove st from needle, insert tapestry needle pwise into next st on front needle, leave st on needle.

Step 4: Insert tapestry needle kwise into st on back needle, remove st from needle, insert tapestry needle pwise into next st on back needle, leave st on needle.

Rep Steps 3 and 4 until 1 st rem on each needle.

Insert tapestry needle kwise into st on front needle and remove st from needle, insert tapestry needle kwise into st on back needle and remove st from needle.

Finishing

Weave in ends. Block to measurements.

EDGING

With smaller needles, CO 7 sts.

Knit 1 row.

Work Rows 1–14 of Edging chart 13 times.

BO all sts. Remove –provisional CO and place sts onto smaller needle. Sew straight selvedge edge of edging to sts on needle. Rep edging for other end of shawl.

BEADS & TREES

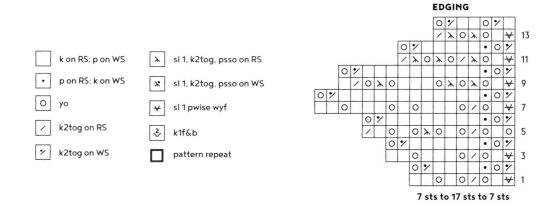

12 st to 14 st to 12 st repeat

Legend

☐	k on RS; p on WS
•	p on RS; k on WS
O	yo
╱	k2tog on RS
╲	k2tog on WS
⅄	sl 1, k2tog, psso on RS
⅄	sl 1, k2tog, psso on WS
⅄	sl 1 pwise wyf
⅀	k1f&b
☐	pattern repeat

EDGING

7 sts to 17 sts to 7 sts

white smoke cardigan

Alison Green

Finished Size

Back width: 16½ (18¾, 20½, 22¾, 24½, 26¾, 28½)".

Cardigan shown measures 18¾" on model with 34" bust.

Yarn

Worsted weight (#4 medium).

Shown here: Berroco Cotolana (47% wool, 47% cotton, 6% nylon; 109 yd [100 m]/1¾ oz [50 g]): #3503 birch, 9 (10, 11, 12, 13, 14, 16) balls.

Needles

Size U.S. 8 (5 mm): 16" and 32" circular (cir) and set of double-pointed (dpn).

Adjust needle size if necessary to obtain the correct gauge.

Notions

Markers (m); removable m; cable needle (cn); stitch holders; tapestry needle.

Gauge

18 sts and 24 rows = 4" in St st.

31 st Back chart = 5¾" wide.

Notes

▪ This cardigan is worked back and forth from the top down. First the back is worked down to the underarm. The fronts begin with neck extensions that will be sewn to the back neck, then front shoulder stitches are picked up from the back shoulders and worked down to the underarm. The back and fronts are then joined and worked in one piece to the lower edge. The sleeves are picked up around the armhole and sleeve caps are worked using short-rows.

▪ A circular needle is used to accommodate the large number of stitches.

Pocket Edgings
(MAKE 2)

With 16" cir needle, CO 19 sts. Do not join.

Next row: (WS) [K1, p1] 9 times, k1.

Next row: (RS) Knit.

Rep last 2 rows 2 more times, then work WS row once more. Place sts on holder.

Back
RIGHT SHOULDER

With 32" cir needle, CO 13 (16, 18, 19, 21, 23, 24) sts. Do not join.

Purl 1 WS row.

Shape shoulder using short-rows as foll:

Short-row 1: (RS) K9 (11, 12, 13, 14, 16, 16), wrap next st, turn.

Short-row 2: (WS) Purl to end.

Short-row 3: K5 (6, 6, 7, 7, 8, 8), wrap next st, turn.

Short-row 4: Purl to end.

Break yarn; leave sts on needle.

LEFT SHOULDER

CO 13 (16, 18, 19, 21, 23, 24) sts onto end of needle without right shoulder on it.

Shape shoulder using short-rows as foll:

Short-row 1: (WS) P9 (11, 12, 13, 14, 16, 16), wrap next st, turn.

Short-row 2: (RS) Knit to end.

Short-row 3: P5 (6, 6, 7, 7, 8, 8), wrap next st, turn.

Short-row 4: Knit to end.

Next row: Purl to end, working wraps tog with wrapped sts.

Next row: (RS) K13 (16, 18, 19, 21, 23, 24) left shoulder sts, then, using the backward-loop method, CO 37 (37, 37, 39, 39, 41, 41) sts, k13 (16, 18, 19, 21, 23, 24) right shoulder sts, working wraps tog with wrapped sts—63 (69, 73, 77, 81, 87, 89) sts total.

Next row: (WS) P16 (19, 21, 23, 25, 28, 29), place marker (pm), work Row 1 of Back chart over 31 sts, pm, p16 (19, 21, 23, 25, 28, 29).

Cont in patt for 36 (36, 36, 36, 36, 38, 36) more rows, ending with Row 7 (7, 7, 7, 7, 9, 7) of chart.

SHAPE ARMHOLES

Inc row: (RS) K2, LLI, work to last 2 sts, RLI, k2—2 sts inc'd.

Rep Inc row every RS row 3 (4, 5, 7, 8, 9, 12) more times—71 (79, 85, 93, 99, 107, 115) sts.

Work 1 WS row (Row 5 [7, 9, 3, 5, 9, 3] of chart).

Break yarn; set aside.

Right Front
NECK EXTENSION

With 16" cir needle and leaving a 12" tail, CO 23 sts. Do not join.

Beg with a WS row, work Right Front chart until piece measures 3½ (3½, 3½, 3¾, 3¾, 4, 4)" from CO, ending with a WS row.

Make a note of last chart row worked. Break yarn, leaving a 24" tail for sewing neck extension later.

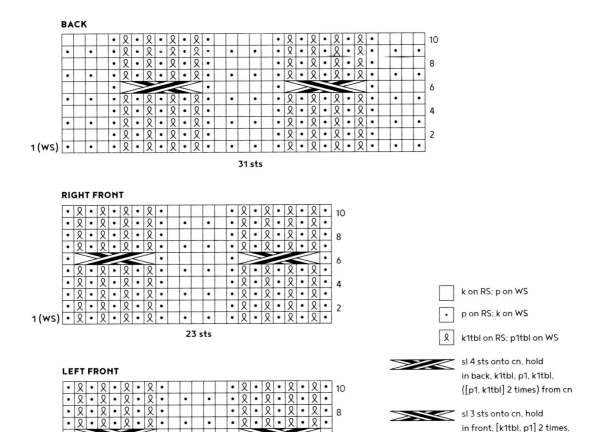

BACK

31 sts

RIGHT FRONT

23 sts

LEFT FRONT

23 sts

□	k on RS; p on WS
·	p on RS; k on WS
ℛ	k1tbl on RS; p1tbl on WS
⧓	sl 4 sts onto cn, hold in back, k1tbl, p1, k1tbl, ([p1, k1tbl] 2 times) from cn
⧓	sl 3 sts onto cn, hold in front, [k1tbl, p1] 2 times, (k1tbl, p1, k1tbl) from cn

FRONT

With RS facing, pick up and knit 13 (16, 18, 19, 21, 23, 24) sts along right back shoulder, pm, work 23 neck extension sts in patt—36 (39, 41, 42, 44, 46, 47) sts total.

Shape shoulder using short-rows as foll:

Short-row 1: (WS) Work in patt to m, sl m, p9 (11, 12, 13, 14, 16, 16), wrap next st, turn.

Short-row 2: (RS) Knit to m, sl m, work in patt to end.

Short-row 3: Work in patt to m, sl m, p5 (6, 6, 7, 7, 8, 8), wrap next st, turn.

Short-row 4: Knit to m, sl m, work in patt to end.

Next row: (WS) Work in patt to m, sl m, purl to end, working wraps tog with wrapped

sts. Cont in patt for 38 (38, 38, 38, 38, 40, 38) rows, ending with a WS row.

Make a note of last chart row worked.

SHAPE ARMHOLE

Inc row: (RS) K2, LLI, work to end—1 st inc'd.

Rep Inc row every RS row 3 (4, 5, 7, 8, 9, 12) more times—40 (44, 47, 50, 53, 56, 60) sts.

Work 1 WS row. Place sts on holder.

Left Front

NECK EXTENSION

With 16" cir needle, CO 23 sts. Do not join. Beg with a WS row, work Left Front chart until piece measures 3½ (3½, 3½, 3¾, 3¾, 4, 4)" from CO, ending with same WS row as right front.

FRONT

Next row: (RS) Work 23 sts in patt, pm, with RS facing, pick up and knit 13 (16, 18, 19, 21, 23, 24) sts along left back shoulder—36 (39, 41, 42, 44, 46, 47) sts total.

Next row: Purl to m, sl m, work in patt to end.

Shape shoulder using short-rows as foll:

Short-row 1: (RS) Work in patt to m, sl m, k9 (11, 12, 13, 14, 16, 16), wrap next st, turn.

Short-row 2: (WS) Purl to m, sl m, work in patt to end.

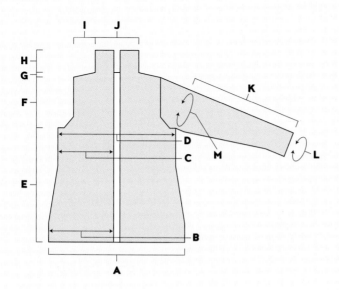

A: 20 (22¼, 24, 26¼, 28, 30¼, 32)"

B: 9¾ (10¾, 11¾, 12½, 13½, 14¼, 15¼)"

C: 8 (9, 10, 10¾, 11¾, 12½, 13½)"

D: 16½ (18¾, 20½, 22¾, 24½, 26¾, 28½)"

E: 18"

F: 7¾ (8, 8¼, 9, 9¼, 10, 10¾)"

G: ¾"

H: 3½ (3½, 3½, 3¾, 3¾, 4, 4)"

I: 3 (3½, 4, 4¼, 4¾, 5, 5¼)"

J: 7 (7, 7, 7½, 7½, 8, 8)"

K: 18"

L: 8 (8, 8½, 8½, 9, 9, 9)"

M: 12 (13, 14¼, 15, 16, 17, 18¼)"

Short-row 3: Work in patt to m, sl m, k5 (6, 6, 7, 7, 8, 8), wrap next st, turn.

Short-row 4: Purl to m, sl m, work in patt to end.

Next row: (RS) Work in patt to m, sl m, knit to end, working wraps tog with wrapped sts.

Cont in patt for 37 (37, 37, 37, 37, 39, 37) rows, ending with same WS row as right front.

SHAPE ARMHOLE

Inc row: (RS) Work to last 2 sts, RLI, k2—1 st inc'd.

Rep Inc row every RS row 3 (4, 5, 7, 8, 9, 12) more times—40 (44, 47, 50, 53, 56, 60) sts.

Work 1 WS row.

Join fronts and back

Next row: (RS) With 32" cir needle and yarn attached to left front, work left front sts, using the backward-loop method, CO 4 (5, 6, 7, 8, 9, 9) sts, pm for side, CO 4 (5, 6, 7, 8, 9, 9) sts, work back sts, CO 4 (5, 6, 7, 8, 9, 9) sts, pm for side, CO 4 (5, 6, 7, 8, 9, 9) sts, work right front sts—167 (187, 203, 221, 237, 255, 271) sts total: 44 (49, 53, 57, 61, 65, 69) sts for each front, 79 (89, 97, 107, 115, 125, 133) sts for back.

Cont in patt until piece measures 6" from underarm, ending with a WS row.

> **Note:** *Pocket edgings are added before shaping is complete; read the foll section all the way through before proceeding.*

Inc row: (RS) *Work to 1 st before side m, LLI, k1, sl m, k1, RLI; rep from * once more, work to end—4 sts inc'd.

Rep Inc row every 8th row 7 more times—199 (219, 235, 253, 269, 287, 303) sts: 52 (57, 61, 65, 69, 73, 77) sts for each front, 95 (105, 113, 123, 131, 141, 149) sts for back.

At the same time, when piece measures 11" from underarm, ending with a WS row, place pockets as foll:

Next row: (RS) Work to m, sl m, k2, place next 19 sts on holder, k19 pocket edging sts, work to 21 sts before last m, place next 19 sts on holder, k19 pocket edging sts, work in patt to end.

Cont in patt, working pocket sts in St st, until side shaping is complete, then work even until piece measures about 15½" from underarm, ending with Row 10 of Front charts.

LOWER EDGING

Next row: (WS) Work to m, sl m, p1, *k1, p1; rep from * to Back chart m, sl m, work in patt to m, sl m, p1, **k1, p1; rep from ** to last m, sl m, work to end.

Next row: Work to m, sl m, knit to Back chart m, sl m, work in patt to m, sl m, knit to last m, sl m, work to end.

Rep last 2 rows until edging measures about 2½", ending with Row 1 of Front charts.

BO all sts in patt.

SLEEVES

Place a removable m in armhole edge 1 (1¼, 1¼, 1½, 1½, 1¾, 1¾)" to each side of shoulder seam and at center of underarm.

With 16" cir needle and RS facing, beg at m before shoulder seam, working ½ st from armhole edge, pick up and knit 10 (12, 12, 14, 14, 16, 16) sts to next m, 18 (18, 20, 20, 21, 21, 24) sts to CO sts at underarm, 1 st in each of 4 (5, 6, 7, 8, 9, 9) CO sts to center of underarm, pm for beg of rnd, 1 st in each of next 4 (5, 6, 7, 8, 9, 9) CO sts, 18 (18, 20, 20, 21, 21, 24) sts to m—54 (58, 64, 68, 72, 76, 82) sts total.

Remove removable m.

> **Note:** *Change to dpn when necessary after cap shaping is complete.*

Shape cap using short-rows as foll:

> **Note:** *Do not work wraps tog with wrapped sts.*

Short-row 1: (RS) K10 (12, 12, 14, 14, 16, 16), wrap next st, turn.

Short-row 2: (WS) P10 (12, 12, 14, 14, 16, 16), wrap next st, turn.

Short-row 3: Knit to wrapped st, knit wrapped st, wrap next st, turn.

Short-row 4: Purl to wrapped st, purl wrapped st, wrap next st, turn.

Rep Short-rows 3 and 4 17 (17, 19, 19, 20, 20, 23) more times—4 (5, 6, 7, 8, 9, 9) sts unworked at each end of rnd.

Next short-row: (RS) Knit to beg-of-rnd m.

Work even in the rnd for 1½".

Dec rnd: K1, k2tog, knit to last 3 sts, ssk, k1—2 sts dec'd.

Rep dec rnd every 8th (7th, 6th, 5th, 5th, 4th, 3rd) rnd 2 (2, 6, 6, 12, 7, 2) more times, then every 10 (8, 7, 6, 6, 5, 4)th rnd 6 (8, 6, 8, 3, 10, 18) times—36 (36, 38, 38, 40, 40, 40) sts rem.

Work even until piece measures 15" from underarm.

EDGING

Next rnd: *K1, p1; rep from * to end.

Next rnd: Knit.

Rep last 2 rnds until edging measures 3", ending with first rnd. BO all sts.

Finishing

POCKET LINING

Place 19 held pocket sts onto needle. Work in St st until piece measures 4". BO all sts.

Weave in ends, except 12" and 24" tails.

Block to measurements.

Sew pocket linings to WS of each front. Sew edges of pocket edgings to RS of each front.

Sew CO edges of neck extensions tog using 12" tail, then sew neck extension to back neck using 24" tail.

roosevelt cardigan

Amanda Scheuzger

Finished Size

Bust circumference, buttoned:
35½ (38, 41, 45½, 49, 54)".

Cardigan shown measures
38", modeled with 4" of
positive ease.

Yarn

Aran weight (#4 medium).

Shown here: Tahki Yarns Tara
Tweed (80% wool, 20%
nylon; 122 yd [112 m]/1¾ oz
[50 g]): #009 moss tweed, 11
(12, 13, 14, 16, 18) balls.

Needles

Size U.S. 6 (4 mm): 32"
circular (cir) and set of
double-pointed (dpn).

Size U.S. 7 (4.5 mm): 32" cir
and set of dpn.

*Adjust needle size if necessary
to obtain the correct gauge.*

Notions

Markers (m); cable needle
(cn); stitch holders; tapestry
needle; five ⅞" buttons.

Gauge

18 sts and 28 rows = 4" in St st
on larger needle.

Notes

▪ The body of this cardigan
is worked back and forth
in one piece from the lower
edge to the underarms. The
pocket fronts are divided from
the body above the rib and
are worked separately, then
joined to the body at the top
of the pocket. The sleeves
are worked separately in the
round, then the sleeves and
body are joined to work the
yoke.

▪ A circular needle is used
to accommodate the large
number of stitches.

Right Sleeve

With smaller dpn, CO 56 (56, 64, 64, 72, 72) sts. Place marker (pm) and join in the rnd.

Set-up rnd: P1, *k6, p2; rep from * to last 7 sts, k6, p1.

Work Rnds 1-6 of Right Sleeve chart 3 times, then work Rnd 1 once more. Change to larger dpn.

Next rnd: [P1, k1, k3tog, k2, p1] 1 (1, 2, 2, 2, 2) time(s), work 40 sts in patt as est, [p1, k1, k3tog, k2, p1] 1 (1, 1, 1, 2, 2) time(s)—52 (52, 58, 58, 64, 64) sts rem.

SIZES 41 (45½)" ONLY

Remove m, k3, pm for new beg of rnd.

ALL SIZES

Next rnd: K5 (5, 8, 8, 11, 11), p1, work 40 sts in patt, p1, knit to end.

Cont in patt through Row 6 of chart, then work Row 1 once more.

Next rnd: K5 (5, 8, 8, 11, 11), p2, k1, k3tog, k2, p1, work 24 sts in patt, p1, k1, k3tog, k2, p2, knit to end—48 (48, 54, 54, 60, 60) sts rem.

Next rnd: K11 (11, 14, 14, 17, 17), p1, work 24 sts in patt, p1, knit to end.

Cont in patt through Rnd 6 of chart, then work Rnd 1 once more.

Next rnd: K11 (11, 14, 14, 17, 17), p2, k1, k3tog, k2, p1, work 8 sts in patt, p1, k1, k3tog, k2, p2, knit to end—44 (44, 50, 50, 56, 56) sts rem.

Next rnd: K17 (17, 20, 20, 23, 23), p1, work 8 sts in patt, p1, knit to end.

Inc rnd: K1, M1L, work in patt to last st, M1R, k1—2 sts inc'd.

Rep Inc rnd every 14 (10, 12, 10, 12, 8) th rnd 6 (8, 7, 5, 2, 4) more times, then every 0 (0, 0, 8, 10, 6) th rnd 0 (0, 0, 4, 6, 9) times—58 (62, 66, 70, 74, 84) sts.

Work even until piece measures 18 (18, 18½, 18½, 19)" from CO, ending with an even-numbered chart rnd.

Remove m, k3 (4, 5, 6, 7, 8), place last 6 (8, 10, 12, 14, 16) sts on holder for underarm—52 (54, 56, 58, 60, 68) sts rem.

Place sts on 2nd holder.

Left Sleeve

With smaller dpn, CO 56 (56, 64, 64, 72, 72) sts. Pm and join in the rnd.

Set-up rnd: P1, *k6, p2; rep from * to last 7 sts, k6, p1.

Work Rnds 1-6 of Left Sleeve chart 3 times, then work Rnd 1 once more. Change to larger dpn.

Next rnd: [P1, k2, sssk, k1, p1] 1 (1, 2, 2, 2) time(s), work 40 sts in patt as est, [p1, k2, sssk, k1, p1] 1 (1, 1, 1, 2) time(s)—52 (52, 58, 58, 64, 64) sts rem.

SIZES 41 (45½)" ONLY

Remove m, k3, pm for new beg of rnd.

ALL SIZES

Next rnd: K5 (5, 8, 8, 11, 11), p1, work 40 sts in patt, p1, knit to end.

Cont in patt through Rnd 6 of chart, then work Rnd 1 once more.

Next rnd: K5 (5, 8, 8, 11, 11), p2, k2, sssk, k1, p1, work 24 sts in patt, p1, k2, sssk, k1, p2, knit to end—48 (48, 54, 54, 60, 60) sts rem.

Next rnd: K11 (11, 14, 14, 17, 17), p1, work 24 sts in patt, p1, knit to end.

Cont in patt through Rnd 6 of chart, then work Rnd 1 once more.

Next rnd: K11 (11, 14, 14, 17, 17), p2, k2, sssk, k1, p1, work 8 sts in patt, p1, k2, sssk, k1, p2, knit to end—44 (44, 50, 50, 56, 56) sts rem.

Next rnd: K17 (17, 20, 20, 23, 23), p1, work 8 sts in patt, p1, knit to end.

Inc rnd: K1, M1L, work in patt to last st, M1R, k1—2 sts inc'd.

Rep Inc rnd every 14 (10, 12, 10, 12, 8) th rnd 6 (8, 7, 5, 2, 4) more times, then every 0 (0, 0, 8, 10, 6) th rnd 0 (0, 0, 4, 6, 9) times—58 (62, 66, 70, 74, 84) sts.

Work even until piece measures 18 (18, 18, 18½, 18½, 19)" from CO, ending with same even-numbered chart row as right sleeve. Remove m, k3 (4, 5, 6, 7, 8), place last 6 (8, 10, 12, 14, 16) sts on holder for underarm—52 (54, 56, 58, 60, 68) sts rem.

Place sts on 2nd holder.

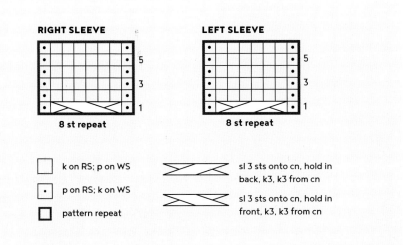

RIGHT SLEEVE

8 st repeat

LEFT SLEEVE

8 st repeat

☐ k on RS; p on WS

• p on RS; k on WS

☐ pattern repeat

⨉⨉ sl 3 sts onto cn, hold in back, k3, k3 from cn

⨉⨉ sl 3 sts onto cn, hold in front, k3, k3 from cn

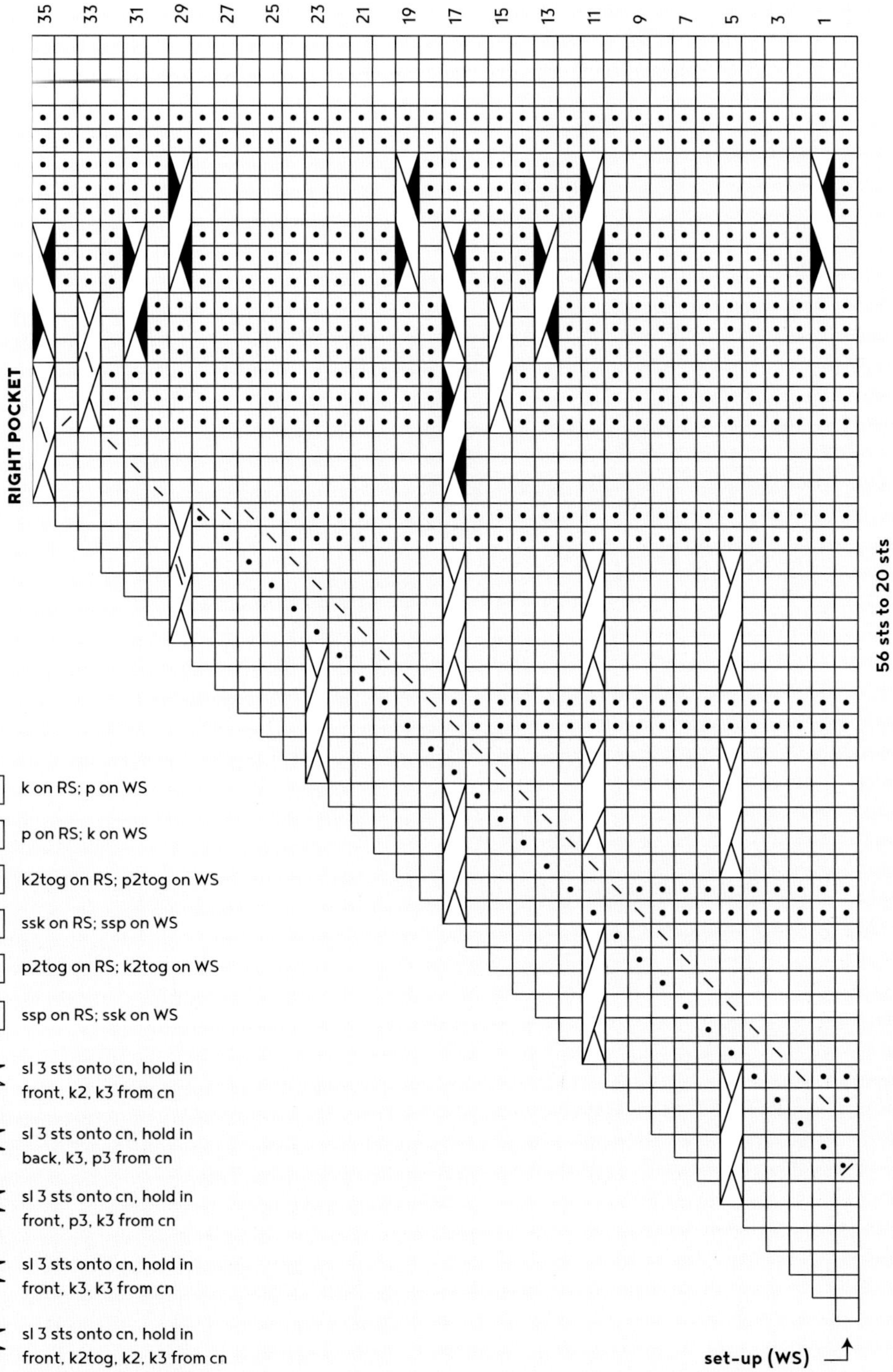

Column numbers (right to left): 35 33 31 29 27 25 23 21 19 17 15 13 11 9 7 5 3 1

RIGHT POCKET

56 sts to 20 sts

Legend:

☐ k on RS; p on WS

• p on RS; k on WS

╱ k2tog on RS; p2tog on WS

╲ ssk on RS; ssp on WS

⟋• p2tog on RS; k2tog on WS

⟍• ssp on RS; ssk on WS

sl 3 sts onto cn, hold in front, k2, k3 from cn

sl 3 sts onto cn, hold in back, k3, p3 from cn

sl 3 sts onto cn, hold in front, p3, k3 from cn

sl 3 sts onto cn, hold in front, k3, k3 from cn

sl 3 sts onto cn, hold in front, k2tog, k2, k3 from cn

sl 1 pwise, sl 3 sts onto cn, hold in front, transfer 1 st from right needle to left needle, k2tog, k2, k3 from cn

set-up (WS)

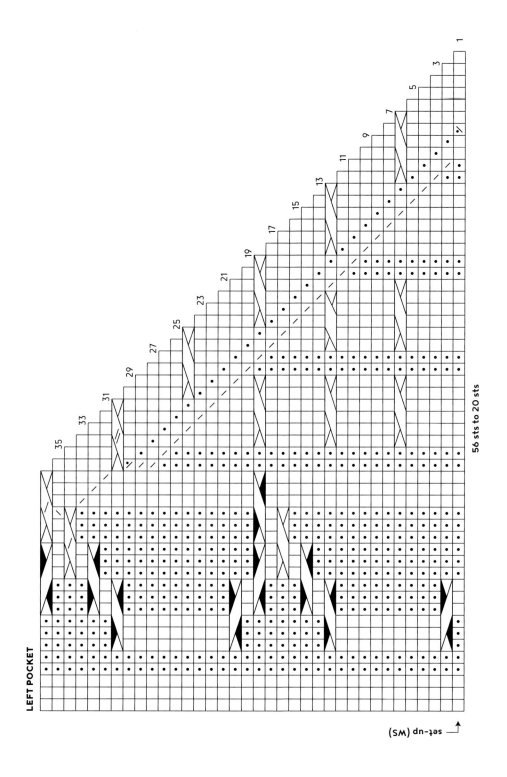

LEFT POCKET

56 sts to 20 sts

set-up (WS)

RIGHT HEM

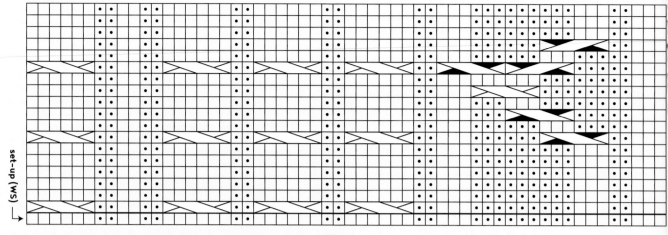

56 sts

RIGHT FRONT

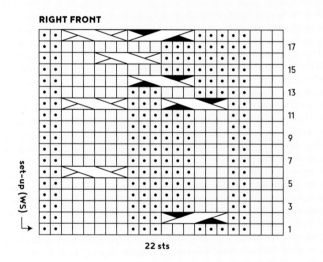

22 sts

	k on RS; p on WS
	p on RS; k on WS
	sl 3 sts onto cn, hold in back, k3, p3 from cn
	sl 3 sts onto cn, hold in front, p3, k3 from cn
	sl 3 sts onto cn, hold in back, k3, k3 from cn
	sl 3 sts onto cn, hold in front, k3, k3 from cn

Lower Body and Pockets

With smaller cir needle, CO 202 (214, 226, 246, 262, 286) sts. Do not join.

Set-up row: (WS) Work Set-up row of Left Hem chart over 56 sts, pm, [k2, p2] 22 (25, 28, 33, 37, 43) times, k2, pm, work Set-up row of Right Hem chart over 56 sts.

Cont in patt through Row 18 of charts. Change to larger cir needle.

Next row: (RS) Work Row 1 of Right Hem chart to m, sl m, p2, knit to 2 sts before m, p2, sl m, work Row 1 of Left Hem chart to end.

Next row: (WS) Work to m, sl m, k2, purl to 2 sts before m, k2, sl m, work to end.

Cont in patt through Row 12 of charts.

DIVIDE FOR POCKETS

Next row: (RS) Work to m, remove m, place last 56 sts on holder for right pocket, knit to m, remove m, place last 90 (102, 114, 134, 150, 174) sts on holder for body, work to end—56 sts rem for left pocket.

Left Pocket

Next row: (WS) Work Set-up row of Left Pocket chart—55 sts rem.

Work through Row 35 of chart—20 sts rem.

Place sts on holder.

Right Pocket

Return 56 right pocket sts to needle and, with WS facing, rejoin yarn.

Next row: (WS) Work Set-up row of Right Pocket chart—55 sts rem.

Work through Row 35 of chart—20 sts rem.

Place sts on holder.

Right Pocket Lining

With larger cir needle, CO 27 sts. Do not join.

Next row: (RS) P5, knit to end.

Next row: (WS) Purl to last 5 sts, k5. Rep last 2 rows 8 more times, then work RS row once more.

Place sts on holder.

Left Pocket Lining

With larger cir needle, CO 27 sts. Do not join.

Next row: (RS) Knit to last 5 sts, p5.

Next row: (WS) K5, purl to end.

Rep last 2 rows 8 more times, then work RS row once more.

Do not break yarn.

Body

JOIN POCKET LININGS TO BODY

Next row: (WS) Working left pocket lining sts, k5, p22, p3 (6, 9, 14, 18, 24) body sts, pm for side, p84 (90, 96, 106, 114, 126), pm for side, p3 (6, 9, 14, 18, 24), p22 right pocket lining sts, k5—144 (156,

168, 188, 204, 228) sts: 30 (33, 36, 41, 45, 51) sts for each front, 84 (90, 96, 106, 114, 126) sts for back.

Work 2 rows even.

SHAPE WAIST

Dec row: (RS) *Work to 3 sts before m, ssk, k1, sl m, k1, k2tog; rep from * once more, work to end—4 sts dec'd.

Rep Dec row every 8th row 3 more times—128 (140, 152, 172, 188, 212) sts rem: 26 (29, 32, 37, 41, 47) sts for each front, 76 (82, 88, 98, 106, 118) sts for back.

Work 7 rows even.

Next row: (RS) BO 3 sts, *work to 3 sts before m, ssk, k1, sl m, k1, k2tog; rep from * once more, work to last 3 sts, BO 3 sts—118 (130, 142, 162, 178, 202) sts rem: 22 (25, 28, 33, 37, 43) sts for each front, 74 (80, 86, 96, 104, 116) sts for back.

Break yarn; leave sts on needle.

JOIN POCKET FRONTS TO BODY

With WS facing, rejoin yarn

Joining row: (WS) Work Set-up row of Left Front chart over 22 sts (20 held pocket sts and 2 body sts), purl to last 2 body sts, work Set-up row of Right Front chart over 22 sts (last 2 body sts and 20 held pocket sts)—158 (170, 182, 202, 218, 242) sts: 42 (45, 48, 53, 57, 63) sts for each front, 74 (80, 86, 96, 104, 116) sts for back.

Next row: (RS) Work Right Front chart over 22 sts, knit to last 22 sts, work Left Front chart over 22 sts.

Cont in patt until piece measures 10½ (10½, 10½, 11, 11, 11)" from CO, ending with a WS row.

Inc row: (RS) *Work to 1 st before m, M1R, k1, sl m, k1, M1L; rep from * once more, work in patt to end—4 sts inc'd.

Rep Inc row every 14th row 2 more times—170 (182, 194, 214, 230, 254) sts: 45 (48, 51, 56, 60, 66) sts for each front, 80 (86, 92, 102, 110, 122) sts for back.

LEFT HEM

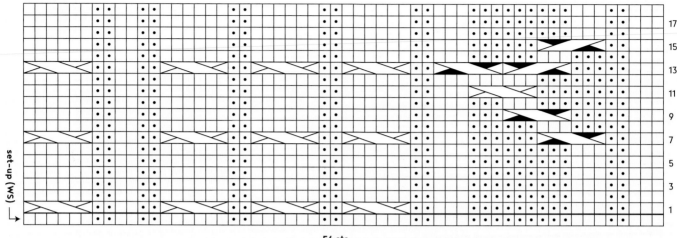

56 sts

LEFT FRONT

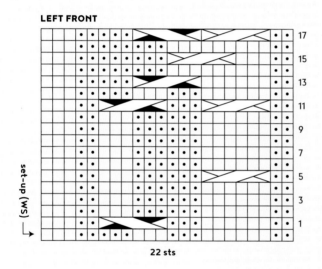

22 sts

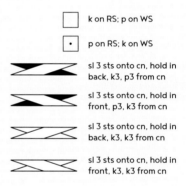

☐ k on RS; p on WS

• p on RS; k on WS

sl 3 sts onto cn, hold in back, k3, p3 from cn

sl 3 sts onto cn, hold in front, p3, k3 from cn

sl 3 sts onto cn, hold in back, k3, k3 from cn

sl 3 sts onto cn, hold in front, k3, k3 from cn

Work even until piece measures 17" from CO, ending with a WS row.

Note: *Sleeves are joined for yoke before neck shaping ends; read the foll section all the way through before proceeding.*

SHAPE NECK

Neck dec row: (RS) Work 22 sts in patt, ssk, work to last 24 sts, k2tog, work to end—2 neck sts dec'd.

Rep Neck dec row every 4th row 10 (9, 11, 12, 10, 11) more times, then every 6th row 1 (2, 1, 1, 3, 3) time(s).

At the same time, when piece measures 18" from CO, ending with a WS row, join sleeves as foll:

Joining row: (RS) Work in patt to 3 (4, 5, 6, 7, 8) sts before side m, place next 6 (8, 10, 12, 14, 16) sts on holder for underarm, removing m, pm, work 52 (54, 56, 58, 60, 68) right sleeve sts in patt, pm, work to 3 (4, 5, 6, 7, 8) sts before side m, place next 6 (8, 10, 12, 14, 16) sts on holder for underarm, removing m, pm, work 52 (54,

56, 58, 60, 68) left sleeve sts in patt, pm, work to end—74 (78, 82, 90, 96, 106) sts for back, 52 (54, 56, 58, 60, 68) sts for each sleeve (front neck shaping is in progress).

Work 1 WS row.

SHAPE ARMHOLES

Armhole dec row: (RS) *Work in patt to 2 sts before m, k2tog, sl m, ssk; rep from * 3 more times, work to end—8 sts dec'd.

Armhole dec row: (WS) *Work to 2 sts before m, ssp, sl m, p2tog; rep from * 3 more times, work to end—8 sts dec'd.

Rep last 2 rows 1 (2, 2, 3, 4, 5) more time(s)—66 (66, 70, 74, 76, 82) sts for back, 44 (42, 44, 42, 40, 44) sts for each sleeve (front neck shaping is in progress).

SIZES 35½ (41, 45½, 49, 54)" ONLY

Next row: (RS) Rep RS Armhole dec row—64 (68, 72, 74, 80) sts for back, 42 (42, 40, 38, 42) sts for each sleeve (front neck shaping is in progress).

Work 1 WS row.

ALL SIZES
SHAPE SLEEVE CAP

Sleeve dec row: (RS) *Work to m, sl m, ssk, work to 2 sts before m, k2tog, sl m; rep from * once more, work to end—4 sts dec'd.

Rep Sleeve dec row every 4th row 3 (4, 4, 6, 8,7) more times, then every RS row 10 (9, 9, 6, 3, 6) times—142 (146, 148, 154, 158, 168) sts rem when all sleeve and neck shaping is complete: 25 (26, 26, 27, 28, 30) sts for each front, 64 (66, 68, 72, 74, 80) sts for back, 14 sts for each sleeve.

SHAPE SHOULDER

> **Note:** On the foll row, m are moved to maintain line of shaping; decs are on fronts and back, but movement of m leaves them with same st counts, and sleeve st count decs.

Next row: (WS) *Work in patt to 1 st before m, sl 1 pwise, remove m, return st to left needle, ssp, pm, work to 1 st before m, sl 1 pwise, remove m, return st to left needle, pm, p2tog; rep from * once more, work to end—138 (142, 144, 150, 154, 164) sts rem: 25 (26, 26, 27, 28, 30) sts for each front, 64 (66, 68, 72, 74, 80) sts for back, 12 sts for each sleeve.

Next row: (RS) *Work to 2 sts before m, k2tog, sl m, work to m, sl m, ssk; rep from * once more, work to end—134 (138, 140, 146, 150, 160) sts rem: 24 (25, 25, 26, 27, 29) sts for each front, 62 (64, 66, 70, 72, 78) sts for back, 12 sts for each sleeve.

Next row: (WS) *Work to 2 sts before m, ssp, sl m, work to m, sl m, p2tog; rep from * once more, work to end—130 (134, 136, 142, 146, 156) sts rem: 23 (24, 24, 25, 26, 28) sts for each front, 60 (62, 64, 68, 70, 76) sts for back, 12 sts for each sleeve.

Right Saddle Shoulder
SIZE 35½" ONLY

Next row: (RS) Work in patt to 2nd m, sl m, ssk, turn—129 (133, 135, 141, 145, 155) sts rem: 23 (24, 24, 25, 26, 28) sts for each front, 59 (61, 63, 67, 69, 75) sts for back, 12 sts for each sleeve.

SIZES 38 (41, 45½, 49, 54)" ONLY

Dec row: (WS) Sl 1 pwise wyf, sl m, work in patt to m, sl m, p2tog, turn—1 st dec'd.

Dec row: (RS) Sl 1 kwise wyb, sl m, work in patt to m, sl m, ssk, turn—1 st dec'd.

Rep last 2 rows 0 (0, 1, 2, 4) more time(s)—131 (133, 137, 139, 145) sts rem: 23 sts for right front, 24 (24, 25, 26, 28) sts for left front, 60 (62, 65, 66, 70) sts for back, 12 sts for each sleeve.

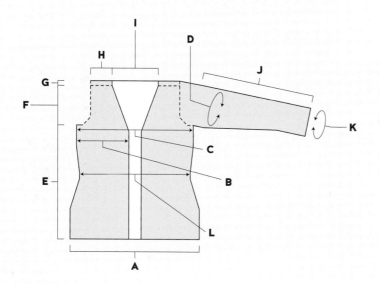

A: 18 (20¾, 23¼, 27¾, 31¼, 36¾)"

B: 7¾ (8½, 9¼, 10¼, 11¼, 12½)"

C: 17¾ (19, 20½, 22¾, 24½, 27)"

D: 12 (12¾, 13¾, 14½, 15½, 17¾)"

E: 18"

F: 5¾ (6¼, 6½, 7, 7½, 8¼)"

G: ¾"

H: 3¼ (3½, 3½, 3¾, 4¼, 4¾)"

I: 7½ (7½, 8, 8½, 8½, 9)"

J: 18 (18, 18, 18½, 18½, 19)"

K: 8¾ (8¾, 10¼, 10¼, 11½, 11½)"

L: 16½ (17¾, 19, 21¼, 23, 25¾)"

ALL SIZES

Row 1: (WS) Sl 1 pwise wyf, sl m, work in patt to m, sl m, p3tog, turn—2 sts dec'd.

Rows 2 and 4: (RS) Sl 1 kwise wyb, sl m, work in patt to m, sl m, ssk, turn—1 st dec'd.

Row 3: Sl 1 pwise wyf, sl m, work in patt to m, sl m, p3tog, turn—2 sts dec'd.

Row 5: Sl 1 pwise wyf, sl m, work in patt to m, sl m, p2tog, turn—1 st dec'd.

Row 6: Sl 1 kwise wyb, sl m, work to m, sl m, ssk, turn—1 st dec'd.

Rep Rows 1–6 three more times, then work Row 5 once more—96 (98, 100, 104, 106, 112) sts rem: 2 sts for right front, 23 (24, 24, 25, 26, 28) sts for left front, 47 (48, 50, 53, 54, 58) sts for back, 12 sts for each sleeve.

Left Saddle Shoulder

SIZE 35½" ONLY

Next row: (RS) Work in patt to 4th m, sl m, sssk, turn—94 sts rem: 2 sts for right front, 21 sts for left front, 47 sts for back, 12 sts for each sleeve.

SIZES 38 (41, 45½, 49, 54)" ONLY

Next row: (RS) Work in patt to 4th m, sl m, ssk, turn—97 (99, 103, 105, 111) sts rem: 2 sts for right front, 23 (23, 24, 25, 27) sts for left front, 48 (50, 53, 54, 58) sts for back, 12 sts for each sleeve.

Next row: Sl 1 pwise wyf, sl m, work to m, sl m, p2tog, turn—96 (98, 102, 104, 110) sts rem: 2 sts for right front, 23 (23, 24, 25, 27) sts for left front, 47 (49, 52, 53, 57) sts for back, 12 sts for each sleeve.

SIZES 45½ (49, 54)" ONLY

Dec row: (RS) Sl 1 kwise wyb, sl m, work to m, sl m, ssk, turn—1 st dec'd.

Dec row: (WS) Sl 1 pwise wyf, sl m, work to m, sl m, p2tog, turn—1 st dec'd.

Rep last 2 rows 0 (1, 3) more time(s)—100 (100, 102) sts rem: 2 sts for right front, 23 sts for left front, 51 (51, 53) sts for back, 12 sts for each sleeve.

SIZES 38 (41, 45½, 49, 54)" ONLY

Next row: (RS) Sl 1 kwise wyb, sl m, work to m, sl m, sssk, turn—94 (96, 98, 98, 100) sts rem: 2 sts for right front, 21 sts for left front, 47 (49, 51, 51, 53) sts for back, 12 sts for each sleeve.

ALL SIZES

Rows 1, 3, and 5: (WS) Sl 1 pwise wyf, sl m, work in patt to m, sl m, p2tog, turn—1 st dec'd.

Row 2: (RS) Sl 1 kwise wyb, sl m, work to m, sl m, sssk, turn—2 sts dec'd.

Row 4: Sl 1 kwise wyb, sl m, work to m, sl m, ssk, turn—1 st dec'd.

Row 6: Sl 1 kwise wyb, sl m, work to m, sl m, sssk, turn—2 sts dec'd.

Rep Rows 1–6 two more times, then work Rows 1–5 again, then work Rows 4 and 5 once more—62 (62, 64, 66, 66, 68) sts rem: 2 sts for each front, 34 (34, 36, 38, 38, 40) sts for back, 12 sts for each sleeve.

Next row: (RS) Work in patt to end.

BO all sts.

Finishing

COLLAR AND FRONT BANDS

With smaller needle and RS facing, beg at right front lower edge, pick up and knit 87 sts to beg of neck shaping, 31 (33, 34, 37, 39, 42) sts along right front neck shaping, 6 sts along first half of saddle, pm, 6 sts along 2nd half of saddle, 32 (32, 34, 36, 36, 38) sts along back neck, 6 sts along first half of saddle, pm, 6 sts along 2nd half of saddle, 31 (33, 34, 37, 39, 42) sts along left front neck shaping, and 87 sts down left front to lower edge—292 (296, 300, 308, 312, 320) sts total.

Next row: (WS) P3, *k2, p2; rep from * to last st, p1.

Shape collar using short-rows as foll:

Short-row 1: (RS) Work to 2nd m, sl m, wrap next st, turn.

Short-row 2: (WS) Sl m, work to m, sl m, wrap next st, turn.

Short-row 3: Work to wrapped st, work wrap tog with wrapped st, work 2 sts, wrap next st, turn.

Short-row 4: Work to wrapped st, work wrap tog with wrapped st, work 2 sts, wrap next st, turn.

Rep last 2 short-rows 6 (6, 7, 10, 10, 11) more times.

Short-row 5: Work to wrapped st, work wrap tog with wrapped st, work 1 st, wrap next st, turn.

Short-row 6: Work to wrapped st, work wrap tog with wrapped st, work 1 st, wrap next st, turn.

Rep last 2 short-rows 5 (6, 5, 2, 3, 3) more times.

Short-row 7: Work to wrapped st, work wrap tog with wrapped st, wrap next st, turn.

Short-row 8: Work to wrapped st, work wrap tog with wrapped st, wrap next st, turn.

Rep last 2 short-rows 3 more times.

Next row: (RS) Work in patt to end, working wrap tog with wrapped st.

Next row: Work to end, working rem wrap.

Cont in patt until band measures 1" along front edge, ending with a WS row. Mark for placement of 5 evenly-spaced buttonholes along right front between bottom edge and beg of neck shaping.

Buttonhole row: (RS) *Work in patt to 1 st before buttonhole m, work 3-st one-row buttonhole; rep from * 4 more times, work in patt to end.

Cont in patt until band measures 2" along front edge. BO all sts in patt.

Graft underarms using Kitchener st. Sew pocket lining to WS of front.

Weave in ends.

Block to measurements.

Sew buttons to left front band opposite buttonholes.

yelena cardigan

Amy Christoffers

Finished Size

Bust circumference: 33 (36¼, 41, 44¼, 47, 50¼)".

Cardigan shown measures 36¼"; modeled with 4¼" of positive ease.

Yarn

Aran weight (#4 medium).

Shown here: Berroco Artisan (80% wool, 20% silk; 123 yd [112 m]/50 g): #6027 Celtic Sea, 10 (11, 12, 13, 14, 15) skeins.

Needles

Size U.S. 6 (4 mm): 24" circular (cir) needle and set of double-pointed (dpn).

Size U.S. 7 (4.5 mm): 24" cir and set of dpn.

Adjust needle size if necessary to obtain the correct gauge.

Notions

Markers (m); cable needle (cn); stitch holders or waste yarn; tapestry needle; six ¾" buttons.

Gauge

20 sts and 30 rows = 4" in Granite st on larger needle.

Notes

▪ The body of this cardigan is worked back and forth in one piece to the underarms, then divided for working the fronts and back separately. The sleeves are worked in the round, with the sleeve cap worked flat.

▪ A circular needle is used to accommodate the large number of stitches.

Granite Stitch in rows: (multiple of 4 sts + 1)

Row 1: (RS) *K1, p3; rep from * to last st, k1.

Row 2: (WS) *P1, k3; rep from * to last st, p1.

Row 3: P2, *k1, p3; rep from * to last 3 sts, k1, p2.

Row 4: K2, *p1, k3; rep from * to last 3 sts, p1, k2.

Rep Rows 1–4 for patt.

Granite Stitch in rnds: (multiple of 4 sts)

Rnds 1 and 2: *K1, p3; rep from * to end.

Rnds 3 and 4: P2, *k1, p3; rep from * to last 2 sts, k1, p1.

Rep Rnds 1–4 for patt.

Body

With smaller cir needle, CO 167 (183, 207, 223, 239, 255) sts. Do not join.

Next row: (WS) [P1tbl] 2 times, *k1tbl, p1tbl; rep from * to last st, p1tbl.

Next row: (RS) [K1tbl] 2 times, *p1tbl, k1tbl; rep from * to last st, k1tbl.

Cont in patt until piece measures 2½" from CO, ending with a WS row.

Change to larger cir needle.

Set-up row: (RS) K1, work Cable chart over 25 (25, 25, 25, 33, 33) sts, place marker (pm), work Granite st in rows (see Stitch Guide) over 37 (45, 57, 65, 57, 65) sts, pm, work Cable chart over 41 (41, 41, 41, 57, 57) sts, pm, work Granite st over 37 (45, 57, 65, 57, 65) sts, pm, work Cable chart over 25 (25, 25, 25, 33, 33) sts, k1.

Work 1 WS row in patt, keeping first and last st in St st.

SHAPE WAIST

Dec row: (RS) *Work in patt to m, sl m, k2tog or p2tog as needed to maintain patt, work in patt to 2 sts before m, ssk or ssp as needed to maintain patt, sl m; rep from * once more, work in patt to end—4 sts dec'd.

Rep Dec row every 12th row 2 more times—155 (171, 195, 211, 227, 243) sts rem.

Work 11 rows even.

Inc row: (RS) *Work in patt to m, sl m, M1R or M1RP as needed to maintain patt, work in patt to m, M1L or M1LP as needed to maintain patt, sl m; rep from * once more, work in patt to end—4 sts inc'd.

Rep Inc row every 12th row 2 more times—167 (183, 207, 223, 239, 255) sts.

Work even until piece measures 15" from CO, ending with a WS row.

DIVIDE FOR FRONTS AND BACK

Next row: (RS) Work 38 (40, 45, 48, 51, 54) sts and place these sts on holder for right front, BO 9 (11, 13, 15, 17, 19) sts, work 73 (81, 91, 97, 103, 109) sts and place these sts on holder for back, BO 9 (11, 13, 15, 17, 19) sts, work in patt to end—38 (40, 45, 48, 51, 54) sts rem for left front.

Left Front

Work 1 WS row.

SHAPE NECK AND ARMHOLE

Dec row: (RS) K1, k2tog or p2tog as needed to maintain patt, work to last 3 sts, ssk or ssp as needed to maintain patt, k1—2 sts dec'd.

Rep Dec row every RS row 3 (4, 5, 6, 7, 7) more times—30 (30, 33, 34, 35, 38) sts rem.

SIZES 44¼(47)" ONLY

Work 1 WS row.

Dec row: (RS) K1, k2tog or p2tog as needed to maintain patt, work to end—33 (34) sts rem.

SIZE 50¼" ONLY

Work 1 WS row.

Dec row: (RS) K1, k2tog or p2tog as needed to maintain patt, work to end—37 sts rem. Work 1 WS row.

Dec row: (RS) K1, k2tog or p2tog as needed to maintain patt, work to last 3 sts, ssk or ssp as needed to maintain patt, k1—35 sts rem.

ALL SIZES

Work 1 (1, 3, 1, 1, 3) row(s) even.

Dec row: (RS) Work to last 3 sts, ssk or ssp as needed to maintain patt, k1—1 st dec'd.

Rep Dec row every RS row 1 (0, 0, 0, 0, 0) more time, then every 4th row 10 (10, 9, 9, 9, 8) times—18 (19, 23, 23, 24, 26) sts rem.

Work even until armhole measures 7½ (7¾, 8, 8¼, 8½, 8¾)", ending with a WS row.

Shape shoulder using short-rows as foll:

Short-row 1: (RS) Work to last 5 (6, 7, 7, 8, 9) sts, wrap next st, turn.

Short-row 2: (WS) Work to end.

Short-row 3: Work to last 11 (12, 14, 14, 16, 18) sts, wrap next st, turn.

Short-row 4: Work to end.

Next row: (RS) Work to end, working wraps tog with wrapped sts.

Work 1 WS row. Place sts on holder.

Back

Return 73 (81, 91, 97, 103, 109) held sts to larger needle and, with WS facing, rejoin yarn.

Work 1 WS row.

SHAPE ARMHOLES

Dec row: (RS) K1, k2tog or p2tog as needed to maintain patt, work to last 3 sts, ssk or ssp as needed to maintain patt, k1—2 sts dec'd.

Rep Dec row every RS row 3 (4, 5, 7, 8, 9) more times—65 (71, 79, 81, 85, 89) sts rem.

Work even until armhole measures 7½ (7¾, 8, 8¼, 8½, 8¾)", ending with a WS row.

Shape shoulders using short-rows as foll:

Short-rows 1 and 2: Work to last 5 (6, 7, 7, 8, 9) sts, wrap next st, turn.

Short-rows 3 and 4: Work to last 11 (12, 14, 14, 16, 18) sts, wrap next st, turn.

Next 2 rows: Work to end, working wraps tog with wrapped sts.

Next row: (RS) Work 18 19, 23, 23, 24, 26) sts, BO 29 (33, 33, 35, 37, 37) sts for neck, work to end—18 (19, 23, 23, 24, 26) sts rem for each shoulder.

Place sts on holders.

CABLE

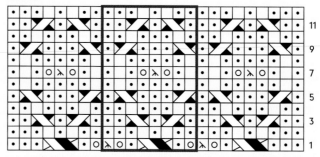

8 st repeat

	k on RS; p on WS
·	p on RS; k on WS
o	yo
⅄	sl 1 kwise, k2tog, psso
	pattern repeat

sl 1 st onto cn, hold in back, k1, p1 from cn

sl 1 st onto cn, hold in front, p1, k1 from cn

sl 2 sts onto cn, hold in front, k1, (p1, k1) from cn

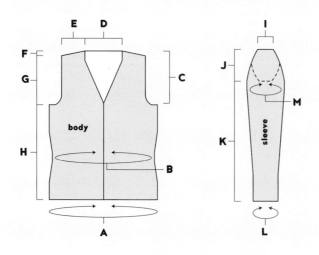

BODY

A: 32 (35¼, 40, 43¼, 46, 49¼)"

B: 29¾ (33, 37¾, 41, 43¾, 46¾)

C: 8 (8¼, 8½, 8¾, 9, 9¼)"

D: 5½ (6¼, 6¼, 6½, 7, 7)"

E: 3½ (3¾, 4½, 4½, 4¾, 5)"

F: ¾"

G: 7½ (7¾, 8, 8¼, 8½, 8¾)"

H: 15"

SLEEVE

I: 2½ (2½, 3½, 3, 3, 2½)"

J: 4¾ (5, 5¼, 5½, 5¾, 7)"

K: 19"

L: 8 (8, 9½, 10½, 11¼, 12)"

M: 11½ (12½, 14, 14¾, 15½, 17¼)"

Right Front

Return 38 (40, 45, 48, 51, 54) held sts to larger needle and, with WS facing, rejoin yarn.

Work 1 WS row.

SHAPE NECK AND ARMHOLE

Dec row: (RS) K1, k2tog or p2tog as needed to maintain patt, work to last 3 sts, ssk or ssp as needed to maintain patt, k1—2 sts dec'd.

Rep Dec row every RS row 3 (4, 5, 6, 7, 7) more times—30 (30, 33, 34, 35, 38) sts rem.

SIZES 44¼ (47)" ONLY

Work 1 WS row.

Dec row: (RS) Work to last 3 sts, ssk or ssp as needed to maintain patt, k1—33 (34) sts rem.

SIZE 50¼" ONLY

Work 1 WS row.

Dec row: (RS) Work to last 3 sts, ssk or ssp as needed to maintain patt, k1—37 sts rem.

Work 1 WS row.

Dec row: (RS) K1, k2tog or p2tog as needed to maintain patt, work to last 3 sts, ssk or ssp as needed to maintain patt, k1—35 sts rem.

ALL SIZES

Work 1 (1, 3, 1, 1, 3) row(s) even.

Dec row: (RS) K1, k2tog or p2tog as needed to maintain patt, work to end—1 st dec'd.

Rep Dec row every RS row 1 (0, 0, 0, 0, 0) more time, then every 4th row 10 (10, 9, 9, 9, 8) times—18 (19, 23, 23, 24, 26) sts rem.

Work even until armhole measures 7½ (7¾, 8, 8¼, 8½, 8¾)", ending with a RS row.

Shape shoulder using short-rows as foll:

Short-row 1: (WS) Work to last 5 (6, 7, 7, 8, 9) sts, wrap next st, turn.

Short-row 2: (RS) Work to end.

Short-row 3: Work to last 11 (12, 14, 14, 16, 18) sts, wrap next st, turn.

Short-row 4: Work to end.

Next row: (WS) Work to end, working wraps tog with wrapped sts. Place sts on holder.

Sleeves

With smaller dpn, CO 40 (40, 48, 52, 56, 60) sts. Pm and join in the rnd.

Next rnd: *K1tbl, p1tbl; rep from * to end.

Work in rib for 2¾". Change to larger dpn. Work in Granite st in rnds (see Stitch Guide) for 12 rnds.

Inc rnd: K1, M1L or M1LP as needed to maintain patt, work to end, M1R or M1RP as needed to maintain patt—2 sts inc'd.

Rep Inc rnd every 12 (10, 10, 8, 8, 8)th rnd 8 (10, 10, 10, 10, 12) more times—58 (62, 70, 74, 78, 86) sts.

Work even until piece measures 19" from CO, ending 4 (5, 6, 7, 8, 9) sts before end of rnd on last rnd.

SHAPE CAP

Next rnd: BO 9 (11, 13, 15, 17, 19) sts, work to end—49 (51, 57, 59, 61, 67) sts rem.

Work back and forth in rows.

Work 1 WS row.

Dec row: (RS) K2, k2tog, work to last 4 sts, ssk, k2—2 sts dec'd.

Rep Dec row every RS row 3 (4, 5, 6, 7, 9) more times, then every 4th row 2 (2, 2, 1, 1, 1) time(s), then every RS row 7 (7, 7, 9, 9, 11) times—23 (23, 27, 25, 25, 23) sts rem.

Dec row: (WS) P2, ssp, work to last 4 sts, p2tog, p2—2 sts dec'd.

Dec 1 st at each end every row 4 more times—13 (13, 17, 15, 15, 13) sts rem. BO all sts.

Finishing

With RS tog, join shoulders using three-needle BO.

Sew sleeves into armholes.

NECKBAND

Mark for placement of 6 buttonholes along right front edge, with top button 1" below beg of neck shaping, bottom button 1" above lower edge, and others evenly spaced between. With cir needle and RS facing, beg at right front lower edge, pick up and knit 3 sts for every 4 rows along right front to shoulder, 1 st for each st along back neck, and 3 sts for every 4 rows along left front to lower edge, making sure to pick up an odd number of sts. Do not join.

Next row: (WS) *P1tbl, k1tbl; rep from * to last st, p1tbl.

Work in rib for 2 more rows.

Buttonhole row: (RS) *Work to m, k2tog, yo; rep from * 5 more times, work to end.

Work in rib for 3 more rows.

With RS facing, BO all sts in patt.

Weave in ends.

Sew buttons to left front band opposite buttonholes.

Block to measurements.

anil cardigan

Amy Christoffers

Finished Size

Bust circumference: 36½ (41, 46, 51, 55½, 60½)" with fronts overlapped about 2½".

Cardigan shown measures 41"; modeled with 8½" of positive ease.

Yarn

Worsted weight (#4 medium).

Shown here: Berroco Indigo (95% cotton, 5% other; 219 yd [200 m]/100 g): #6463 denim 5 (6, 6, 7, 8, 9) skeins.

Needles

Size U.S. 7 (4.5 mm): 32" circular (cir) and set of double-pointed (dpn).

Size U.S. 6 (4 mm): 32" cir and set of dpn.

Adjust needle size if necessary to obtain the correct gauge.

Notions

Markers (m); stitch holders or waste yarn; tapestry needle.

Gauge

20 sts and 28 rows = 4" in St st on larger needle.

Notes

■ The body of this cardigan is worked back and forth in one piece to the underarm, then divided for working the fronts and back separately. Stitches for the sleeves are picked up around the armhole and the sleeves are worked in the round from the top down.

■ A circular needle is used to accommodate the large number of stitches.

■ The shoulder shaping is worked in stockinette short-rows below the lace yoke to avoid interrupting the lace pattern.

■ During shaping, if there are not enough stitches to work each decrease with its companion yarnover, or each double decrease with both its yarnovers, work the remaining stitch(es) in stockinette instead.

Body

With smaller cir needle, CO 195 (219, 243, 267, 291, 315) sts. Do not join.

Knit 6 rows, ending with a RS row. Change to larger cir needle.

Next row: (WS) K3, purl to last 3 sts, k3.

Next row: (RS) Knit.

Rep last 2 rows until piece measures 15" from CO, ending with a WS row.

DIVIDE FOR FRONTS AND BACK

Next row: (RS) K52 (58, 64, 70, 76, 82) and place these sts on holder for right front, k91 (103, 115, 127, 139, 151) and place these sts on holder for back, knit to end—52 (58, 64, 70, 76, 82) sts rem for left front.

Left Front

Next row: (WS) K3 front edge sts, purl to end.

Next row: (RS) Using the backward-loop method, CO 1 st for armhole selvedge st, knit to end—53 (59, 65, 71, 77, 83) sts.

Keeping front edge sts in garter st, and working selvedge st in St st, work even until armhole measures 2¼ (2¾, 3¼, 3¾, 4¼, 4¾)", ending with a RS row.

Shape shoulder (see Notes) using short-rows as foll:

Short-row 1: (WS) K3, purl to last 6 (7, 8, 8, 9, 10) sts, wrap next st, turn.

Short-row 2: (RS) Knit to end.

Short-row 3: K3, purl to 4 (5, 6, 6, 7, 8) sts before wrapped st, wrap next st, turn.

Short-row 4: Knit to end.

Rep last 2 short-rows 4 more times.

Next row: (WS) K3, purl to end, working wraps tog with wrapped sts—armhole measures 2½ (3, 3½, 4, 4½, 5)".

Next row: (RS) K1, work Row 1 of Lace chart over 49 (55, 61, 67, 73, 79) sts, k3.

Keeping front edge sts in garter st and selvedge st in St st, work Rows 2-24 of chart once—armhole measures 6 (6½, 7, 7½, 8, 8½)".

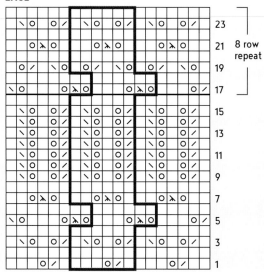

LACE

6 st repeat

8 row repeat

Rows: 23, 21, 19, 17, 15, 13, 11, 9, 7, 5, 3, 1

☐ k on RS; p on WS

○ yo

╱ k2tog on RS; p2tog on WS

╲ ssk on RS; ssp on WS

⋏ sl 1 kwise, k2tog, psso

▢ pattern repeat

Note: *From here, rep Rows 17-24 of chart only.*

Next row: (RS) BO 26 (32, 38, 38, 44, 50) shoulder sts, work in patt to end (see Notes)—27 (27, 27, 33, 33, 33) sts rem.

COLLAR EXTENSION

Work 1 WS row even.

Next row: (RS) CO 1 st for back neck selvedge st, knit new CO st, work in patt to end—28 (28, 28, 34, 34, 34) sts.

Keeping front edge sts in garter st and selvedge st in St st, work even until collar extension measures 4 (4, 4, 5, 5, 5)" ending with a WS row.

BO all sts.

Back

Return 91 (103, 115, 127, 139, 151) held back sts to larger cir needle and, with WS facing, rejoin yarn.

Next row: (WS) CO 1 st for armhole selvedge st, purl to end—1 st inc'd.

Next row: (RS) CO 1 st for armhole selvedge st, knit to end—93 (105, 117, 129, 141, 153) sts.

Work even in St st until armhole measures 2¼ (2¾, 3¼, 3¾, 4¼, 4¾)", ending with a RS row.

Shape shoulders using short-rows as foll:

Short-row 1: (WS) Purl to last 6 (7, 8, 8, 9, 10) sts, wrap next st, turn.

Short-row 2: (RS) Knit to last 6 (7, 8, 8, 9, 10) sts, wrap next st, turn.

Short-row 3: Purl to 4 (5, 6, 6, 7, 8) sts before wrapped st, wrap next st, turn.

Short-row 4: Knit to 4 (5, 6, 6, 7, 8) sts before wrapped st, wrap next st, turn.

Rep last 2 short-rows 4 more times.

Next row: (WS) Purl to end, working wraps tog with wrapped sts.

Next row: (RS) Working rem wraps tog with wrapped sts, k1, work Row 1 of Lace chart over 91 (103, 115, 127, 139, 151) sts, k1.

Keeping selvedge sts in St st, work Rows 2–24 of chart once—armhole measures 6 (6½, 7, 7½, 8, 8½)".

BO all sts.

Right Front

Return 52 (58, 64, 70, 76, 82) held sts to larger cir needle and, with WS facing, rejoin yarn.

Next row: (WS) CO 1 st for armhole selvedge st, purl to last 3 sts, k3—53 (59, 65, 71, 77, 83) sts.

Keeping front edge sts in garter st, and working selvedge st in St st, work even until armhole measures 2¼ (2¾, 3¼, 3¾, 4¼, 4¾)", ending with a WS row.

Shape shoulder using short-rows as foll:

Short-row 1: (RS) Knit to last 6 (7, 8, 8, 9, 10) sts, wrap next st, turn.

Short-row 2: (WS) Purl to last 3 sts, k3.

Short-row 3: Knit to 4 (5, 6, 6, 7, 8) sts before wrapped st, wrap next st, turn.

Short-row 4: Purl to last 3 sts, k3.

Rep last 2 short-rows 4 more times.

Next row: (RS) Knit to end, working wraps tog with wrapped sts.

Work 1 WS row.

Next row: (RS) K3, work Row 1 of Lace chart over 49 (55, 61, 67, 73, 79) sts, k1.

Keeping front edge sts in garter st and selvedge st in St st, work Rows 2–24 of chart once—armhole measures 6 (6½, 7, 7½, 8, 8½)".

▎ **Note:** *Rep only Rows 17–24 of chart from here.*

Work 1 RS row.

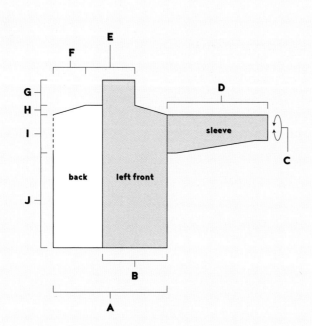

A: 18¼ (20½, 23, 25½, 27¾, 30¼)"

B: 10½ (11½, 12¾, 14, 15¼, 16½)"

C: 8 (8¾, 10, 10¾, 10¾, 11½)"

D: 16¼ (16¼, 16¼, 16¼, 17, 17)"

E: 8 (8, 8½, 10¾, 10¾, 10½)"

F: 5¼ (6½, 7½, 7½, 8¾, 10)"

G: 4 (4, 4, 5, 5, 5)"

H: 1½"

I: 6 (6½, 7, 7½, 8, 8½)"

J: 15"

Next row: (WS) BO 26 (32, 38, 38, 44, 50) shoulder sts, work in patt to end—27 (27, 27, 33, 33, 33) sts rem.

COLLAR EXTENSION

Work 1 RS row even.

Next row: (WS) CO 1 st for back neck selvedge st, purl new CO st, work in patt to end—28 (28, 28, 34, 34, 34) sts.

Keeping front edge sts in garter st and selvedge st in St st, work even until collar extension measures 4 (4, 4, 5, 5, 5)" ending with a WS row.

BO all sts.

Sleeves

Sew shoulder seams. With larger dpn and RS facing, beg at center of underarm, pick up and knit 60 (64, 70, 74, 80, 84) sts evenly around armhole edge. Pm and join in the rnd.

Knit 10 (10, 10, 10, 8, 8) rnds.

Dec rnd: K1, k2tog, knit to last 2 sts, ssk—2 sts dec'd.

Rep Dec rnd every 10 (10, 10, 10, 8, 8)th rnd 9 (9, 9, 9, 12, 12) more times—40 (44, 50, 54, 54, 58) sts rem.

Work even until piece measures 15¾ (15¾, 15¾, 15¾, 16½, 16½)" from underarm.

Change to smaller dpn. [Purl 1 rnd, knit 1 rnd] 2 times, then purl 1 rnd—sleeve measures 16¼ (16¼, 16¼, 16¼, 17, 17)" from underarm.

BO all sts.

Finishing

Sew collar extensions tog at center back neck. Sew selvedge of collar along back neck edge, easing to fit.

Weave in ends.

Block to measurements.

benton cardigan

Amy Christoffers

Finished Size

Bust circumference: about 38 (42, 46, 50, 54)" with 3½" opening at front.

Cardigan shown measures 38".

Yarn

Worsted weight (#4 medium).

Shown here: O-Wool Classic Worsted (100% wool; 99 yd [90 m]/50 g): #5401 Garnet, 12 (14, 15, 16, 17) skeins.

Needles

Size U.S. 9 (5.5 mm): 32" circular (cir) and set of 4 or 5 double-pointed (dpn).

Size U.S. 8 (5 mm): 32" cir and set of 4 or 5 dpn.

Adjust needle size if necessary to obtain the correct gauge.

Notions

Markers (m); stitch holders or waste yarn; tapestry needle.

Gauge

16 sts and 21 rows = 4" in St st on larger needles.

26 sts = 4½" in Front charts on larger needles.

Note: *Circular needle is used to accommodate a large number of stitches. Do not join; work back and forth in rows.*

Sleeve

With smaller needle, CO 40 (44, 44, 48, 52) sts. Divide sts evenly over 3 or 4 smaller dpn, place marker (pm), and join for working in the rnd, being careful not to twist sts.

Est rib: *K1, p2, k1, rep from *.

Rep the last rnd until piece measures 3¾" from CO.

Change to larger dpn and St st (knit every rnd).

SHAPE SLEEVE

Knit 11 (11, 7, 7, 7) rnds.

Inc rnd: K1, M1L, knit to last st, M1R, k1—2 sts inc'd.

Rep the last 12 (12, 8, 8, 8) rnds 4 (5, 7, 8, 8) times—50 (56, 60, 66, 70) sts.

Work even until piece measures 19" from CO, ending 3 (3, 4, 6, 7) sts before the end of rnd. Break yarn, leaving at least a 9" tail, and place the next 6 (6, 8, 12, 14) sts onto st holder or waste yarn for underarm. Place the rem 44 (50, 52, 54, 56) onto st holder or waste yarn for the yoke.

Make a second sleeve the same as the first.

Body

With smaller cir, CO 156 (172, 188, 204, 220) sts. Do not join; work back and forth in rows.

Est rib: (WS) P2, *p1, k2, p1; rep from * to last 2 sts, p2.

Next row: (RS) K2, *k1, p2, k1; rep from * to last 2 sts, k2.

Rep the last 2 rows until piece measures 2¼", ending after a WS row.

Change to larger cir.

Est Front charts: (RS) Work 3 sts in St st, 26 sts in Right Front chart, 11 (15, 19, 23, 27) sts in St st, pm for side, work 76 (84, 92, 100, 108) sts in St st, pm for side, work 11 (15, 19, 23, 27) sts in St st, 26 sts in Left Front chart, 3 sts in St st.

SHAPE WAIST

Work 11 rows even as est, ending after a WS row.

Dec row: (RS) *Work as est to 3 sts before m, ssk, k1, sl m, k1, k2tog; rep from * once more, work to end as est—4 sts dec'd.

Rep the last 12 rows 2 times—144 (160, 176, 192, 208) sts.

Work 11 rows even as est, ending after a WS row.

Inc row: (RS) *Work as est to 1 st before m, M1R, k1, sl m, k1, M1R; rep from * once more, work to end as est—4 sts inc'd.

Work 5 rows even as est, ending after a WS row.

Rep the last 6 rows 2 times—156 (172, 188, 204, 220) sts.

Cont working as est until six 12-row repeats of the Front charts are completed, ending after WS Row 12. Piece measures about 16".

RIGHT FRONT ANGLE

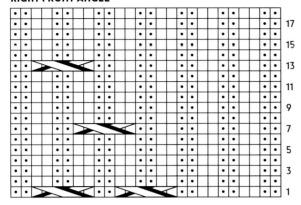

RIGHT FRONT

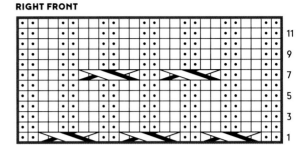

LEFT FRONT ANGLE

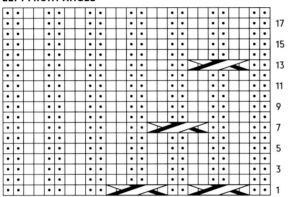

LEFT FRONT

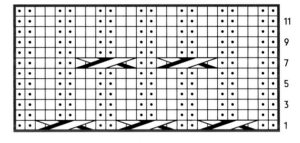

	knit on RS, purl on WS
•	purl on RS, knit on WS
	sl 3 sts to cn and hold in front, k2, p1 from left needle, p1, k2 from cn
	sl 3 sts to cn and hold in back, k2, p1 from left needle, p1, k2 from cn
	pattern repeat

Est Front Angle charts: (RS) Work 3 sts in St st, 26 sts in Right Front Angle chart, work in St st to Left Front chart, work 26 sts in Left Front Angle chart, work 3 sts in St st.

Cont working even as est until piece measures 18" from CO, ending after a WS row.

Yoke

❚ *Note: While working yoke, cont working Front Angle charts until all 18 rows are completed, then continue working those 26 sts in ribbing as est.*

Joining row: (RS) Work 37 (41, 44, 46, 49) right front sts, place the next 6 (6, 8, 12, 14) sts onto st holder or waste yarn for underarm, pm, return 44 (50, 52, 54, 56)

held sleeve sts onto dpn and work across, pm and work 70 (78, 84, 88, 94) back sts, place the next 6 (6, 8, 12, 14) sts onto st holder or waste yarn for underarm, pm, return 44 (50, 52, 54, 56) held sleeve sts to dpn and work across, pm, and work rem 37 (41, 44, 46, 49) left front sts to end—232 (260, 276, 288, 304) sts.

Work 1 WS row even as est.

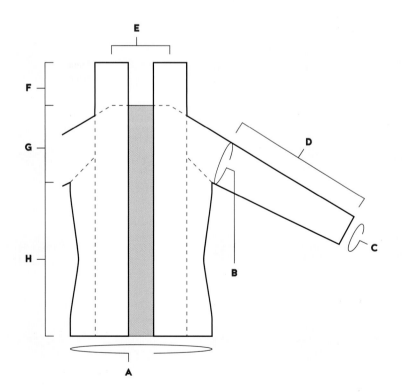

A: 38 (42, 46, 50, 54)"
with 3½" gap

B: 12½ (14, 15, 16½, 17½)"

C: 10 (11, 11, 12, 13)"

D: 19"

E: Back neck width:
7½ (8, 9, 9½, 10½)"

F: 4¼ (4½, 5, 5¼, 5¾)"

G: 8¾ (9½, 10, 10¼, 10¾)"

H: 18"

SHAPE RAGLAN

Front, Back, and Sleeve Dec row: (RS) *Work to 3 sts before next m, ssk, k1, sl m, k1, k2tog; rep from * 3 more times, work to end—8 sts dec'd.

Work 1 WS row even as est.

Rep the last 2 rows 5 (9, 12, 14, 17) times—184 (180, 172, 168, 160) sts rem: 31 sts each front, 32 (30, 26, 24, 20) sts each sleeve, and 58 sts for back.

Back and Sleeve Dec row: (RS) Work as est to m, *sl m, k1, k2tog, work to 3 sts before next m, ssk, k1, sl m; rep from * 2 more times, work to end as est—6 sts dec'd.

Work 3 rows even as est.

Rep the last 4 rows 1 (0, 0, 0, 0) times—172 (174, 166, 162, 154) sts rem: 31 sts each front, 28 (28, 24, 22, 18) sts each sleeve, and 54 (56, 56, 56, 56) sts for back.

[Work back and sleeve dec row, then work 1 WS row even] 12 (12, 10, 9, 7) times—100 (102, 106, 108, 112) sts rem: 31 sts each front, 4 sts each sleeve, and 30 (32, 36, 38, 42) sts for back.

SHAPE NECK

Next row: (RS) Work 31 sts as est for right neck, BO the next 38 (40, 44, 46, 50) sts, work rem 31 sts as est for left neck.

Cont working back and forth on the left neck sts, keeping the right neck sts on needle to be worked later.

LEFT NECK EXTENSION

Work in rib as est until piece measures 4¼ (4½, 5, 5¼, 5¾)" from neck BO. Place left neck extension sts on a st holder or waste yarn and break yarn.

RIGHT NECK EXTENSION

Rejoin yarn to right neck sts, preparing to work a WS row. Work the same as the left neck extension.

Finishing

Block piece to measurements.

Return held neck extension sts onto two needles and join them together by grafting in rib.

With yarn threaded on a tapestry needle, sew selvedge edge of neck extensions to the BO neck edge, stretching the extensions gently to fit.

Return the held underarm sts to the needles and use the 9" tail from the sleeve and the Kitchener st to graft sleeve and body sts together.

FRONT BAND

With smaller cir, beg at right front hem, pick up and knit 250 (254, 258, 262, 270) sts (about 3 sts for every 4 rows) along front edge up the right front, along the neck back, and down the left front.

Est rib: (WS) P2, *k2, p2; rep from *.

Next row: (RS) K2, *p2, k2; rep from *.

Rep the last 2 rows once more, then work one more WS row.

BO all sts in rib.

Weave in ends.

Block again if desired.

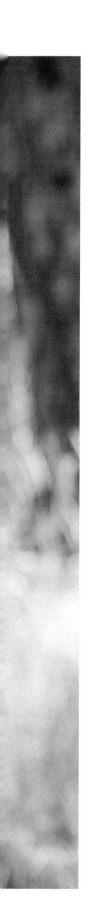

zephirine cardigan

Angela Hahn

Finished Size

Bust circumference: 37¼ (41½, 45¾, 50, 54)".

Cardigan shown measures 37¼", modeled with 2¾" of positive ease.

Yarn

Worsted weight (#4 medium).

Shown here: Universal Yarn Nettle Lana (70% organic wool, 30% nettle; 98 yd [90 m]/1¾ oz [50 g]): #109 linen, 11 (12, 14, 15, 17) balls.

Needles

Size U.S. 5 (3.75 mm): 24-47" circular (cir), depending on size you are making, and set of double-pointed (dpn).

Size U.S. 7 (4.5 mm): cir depending on size you are making, and dpn.

Adjust needle size if necessary to obtain the correct gauge.

Notions

Markers (m); stitch holders; tapestry needle; two ⅝" buttons.

Gauge

19 sts and 27 rows = 4" in body patt on larger needle.

Notes

■ The body of this cardigan is worked back and forth in one piece from the lower edge to the underarms. The sleeves are worked separately in the round, then the sleeves and body are joined to work the yoke.

■ A circular needle is used to accommodate the large number of stitches.

Body

With smaller cir needle, CO 177 (197, 217, 237, 257) sts. Do not join.

RIB

Row 1: (RS) K1, *k1, p1; rep from * to last 2 sts, k2.

Row 2: K1, *p1, k1; rep from * to end.

Rep Rows 1 and 2 two more times. Change to larger cir needle.

Next row: (RS) Knit.

Next row: [K1, p13] 3 (3, 3, 4, 4) times, k1, p1 (6, 11, 2, 7), place marker (pm) for side, p2 (7, 12, 3, 8), [k1, p13] 6 (6, 6, 8, 8) times, k1, p1 (6, 11, 2, 7), pm for side, p2 (7, 12, 3, 8), [k1, p13] 3 (3, 3, 4, 4) times, k1.

Rep last 2 rows until piece measures 14½ (15¼, 15¾, 15½, 15¼)" from CO, ending with a WS row. Do not break yarn. Set aside.

Sleeves

With smaller dpn, CO 62 (68, 72, 78, 86) sts. Pm and join in the rnd.

Next rnd: Beg with k1 (p1, k1, p1, k1), work in k1, p1 rib to end.

Cont in rib for 5 more rnds. Change to larger dpn.

Next rnd: Knit.

Next rnd: K3 (6, 1, 4, 1), [p1, k13] 4 (4, 5, 5, 6) times, p1, k2 (5, 0, 3, 0).

Rep last 2 rnds until piece measures 9 (9½, 10¼, 10½, 10½)" from CO, ending 4 (5, 6, 7, 8) sts before end of rnd on last rnd.

Place next 9 (11, 13, 15, 17) sts on holder for underarm (remove m), then place foll 53 (57, 59, 63, 69) sts on another holder for sleeve. Break yarn, leaving a 1-yd tail.

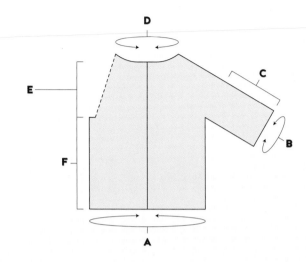

A: 37¼ (41½, 45¾, 50, 54)"

B: 13 (14¼, 15¼, 16½, 18)"

C: 9 (9½, 10¼, 10½, 10½)"

D: 20 (20, 22½, 22½, 25)"

E: 8¾ (9¼, 10, 10¼, 10½)"

F: 14½ (15¼, 15¾, 15½, 15¼)"

Yoke

Joining row: With RS facing and using working yarn from body, larger cir needle, and working all sts in patt, work 40 (44, 48, 52, 56) right front sts, place next 9 (11, 13, 15, 17) sts on holder for underarm, removing m, pm, work 53 (57, 59, 63, 69) sleeve sts, pm, work 79 (87, 95, 103, 111) back sts, place next 9 (11, 13, 15, 17) sts on holder for underarm, removing m, pm, work 53 (57, 59, 63, 69) sleeve sts, pm, work 40 (44, 48, 52, 56) left front sts—265 (289, 309, 333, 361) sts total.

Work 1 WS row.

Raglan dec row: (RS) *Work to 3 sts before m, ssk, k1, sl m, k1, k2tog; rep from * 3 more times, work to end—8 sts dec'd.

Rep Raglan dec row every RS row 1 (5, 1, 6, 5) more time(s), then every 4th row 3 (2, 5, 3, 4) times—225 (225, 253, 253, 281) sts rem.

Work 3 rows even, ending with a WS row and removing m.

Work Rows 1–16 of Lace chart. Change to smaller needle.

Work Rows 17–39 of chart—65 (65, 73, 73, 81) sts rem.

BO all sts in patt.

Finishing

Place held underarm sts from sleeve and body onto 2 larger dpn. With RS tog and using yarn tail from sleeve, join underarm sts using three-needle BO.

Weave in ends, closing any holes at sides of underarms.

Block to measurements.

Sew buttons to edge of left front opposite button loops.

LACE

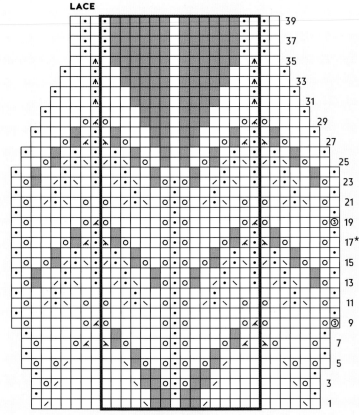

14 st to 4 st repeat
* change needle size

☐ k on RS; p on WS	⅄ sssk
• p on RS; k on WS	⋏ sl 2 as if to k2tog, k1, p2sso
O yo	③ button loop: [k1, transfer st to left needle] 2 times, k1
╱ k2tog	
╲ ssk	▨ no stitch
⟋ k3tog	☐ pattern repeat

snowbowl hoodie

Anne Podlesak

Finished Size

Bust circumference: About 38 (39, 41, 42¾, 44¼, 47½, 50¼, 54)".

Length from neck at center back: 23¼ (23½, 24½, 25, 25¾, 26½, 27, 27½)".

Hoodie shown measures 41".

Yarn

DK weight (#3 light).

Shown here: Green Mountain Spinnery New Mexico Organic (100% fine wool; 180 yd/2 oz [57 g]): grey 10 (10, 10, 11, 11, 12, 12,13) skeins.

Needles

Size U.S. 5 (3.75 mm) 32" or longer circular (cir) and set of double-pointed (dpn).

Adjust needle size if necessary to obtain the correct gauge.

Notions

Stitch markers (m); cable needle (cn); stitch holders or waste yarn; tapestry needle; zipper to fit length from bottom hem to top of front neckband; sewing needle; matching sewing thread.

Gauge

20 sts and 29 rows = 4" in St st, after blocking; 15-st Moguls Cable panel = about 2" wide, after blocking.

66-st Ski Run Cable panel = 9" (23 cm) wide, after blocking.

Notes

■ This is a woman's cardigan sweater with a hood. The back features large ski-run cables extending from the hood all the way down the center back. The front features a smaller set of mogul cables along the front bands, which have a zippered closure. The yoke is shaped with raglan armhole seams. Matching mogul cables run down the center of each sleeve.

■ Both charts are worked back and forth for the body. Read the right-side (odd-numbered) rows from right to left and the wrong-side (even-numbered) rows from left to right. The Moguls chart is worked in the round for the sleeves. Read all rows from right to left.

■ The front edges have two edge sts used to sew in the zipper. Slip the first stitch of each row to help create a smooth edge.

■ A circular needle is used for the body to accommodate the large number of stitches. Do not join, work back and forth.

1/1 LC (1 over 1 left cross): Slip 1 st to cn and hold in front, k1, k1 from cn.

1/1 RC (1 over 1 right cross) : Slip 1 st to cn and hold in back, k1, k1 from cn.

2/2 LC (2 over 2 left cross): Slip 2 sts to cn and hold in front, k2, k2 from cn.

2/2 LPC (2 over 2 left purl cross): Slip 2 sts to cn and hold in front, p2, k2 from cn.

2/2 RC (2 over 2 right cross): Slip 2 sts to cn and hold in back, k2, k2 from cn.

2/2 RPC (2 over 2 right purl cross): Slip 2 sts to cn and hold in back, k2, p2 from cn.

3/3 RC (3 over 3 right cross): Slip 3 sts to cn and hold in back, k3, k3 from cn.

Body

With cir needle, CO 202 (208, 218, 226, 234, 250, 264, 282) sts using the long-tail cast-on method. Do not join.

Next row: (WS) P2 (edge sts), place marker (pm), p2, k2, p4, [k2, p2] 10 (10, 11, 11, 12, 13, 14, 15) times, k0 (2, 0, 2, 0, 0, 0, 0), pm for left side, [k2, p2] 4 (4, 5, 6, 6, 7, 8, 9) times, k2 (3, 2, 0, 2, 2, 1, 2), pm, p2, k2, [p4, k2] twice, p2, k4, [p2, k2] 5 times, p2, k4, p2, k2, [p4, k2] twice, p2, pm, [k2, p2] 4 (4, 5, 6, 6, 7, 8, 9) times, k2 (3, 2, 0, 2, 2, 1, 2), pm for right side, p0 (2, 0, 2, 0, 0, 0, 0), [p2, k2] 10 (10, 11, 11, 12, 13, 14, 15) times, p4, k2, p2, pm, p2 edge sts.

Slipping m as you come to them, work 18 more rows in est ribbing, ending with a WS row.

Set-up row: (RS) Sl 1, k1, sm, work Row 1 of Left Moguls chart over next 15 sts, pm, (knit to next m, sm) twice, work Row 1 of Ski Run chart over next 66 sts, sm, knit to next m, sm, k33 (35, 37, 39, 41, 45, 49, 53), work Row 1 of Right Moguls chart over next 15 sts, sm, k2.

Next row: (WS) Sl 1, p1, sm, work Row 2 of Right Moguls chart over next 15 sts, sm, (purl to next m, sm) twice, work Row 2 of Ski Run chart over next 66 sts, sm, (purl to next m, sm) twice, work Row 2 of Left Moguls chart over next 15 sts, sm, p2.

SKI RUN

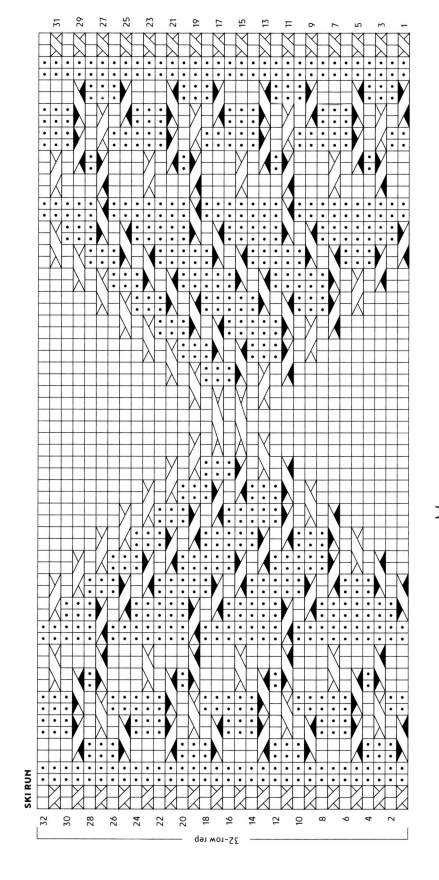

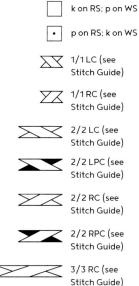

	k on RS; p on WS
	p on RS; k on WS
	1/1 LC (see Stitch Guide)
	1/1 RC (see Stitch Guide)
	2/2 LC (see Stitch Guide)
	2/2 LPC (see Stitch Guide)
	2/2 RC (see Stitch Guide)
	2/2 RPC (see Stitch Guide)
	3/3 RC (see Stitch Guide)

32-row rep

Cont in est patts until piece measures 15 (15, 15½, 15½, 16, 16, 16½, 16½)" from beg, ending with a RS row. Make a note of which row you ended each Moguls chart so the pattern can be matched on sleeves.

ARMHOLES

Next row: (WS) *Work in est patt to 4 (4, 4, 5, 5, 5, 6, 6) sts before side m, BO 8 (8, 8, 10, 10, 10, 12, 12) sts for armhole, removing m; rep from * once more, then work to end of row—186 (192, 202, 206, 214, 230, 240, 258) sts rem; 46 (48, 50, 51, 53, 57, 60, 64) sts for each front, and 94 (96, 102, 104, 108, 116, 120, 130) sts for back.

Set aside.

Sleeves

With dpn, CO 54 (54, 54, 62, 62, 62, 70, 70) sts using the long-tail cast-on method. Pm and join for working in rnds, being careful not to twist sts.

Set-up rnd: [K2, p2] 3 (3, 3, 4, 4, 4, 5, 5) times, pm, k2, p2, k4, [p2, k2] 3 times, p2, k4, p2, k2, pm, [p2, k2] 3 (3, 3, 4, 4, 4, 5, 5) times.

Slipping m as you come to them, work 18 more rnds in est ribbing.

Next rnd: K12 (12, 12, 16, 16, 16, 20, 20) sts, sm, work Row 1 of Left Moguls chart over next 15 sts, and Row 1 of Right Moguls chart over next 15 sts, sm, knit to end.

Work 7 (7, 6, 7, 5, 4, 5, 5) rnds even.

Inc rnd: K1, m1l, work to last st, m1r, k1—2 sts inc'd.

Rep last 8 (8, 7, 8, 6, 5, 6, 6) rnds 11 (12, 14, 12, 15, 18, 16, 17) more times—78 (80, 84, 88, 94, 100, 104, 106) sts.

Cont even until piece measures about 17¾ (18, 18, 18¼, 18½, 18½, 18¾, 19)" from beg, ending 1 row before the end point on Moguls Cable charts as with body, and ending 4 (4, 5, 5, 5, 6, 6) sts before end of last rnd.

BO 8 (8, 8, 10, 10, 10, 12, 12) sts, removing m, then work to end of rnd—70 (72, 76, 78, 84, 90, 92, 94) sts rem.

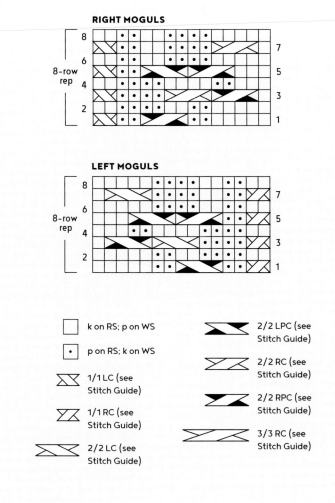

JOIN BODY AND SLEEVES

With RS facing, cont in est patts, work 46 (48, 50, 51, 53, 57, 60, 64) right front sts, pm, work 70 (72, 76, 78, 84, 90, 92, 94) sleeve sts, pm, work 94 (96, 102, 104, 108, 116, 120, 130) back sts, pm, work 70 (72, 76, 78, 84, 90, 92, 94) sleeve sts, pm, then work 46 (48, 50, 51, 53, 57, 60, 64) left front sts—326 (336, 354, 362, 382, 410, 424, 446) sts.

Work 3 rows even.

SHAPE RAGLAN

SIZES 47½ (50¼, 54)" ONLY

Double dec row: (RS) *Work to 2 sts before marker, k3tog, sm, sssk; rep from * 3 more times, work to end of row—16 sts dec'd.

Work 1 WS row even.

Rep last 2 rows 0 (1, 2) more time(s)—394 (392, 398) sts rem; 55 (56, 58) sts for each front, 86 (84, 82) sts for each sleeve, and 112 (112, 118) sts for back.

ALL SIZES

Dec row: (RS) *Work to 2 sts before m, k2tog, sm, ssk; rep from * 3 more times, work to end of row—8 sts dec'd.

Work 1 WS row even.

Rep last 2 rows 27 (28, 30, 31, 32, 34, 33, 34) more times—102 (104, 106, 106, 118, 114, 120, 118) sts rem; 18 (19, 19, 19, 20, 20, 22, 23) for each front, 14 (14, 14, 14, 18, 16, 16, 12) for each sleeve, and 38 (38, 40, 40, 42, 42, 44, 48) sts for back.

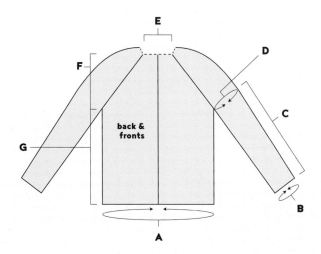

A: 38 (39, 41, 42¾, 44¼, 47½, 50¼, 54)"

B: 8¾ (8¾, 8¾, 10½, 10½, 10½, 12, 12)"

C: 17¾ (18, 18, 18¼, 18½, 18½, 18¾, 19)"

D: 13½ (14, 14¾, 15½, 16¾, 18, 18¾, 19¼)"

E: 5¼ (5¼, 5½, 5½, 5¾, 5¾, 6, 6½)"

F: 8¼ (8½, 9, 9½, 9¾, 10½, 10½, 11)"

G: 15 (15, 15½, 15½, 16, 16, 16½, 16½)"

Hood

Next row: (RS) Sl 1, k1, work next row of Left Moguls chart over next 15 sts, knit to last 17 sts removing m, work next row of Right Moguls chart over next 15 sts, k2.

Next row: (WS) Sl 1, p1, work next row of Right Moguls chart over next 15 sts, purl to last 17 sts work next row of Left Moguls chart over next 15 sts, p2.

Cont in est patt until hood measures 11 (11, 11, 11, 11, 11¼, 11, 11¼)" from last row of Ski Run Cable panel at center back, ending with a RS row.

SHAPE HOOD

Set-up row: (WS) Work 51 (52, 53, 53, 59, 57, 60, 59), pm, work 51 (52, 53, 53, 59, 57, 60, 59).

Dec row: (RS) Work to 3 sts before marker, k2tog, k1, sm, k1, ssk, work to end—2 sts dec'd.

Work 1 WS row even.

Rep last 2 rows 4 (4, 5, 5, 6, 5, 7, 6) more times, then rep Dec row once more—90 (92, 92, 92, 102, 100, 102, 102) sts rem.

Divide sts evenly with 45 (46, 46, 46, 51, 50, 51, 51) sts on each end of cir needle. Join sts using Kitchener st.

Finishing

Weave in all the loose ends using the ends at the armholes to close up any gaps at the sleeve and body join.

Allow the garment to soak in lukewarm water until thoroughly saturated. Gently press or spin out the excess water.

Block the garment to measurements.

Allow the garment to dry completely.

Sew in the zipper.

aspens sweater

Anne Podlesak

Finished Size

Bust circumference:
About 34¼ (36, 38¼, 40½, 44¾, 49, 53)".

Long: 20¾ (21½, 22½, 23, 23½, 24, 24¾)" long.

Sweater shown measures 36".

Yarn

Fingering weight
(#1 super fine).

Shown here: Brooklyn Tweed Loft (100% American wool; 275 yd/1¾ oz [50 g]): #21 hayloft, 5 (5, 5, 6, 6, 7, 7) skeins.

Needles

Size U.S. 4 (3.5 mm) 24" or longer circular (cir) and set of double-pointed (dpn).

Adjust needle size if necessary to obtain the correct gauge.

Notions

Stitch markers (m); stitch holders or waste yarn; tapestry needle; 7 (7, 7, 7, 9, 9, 9) ⅝" buttons

Gauge

26 sts and 37 rows = 4" in St st, after blocking.

15-st Aspen Leaf panel = 2½" wide.

Notes

■ This project is a woman's cardigan sweater with waist shaping for a tailored silhouette. The sweater is knitted in one piece from the bottom up to the armholes. The fronts and back are then shaped separately and joined at the shoulders with three-needle bind-off. The cap sleeves are worked flat, seamed, and set into the armholes. A wide panel of leaf lace adorns the back, while a single panel of the same motif highlights the front cardigan opening and the sleeves. A simple garter stitch finishes the hems, the neckband, and the front bands.

■ The chart is worked back and forth. Read all right-side (odd-numbered) rows from right to left and all wrong-side (even-numbered) rows from left to right.

■ The lace chart begins with 15 stitches, increases to 17 sts on Row 5, to 19 sts on Row 7, then decreases to 17 sts on Row 9, and to 15 sts on Row 11. Stitch counts should not be taken on chart Rows 5 through 10. To ensure your stitch counts will match those in the pattern, begin the armhole and neck decreases on Aspen Leaf chart Row 2, 4, or 11.

■ Slip the first stitch of each row of the body to help provide a smooth, even edge to pick up the buttonband sts.

■ A cir needle is used to accommodate the large number of stitches. Work back and forth.

Body

With cir needle, CO 221 (233, 247, 261, 287, 313, 339) sts using the long-tail cast-on method: Do not join.

Set-up row: (WS) Sl 1, k1, place marker (pm), k15, pm, k38 (41, 45, 48, 54, 61, 67), pm for left side, k32 (35, 38, 42, 49, 55, 62), pm, k47, pm, k32 (35, 38, 42, 49, 55, 62), pm for right side, k38 (41, 45, 48, 54, 61, 67), pm, k15, pm, k2.

Next row: Sl 1, k1, *sm, knit to m; rep from * 7 more times, work to end.

Rep last row once more.

Next row: (RS) Sl 1, k1, sm, work Row 1 of Aspen Leaf chart over next 15 sts, sm, [knit to next m, sm] twice, [work Row 1 of Aspen Leaf chart over next 15 sts, k1] twice, work Row 1 of Aspen Leaf chart over next 15 sts, sm, [knit to m, sm] twice, work Row 1 of Aspen Leaf chart over next 15 sts, sm, k2

Next row: (WS) Sl 1, p1, sm, work Row 2 of Aspen Leaf chart over next 15 sts, sm, [purl to next m, sm] twice, [work Row 2 of Aspen Leaf chart over next 15 sts, p1] twice, work Row 2 of Aspen Leaf chart over next 15 sts, sm, [purl to m, sm] twice, work Row 2 of Aspen Leaf chart over next 15 sts, sm, p2.

Work 12 more rows as est.

SHAPE WAIST

Dec row: (RS) *Work to 3 st before side m, ssk, k1, sm, k1, k2tog; rep from * once more, work to end—4 sts dec'd.

Rep Dec row every 12 rows 4 more times—201 (213, 227, 241, 267, 293, 319) sts rem.

Work 11 rows even. Piece should measure 8¼" from beg.

SHAPE BUST

Inc row: (RS) *Work to 1 st before side m, m1r, k1, sm, k1, m1l; rep from * once more, work to end—4 sts inc'd.

Rep Inc row every 14 rows once more—209 (221, 235, 249, 275, 301, 327) sts.

Cont even until piece measures 13 (13¼, 13¾, 13¾, 13¾, 13¾, 14)" from beg, ending with a WS row.

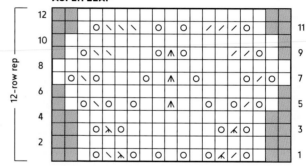

ASPEN LEAF

	k on RS; p on WS		⋏	sk2p
○	yo		⋌	k3tog
╱	k2tog		⋋	sssk
╲	ssk			no stitch

SHAPE ARMHOLES

Next row: (RS) *Work to 4 (4, 4, 5, 5, 6, 6) sts before side m, BO 8 (8, 8, 10, 10, 12, 12) sts, removing m; rep from * once more, work to end—48 (51, 55, 57, 63, 69, 75) sts rem for each front, and 97 (103, 109, 115, 129, 139, 153) sts rem for back.

LEFT FRONT

Work 1 WS row even.

BO at beg of RS rows 2 (2, 2, 3, 3, 3) sts once, then 1 st 2 (2, 2, 3, 3, 3) times—44 (47, 51, 53, 57, 63, 69) sts rem.

Cont even until armhole measures 6 (6¼, 6½, 6½, 6½, 6¾, 7)", ending with a RS row.

SHAPE NECK

BO at beg of WS rows 12 sts once, 3 (3, 3, 4, 4, 4, 4) sts twice, then 1 (1, 2, 1, 2, 2, 2) st(s) 1 (2, 3, 6, 5, 6, 8) time(s)—25 (27, 27, 27, 27, 31, 33) sts rem.

Work even until armhole measures 7¾ (8¼, 8¾, 9¼, 9¾, 10¼, 10¾)", ending with WS row. Place rem sts on holder.

RIGHT FRONT

Join yarn to beg with a WS row.

BO at beg of WS rows 2 (2, 2, 2, 3, 3, 3) sts once, then 1 st 2 (2, 2, 2, 3, 3, 3) times—44 (47, 51, 53, 57, 63, 69) sts rem.

Cont even until armhole measures 6 (6¼, 6½, 6½, 6½, 6¾, 7)", ending with a WS row.

SHAPE NECK

At beg of RS rows, BO 12 sts once, 3 (3, 3, 4, 4, 4, 4) sts twice, then 1 (1, 2, 1, 2, 2, 2) st(s) 1 (2, 3, 6, 5, 6, 8) time(s)—25 (27, 27, 27, 27, 31, 33) sts rem.

Work even until armhole measures 7¾ (8¼, 8¾, 9¼, 9¾, 10¼, 10¾)", ending with WS row. Place rem sts on holder.

Back

Join yarn to beg with a WS row.

BO 2 (2, 2, 2, 3, 3, 3) sts at beg of next 2 rows—93 (99, 105, 111, 123, 133, 147) sts rem. Dec 1 st at each end of every RS row 2 (2, 2, 2, 3, 3, 3) times—89 (95, 101, 107, 117, 127, 141) sts rem.

Work even until armholes measure 7¾ (8¼, 8¾, 9¼, 9¾, 10¼, 10¾)", ending with a RS row.

Next row: (WS) Purl, removing m.

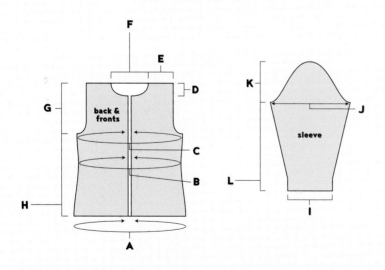

BODY

A: 36 (38, 40¼, 42½, 46¾, 50¾, 55)"

B: 33 (34¾, 37, 39¼, 43½, 47¾, 51¾)"

C: 34¼ (36, 38¼, 40½, 44¾, 49, 53)"

D: 1¾ (2, 2¼, 2¾, 3¼, 3½, 3¾)"

E: 4 (4¼, 4¼, 4¼, 4¼, 5, 5¼)"

F: 5¾ (6, 7, 7¾, 9¼, 9¾, 11)"

G: 7¾ (8¼, 8¾, 9¼, 9¾, 10¼, 10¾)"

H: 13 (13¼, 13¾, 13¾, 13¾, 13¾, 14)"

SLEEVE

I: 9½ (9½, 9¾, 10¼, 10½, 11¼, 11½)"

J: 15¾ (15¾, 16, 16½, 17¼, 18¼, 18¾)"

K: 8 (8, 8, 8, 8¼, 8½, 9)"

L: 17½ (17½, 18, 18¼, 18¼, 18½, 18½)"

With RS facing, place first 25 (27, 27, 27, 27, 31, 33) sts on holder for shoulder, center 39 (41, 47, 53, 63, 65, 75) sts on holder for neck, then rem 25 (27, 27, 27, 27, 31, 33) sts on holder for shoulder.

Sleeves

With cir needle, CO 59 (59, 61, 63, 65, 69, 71) sts using long-tail cast-on method. Do not join.

Set-up row: (WS) K22 (22, 23, 24, 25, 27, 28) sts, pm, k15, pm, k22 (22, 23, 24, 25, 27, 28).

Next row: (RS) *Knit to m, sm; rep from * once more, work to end.

Rep last row once more.

Next row: (RS) Knit to m, sm, work Row 1 of Aspen Leaf chart over next 15 sts, sm, knit to end.

Next row: (WS) Purl to m, sm, work Row 2 of Aspen Leaf chart over next 15 sts, sm, purl to end.

Work 22 (22, 22, 22, 22, 10, 10) more rows in est patt.

Inc row: (RS) K1, m1l, work in est patt to last st , m1r, k1—2 sts inc'd.

Rep Inc row every 6 rows 9 (9, 9, 10, 10, 10, 13) times, then every 8 rows 9 (9, 9, 9, 10, 11, 9) times—97 (97, 99, 103, 107, 113, 117) sts.

Cont even until piece measures 17½ (17½, 18, 18¼, 18¼, 18½, 18½)", from beg, ending with a WS row.

SHAPE CAP

BO 4 (4, 4, 5, 5, 6, 6) sts at beg of next 2 rows, then 3 (3, 3, 3, 4, 4, 4) sts at beg of next 2 rows. Dec 1 st at each end of every RS row 32 (32, 32, 33, 34, 35, 37) times—19 (19, 21, 21, 21, 23, 23) sts rem.

BO 2 sts at beg of next 4 rows—11 (11, 13, 13, 13, 15, 15) sts rem.

Work 1 WS row even.

BO rem sts kwise.

Finishing

Weave in all the loose ends. Join the shoulders using the three-needle bind-off.

NECKBAND

With cir needle and RS facing, pick up and k21 (22, 24, 27, 28, 30, 30) sts along right front neck, k39 (41, 47, 53, 61, 65, 75) held sts for back neck, then pick up and k21 (22, 24, 27, 28, 30, 30) sts along left front neck—81 (85, 95, 107, 117, 125, 135) sts.

Knit 3 rows. BO all sts loosely kwise.

BUTTONBAND

With cir needle and RS facing, beg at left neck edge, pick up and k3 sts in neckband, 1 st in every sl st along left front edge, then 3 sts in garter st band at bottom.

Knit 3 rows. BO all sts loosely kwise.

Pm for buttons as foll: Bottom button ½" from CO edge, top button ½" from BO edge of neckband, then evenly space rem buttons in between.

BUTTONHOLE BAND

With cir needle and RS facing, beg at bottom edge, pick up and k3 sts in garter st band at bottom, 1 st in every sl st along right front edge, then 3 sts in neckband.

Next row. (WS) *Knit to 1 st before m, k2tog, yo; rep from * 6 (6, 6, 6, 8, 8, 8) more times, knit to end.

Knit 1 row.

BO all sts loosely kwise.

Sew the underarm seams. Sew in the sleeves.

Allow the garment to soak in lukewarm water until thoroughly saturated. Gently press or spin out the excess water. Lay garment out to measurements, pinning hems so that they dry flat. Allow the garment to dry completely.

Sew buttons to the buttonband opposite the buttonholes.

union station cardigan

Beatrice Perron Dahlen

Finished Size

Bust circumference: 28½ (32, 37, 40, 44)".

Cardigan shown measures 32", modeled with 1½" of negative ease.

Yarn

Sport weight (#2 fine).

Shown here: Quince & Co. Chickadee (100% wool; 181 yd [166 m]/1¾ oz [50 g]): #129 parsley, 6 (6, 6, 7, 7) skeins.

Needles

Size U.S. 6 (4 mm): 32" circular (cir) and set of double-pointed (dpn).

Adjust needle size if necessary to obtain the correct gauge.

Notions

Markers (m); stitch holders; waste yarn for provisional CO; tapestry needle.

Gauge

19 sts and 26 rows = 4" in St st.

Notes

■ This cardigan is worked back and forth from the top down. The sleeves are worked in the round from the top down.

■ The lace pattern incorporates all increases for the yoke and front opening.

■ A circular needle is used to accommodate the large number of stitches.

STITCH GUIDE

Seed Stitch in rows: (even number of sts)

Row 1: (RS) *K1, p1; rep from * to end.

Row 2: (WS) *P1, k1; rep from * to end.

Rep Rows 1 and 2 for patt.

Seed Stitch in rnds: (odd number of sts)

Rnd 1: K1, *p1, k1; rep from * to end.

Rnd 2: P1, *k1, p1; rep from * to end.

Rep Rnds 1 and 2 for patt.

Yoke

NECKBAND

With dpn and using a provisional method, CO 6 sts. Do not join.

Work Seed st in rows (see Stitch Guide) until piece measures 15½ (16½, 17¾, 19, 20¼)" from CO, ending with a WS row.

Change to cir needle.

Next row: (RS) Work to end, place marker (pm), rotate work and pick up and knit 65 (70, 75, 80, 85) sts along left edge of neckband, pm, remove waste yarn from CO sts and place 6 sts onto left needle, [k1, p1] 3 times for Seed st—77 (82, 87, 92, 97) sts.

Next row: (WS) Work Seed st to m, sl m, purl to m, sl m, work Seed st to end. Next row (RS) Work in patt to m, sl m, work Yoke chart to m, sl m, work to end. Cont in patt through Row 53 of chart—233 (250, 267, 284, 301) sts.

DIVIDE FOR BODY AND SLEEVES

Next row: (WS) Work to m, sl m, p34, pm, p0 (4, 4, 5, 4), place next 45 (46, 49, 53, 58) sts on holder for sleeve, then, using the backward-loop method, CO 5 (6, 7, 7, 8) sts, p63 (70, 81, 88, 97) for back, place next 45 (46, 49, 53, 58) sts on holder for sleeve, CO 5 (6, 7, 7, 8) sts, p0 (4, 4, 5, 4), pm, p34, sl m, work to end—153 (170, 183, 192, 201) sts rem for body.

YOKE

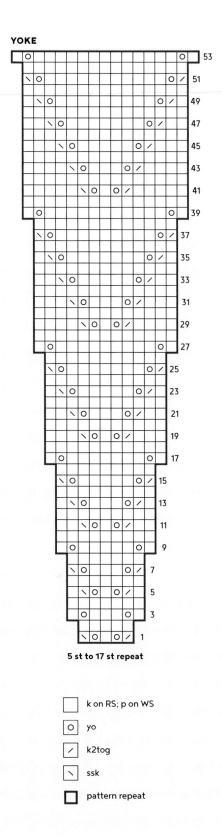

5 st to 17 st repeat

	k on RS; p on WS
○	yo
╱	k2tog
╲	ssk
▢	pattern repeat

Body

Next row: (RS) Work to m, sl m, work Front Panel chart over 34 sts, sl m, knit to m, sl m, work Front Panel chart over 34 sts, sl m, work in patt to end. Cont in patt through Row 75 of chart—185 (202, 215, 224, 233) sts.

SIZES 28½ (37, 44)" ONLY

Next row :(WS) Work to m, sl m, p85 (100, 109), p2tog, work in patt to end—184 (214, 232) sts rem.

SIZES 32 (40)" ONLY

Work 1 WS row even.

ALL SIZES

Next row: (RS) Work in Seed st over all sts.

Dec row: (WS) Work 2 sts tog in patt, work Seed st to last 2 sts, work 2 sts tog—2 sts dec'd. Rep last 2 rows 2 more times—178 (196, 208, 218, 226) sts rem.

Work 1 RS row.

With WS facing, BO all sts kwise.

Sleeves

With dpn and RS facing, beg at center of underarm, pick up and knit 2 (3, 3, 3, 4) sts along underarm CO, k45 (46, 49, 53, 58) held sleeve sts, then pick up and knit 3 (3, 4, 4, 4) sts along underarm CO—50 (52, 56, 60, 66) sts total.

Pm and join in the rnd.

Work in St st until piece measures 3" from underarm.

	k on RS; p on WS
o	yo
/	k2tog
\	ssk
▭	pattern repeat

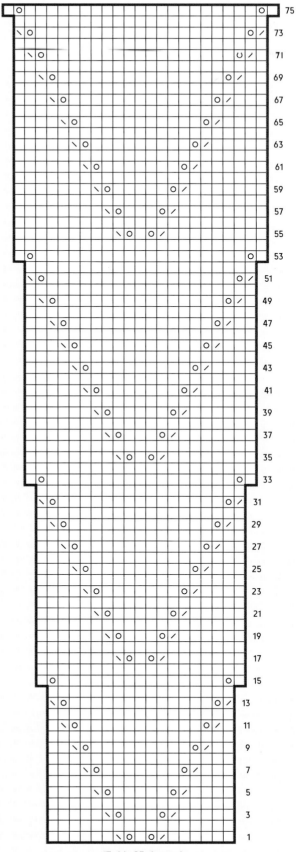

FRONT PANEL

17 st to 25 st repeat

Dec rnd: K1, k2tog, knit to last 3 sts, ssk, k1—2 sts dec'd.

Rep Dec rnd every 9 (10, 10, 8, 6)th rnd 5 (5, 5, 7, 9) more times—38 (40, 44, 44, 46) sts rem.

Work even until piece measures 11¼ (11¼, 11¾, 12, 12)" from underarm, dec 1 st on last rnd—37 (39, 43, 43, 45) sts rem.

Work Seed st in rnds (see Stitch Guide) for 6 rnds.

BO all sts pwise.

Finishing

Weave in ends.

Block to measurements.

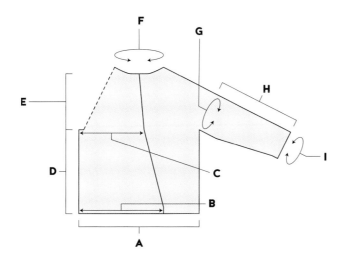

A: 14¼ (16, 18½, 20, 22)"

B: 12¼ (13¼, 13¼, 13½, 13½)"

C: 9 (10, 10, 10¼, 10)"

D: 12¾"

E: 8½"

F: 15½ (16½, 17¾, 19, 20¼)"

G: 10½ (11, 11¾, 12¾, 14)"

H: 12¼ (12¼, 12¾, 13, 13)"

I: 8 (8½, 9¼, 9¼, 9¾)"

chili pepper cardigan

Bonnie Sennott

Finished Size

Bust circumference: About 32 (36, 40, 44, 48, 52)" with fronts meeting at center.

Cardigan shown measures 36"; modeled with 4" of positive ease.

Yarn

DK weight (#3 light).

Shown here: Valley Yarns Northfield (70% Merino wool, 20% baby alpaca, 10% silk; 124 yd [114 m] / 1¾ oz [50 g]): #03 chestnut, 9 (10, 11, 13, 14, 15) skeins.

Needles

Size U.S. 5 (3.75 mm): 32" circular (cir) and set of double-pointed (dpn).

Adjust needle size if necessary to obtain the correct gauge.

Notions

Markers (m); stitch holders or waste yarn; tapestry needle.

Gauge

20 sts and 27 rows = 4" in St st.

25 sts and 27 rows = 4" in Lozenge patt.

Notes

■ The body of this cardigan is worked back and forth in one piece from the lower edge to the underarm, then the upper fronts and back are worked separately. Stitches for the sleeves are picked up around the armhole and the sleeves are worked in the round from the top down with short-rows to shape the sleeve cap. When working short-rows on the sleeve cap, do not work the wraps together with the wrapped stitches.

■ A circular needle is used to accommodate the large number of stitches.

■ The Lozenge pattern in Rows begins as a multiple of 6 stitches plus 3, temporarily increases to a multiple of 6 stitches plus 5 for Rows 2–4, then decreases back to a multiple of 6 stitches plus 3 in Row 5. Always count the stitches as the original number, and do not include the temporary increase stitches.

K1fb&f

Knit into a stitch and leave it on the needle, knit through the back loop of the same stitch, knit through the front loop once more, then slip the stitch from the needle—2 sts inc'd.

Sk2p

Sl 1 kwise, k2tog, pass sl st over—2 sts dec'd.

Lozenge Pattern in Rows: (multiple of 6 sts +3; see Notes)

Row 1: (RS) P1, k1fb&f, p1, *sk2p, p1, k1fb&f, p1; rep from * to end—patt has inc'd to a multiple of 6 sts + 5.

Row 2: (WS) K1, p3, *k3, p3; rep from * to last st, k1.

Row 3: P1, k3, *p3, k3; rep from * to last st, p1.

Row 4: K1, p3, *k3, p3; rep from * to last st, k1.

Row 5: P1, sk2p, p1, *k1fb&f, p1, sk2p, p1; rep from * to end—patt has dec'd to a multiple of 6 sts + 3.

Row 6: K3, *p3, k3; rep from * to end.

Row 7: P3, *k3, p3; rep from * to end.

Row 8: Rep Row 6.

Rep Rows 1-8 for patt.

Lozenge Pattern in Rnds: (multiple of 6 sts)

Rnd 1: *Sk2p, p1, kfb&f, p1; rep from * to end.

Rnd 2: P2, *k3, p3; rep from * to last 4 sts, k3, sl 1 pwise wyb, remove m, sl st back to left needle, replace m.

Rnds 3 and 4: *P3, k3; rep from * to end.

Rnd 5: *P1, k1fb&f, p1, sk2p; rep from * to end.

Rnd 6: Remove m, p1, replace m, *k3, p3; rep from * to end.

Rnds 7 and 8: *K3, p3; rep from * to end.

Rep Rnds 1-8 for patt.

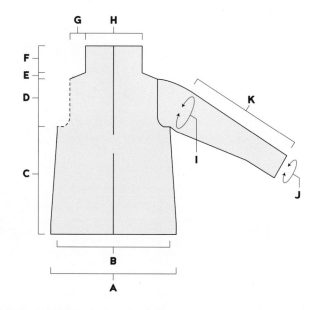

A: 18 (20, 22, 24, 26, 28)"

B: 16 (18, 20, 22, 24, 26)"

C: 17"

D: 7 (7½, 8, 8½, 9, 9½)"

E: 1"

F: 4¼"

G: 2 (2½, 3¼, 3¾, 4½, 5)"

H: 8¾"

I: 11½ (12¾, 13½, 14¾, 15½, 16¾)"

J: 7¾ (7¾, 8¾, 8¾, 9½, 9½)"

K: 18¼ (18¼, 18½, 18½, 18¾, 18¾)"

Body

With cir needle, CO 192 (212, 232, 252, 272, 292) sts. Do not join.

Set-up row: (WS) K4, [p3, k3] 4 times, place marker (pm) at end of left front band, k23 (28, 33, 38, 43, 48), pm for left side, k90 (100, 110, 120, 130, 140), pm for right side, k23 (28, 33, 38, 43, 48), pm at start of right front band, [k3, p3] 4 times, k4.

Next row: (RS) P1, work Lozenge patt in Rows (see Stitch Guide and Notes) over 27 sts, sl m; knit to last 28 sts, slipping side m; sl m, work Lozenge patt over 27 sts, p1.

Next row: (WS) K1, work Lozenge patt over 27 sts, sl m; knit to last 28 sts, slipping side m; sl m, work Lozenge patt over 27 sts, k1.

Rep last 2 rows 6 more times, then work RS row once more.

Next row: (WS) K1, work Lozenge patt over 27 sts, sl m, [purl to m, sl m] 3 times, work Lozenge patt over 27 sts, k1.

Change to working all sts outside Lozenge patt bands in St st.

Dec row: (RS) Work in patt to 3 sts before right side m, ssk, k1, sl m, k1, k2tog, work in patt to 3 sts before left side m, ssk, k1, sl m, k1, k2tog, work in patt to end—4 sts dec'd.

Rep dec row every 24th row 4 more times—172 (192, 212, 232, 252, 272) sts rem: 46 (51, 56, 61, 66, 71) sts for each front and 80 (90, 100, 110, 120, 130) back sts.

Work even until piece measures 17" from CO, ending with a WS row.

DIVIDE FOR FRONTS AND BACK
Next row :(RS) *Work in patt to 4 (5, 6, 7, 9, 10) sts before side m, BO 8 (10, 12, 14, 18, 20) sts, removing side m; rep from * once more, work in patt to end—42 (46, 50, 54, 57, 61) sts rem for each front and 72 (80, 88, 96, 102, 110) sts rem for back.

Place left and right front sts on holders, leaving yarn attached to left front.

Back
With WS facing, rejoin yarn. Work 1 WS row even.

SHAPE ARMHOLES
Dec row: (RS) K1, ssk, work in patt to last 3 sts, k2tog, k1—2 sts dec'd.

Rep dec row every RS row 2 (3, 4, 5, 5, 6) more times, then every 4th row once—64 (70, 76, 82, 88, 94) sts rem. Work even until armhole measures 7 (7½, 8, 8½, 9, 9½)", ending with a WS row.

SHAPE SHOULDERS

BO 4 (5, 6, 7, 8, 9) sts at beg of next 2 rows, then BO 3 (4, 5, 6, 7, 8) sts at beg of next 4 rows—44 sts rem.

Work 1 WS row even. BO all sts.

Right Front

Return 42 (46, 50, 54, 57, 61) held right front sts to needle and, with WS facing, rejoin yarn. Work 1 WS row even.

SHAPE ARMHOLE

Dec row: (RS) Work in patt to last 3 sts, k2tog, k1—1 st dec'd.

Rep dec row every RS row 2 (3, 4, 5, 5, 6) more times, then every 4th row once—38 (41, 44, 47, 50, 53) sts rem. Work even until armhole measures 7 (7½, 8, 8½, 9, 9½)", ending with a RS row.

SHAPE SHOULDER

At beg of WS rows, BO 4 (5, 6, 7, 8, 9) sts once, then BO 3 (4, 5, 6, 7, 8) sts 2 times, removing band m when necessary—28 sts rem.

Work even until neckband extension measures 4¼" from last shoulder BO row or slightly less than half the width of back neck, ending with Row 4 or 8 of patt.

Next row: (RS) BO all sts, working sk2p over each group of 3 knit sts as you bind off to prevent the edge from flaring.

Left Front

Return 42 (46, 50, 54, 57, 61) held left front sts to needle. Using yarn attached at front edge, work 1 WS row even.

SHAPE ARMHOLE

Dec row: (RS) K1, ssk, work in patt to end—1 st dec'd.

Rep dec row every RS row 2 (3, 4, 5, 5, 6) more times, then every 4th row once—38 (41, 44, 47, 50, 53) sts rem. Work even until armhole measures 7 (7½, 8, 8½, 9, 9½)", ending with a WS row.

SHAPE SHOULDER

At beg of RS rows, BO 4 (5, 6, 7, 8, 9) sts once, then BO 3 (4, 5, 6, 7, 8) sts 2 times—28 sts rem.

Work even until neckband extension measures 4¼" from last shoulder BO row, ending with same WS patt row as right front band.

Next row: (RS) BO all sts, working sk2p over each group of 3 knit sts as you bind off.

Sleeves

Sew shoulder seams.

With dpn and RS facing, beg at center of underarm, pick up and knit 4 (5, 6, 7, 9, 10) sts along underarm BO sts, 25 (27, 28, 30, 30, 32) sts along armhole edge to shoulder seam, pm, 25 (27, 28, 30, 30, 32) sts to beg of underarm BO sts, and 4 (5, 6, 7, 9, 10) sts along BO sts—58 (64, 68, 74, 78, 84) sts total. Pm and join in the rnd.

Shape cap using short-rows as foll:

Short-row 1: (RS) Knit to shoulder m, sl m, k7, wrap next st, turn.

Short-row 2: (WS) Purl to shoulder m, sl m, p7, wrap next st, turn.

Short-row 3: (RS) Knit to wrapped st, knit wrapped st (see Notes), wrap next st, turn.

Short-row 4: (WS) Purl to wrapped st, purl wrapped st, wrap next st, turn.

Rep last 2 short-rows 16 (18, 19, 21, 21, 23) more times—4 (5, 6, 7, 9, 10) sts rem unworked between last wrapped st at each side and underarm m.

Next short-row: (RS) Knit to m.

Resume working in rnds. Knit 5 rnds.

Dec rnd: K1, k2tog, knit to last 3 sts, ssk, k1—2 sts dec'd.

Rep dec rnd every 18 (12, 12, 10, 10, 8)th rnd 4 (4, 6, 4, 8, 7) more times, then every 0 (10, 0, 8, 0, 6)th rnd 0 (3, 0, 5, 0, 4) times—48 (48, 54, 54, 60, 60) sts rem.

Work even until piece measures 13 (13, 13¼, 13¼, 13½, 13½)" from underarm, or 5¼" less than desired length.

Next 3 rnds: *K3, p3; rep from * to end.

Work Rnds 1–8 of Lozenge patt in Rnds (see Stitch Guide) 4 times—sleeve measures about 18¼ (18¼, 18½, 18½, 18¾, 18¾)" from underarm.

Next rnd: BO all sts as foll: Sk2p, *[p1, pass first st on right needle over 2nd st] 3 times, sk2p, pass first st on right needle over 2nd st; rep from * to last 3 sts, [p1, pass first st on right needle over 2nd st] 3 times, fasten off last st.

Finishing

Sew BO edges of neckband extensions tog. Sew neck edge of joined extensions to back neck.

Weave in ends.

Block to measurements.

drafter's cardigan

Bonnie Sennott

Finished Size

Bust circumference, buttoned: about 33½ (38, 42¼, 47, 51¼, 55¼)".

Cardigan shown measures 38"; modeled with 4" of positive ease.

Yarn

Sport weight (#2 fine).

Shown here: The Plucky Knitter Traveler Sport (65% Merino wool, 20% mulberry silk, 15% yak; 325 yd [298 m]/3½ oz [100 g]): dovecote, 4 (5, 5, 5, 6, 6) skeins.

Needles

Sizes U.S. 4 (3.5 mm) and U.S. 6 (4 mm): 32" circular (cir).

Sizes U.S. 4 (3.5 mm) and U.S. 5 (3.75 mm): set of double-pointed (dpn).

Adjust needle size if necessary to obtain the correct gauge.

Notions

Markers (m); stitch holders or waste yarn; tapestry needle; nine ½" buttons.

Gauge

25 sts and 34 rnds = 4" in St st on larger dpn.

22 sts and 37½ rows in Lace patt on larger cir needle, blocked (see Notes).

Notes

■ The body of this cardigan is worked back and forth in one piece from the lower edge to the underarm, then the upper fronts and back are worked separately. Stitches for the sleeves are picked up around the armhole and the sleeves are worked from the top down in the round with short-rows to shape the sleeve cap.

■ When working short-rows on the sleeve cap, do not work the wraps together with the wrapped stitches.

■ A circular needle is used to accommodate the large number of stitches.

■ When increasing and decreasing in the lace pattern, work the stitches of partial repeats into the lace pattern when they are available; however, do not work any yarnover(s) unless there are enough stitches to work the corresponding decrease.

■ The stitch counts of the Lace chart temporarily increase to a multiple of 8 stitches plus 11 after Rows 3 and 9, and then decrease back to the original multiple of 6 stitches plus 9 on Rows 5 and 11. Stitch counts given throughout pattern do not include the temporary increase stitches.

Body

With larger cir needle, CO 181 (205, 229, 253, 277, 301) sts. Do not join.

Next row: (WS) P2, *k1, p1; rep from * to last 3 sts, k1, p2.

Next row: (RS) K2, *p1, k1; rep from * to last 3 sts, p1, k2.

Rep last 2 rows until piece measures 1¾" from CO, ending with a RS row.

Next row: (WS) P46 (52, 58, 64, 70, 76), place marker (pm), k1, p87 (99, 111, 123, 135, 147), k1, pm, p46 (52, 58, 64, 70, 76).

Next row: (RS) K1, work Lace chart over 45 (51, 57, 63, 69, 75) sts, sl m, p1, work Lace chart over 87 (99, 111, 123, 135, 147) sts, p1, sl m, work Lace chart over 45 (51, 57, 63, 69, 75) sts, k1.

Next row: (WS) P1, work in chart patt to m, sl m, k1, work in chart patt to 1 st before m, k1, sl m, work in chart patt to last st, p1.

Cont in patt as est until piece measures about 14¾" from CO, ending with Row 11 of chart.

Next row: (WS) Work in patt to 2 sts before m, p2tog, sl m, work in patt to m, sl m, p2tog, work in patt to end—179 (203, 227, 251, 275, 299) sts rem: 45 (51, 57, 63, 69, 75) sts for each front and 89 (101, 113, 125, 137, 149) back sts.

DIVIDE FOR FRONTS AND BACK

Next row: (RS) *Work in patt to 3 (4, 6, 7, 9, 10) sts before m, BO 6 (8, 12, 14, 18, 20) sts, removing m; rep from * once more, work in patt to end—42 (47, 51, 56, 60, 65) sts rem for each front and 83 (93, 101, 111, 119, 129) sts rem for back.

Place left and right front sts on holders, leaving yarn attached to left front.

Back

With WS facing, rejoin yarn. Work 1 WS row even.

SHAPE ARMHOLES

Dec row: (RS) K1, ssk, work in patt to last 3 sts, k2tog, k1—2 sts dec'd.

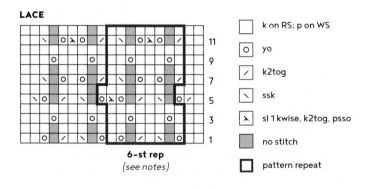

LACE

6-st rep
(see notes)

- ☐ k on RS; p on WS
- ○ yo
- ⟋ k2tog
- ⟍ ssk
- ⊼ sl 1 kwise, k2tog, psso
- ▨ no stitch
- ☐ pattern repeat

Rep dec row every RS row 2 (3, 4, 6, 7, 8) more times, then every 4th row 1 (2, 2, 2, 3, 3) time(s)—75 (81, 87, 93, 97, 105) sts rem.

Work even until armhole measures 7 (7½, 8, 8½, 8½, 9)", ending with Row 6 or 12 of chart.

Shape shoulder and neck.

Next row: (RS) BO 6 (6, 7, 7, 8, 8) sts, work until there are 13 (15, 16, 17, 17, 19) sts on right needle and place these sts on holder for right shoulder, join new yarn and BO 37 (39, 41, 45, 47, 51) sts, work in patt to last 7 (7, 8, 8, 9, 9) sts, knit to end—19 (21, 23, 24, 25, 27) sts rem for left shoulder.

LEFT SHOULDER

Next row: (WS) BO 6 (6, 7, 7, 8, 8) sts, purl to end—13 (15, 16, 17, 17, 19) sts rem.

Next row: (RS) BO 3 sts, knit to end—10 (12, 13, 14, 14, 16) sts rem.

Next row: (WS) BO 5 (6, 7, 7, 7, 8) sts, purl to end—5 (6, 6, 7, 7, 8) sts rem.

Next row: (RS) Knit. BO all sts.

RIGHT SHOULDER

Return 13 (15, 16, 17, 17, 19) held sts to needle.

Next row: (WS) BO 3 sts, purl to end—10 (12, 13, 14, 14, 16) sts rem.

Next row: (RS) BO 5 (6, 7, 7, 7, 8) sts, knit to end—5 (6, 6, 7, 7, 8) sts rem.

Next row: (WS) Purl. BO all sts.

Right Front

Return 42 (47, 51, 56, 60, 65) held right front sts to needle and, with WS facing, rejoin yarn.

Next row: (WS) Work in patt to end.

SHAPE ARMHOLE

Dec row: (RS) Work in patt to last 3 sts, k2tog, k1—1 st dec'd.

Rep dec row every RS row 2 (3, 4, 6, 7, 8) more times, then every 4th row 1 (2, 2, 2, 3, 3) time(s)—38 (41, 44, 47, 49, 53) sts rem.

Work even until armhole measures 3¾", ending with Row 12 of chart.

SHAPE NECK

At beg of RS rows, BO 5 sts once, then BO 4 sts once, then BO 3 sts 2 times, then BO 2 sts 2 (2, 2, 3, 3, 4) times, then BO 1 st 3 (4, 5, 5, 6, 6) times—16 (18, 20, 21, 22, 24) sts rem.

Work even until armhole measures 7 (7½, 8, 8½, 8½, 9)", ending with Row 12 of chart.

SHAPE SHOULDER

Next row: (RS) Work in patt to last 7 (7, 8, 8, 9, 9) sts, knit to end.

Cont in St st.

At beg of WS rows, BO 6 (6, 7, 7, 8, 8) sts once, BO 5 (6, 7, 7, 7, 8) sts once, then BO 5 (6, 6, 7, 7, 8) sts once—no sts rem.

Left Front

Return 42 (47, 51, 56, 60, 65) held left front sts to needle.

Next row: (WS) Using yarn attached at front edge, work in patt to end.

SHAPE ARMHOLE

Dec row: (RS) K1, ssk, work in patt to end—1 st dec'd.

Rep dec row every RS row 2 (3, 4, 6, 7, 8) more times, then every 4th row 1 (2, 2, 2, 3, 3) time(s)—38 (41, 44, 47, 49, 53) sts rem.

Work even until armhole measures 3¾", ending with Row 12 of chart.

SHAPE NECK

Note: *During left front neck shaping, at end of every RS row, work in St st for at least 1 st more than the number of sts to be BO on next WS row.*

Next row: (RS) Work in patt to last 6 sts, knit to end. At beg of WS rows, BO 5 sts once, then BO 4 sts once, then BO 3 sts 2 times, then BO 2 sts 2 (2, 2, 3, 3, 4) times, then BO 1 st 3 (4, 5, 5, 6, 6) times—16 (18, 20, 21, 22, 24) sts rem.

Work even until armhole measures 7 (7½, 8, 8½, 8½, 9)", ending with Row 12 of chart.

SHAPE SHOULDER

Working in St st, at beg of RS rows, BO 6 (6, 7, 7, 8, 8) sts once, BO 5 (6, 7, 7, 8, 8) sts once, then BO 5 (6, 6, 7, 7, 8) sts once—no sts rem.

Sleeves

Sew shoulder seams.

With larger dpn and RS facing, beg at center of underarm, pick up and knit 3 (4, 6, 7, 9, 10) sts along underarm BO sts, 31 (34, 35, 37, 37, 38) sts along armhole edge to shoulder seam, pm, 31 (34, 35, 37, 37, 38) sts to beg of underarm BO sts, and 3 (4, 6, 7, 9, 10) sts along BO sts—68 (76, 82, 88, 92, 96) sts total.

Pm and join in the rnd.

Shape cap using short-rows as foll:

Short-row 1: (RS) Knit to shoulder m, sl m, k8, wrap next st, turn.

Short-row 2: (WS) Purl to shoulder m, sl m, p8, wrap next st, turn.

Short-row 3: Knit to wrapped st, knit wrapped st (see Notes), wrap next st, turn.

Short-row 4: Purl to wrapped st, purl wrapped st, wrap next st, turn.

Rep last 2 short-rows 21 (24, 25, 27, 27, 28) more times—3 (4, 6, 7, 9, 10) sts rem unworked between last wrapped st at each side and underarm m.

Next short-row: (RS) Knit to m.

Resume working in rnds. Knit 6 rnds.

Dec rnd: K1, k2tog, knit to last 3 sts, ssk, k1—2 sts dec'd.

Rep dec rnd every 14th rnd 5 (0, 0, 0, 0, 0) more times, then every 12th rnd 0 (6, 5, 1, 0, 0) time(s), then every 8th rnd 0 (1, 3, 9, 12, 12) time(s)—56 (60, 64, 66, 66, 70) sts rem.

Work even until piece measures 11 (11¼, 11½, 11¾, 12, 12)" from underarm.

Change to smaller dpn.

Work in k1, p1 rib for 1¾"—piece measures 12¾ (13, 13¼, 13½, 13¾, 13¾)".

BO all sts in patt.

Finishing

Block to measurements.

BUTTONBAND
With smaller cir needle and RS facing, pick up and knit 120 sts evenly spaced along left front edge.

Next row: (WS) P2, *k1, p1; rep from * to end.

Next row: (RS) *K1, p1; rep from * to last 2 sts, k2.

Rep last 2 rows until band measures ¾", ending with a WS row.

BO all sts in patt.

BUTTONHOLE BAND
Mark placement for 9 buttonholes along right front, with the lowest ½" up from the CO edge and the highest ½" below neck edge.

With smaller cir needle and RS facing, pick up and knit 120 sts evenly spaced along right front edge.

Next row: (WS) *P1, k1; rep from * to last 2 sts, p2.

Next row: (RS) K2, *p1, k1; rep from * to end.

Work 1 row in rib patt as est.

Buttonhole row: (RS) Keeping in patt, work a 2-st one-row buttonhole to correspond to each buttonhole m.

Cont in rib patt as est until band measures ¾", ending with a WS row.

BO all sts in patt.

NECKBAND
With smaller cir needle and RS facing, pick up and knit 40 (43, 45, 48, 48, 51) sts along right front neck, 43 (45, 47, 51, 53, 57) sts along back neck, and 40 (43, 45, 48, 48, 51) sts along left front neck—123 (131, 137, 147, 149, 159) sts total.

Next row: Knit 1 row.

Purl 1 row.

Knit 1 row.

BO all sts.

Weave in ends.

> **Note:** If a small gap occurs where the last wrap and turn was worked on the underarms, use duplicate st to fill it in.

Sew buttons to buttonband opposite buttonholes.

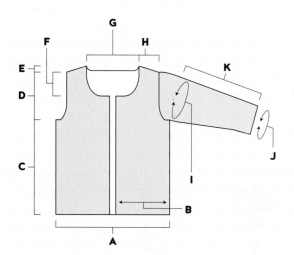

A: 16¼ (18¼, 20½, 22¾, 25, 27)"

B: 8¼ (9½, 10½, 11¾, 12¾, 13¾)"

C: 14¾"

D: 7 (7½, 8, 8½, 8½, 9)"

E: ¾"

F: 3¼ (3¾, 4¼, 4¾, 4¾, 5¼)"

G: 7¾ (8¼, 8½, 9¼, 9¾, 10¼)"

H: 3 (3¼, 3¾, 3¾, 4, 4¼)"

I: 11 (12¼, 13, 14, 14¾, 15¼)"

J: 9 (9½, 10¼, 10½, 10½, 11¼)"

K: 12¾ (13, 13¼, 13½, 13¾, 13¾)"

l'acadie cardigan

Bristol Ivy

Finished Size

Back width at bust: 13¼ (15, 17, 18¾, 20¾, 23½)".

Cardigan shown measures 15".

Yarn

Aran weight (#4 medium).

Shown here: Filatura di Crosa Zara Plus (100% Merino wool; 77 yd [70 m]/1¾ oz [50 g]): #455 fawn, 18 (20, 22, 23, 25, 27) balls.

Needles

Size U.S. 7 (4.5 mm): set of double-pointed (dpn).

Size U.S. 8 (5 mm): 32" circular (cir) and set of dpn.

Adjust needle size if necessary to obtain the correct gauge.

Notions

Markers (m); cable needle (cn); stitch holders or waste yarn; tapestry needle.

Gauge

17 sts and 24 rows = 4" in St st on larger needle.

52 sts of Body Cable chart = 7½" wide.

Notes

■ The body of this sweater is worked back and forth in one piece from the lower edge to the underarm, then the upper fronts and back are worked separately. The sleeves are picked up from the armholes and worked in the round from the top down.

■ The cable panels are continued up and around the neck and joined at the center back neck with a three-needle bind-off to create a shawl collar.

■ A circular needle is used to accommodate the large number of stitches.

STITCH GUIDE

K2, P2 Rib in rows:
(multiple of 4 sts + 2)

Row 1: (WS) P2, *k2, p2; rep from * to end.

Row 2: (RS) K2, *p2, k2; rep from * to end.

Rep Rows 1 and 2 for patt.

K2, P2 Rib in rnds:
(multiple of 4 sts)

Rnd 1: *K2, p2; rep from * to end.

Rep Rnd 1 every rnd for patt.

Body

With cir needle and using the long-tail method, CO 210 (226, 242, 258, 274, 294) sts. Do not join.

Work K2, P2 Rib in rows (see Stitch Guide) until piece measures 4" from CO, ending with a WS row.

Next row: (RS) K2, work Body Cable chart over 54 sts (dec'd to 52 sts), place marker (pm), k18 (22, 26, 30, 34, 38), pm for side, k62 (70, 78, 86, 94, 106), pm for side, k18 (22, 26, 30, 34, 38), pm, work Body Cable chart over 54 sts (dec'd to 52 sts), k2—206 (222, 238, 254, 270, 290) sts rem.

Cont working in St st and charts as est for 25 (25, 27, 27, 27, 27) more rows, ending with a WS row.

Dec row: (RS) Work to side m, sl m, k1, ssk, work to 3 sts before side m, k2tog, k1, sl m, work to end—2 sts dec'd.

Rep Dec row every 26 (26, 28, 28, 28, 28) the row 2 more times—200 (216, 232, 248, 264, 284) sts rem: 72 (76, 80, 84, 88, 92) sts each front and 56 (64, 72, 80, 88, 100) sts for back.

Work even until piece measures 17½ (17¾, 19, 19¼, 19½, 20¼)" from CO, ending with a WS row.

DIVIDE FOR FRONTS AND BACK

Next row: (RS) *Work to 2 (2, 3, 4, 4, 5) sts before side m, BO 4 (4, 6, 8, 8, 10) sts, removing m; rep from * once more, work to end—70 (74, 77, 80, 84, 87) sts rem each front; 52 (60, 66, 72, 80, 90) sts rem for back.

Place right front and back sts on holders.

Left Front

Work 1 WS row even.

SIZES 18¾ (20¾, 23½)" ONLY

SHAPE ARMHOLE

Dec row: (RS) K1, ssk, work to end—1 st dec'd.

Dec row: (WS) Work to last 3 sts, ssp, p1—1 st dec'd.

Rep last 2 rows 0 (1, 2) more time(s)—78 (80, 81) sts rem.

SIZES 17 (18¾, 20¾, 23½)" ONLY

SHAPE ARMHOLE

Dec row: (RS) K1, ssk, work to end—1 st dec'd.

Rep Dec row every other row 1 (1, 2, 3) more time(s)—75 (76, 77, 77) sts rem.

ALL SIZES

Work even until armhole measures 7 (7¼, 7½, 7¾, 8¼, 8½)", ending with a WS row.

SHAPE SHOULDER

At beg of RS rows, BO 5 (6, 7, 7, 7, 7) sts 2 (1, 3, 2, 1, 1) time(s), then BO 6 (7, 0, 8, 8, 8) sts 1 (2, 0, 1, 2, 2) time(s)—54 sts rem. Do not break yarn.

Place sts on holder.

Right Front

Return 70 (74, 77, 80, 84, 87) held right front sts to needle. With WS facing, rejoin yarn.

Work 1 WS row even.

SIZES 18¾ (20¾, 23½)" ONLY

SHAPE ARMHOLE

Dec row: (RS) Work to last 3 sts, k2tog, k1—1 st dec'd.

Dec row: (WS) P1, p2tog, work to end—1 st dec'd. Rep last 2 rows 0 (1, 2) more time(s)—78 (80, 81) sts rem.

BODY CABLE

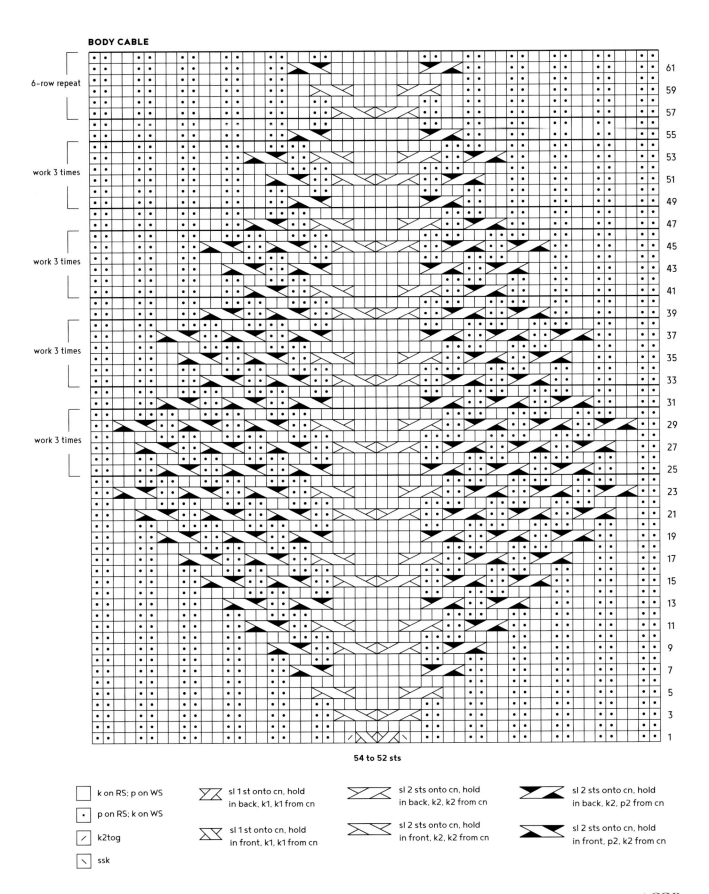

6-row repeat

work 3 times

work 3 times

work 3 times

work 3 times

61
59
57
55
53
51
49
47
45
43
41
39
37
35
33
31
29
27
25
23
21
19
17
15
13
11
9
7
5
3
1

54 to 52 sts

☐ k on RS; p on WS	sl 1 st onto cn, hold in back, k1, k1 from cn	sl 2 sts onto cn, hold in back, k2, k2 from cn	sl 2 sts onto cn, hold in back, k2, p2 from cn
• p on RS; k on WS	sl 1 st onto cn, hold in front, k1, k1 from cn	sl 2 sts onto cn, hold in front, k2, k2 from cn	sl 2 sts onto cn, hold in front, p2, k2 from cn
∕ k2tog		
∖ ssk		

SHAPE ARMHOLE

Dec row: (RS) Work to last 3 sts, k2tog, k1—1 st dec'd.

Rep Dec row every other row 1 (1, 2, 3) more time(s)—75 (76, 77, 77) sts rem.

ALL SIZES

Work even until armhole measures 7 (7¼, 7½, 7¾, 8¼, 8½)", ending with a RS row.

SHAPE SHOULDER:

At beg of WS rows, BO 5 (6, 7, 7, 7, 7) sts 2 (1, 3, 2, 1, 1) time(s), then BO 6 (7, 0, 8, 8, 8) sts 1 (2, 0, 1, 2, 2) time(s)—54 sts rem. Do not break yarn.

Place sts on holder.

Back

Return 52 (60, 66, 72, 80, 90) held back sts to needle. With WS facing, rejoin yarn.

Work 1 WS row even.

SIZES 18¾ (20¾, 23½)" ONLY

SHAPE ARMHOLES

Dec row: (RS) K1, ssk, work to last 3 sts, k2tog, k1—2 sts dec'd.

Dec row: (WS) P1, p2tog, work to last 3 sts, ssp, p1—2 sts dec'd.

SIZES 17 (18¾, 20¾, 23½)" ONLY

Dec row: (RS) K1, ssk, work to last 3 sts, k2tog, k1—2 sts dec'd.

Rep Dec row every other row 1 (1, 2, 3) more time(s)—62 (64, 66, 70) sts rem.

ALL SIZES

Work even until armhole measures 7 (7¼, 7½, 7¾, 8¼, 8½)", ending with a WS row.

SHAPE SHOULDERS

BO 5 (6, 7, 7, 7, 7) sts at beg of next 4 (2, 6, 4, 2, 2) rows, then BO 6 (7, 0, 8, 8, 8) sts at beg of foll 2 (4, 0, 2, 4, 4) rows—20 (20, 20, 20, 20, 24) sts rem. Break yarn.

Place sts on holder.

Collar

Sew shoulders.

Return 54 left front and 20 (20, 20, 20, 20, 24) back sts to needle with WS facing—74 (74, 74, 74, 74, 78) sts.

Next row: (WS) Work in patt to last st of left front, ssk (last left front st tog with first back st), turn—1 back st dec'd.

Next row: (RS) Work in patt to end.

Rep last 2 rows 8 (8, 8, 8, 8, 10) more times, then work WS row once more—10 (10, 10, 10, 10, 12) back sts rem. Break yarn.

Place 54 left front sts on holder. Return 54 right front sts to needle with RS facing.

Next row: (RS) Work in patt to last st of right front, ssp (last right front st tog with first back st), turn—1 back st dec'd.

Next row: (WS) Work in patt to end. Rep last 2 rows 9 (9, 9, 9, 9, 11) more times—no back sts rem.

Return 54 left front sts to needle. With right sides facing, join left and right collars using three-needle BO.

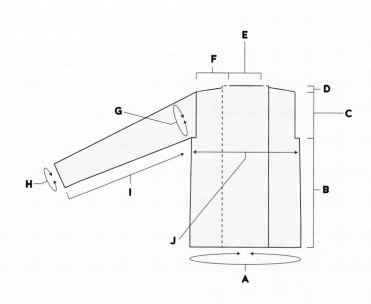

A: 31½ (35¼, 39, 42¾, 46½, 51¼)"

B: 17½ (17¾, 19, 19¼, 19½, 20¼)"

C: 7 (7¼, 7½, 7¾, 8¼, 8½)"

D: 1"

E: 4¾ (4¾, 4¾, 4¾, 4¾, 5¾)"

F: 3¾ (4¾, 5, 5¼, 5½, 5½)"

G: 11¼ (12¼, 13¼, 14, 15½, 17½)"

H: 8½ (9½, 9½, 9½, 10¼, 10¼)"

I: 22"

J: 13¼ (15, 17, 18¾, 20¾, 23½)"

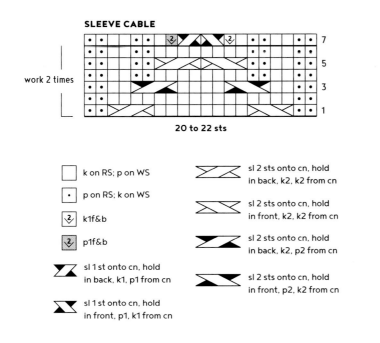

SLEEVE CABLE

work 2 times

20 to 22 sts

- ☐ k on RS; p on WS
- ▪ p on RS; k on WS
- k1f&b
- p1f&b
- sl 1 st onto cn, hold in back, k1, p1 from cn
- sl 1 st onto cn, hold in front, p1, k1 from cn
- sl 2 sts onto cn, hold in back, k2, k2 from cn
- sl 2 sts onto cn, hold in front, k2, k2 from cn
- sl 2 sts onto cn, hold in back, k2, p2 from cn
- sl 2 sts onto cn, hold in front, p2, k2 from cn

Sleeves

With larger dpn and RS facing, beg at center of underarm, pick up and knit 2 (2, 3, 4, 4, 5) sts from first half of underarm, 44 (48, 50, 52, 58, 64) sts around armhole, and 2 (2, 3, 4, 4, 5) sts from 2nd half of underarm—48 (52, 56, 60, 66, 74) sts. Pm and join in the rnd.

Next rnd: K14 (16, 18, 20, 22, 25), pm for shoulder, k0 (0, 0, 0, 1, 2), p2, k2, p2, k8, p2, k2, p2, k0 (0, 0, 0, 1, 2), pm for shoulder, knit to end.

Shape cap using short-rows as foll:

Short-row 1: (RS) Work in patt as est to 2nd shoulder m, sl m, wrap next st, turn.

Short-row 2: (WS) Sl m, work to next shoulder m, sl m, wrap next st, turn.

Short-row 3: Work to previously wrapped st, work wrap tog with wrapped st, wrap next st, turn.

Short-row 4: Work to previously wrapped st, work wrap tog with wrapped st, wrap next st, turn.

Rep Short-rows 3 and 4 eight (ten, ten, ten, twelve, thirteen) more times—8 (8, 12, 16, 16, 20) sts rem unwrapped at underarm.

Next rnd: Work to previously wrapped st, work wrap tog with wrapped st, work to end.

Next rnd: Work to end, working rem wrap tog with wrapped st. Work 15 (15, 9, 3, 9, 8) rnds even.

Dec rnd: K1, k2tog, work to last 3 sts, ssk, k1—2 sts dec'd.

Rep Dec rnd every 21st (21st, 15th, 12th, 10th, 7th) rnd 4 (4, 6, 8, 9, 13) more times—38 (42, 42, 42, 46, 46) sts rem.

Work even until sleeve measures 18¼ " from underarm.

BEG SLEEVE CABLE

Knit to shoulder m, remove m, k0 (0, 0, 0, 1, 2), pm for cable, work Rnd 1 of Sleeve Cable chart over 20 sts, pm for cable, k0 (0, 0, 0, 1, 2), remove shoulder m, knit to end.

Cont in patt as est, work Rnds 2–6 of chart once, then Rnds 1–7 of chart once—40 (44, 44, 44, 48, 48) sts.

Next rnd: K1, k2tog, work to 2 sts before cable m, k2tog, sl m, [p2, k2] 5 times, p2, sl m, ssk, work to last 3 sts, ssk, k1—36 (40, 40, 40, 44, 44) sts rem.

Change to smaller needles.

Next rnd: P1 (0, 0, 0, 1, 1), k2 (1, 1, 1, 2, 2), *p2, k2; rep from * to last 3 (1, 1, 1, 3, 3) st(s), k2 (1, 1, 1, 2, 2), p1 (0, 0, 0, 1, 1).

Cont in rib patt until sleeve measures 22" from underarm.

BO all sts loosely.

Finishing

Weave in ends.

Block to measurements.

fête cardigan

Cheryl Chow

Finished Size

Bust circumference, buttoned: 37 (41¼, 45¼, 48¾, 53¼)".

Cardigan shown measures 37"; modeled with 5" of positive ease.

Yarn

Sport weight (#2 fine).

Shown here: Imperial Yarn Tracie Too (100% wool; 395 yd [361 m]/4 oz [113 g]): #02 pearl gray, 4 (5, 5, 5, 6) balls.

Needles

Size U.S. 3 (3.25 mm): 40" circular (cir) and set of double-pointed (dpn).

Size U.S. 4 (3.5 mm): 40" cir and set of dpn.

Adjust needle size if necessary to obtain the correct gauge.

Notions

Markers (m); cable needle (cn); stitch holders or waste yarn; tapestry needle; 8 (8, 9, 9, 9) ¾" buttons.

Gauge

24 sts and 34 rows = 4" in St st on larger needle.

Notes

■ This cardigan is worked back and forth from the top down with raglan shaping. The sleeves are worked in the round from the top down. Circular needles are used to accommodate the large number of stitches.

■ For the front charts, work the stitches outlined in the color indicated for your size. For the back chart, work the stitches between the beginning and ending points for your size.

■ When working the chart patterns, if there are not enough stitches to work a complete 3- or 4-stitch cable, 4-stitch wrap, or 3-stitch [pass, k1, yo, k1] because the size outline cuts through the multistitch symbol, work the remaining stitches as they appear instead. If there are not enough stitches to work both a decrease and its companion yarnover, work the remaining stitch in stockinette stitch.

■ The M1L and M1R increases for the raglan shaping and k1f&b increases for the neck shaping are not shown on the charts. New stitches make their first appearance in the wrong-side chart row following the increase row, when they are worked into the pattern.

■ Cast-on stitches added at the neck edges are cast on at the beginning of the row, and then immediately worked in the chart pattern for that row.

■ The sleeve chart is worked back and forth in rows and in the round. When working in rounds, work every chart row as a right-side row.

Yoke

With larger cir needle, CO 76 (84, 92, 100, 112) sts. Do not join.

Work chart patts (see Notes) as foll:

Set-up row: (WS) Work Right Front chart over 1 st, place marker (pm), p1, work Sleeve chart over 12 sts, p1, pm, beg and ending as indicated for your size, work Back chart over 46 (54, 62, 70, 82) sts, pm, p1, work Sleeve chart over 12 sts, p1, pm, work Left Front chart over 1 st.

Next row: (RS) Work Left Front chart over 1 st, M1R, sl m, k1, M1L, work Sleeve chart over 12 sts, M1R, k1, sl m, M1L, work Back chart over 46 (54, 62, 70, 82) sts, M1R, sl m, k1, M1L, work Sleeve chart over 12 sts, M1R, k1, sl m, M1L, work Right Front chart over 1 st—84 (92, 100, 108, 120) sts: 2 sts each front, 16 sts each sleeve, and 48 (56, 64, 72, 84) back sts.

Next row: (WS) Work Right Front chart over 2 sts, sl m, p2, work Sleeve chart over 12 sts, p2, sl m, work Back chart over 48 (56, 64, 72, 84) sts, sl m, p2, work Sleeve chart over 12 sts, p2, sl m, work Left Front chart over 2 sts.

Inc row: (RS) *Work in patt to m, M1R, sl m, k1, M1L, work in patt to 1 st before m, M1R, k1, sl m, M1L; rep from * once more, work in patt to end--8 sts inc'd: 1 st each front, 2 sts each sleeve, and 2 back sts.

Next row: (WS) Work even, working new sleeve sts into St st. Rep last 2 rows 5 (5, 6, 6, 7) more times, ending with Row 14 (14, 16, 16, 18) of charts—132 (140, 156, 164, 184) sts: 8 (8, 9, 9, 10) sts each front, 28 (28, 30, 30, 32) sts each sleeve, and 60 (68, 78, 86, 100) back sts.

> **Note:** As you work the following shaping, once the raglan increase outline for your size has reached the edge of the front or back charts, work any additional raglan increases outside the chart in stockinette stitch.

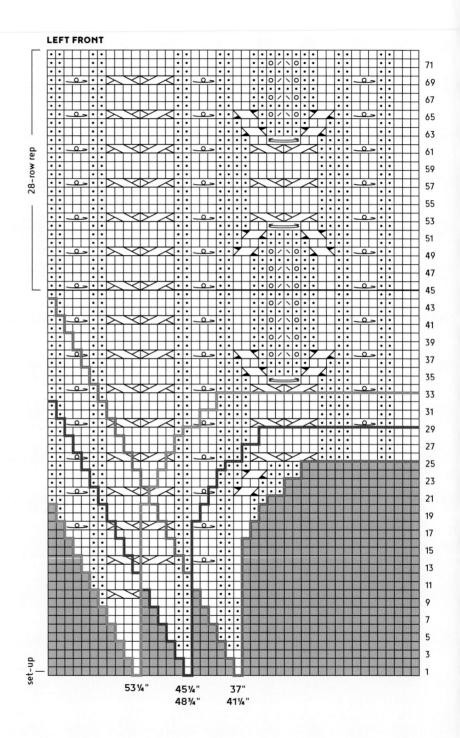

LEFT FRONT

28-row rep

set-up

71 69 67 65 63 61 59 57 55 53 51 49 47 45 43 41 39 37 35 33 31 29 27 25 23 21 19 17 15 13 11 9 7 5 3 1

53¼" 45¼" 37"
48¾" 41¼"

RIGHT FRONT

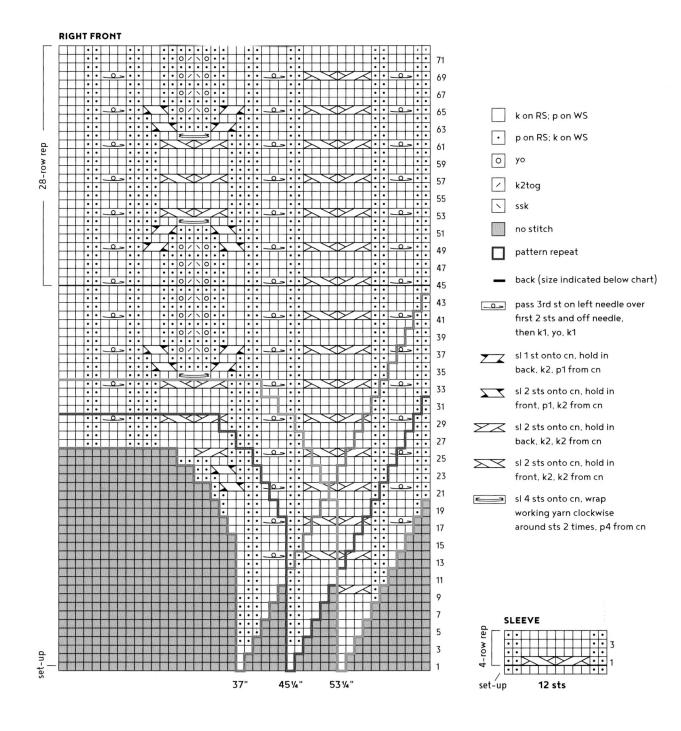

k on RS; p on WS

· p on RS; k on WS

○ yo

╱ k2tog

╲ ssk

no stitch

pattern repeat

— back (size indicated below chart)

pass 3rd st on left needle over first 2 sts and off needle, then k1, yo, k1

sl 1 st onto cn, hold in back, k2, p1 from cn

sl 2 sts onto cn, hold in front, p1, k2 from cn

sl 2 sts onto cn, hold in back, k2, k2 from cn

sl 2 sts onto cn, hold in front, k2, k2 from cn

sl 4 sts onto cn, wrap working yarn clockwise around sts 2 times, p4 from cn

SLEEVE

4-row rep

set-up   **12 sts**

SHAPE FRONT NECK

Neck and Raglan inc row: (RS) K1f&b, *work in patt to m, M1R, sl m, k1, M1L, work in patt to 1 st before m, M1R, k1, sl m, M1L; rep from * once more, work in patt to last st, k1f&b—10 sts inc'd; 2 sts each front, 2 sts each sleeve, and 2 back sts.

Rep Neck and Raglan inc row every RS row 2 (2, 3, 3, 4) more times—162 (170, 196, 204, 234) sts: 14 (14, 17, 17, 20) sts each front, 34 (34, 38, 38, 42) sts each sleeve, and 66 (74, 86, 94, 110) back sts.

Work 1 WS row even.

Cont working 8 Raglan incs as est every RS row 3 more times, **at the same time**, CO 2 sts at beg of next 4 rows (see Notes), then CO 14 (14, 19, 19, 24) sts at beg of foll 2 rows, ending with Row 26 (26, 30, 30, 34) of charts—222 (230, 266, 274, 314) sts: 35 (35, 43, 43, 51) sts each front, 40 (40, 44, 44, 48) sts each sleeve, and 72 (80, 92, 100, 116) back sts.

Cont working 8 Raglan incs as est every RS row 17 (20, 18, 24, 25) more times—358 (390, 410, 466, 514) sts: 52 (55, 61, 67, 76) sts each front, 74 (80, 80, 92, 98) sts each sleeve, 106 (120, 128, 148, 166) back sts.

Work 1 WS row even.

SIZES 37 (41¼, 45¼, 48¾)" ONLY

Body inc row: (RS) *Work in patt to m, M1R, sl m, work in patt to m, sl m, M1L; rep from * once more, work in patt to end—4 sts inc'd; 1 st each front and 2 back sts.

Rep Body inc row every RS row 3 (4, 4, 1) more times—374 (410, 430, 474) sts: 56 (60, 66, 69) sts each front, 74 (80, 80, 92) sts each sleeve, and 114 (130, 138, 152) back sts.

Work 1 WS row even.

ALL SIZES

DIVIDE FOR BODY AND SLEEVES

Next row: (RS) *Work in patt to m, remove m, place 74 (80, 80, 92, 98) sleeve sts on holder, remove m, CO 6 (7, 8, 9, 9) sts, pm for side, CO 6 (7, 8, 9, 9) sts; rep from * once more, work in patt to end—250 (278, 302, 326, 354) body sts rem.

Body

Work even until piece measures 2½ (2¾, 3½, 3½, 3½)" from underarm, ending with a WS row.

SHAPE WAIST

Dec row: (RS) *Work in patt to 2 sts before m, ssk, sl m, k2tog; rep from * once more, work in patt to end—4 sts dec'd.

Rep Dec row every 8th row 3 (3, 2, 2, 2) more times—234 (262, 290, 314, 342) sts rem.

Work even until piece measures 6½" from underarm, ending with a WS row.

BACK

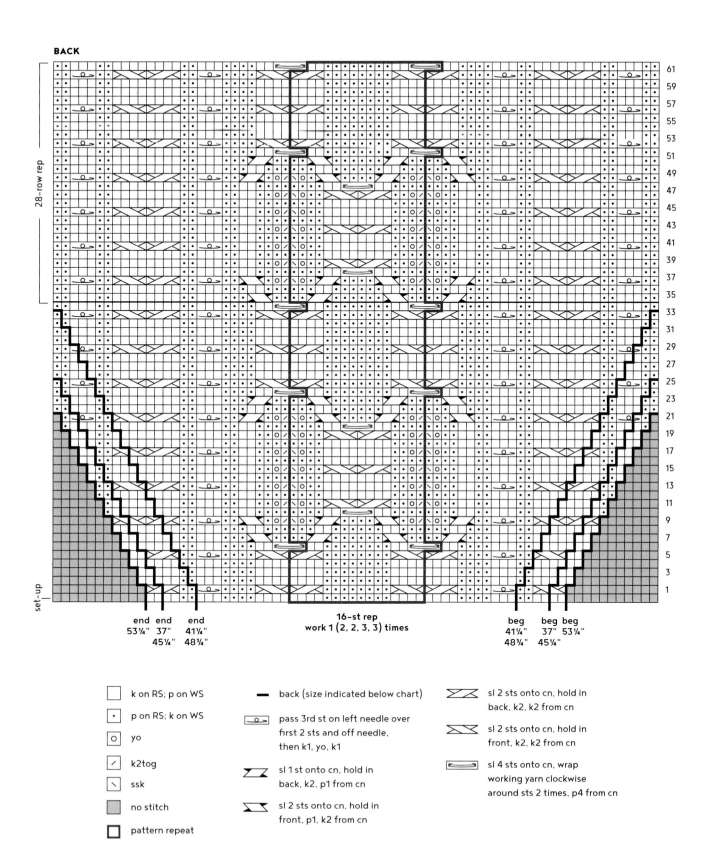

28-row rep

set-up

end 53¼" end 37" end 41¼"
45¼" 48¾"

16-st rep
work 1 (2, 2, 3, 3) times

beg 41¼" beg 37" beg 53¼"
48¾" 45¼"

	k on RS; p on WS		—	back (size indicated below chart)		sl 2 sts onto cn, hold in back, k2, k2 from cn
·	p on RS; k on WS		-o→	pass 3rd st on left needle over first 2 sts and off needle, then k1, yo, k1		sl 2 sts onto cn, hold in front, k2, k2 from cn
o	yo			sl 1 st onto cn, hold in back, k2, p1 from cn		sl 4 sts onto cn, wrap working yarn clockwise around sts 2 times, p4 from cn
╱	k2tog					
╲	ssk			sl 2 sts onto cn, hold in front, p1, k2 from cn		
	no stitch					
	pattern repeat					

Cardigans | **259**

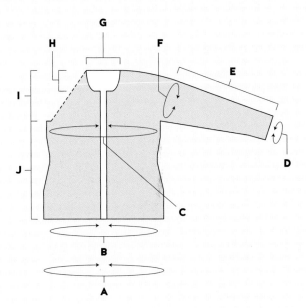

A: 39 (43¼, 47¼, 49¼, 54)"

B: 34½ (38½, 43¼, 46¾, 51¼)"

C: 37 (41¼, 45¼, 48¾, 53¼)"

D: 8¼ (8¾, 9¼, 9¾, 10½)"

E: 17 (17¼, 17½, 17¾, 18)"

F: 14¼ (15½, 16, 18¼, 19¼)"

G: 6¼ (7¼, 8¼, 9¼, 11)"

H: 3¼ (3¼, 3¾, 3¾, 4)"

I: 8 (9, 9, 9¾, 10)"

J: 15½ (16, 16½, 16½, 16½)"

Inc row: (RS) *Work in patt to 1 st before m, M1R, k1, sl m, k1, M1L, rep from * once more, work in patt to end—4 sts inc'd.

Rep Inc row every 6 (6, 6, 8, 8)th row 6 (6, 5, 3, 3) more times—262 (290, 314, 330, 358) sts.

Work even until piece measures 14½ (15, 15½, 15½, 15½)" from underarm, dec 1 st on last WS row—261 (289, 313, 329, 357) sts rem.

Change to smaller cir needle.

Next row: (RS) K1, *p1, k1; rep from * to end.

Next row: (WS) P1, *k1, p1; rep from * to end.

Rep last 2 rows until rib measures 1".

Loosely BO all sts in patt.

Sleeves

With larger dpn and RS facing, beg at center of underarm, pick up and knit 7 (8, 9, 10, 10) sts along underarm CO, work 74 (80, 80, 92, 98) held sleeve sts in patt, pick up and knit 7 (8, 9, 10, 10) sts along underarm CO—88 (96, 98, 112, 118) sts. Pm and join in the rnd.

Dec rnd: K2tog, work in patt to last 2 sts, ssk—2 sts dec'd.

Rep Dec rnd every 7 (7, 7, 6, 6)th rnd 17 (19, 19, 24, 25) more times—52 (56, 58, 62, 66) sts rem.

Work even until piece measures 16 (16¼, 16½, 16¾, 17)" from underarm.

Change to smaller dpn.

Work in k1, p1 rib for 1".

Loosely BO all sts in patt.

Finishing

NECKBAND

With smaller cir needle and RS facing, beg at right front neck, pick up and knit 14 (14, 19, 19, 24) sts along CO sts, 21 (24, 24, 24, 24) sts along right neck to beg of sleeve, 9 sts along top of right sleeve, 47 (55, 61, 69, 77) sts along back neck to beg of sleeve, 9 sts along top of left sleeve, 21 (24, 24, 24, 24) sts along left neck, and 14 (14, 19, 19, 24) sts along left front CO sts—135 (149, 165, 173, 191) sts.

Next row: (WS) K1, *p1, k1; rep from * to end.

Next row: (RS) P1, *k1, p1; rep from * to end.

Rep last 2 rows 2 more times, then work WS row once more.

BO all sts in patt.

BUTTONHOLE BAND

With smaller cir needle and RS facing, pick up and knit 155 (157, 161, 163, 163) sts evenly along right front edge.

Next row: (WS) P1, *k1, p1; rep from * to end.

Next row: (RS) K1, *p1, k1; rep from * to end.

Work WS row once more.

Buttonhole row: (RS) Work 2 (3, 2, 4, 4) sts in patt, *work 3-st one-row buttonhole, work in patt until there are 17 (17, 15, 15, 15) sts on right needle after last buttonhole st; rep from * 6 (6, 7, 7, 7) more times, work 3-st one-row buttonhole, work in patt to end.

Work 3 more rows in rib patt.

BO all sts in patt.

BUTTONBAND

With smaller cir needle and RS facing, pick up and knit 155 (157, 161, 163, 163) sts evenly along left front edge.

Next row: (WS) P1, *k1, p1; rep from * to end.

Next row: (RS) K1, *p1, k1; rep from * to end.

Rep last 2 rows 2 more times, then work WS row once more.

BO all sts in patt.

Weave in ends.

Block.

Sew on buttons.

central park hoodie

Heather Lodinsky

Finished Size

Bust: 32 (36, 40, 44, 48, 52, 56, 60)".

Cardigan shown measures 36".

Yarn

Aran weight (#4 medium).

Shown here: Tahki Donegal Tweed (100% wool; 183 yd (167 m)/110 g): #803 yellow-green: 6 (7, 8, 9, 10, 16,18, 20) skeins.

Needles

Size U.S. 6 (4 mm): 32–40" circular (cir) and set of double-pointed (dpn).

Size U.S. 8 (5 mm): 32–40" cir and set of dpn.

Adjust needle size if necessary to obtain the correct gauge.

Notions

Markers (m); cable needle (cn); stitch holders or waste yarn; tapestry needle; Size G/6 (4 mm) crochet hook (optional); buttons (optional).

Gauge

17 sts and 24 rows = 4" in St st on larger needles (see Notes if making three largest sizes).

Notes

■ For the three largest sizes, the pattern was configured with a stitch gauge of 18 stitches per four inches. If you are making one of these sizes, adjust needle size to achieve this gauge.

■ The pieces are worked separately, then sewn together, then hood is picked up and worked around neck.

■ For the three largest sizes, the instructions differ in some places. It may be helpful to go through the pattern and highlight your relevant directions before beginning.

Back

With smaller needles, CO 78 (86, 94, 102, 110, 122, 138, 146) sts.

SIZES 32 (36, 40, 44, 48)" ONLY

Row 1: (RS) *K2, p2; rep from * to last 2 sts, k2.

Row 2: (WS) *P2, k2; rep from * to last 2 sts, p2.

SIZES 52 (56, 60)" ONLY

Row 1: (RS) *P2, k2; rep from * to last 2 sts, p2.

Row 2: (WS) *K2, p2; rep from * to last 2 sts, k2.

ALL SIZES

Rep Rows 1 and 2 for 4 (4, 4, 4, 4, 4¼, 4½, 4½)", ending with a WS row.

Change to larger needles.

Row 1: (RS) K14 (14, 14, 18, 18, 24, 32, 36), place marker (pm), work Row 1 of Chart A over 10 sts, pm, k6 (10, 14, 14, 18, 18, 18, 18), pm, work Row 1 of Chart B over 18 sts, pm, k6 (10, 14, 14, 18, 18, 18, 18), pm, work Row 1 of Chart C over 10 sts, pm, k14 (14, 14, 18, 18, 24, 32, 36).

Row 2: (WS) P14 (14, 14, 18, 18, 24, 32, 36), work Row 2 of Chart C, p6 (10, 14, 14, 18, 18, 18, 18), work Row 2 of Chart B, p6 (10, 14, 14, 18, 18, 18, 18), work Row 2 of Chart A, p14 (14, 14, 18, 18, 24, 32, 36).

Cont in patt until back measures 13½ (14, 14, 14½, 14½, 16¼, 17, 17¾)", ending with a WS row.

ARMHOLES

BO 4 (5, 6, 7, 8, 8, 8, 8) sts at beg of next 2 rows, then 2 sts at beg of foll 2 rows— 66 (72, 78, 84, 90, 102, 118, 126) sts rem.

Dec row: (RS) K2, ssk, work in patt to last 4 sts, k2tog, k2—2 sts dec'd.

Work 1 WS row.

Rep last 2 rows 1 (1, 1, 1, 1, 3, 5, 7) more time, then work Dec row every other RS row 0 (0, 0, 0, 0, 7, 7, 7) times—62 (68, 74, 80, 86, 80, 92, 96) sts rem.

Work even in patt until armhole measures 8 (8, 8½, 8½, 9, 8½, 9¼, 9¾)", ending with a WS row.

SHOULDERS

Keeping in patt, BO 5 (6, 6, 7, 8, 6, 7, 8) sts at beg of next 6 rows, then 0 (0, 0, 0, 0, 5, 8, 7) sts at beg of foll 2 rows—32 (32, 38, 38, 38, 34, 34, 34) sts rem.

Place all sts on a holder for back neck.

Block back to schematic measurements.

Left Front

With smaller needles, CO 36 (40, 44, 48, 52, 55, 63, 71) sts.

SIZES 32 (36, 40, 44, 48)" ONLY

Row 1: (RS) *K2, p2; rep from * to end of row.

Row 2: (WS) *K2, p2; rep from * to end.

SIZES 52 (56, 60)" ONLY

Row 1: (RS) *P2, k2; rep from* to last 3 sts, p2, k1.

Row 2: (WS) P1, k2, *p2, k2; rep from * to end.

ALL SIZES

Rep Rows 1 and 2 for 4 (4, 4, 4, 4, 4¼, 4½, 4½)", ending with a WS row.

Change to larger needles.

Row 1: (RS) K14 (14, 14, 18, 18, 24, 32, 36), pm, work Row 1 of Chart A over 10 sts, pm, k2 (6, 10, 10, 14, 10, 10, 14), pm, work Row 1 of Chart A over 10 sts, k0 (0, 0, 0, 0, 1, 1, 1).

Row 2: (WS) P0 (0, 0, 0, 0, 1, 1, 1), work Row 2 of Chart A, p2 (6, 10, 10, 14, 10, 10, 14), work Row 2 of Chart A, p14 (14, 14, 18, 18, 24, 32, 36).

Cont in patt until piece measures 13½ (14, 14, 14½, 14½, 16¼, 17, 17¾)", ending with a WS row.

ARMHOLE

> **Note:** Read foll section all the way through before beginning.

Next row: (RS) BO 4 (5, 6, 7, 8, 8, 8, 8), work in patt to end.

Work 1 WS row.

Next row: (RS) BO 2 sts, work in patt to end.

Work 1 WS row.

Dec row: (RS) K2, ssk, work in patt to end—1 st dec'd.

Work 1 WS row.

Rep last 2 rows 1 (1, 1, 1, 1, 3, 5, 7) more time(s), then rep Dec row every other RS row 0 (0, 0, 0, 0, 7, 7, 7) times—28 (31, 34, 37, 40, 34, 40, 46) sts rem.

At the same time, for sizes 52 (56, 60)" only, work as foll; all other sizes move to neck shaping.

SIZES 52 (56, 60)" ONLY

When armhole measures 5 (6, 6½)", end with a WS row.

Next row: (RS) Work in patt to last 11 sts, incl any armhole shaping, then place last 11 sts of row on holder. Cont working rem sts on needle in patt—23 (29, 35) sts rem after armhole shaping is completed.

Work even in patt until armhole measures 8½ (9¼, 9¾)", ending with a WS row.

Move to shoulder shaping directions.

NECK SHAPING
SIZES 32 (36, 40, 44, 48)" ONLY

Work even in patt until armhole measures 6 (6, 6½, 6½, 7)", ending with a RS row.

Next row: (WS) Work in patt across 10 sts, then place these sts on a holder. Make note of last cable row worked in charts.

Work to end of row.

Keeping in patt, BO 1 (1, 2, 2, 2) st(s) at neck edge every other row 3 times—15 (18, 18, 21, 24) sts rem.

Work even in patt until front measures same as back to beg of shoulder shaping, ending with a WS row.

ALL SIZES
SHOULDER SHAPING
Keeping in patt, BO 5 (6, 6, 7, 8, 6, 7, 8) sts at beg of next 3 RS rows, then 0 (0, 0, 0, 0, 5, 8, 11) sts at beg of next RS row—no sts rem on needle.

Block front to schematic measurements.

Right Front
With smaller needles, CO 36 (40, 44, 48, 52, 55, 63, 71) sts.

SIZES 32 (36, 40, 44, 48)" ONLY
Row 1: (RS) *P2, k2; rep from * to end of row.

Row 2: (WS) *P2, k2; rep from * to end of row.

SIZES 52 (56, 60)" ONLY
Row 1: (RS) K1, p2, *k2, p2; rep from * to end.

Row 2: (WS) *K2, p2; rep from * to last 3 sts, k2, p1.

ALL SIZES
Rep Rows 1 and 2 for 4 (4, 4, 4, 4, 4¼, 4½, 4½)", ending with a WS row.

Change to larger needles.

Row 1: (RS) K0 (0, 0, 0, 0, 1, 1, 1), work Row 1 of Chart C over 10 sts, pm, k2 (6, 10, 10, 14, 10, 10, 14), pm, work Row 1 of Chart C over 10 sts, pm, k14 (14, 14, 18, 18, 24, 32, 36).

Row 2: (WS) P14 (14, 14, 18, 18, 24, 32, 36), work Row 2 of Chart C, p2 (6, 10, 10, 14, 10, 10, 14), work Row 2 of Chart C, p0 (0, 0, 0, 0, 1, 1, 1).

Cont in patt until piece measures 13½ (14, 14, 14½, 14½, 16¼, 17, 17¾)", ending with a RS row.

ARMHOLE
❙ Note: *Read foll section all the way through before beginning.*

Next row: (WS) BO 4 (5, 6, 7, 8, 8, 8, 8) sts, work in patt to end.

Work 1 RS row.

Next row: (WS) BO 2 sts, work in patt to end.

Next row: (RS) Work in patt to last 4 sts, k2tog, k2—1 st dec'd.

Work 1 WS row.

Rep last 2 rows 1 (1, 1, 1, 1, 3, 5, 7) more time(s), then rep Dec row every other RS row 0 (0, 0, 0, 0, 7, 7, 7) times—28 (31, 34, 37, 40, 34, 40, 46) sts rem.

At the same time, for sizes 52 (56, 60)" only, work as foll; all other sizes move to neck shaping.

SIZES 52 (56, 60)" ONLY
When armhole measures 5 (6, 6½)", end with a RS row.

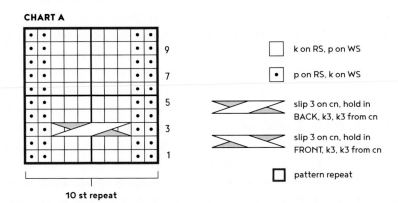

CHART A

9
7
5
3
1

10 st repeat

☐ k on RS, p on WS

▣ p on RS, k on WS

slip 3 on cn, hold in BACK, k3, k3 from cn

slip 3 on cn, hold in FRONT, k3, k3 from cn

☐ pattern repeat

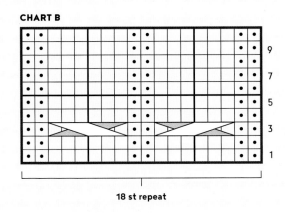

CHART B

9
7
5
3
1

18 st repeat

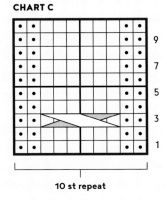

CHART C

9
7
5
3
1

10 st repeat

Next row: (WS) Work in patt to last 11 sts, then place last 11 sts of row on holder.

Cont working rem sts on needle in patt—23 (29, 35) sts rem after armhole shaping is completed.

Work even in patt until armhole measures 8½ (9¼, 9¾)", ending with a WS row.

Move to shoulder shaping directions.

NECK SHAPING
SIZES 32 (36, 40, 44, 48)" ONLY
Work even in pattern until armhole measures 6 (6, 6½, 6½, 7)", ending with a WS row.

Next row: (RS) Work in patt across 10 sts, then place these sts on a holder. Make note of last cable row worked in charts (should match left front).

Work to end of row.

Keeping in patt, BO 1 (1, 2, 2, 2) st(s) at neck edge every other row 3 times—15 (18, 18, 21, 24) sts rem.

Work even in patt until front measures same as back to beg of shoulder shaping, ending with a RS row.

ALL SIZES
SHOULDER SHAPING
Keeping in patt, BO 5 (6, 6, 7, 8, 6, 7, 8) sts at beg of next 3 WS rows, then 0 (0, 0, 0, 0, 5, 8, 11) sts at beg of next WS row—no sts rem.

Block front to schematic measurements.

Sleeves
With smaller needles, CO 38 (38, 46, 46, 54, 54, 62, 62) sts.

Work ribbing for all sizes as foll:

Row 1: (RS) *K2, p2; rep from * to last 2 sts, k2.

Row 2: (WS) *P2, k2; rep from * to last 2 sts, p2.

Cont in rib for 5 (5, 5, 5, 5, 4¼, 4¼, 4¼)", ending with a WS row.

Change to larger needles.

Row 1: (RS) K10 (10, 14, 14, 18, 18, 22, 22), pm, work Row 1 of Chart B over 18 sts, pm, k10 (10, 14, 14, 18, 18, 22, 22).

Row 2: (WS) P10 (10, 14, 14, 18, 18, 22, 22), work Row 2 of Chart B, p10 (10, 14, 14, 18, 18, 22, 22).

Cont in patt and **at the same time**, inc 1 st each end of needle every 8th row 9 (10, 9, 10, 9, 8, 8, 7) times, then every 4th row 0 (0, 0, 0, 0, 4, 5, 7) times—56 (58, 64, 66, 72, 78, 88, 90) sts.

Work even in patt until sleeve measures 18½ (19, 19½, 20, 20½, 20½, 21, 21)" from CO, ending with a WS row.

SLEEVE CAP
Cont in patt. BO 4 (5, 6, 7, 8, 8, 8, 8) sts at beg of next 2 rows, then 2 sts at beg of foll 2 rows, then 2 sts at beg of foll 0 (0, 0, 0, 0, 0, 2, 2) rows—44 (44, 48, 48, 52, 58, 64, 66) sts rem.

SIZES 32 (36, 40, 44, 48)" ONLY
Dec row: (RS) K2, ssk, work to last 4 sts, k2tog, k2—2 sts dec'd.

Rep Dec row every RS row 3 times, then every 4th row 5 times.

BO 2 sts at beg of next 4 rows—18 (18, 22, 22, 26) sts rem.

BO all sts.

SIZES 52 (56, 60)" ONLY
Dec row (RS) K2, ssk, work to last 4 sts, k2tog, k2—2 sts dec'd.

Rep Dec row on every RS row 11 (12, 12) more times—34 (38, 40) sts rem. BO 2 sts at beg of next 4 rows—26 (30, 32) sts rem.

BO all sts.

Block sleeves to schematic measurements.

Finishing

Sew shoulder seams.

HOOD

With larger needles, RS facing, and starting at right front neck, work across 10 (10, 10, 10, 10, 11, 11, 11) sts on holder in patt, pick up and knit 11 (11, 14, 14, 14, 17, 21, 23) sts along right-front neckline (for three largest sizes, this is the straight edge along the right front), k32 (32, 38, 38, 38, 34, 34, 34) across sts on back holder, pick up and knit 11 (11, 14, 14, 14, 17, 21, 23) sts down left-front neck, then work sts on holder in patt—74 (74, 86, 86, 86, 90, 98, 102) sts total.

Next row: (WS) Work charted sts in patt, pm, purl to next cabled section, pm, work in patt.

> **Note:** You can cont the cable onto the hood, or cease work cable patt and work hood in plain St st.

Cont in patt until hood measures 11 (11, 11½, 11½, 12, 12¼, 12¼ 12½)" from shoulder, ending with a RS row.

Next row: (WS) Work 37 (37, 43, 43, 43, 45, 49, 51) sts, pm, work rem 37 (37, 43, 43, 43, 45, 49, 51) sts.

Dec row: (RS) Work to 3 sts before m, k2tog, k1, sl m, k1, ssk, work to end—2 sts dec'd.

Rep Dec row on every RS row 4 more times—64 (64, 76, 76, 76, 80, 88, 92) sts rem. BO all sts, or seam top of hood with three-needle BO.

SIZES 32 (36, 40, 44, 48)" ONLY

FRONT BANDS AND HOOD EDGING

With smaller cir needle, RS facing, and starting at upper edge of hood, evenly pick up and knit 146 (150, 154, 158, 162) sts to the lower bottom edge of the left front.

Next row: (WS) *P2, k2; rep from * to last 2 sts, p2.

Work in rib as est until band measures 1½".

BO all sts in rib.

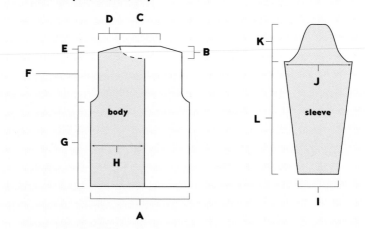

SIZES 32 (36, 40, 44, 48)"

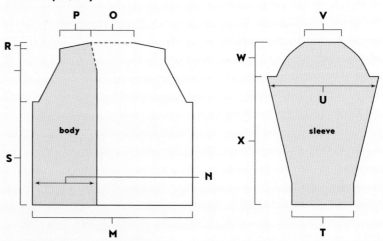

SIZES 52 (56, 60)"

**SIZES 32 (36, 40, 44, 48)"
BODY**

A: 16 (18, 20, 22, 24)"

B: 2"

C: 6¼ (6¼, 8, 8, 8)"

D: 3½ (3¾, 3¾, 4¼, 4¾)"

E: 1"

F: 8 (8, 8¾, 8½, 9)"

G: 13½ (14, 14, 14½, 14½)"

H: 8½ (9½, 10½, 11½, 12½)"

SLEEVE

I: 6½ (6½, 7¾, 7¾, 9)"

J: 11 (11½, 12½, 13, 14)"

K: 6"

L: 18½ (19, 19½, 20, 20½)"

**SIZES 52 (56, 60)"
BODY**

M: 26¼ (28½, 30½)"

N: 11½ (13¼, 14¾)"

O: 7¼"

P: 5 (6¼, 7¼)"

Q: 1¼"

R: 8½ (9¼, 9¾)"

S: 16¼ (17, 17¾)"

SLEEVE

T: 12 (13¾, 13¾)"

U: 17¼ (19½, 20)"

V: 5¾ (6½, 7¼)"

W: 5½ (6, 6)"

X: 20½ (21, 21)"

With smaller needles, RS facing, and starting at lower edge of right front, evenly pick up and knit 146 (150, 154, 158, 162) sts along edge of right front and edge of right side of hood.

Next row: (WS) *P2, k2; rep from * to last 2 sts, p2.

Work in rib as est until band measures 1½".

BO all sts in rib.

BUTTON/BUTTONHOLE OPTION

After working the left-front band, mark the placement for 5 or 6 buttons along band. On right-front band, work rib for 3 rows. On the 4th row, BO 2 sts at points marked for buttonhole placement. On next row, CO 2 sts above each place where sts were BO.

Cont in rib until band measures 1½".

BO all sts in rib. Sew top of hood tog.

Sew in sleeves. Sew side and sleeve seams.

Weave in ends.

Sew on buttons.

SIZES 52 (56, 60)" ONLY

Seam the top of the hood, if you did not use the three-needle BO already.

FRONT BANDS AND HOOD EDGINGS

With smaller cir needle, RS facing, and beg at bottom corner of right front, pick up and knit 181 (189, 197) sts evenly along right front and right-front edge of hood, ending at seam at top of hood.

Pick up and knit 181 (189, 197) sts evenly down left-front edge of hood and left front—362 (378, 394) sts total.

Next row: (WS) *P2, k2; rep from * to last 2 sts, p2.

Cont in rib until band measures 2½". BO all sts in rib.

OPTIONAL CROCHET BUTTONLOOPS

With size G/6 (4 mm) crochet hook, join yarn with sl st to rightfront band edge, about ½" up from the bottom edge.

Ch 7, join with sl st to band edge about 1" above starting point, turn, sc in each ch, join with sl st to knitted edge, fasten off.

Keeping loops spaced by about 1", rep buttonloops along right-front edge, ending at a point level with the underarm—you should be able to fit 6-7 buttonloops.

Sew buttons to corresponding points on leftfront band, offcenter (closer to the body of the left front).

Sew in sleeves.

Sew side seams and sleeve seams.

Weave in all loose ends.

dahlia cardigan

Heather Zoppetti

Finished Size

Bust circumference: 30 (35½, 40½, 45½, 50)", with fronts overlapped about 4".

Cardigan shown measures 35½".

Yarn

Sportweight (#2 fine).

Shown here: Manos del Uruguay Serena (60% baby alpaca, 40% pima cotton; 170 yd [155 m]/1¾ oz [50 g]): #2150 fig, 5 (6, 7, 8, 9) skeins.

Needles

Size U.S. 5 (3.75 mm): 32" circular (cir) and set of double-pointed (dpn).

Adjust needle size if necessary to obtain the correct gauge.

Notions

Markers (m); size E/4 (3.5 mm) crochet hook for provisional CO; stitch holders or waste yarn; tapestry needle.

Gauge

24 sts and 32 rows = 4" in St st; lace panel measures about 13" square, after blocking.

Notes

■ The square back lace panel is worked first in the round from the center out. Stitches are bound off along the upper and lower edges of the panel, leaving live stitches on holders along the remaining two sides.

■ The upper and lower back each begin with a provisional cast-on at center back and are worked separately from the middle of the back outward. For the back sides, the upper and lower back stitches are joined to the live stitches from one side of the lace panel, and the joined stitches are worked in one piece out to the side of the body (see Back Diagram). During finishing, the upper and lower back sections are seamed to the bound-off top and bottom edges of the lace panel.

■ The afterthought armhole positions are marked by working a set of stitches at each side using waste yarn. Both fronts are worked from the side of the body inward and finished with a seed-stitch border. The sleeve stitches are picked up around the armhole openings and worked in the round down to the cuffs. The left sleeve is not shown on the schematic.

■ On right-side rows, slip stitches knitwise with yarn in back; on wrong-side rows, slip stitches purlwise with yarn in front.

Lace Panel

Using the crochet provisional method, CO 4 sts.

Next row: [K1f&b] 4 times—8 sts. Divide sts evenly over 4 dpn. Place marker (pm), and join in the rnd.

Work Rnds 1–26 of Chart A, working chart patt 4 times around (once on each needle)—136 sts total; 34 sts on each needle.

Work Rnds 1–30 of Chart B, changing to cir needle when necessary, and pm after each patt rep—280 sts total; 4 patt reps of 70 sts each.

Next rnd: K70 for right side, BO 70 sts for upper edge, k70 for left side, BO 70 sts for bottom edge. Place 70 sts for each side on separate waste yarn holders.

Right Back and Side

UPPER BACK

With cir needle and using the crochet provisional method, CO 44 (44, 50, 56, 62) sts.

Row 1: (RS) Sl 1, k23 (23, 26, 29, 32), pm, purl to last 5 sts, [k1, p1] 2 times, k1.

Row 2: (WS) Sl 1, [p1, k1] 2 times, p1, knit to m, sl m, purl to end.

Rep last 2 rows 25 more times, ending with a WS row—piece measures 6½" from CO. Place sts on waste yarn, leaving m in position.

LOWER BACK

With cir needle and using the crochet provisional method, CO 32 (32, 35, 38, 41) sts.

Row 1: (RS) Sl 1, [k1, p1] 2 times, knit to end.

Row 2: (WS) Sl 1, purl to last 6 sts, [k1, p1] 3 times.

Rep last 2 rows 25 more times, ending with a WS row—piece measures 6½" from CO. Leave sts on needle.

CHART A

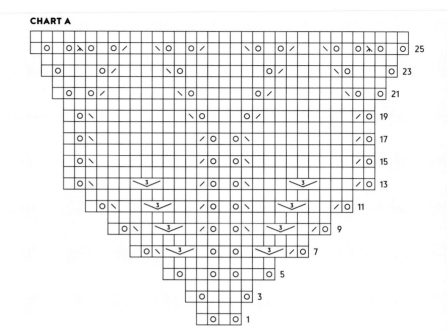

CHART C

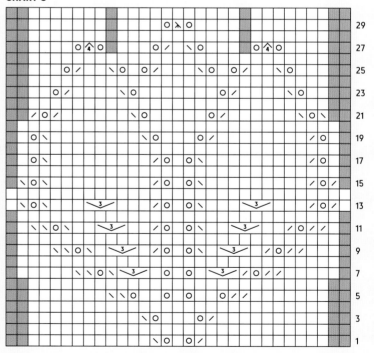

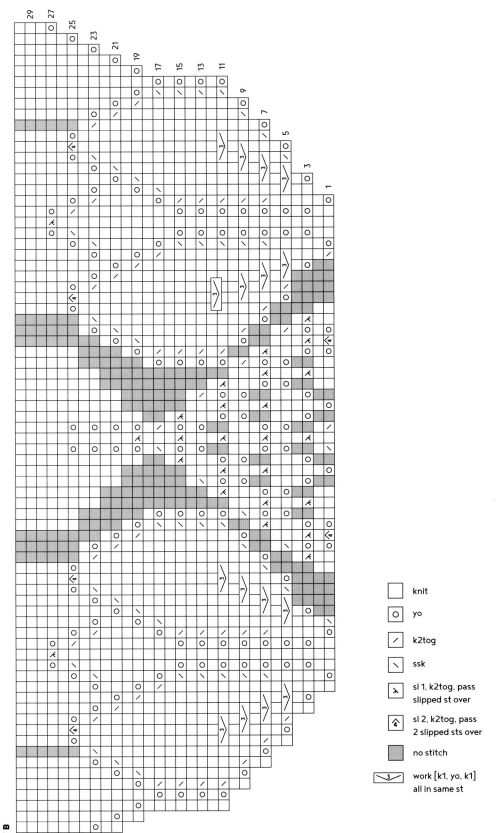

CHART B

knit				
yo				
k2tog				
ssk				
sl 1, k2tog, pass slipped st over				
sl 2, k2tog, pass 2 slipped sts over				
no stitch				
work [k1, yo, k1] all in same st				

RIGHT SIDE

Return 70 held right side lace panel sts and 44 (44, 50, 56, 62) held upper back sts (including m) to cir needle with RS facing so that pieces will be worked in this order on next RS row: lower back, lace panel, upper back—146 (146, 155, 164, 173) sts total.

Row 1: (RS) Sl 1, [k1, p1] 2 times, k26 (26, 29, 32, 35), ssk (last lower-back st tog with first lace panel st), k68 center lace panel sts, k2tog (last lace panel st tog with first upper-back st), knit to m, sl m, purl to last 5 sts, [k1, p1] 2 times, k1—144 (144, 153, 162, 171) sts rem.

Row 2: (WS) Sl 1, [p1, k1] 2 times, p1, knit to m, sl m, purl to last 6 sts, [k1, p1] 3 times.

Row 3: Sl 1, [k1, p1] 2 times, knit to m, sl m, purl to last 5 sts, [k1, p1] 2 times, k1.

Rep last 2 rows 0 (2, 4, 6, 8) more times, then work Row 2 once more—4 (8, 12, 16, 20) side rows completed; piece measures ½ (1, 1½, 2, 2½)" from end of lace panel, and 7 (7½, 8, 8½, 9)" from provisional CO of upper and lower back.

Mark right armhole: (RS) Sl 1, [k1, p1] 2 times, k60 (57, 57, 56, 53), knit next 36 (39, 42, 46, 52) sts using waste yarn, then return these sts to left needle and knit across them again using main yarn, knit to m, purl to last 5 sts, [k1, p1] 2 times, k1.

RIGHT FRONT

Rep Rows 2 and 3 of right side 36 (45, 53, 61, 68) times—front measures 9 (11¼, 13¼, 15¼, 17)" from afterthought armhole.

Work seed st front border as foll:

Next row: (WS) Sl 1, *p1, k1; rep from * to last 1 (1, 2, 1, 2) st(s), p1 (p1, p2tog, p1, p2tog)—144 (144, 152, 162, 170) sts.

Next row: (RS) Sl 1, *k1, p1; rep from * to last st, k1.

Rep last row until seed st border measures 1"—front measures 10 (12¼, 14¼, 16¼, 18)" from afterthought armhole.

BO loosely in patt.

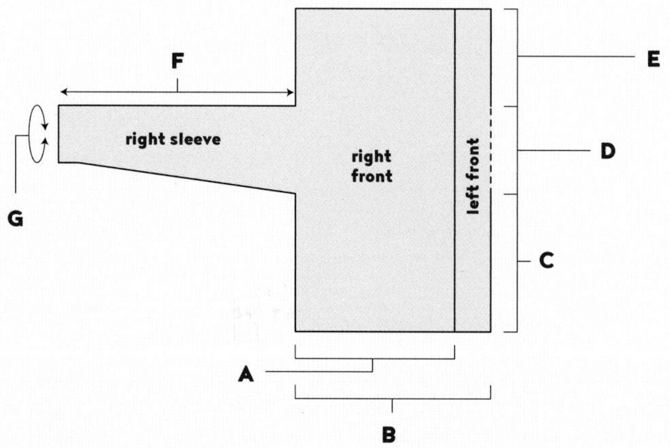

Left Back and Side

LOWER BACK

Carefully unzip provisional CO at start of right lower back, and place 31 (31, 34, 37, 40) live sts on cir needle. Join main yarn with WS facing.

Set-up row: (WS) Sl 1, [k1, p1] 2 times, k1, purl to last st, M1, p1—32 (32, 35, 38, 41) sts.

Row 1: (RS) Sl 1, knit to last 5 sts, [p1, k1] 2 times, p1.

Row 2: Sl 1, [k1, p1] 2 times, k1, purl to end.

Rep last 2 rows 25 more times, ending with a WS row—piece measures 6½" from CO. Place sts on waste yarn.

UPPER BACK

Carefully unzip provisional CO at start of right upper back, and place 43 (43, 49, 55, 61) live sts on cir needle. Join main yarn with WS facing.

Set-up row: (WS) Sl 1, M1, p22 (22, 25, 28, 31) pm, knit to last 6 sts, [p1, k1] 3 times—44 (44, 50, 56, 62) sts.

Row 1: (RS) Sl 1, [p1, k1] 2 times, purl to m, sl m, knit to end.

Row 2: (WS) Sl 1, purl to m, sl m, knit to last 6 sts, [p1, k1] 3 times.

Rep last 2 rows 25 more times, slipping m as you come to it, and ending with a WS row—piece measures 6½" from CO. Leave sts on needle.

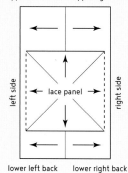

BACK DIAGRAM
Arrows show direction of knitting

upper left back   upper right back

left side   lace panel   right side

lower left back   lower right back

A: Front: 10 (12¼, 14¼, 16¼, 18)"

B: Back: 14 (15, 16, 17, 18)"

C: 10¾ (10¼, 10¼, 10, 9¾)"

D: 6 (6½, 7, 7¾, 8¾)"

E: 7¼ (7¼, 8¼, 9¼, 10¼)"

F: 18 (18, 19, 19, 20)"

G: 7¾ (8½, 9½, 9¾, 10½)"

LEFT SIDE

Return 70 held left-side lace panel sts and 32 (32, 35, 38, 41) held lower back sts to cir needle with RS facing so that the pieces will be worked in this order on the next RS row: upper back, lace panel, lower back—146 (146, 155, 164, 173) sts total.

Row 1: (RS) Sl 1, [p1, k1] 2 times, purl to m, sl m, k23 (23, 26, 29, 32), ssk (last upper-back st tog with first lace panel st), k68 center lace panel sts, k2tog (last lace panel st tog with first lower-back st), knit to last 5 sts [p1, k1] 2 times, p1—144 (144, 153, 162, 171) sts total.

Row 2: (WS) Sl 1, [k1, p1] 2 times, k1, purl to m, sl m, knit to last 6 sts, [p1, k1] 3 times.

Row 3: Sl 1, [p1, k1] 2 times, purl to m, sl m, knit to last 5 sts, [p1, k1] 2 times, p1.

Rep last 2 rows 0 (2, 4, 6, 8) more times, then work Row 2 once more—4 (8, 12, 16, 20) side rows completed; piece measures ½ (1, 1½, 2, 2½)" from end of lace panel, and 7 (7½, 8, 8½, 9)" from provisional CO of upper and lower back.

Mark left armhole: (RS) Sl 1, [p1, k1] 2 times, purl to m, sl m, k23 (23, 26, 29, 32), knit next 36 (39, 42, 46, 52) sts using waste yarn, then return these sts to left needle and knit across them again using main yarn, knit to last 5 sts, [p1, k1] 2 times, p1.

LEFT FRONT

Rep Rows 2 and 3 of left side 36 (45, 53, 61, 68) times—front measures 9 (11¼, 13¼, 15¼, 17)" from afterthought armhole.

Work seed st front border as foll:

Next row: (WS) Sl 1, *k1, p1; rep from * to last 1 (1, 2, 1, 2) st(s), k1 (k1, k2tog, k1, k2tog)— 144 (144, 152, 162, 170) sts.

Next row: (RS) Sl 1, *p1, k1; rep from * to last st, p1.

Rep last row until seed st border measures 1"—front measures 10 (12¼, 14¼, 16¼, 18)" from afterthought armhole.

BO loosely in patt.

Sleeves

Starting at base of underarm, carefully remove waste yarn from afterthought armhole, and place live sts on dpns—71 (77, 83, 91, 103) sts total; 36 (39, 42, 46, 52) sts on side of armhole opening closer to lace panel, and 35 (38, 41, 45, 51) sts on other side. Arrange sts as evenly as possible on dpn, and join yarn with RS facing at base of armhole.

Next rnd: Knit to top of armhole, pick up and knit 1 st between two sets of armhole sts, knit to bottom of armhole, pick up and knit 1 st between two sets of armhole sts—73 (79, 85, 93, 105) sts. Pm and join in the rnd. Work in St st until sleeve measures 2½ (2½, 2½, 2¼, 2)" from body.

Dec rnd: K1, k2tog, knit to last 2 sts, ssk—2 sts dec'd. Rep Dec rnd every 8 (8, 8, 7, 6)th rnd 10 (10, 11, 13, 17) more times—51 (57, 61, 65, 69) sts rem; sleeve measures 12¾ (12¾, 13¾, 13¾, 14¾)" from underarm.

Next rnd: K12 (15, 17, 19, 21), pm, work Rnd 1 of Chart C over 27 sts, pm, k12 (15, 17, 19, 21).

Work Rnds 2-30 of chart (25 chart sts rem after Rnd 27) and ***at the same time*** cont to work sleeve dec rnd every 8 (8, 8, 7, 6)th rnd as est 1 (2, 1, 2, 2) more time(s)—47 (51, 57, 59, 63) sts rem; 25 center chart sts, 11 (13, 16, 17, 19) sts each side; sleeve measures 16½ (16½, 17½, 17½, 18½)" from underarm.

Work even in St st for ½".

Work seed st edging as foll:

Next rnd: K1, *p1, k1; rep from *.

Next rnd: P1, *k1, p1; rep from *.

Rep last 2 rnds until seed st measures 1½", and sleeve measures 18 (18, 19, 19, 20)" from underarm.

BO all sts in patt.

Finishing

Carefully remove provisional CO from center of lace panel, thread tail on a tapestry needle, draw tail through 4 CO sts, and pull gently to close hole in center.

Block to measurements, blocking lace panel to 13" square.

Sew upper edge of lace panel to right and left upper back, then sew lower edge of lace panel to right and left lower back.

Weave in ends.

augusta cardigan

Kephren Pritchett

Finished Size

Width at back hip: 18 (20, 22, 24, 26, 28)".

Cardigan shown measures 20".

Yarn

Worsted weight (#4 medium).

Shown here: Woolfolk Får (100% Ovis 21 ultimate Merino wool; 142 yd [130 m]/1¾ oz [50 g]): #6 parchment, 10 (11, 13, 14, 16, 17) skeins.

Needles

Size U.S. 8 (5 mm): 32" circular (cir).

Size U.S. 7 (4.5 mm): set of double-pointed (dpn).

Adjust needle size if necessary to obtain the correct gauge.

Notions

Markers (m); stitch holders or waste yarn; tapestry needle.

Gauge

18 sts and 28 rows = 4" in St st on larger needle.

57 sts of cable panel = 7½" wide.

Notes

■ This cardigan is worked mostly in a modular fashion. First the back cable panel is worked from the bottom up. The sides are worked by picking up stitches from the sides of the cable panel and working outward toward the sleeve cuffs. Stitches for the ribbed lower edging are picked up from the body and worked downward. Stitches for the collar are worked from held cable panel stitches and picked up from the body, then worked outward.

■ A circular needle is used to accommodate the large number of stitches.

Back Cable Panel

With cir needle, CO 49 sts. Do not join.

Beg with a WS row, work Rows 1–28 of Cable chart 5 (5, 6, 6, 6, 6) times, then work Rows 1–10 (1–10, 1–2, 1–2, 1–10, 1–10) once more. Do not break yarn.

Place sts on holder.

Left Side

With cir needle and RS facing, using yarn from back cable panel, pick up and knit 100 (100, 112, 112, 118, 118) sts evenly along left edge of back cable panel (see Assembly Diagram 1). Do not join.

Work in St st for 1", ending with a WS row.

Inc row: (RS) K2, M1L, knit to end—1 st inc'd.

Rep Inc row every 6th row 5 (7, 9, 11, 13, 15) more times—106 (108, 122, 124, 132, 134) sts.

Work even until piece measures 13½ (14, 16, 16½, 17½, 18)" from pick-up row, ending with a WS row. Break yarn, leaving a 25" tail.

Fold in half and, with tail threaded on a tapestry needle, graft first 29 (28, 31, 30, 32, 31) sts to last 29 (28, 31, 30, 32, 31) sts using Kitchener st—48 (52, 60, 64, 68, 72) sts rem (see Assembly Diagram 2).

CUFF

Transfer sts to smaller dpn and, with RS facing, rejoin yarn at grafted row. Place marker (pm) and join in the rnd.

Next rnd: Knit to last st, sl 1 kwise wyb, pick up and knit 1 st from gap at join, return these 2 sts to left needle and k2tog tbl.

Next rnd: *K1, p2, k1; rep from * to end.

Work 18 (18, 8, 8, 8, 8) more rnds in rib patt as est.

Dec rnd: Ssk, work in patt to last 2 sts, k2tog—2 sts dec'd.

Rep Dec rnd every 20 (20, 10, 10, 10, 10)th rnd 3 (3, 7, 7, 7, 7) more times—40 (44, 44, 48, 52, 56) sts rem.

Work even until cuff measures 12".

BO all sts in patt.

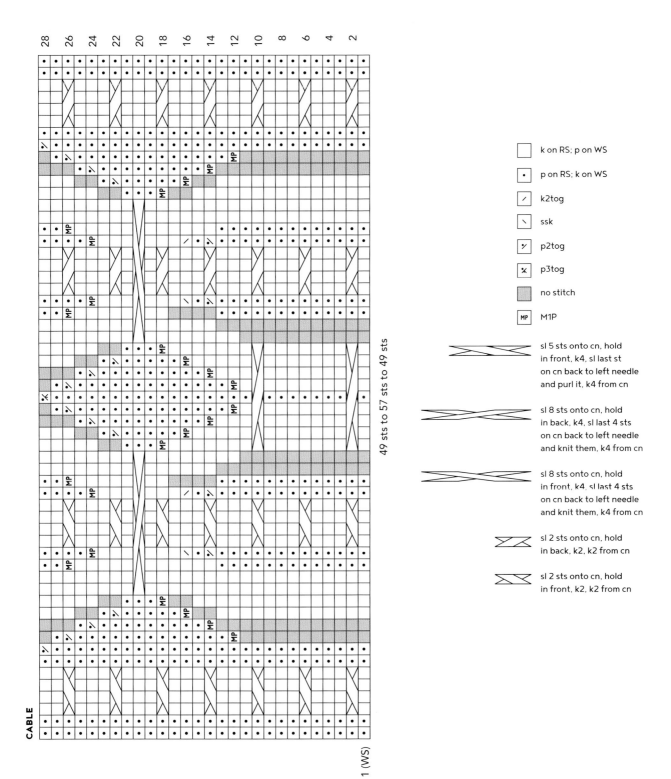

28 26 24 22 20 18 16 14 12 10 8 6 4 2

49 sts to 57 sts to 49 sts

CABLE

1 (WS)

k on RS; p on WS

• p on RS; k on WS

∕ k2tog

＼ ssk

∕ p2tog

✕ p3tog

no stitch

MP M1P

sl 5 sts onto cn, hold
in front, k4, sl last st
on cn back to left needle
and purl it, k4 from cn

sl 8 sts onto cn, hold
in back, k4, sl last 4 sts
on cn back to left needle
and knit them, k4 from cn

sl 8 sts onto cn, hold
in front, k4, sl last 4 sts
on cn back to left needle
and knit them, k4 from cn

sl 2 sts onto cn, hold
in back, k2, k2 from cn

sl 2 sts onto cn, hold
in front, k2, k2 from cn

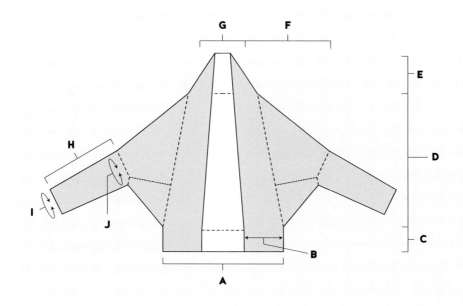

A: 18 (20, 22, 24, 26, 28)"

B: 5½ (6½, 7½, 8½, 9½, 10½)"

C: 4"

D: 21½ (21½, 24¼, 24¼, 25½, 25½)"

E: 5½ (6½, 7½, 8½, 9½, 10½)"

F: 13½ (14, 16, 16½, 17½, 18)"

G: 7½"

H: 12"

I: 7¼ (8, 8, 8¾, 9½, 10¼)"

J: 10¾ (11½, 13¼, 14¼, 15, 16)"

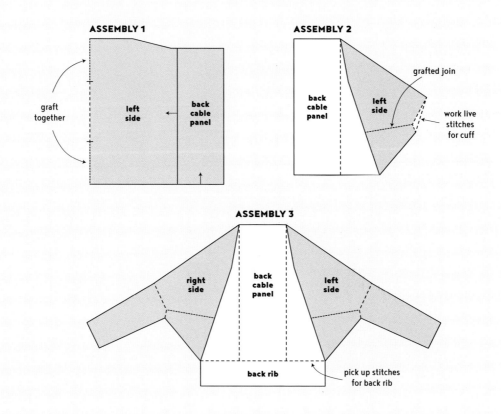

Right Side

With cir needle and RS facing, pick up and knit 100 (100, 112, 112, 118, 118) sts along right edge of back cable panel. Do not join.

Work in St st for 1", ending with a WS row.

Inc row: (RS) Knit to last 2 sts, M1R, k2—1 st inc'd.

Rep Inc row every 6th row 5 (7, 9, 11, 13, 15) more times—106 (108, 122, 124, 132, 134) sts.

Work even until piece measures 13½ (14, 16, 16½, 17½, 18)" from pick-up row, ending with a WS row. Break yarn, leaving a 25" tail.

Fold in half and, with tail threaded on a tapestry needle, graft first 29 (28, 31, 30, 32, 31) sts to last 29 (28, 31, 30, 32, 31) sts using Kitchener st—48 (52, 60, 64, 68, 72) sts rem.

CUFF
Work as for left side.

Back Rib

With cir needle and RS facing, beg at CO edge 5¼ (6¼, 7¼, 8¼, 9¼, 10¼)" to right of cable panel, pick up and knit 31 (37, 43, 49, 55, 61) sts evenly along left side edge, 49 sts along cable panel, and 31 (37, 43, 49, 55, 61) sts along right side edge, ending 5¼ (6¼, 7¼, 8¼, 9¼, 10¼)" to left of cable panel (see Assembly Diagram 3)—111 (123, 135, 147, 159, 171) sts total.

Row 1: (WS) P1, [k2, p4] 9 (10, 11, 12, 13, 14) times, k1, [p4, k2] 9 (10, 11, 12, 13, 14) times, p1.

Row 2: (RS) K1, [p2, k4] 9 (10, 11, 12, 13, 14) times, p1, [k4, p2] 9 (10, 11, 12, 13, 14) times, k1.

Row 3: Rep Row 1.

Row 4: K1, p2 (0, 2, 0, 2, 0), k4 (0, 4, 0, 4, 0), [p2, sl 2 sts onto cn, hold in back, k2, k2 from cn, p2, k4] 4 (5, 5, 6, 6, 7) times, p1, [k4, p2, sl 2 sts onto cn, hold in front, k2, k2 from cn, p2] 4 (5, 5, 6, 6, 7) times, k4 (0, 4, 0, 4, 0), p2 (0, 2, 0, 2, 0), k1.

Rep Rows 1–4 until rib measures 4", ending with Row 1.

BO all sts in patt.

Front Rib

With cir needle and RS facing, beg at bottom edge of right front, pick up and knit 20 sts along right edge of back rib, 100 (100, 108, 108, 116, 116) sts along edge of right side, return 49 held sts to left needle and knit them, dec 5 sts evenly spaced, pick up and knit 100 (100, 108, 108, 116, 116) sts along edge of left side, and 20 sts along left edge of back rib to bottom edge of left front—284 (284, 300, 300, 316, 316) sts total.

Next row: (WS) *P4, k4; rep from * to last 4 sts, p4.

Work in rib patt as est for 5½ (6½, 7½, 8½, 9½, 10½)", ending with a WS row. BO all sts in patt.

Finishing

Weave in ends.

Block to measurements.

alice hoodie

Kristen TenDyke

Finished Size

Bust circumference, buttoned: 33 (37, 41, 45, 49, 53)".

Cardigan shown measures 33"; modeled with 1" of negative ease.

Yarn

Worsted weight (#4 medium).

Shown here: O-Wool Local (50% alpaca, 50% certified organic Merino wool; 240 yd [219 m]/3½ oz [100 g]): bluebell, 5 (5, 6, 6, 6, 7) skeins.

Needles

Size U.S. 9 (5.5 mm): 32" circular (cir) and set of double-pointed (dpn).

Adjust needle size if necessary to obtain the correct gauge.

Notions

Markers (m); stitch holders or waste yarn; tapestry needle; seven 1" buttons.

Gauge

16 sts and 25 rows = 4" in St st.

10-st right or left cable = 1¼" wide.

Notes

- The body of this cardigan is worked back and forth in one piece from the lower edge to the underarms. The sleeves are worked separately in the round, then the sleeves and body are joined to work the yoke back and forth.
- A circular needle is used to accommodate the large number of stitches.

STITCH GUIDE

Garter Ridge Pattern:

Rows 1 and 3: (RS) Knit.

Row 2: Purl.

Row 4: Knit.

Rep Rows 1-4 for patt.

Body

With cir needle, CO 133 (149, 165, 181, 197, 213) sts. Do not join.

Next row: (RS) K4 (5, 5, 6, 6, 7), place marker (pm), p1, k4, p1, pm, k44 (50, 58, 64, 72, 78), pm, p1, k4, p1, pm, k13 (15, 15, 17, 17, 19), pm, p1, k4, p1, pm, k44 (50, 58, 64, 72, 78), pm, p1, k4, p1, pm, k4 (5, 5, 6, 6, 7).

Next row: (WS) *Knit to m, sl m, k1, p4, k1, sl m; rep from * 3 more times, knit to end.

Cont in patt as est for 3 more rows.

Inc row: (WS) *Purl to m, sl m, k1, [RLPI, p1] 4 times, k1, sl m; rep from * 3 more times, purl to end—149 (165, 181, 197, 213, 229) sts.

Next row: (RS) Knit to m, sl m, work Right Cable chart over 10 sts, sl m, k22 (25, 29, 32, 36, 39), pm for side, k22 (25, 29, 32, 36, 39), sl m, work Left Cable chart over 10 sts, sl m, work in Garter Ridge patt (see Stitch Guide) to m, sl m, work Right Cable chart over 10 sts, sl m, k22 (25, 29, 32, 36, 39), pm for side, k22 (25, 29, 32, 36, 39), sl m, work Left Cable chart over 10 sts, sl m, knit to end.

Next row: (WS) Purl to m, sl m, work chart patt to m, sl m, [purl to m, sl m] 2 times, work chart patt to m, sl m, work Garter Ridge patt to m, sl m, work chart patt to m, sl m, [purl to m, sl m] 2 times, work chart patt to m, sl m, purl to end.

Cont in patt as est until piece measures 3" from CO, ending with a WS row.

SHAPE WAIST

Dec row: (RS) *Work in patt to 4 sts before side m, ssk, k2, sl m, k2, k2tog; rep from * once more, work in patt to end—4 sts dec'd.

Rep Dec row every 10th row 3 more times—133 (149, 165, 181, 197, 213) sts rem.

Work even for 11 rows, ending with a WS row.

Inc row: (RS) *Work in patt to 2 sts before side m, M1L, k2, sl m, k2, M1R; rep from * once more, work in patt to end—4 sts inc'd.

Rep Inc row every 8th row 3 more times—149 (165, 181, 197, 213, 229) sts.

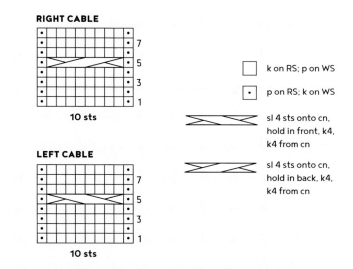

RIGHT CABLE

10 sts

LEFT CABLE

10 sts

☐ k on RS; p on WS

· p on RS; k on WS

sl 4 sts onto cn, hold in front, k4, k4 from cn

sl 4 sts onto cn, hold in back, k4, k4 from cn

Work even until piece measures 16½" from CO, ending with a RS row.

DIVIDE FOR FRONTS AND BACK

Next row: (WS) *Work in patt to side m, remove m, p5 (6, 7, 8, 9, 11), place last 10 (12, 14, 16, 18, 22) sts worked on holder for underarm; rep from * once more, work in patt to end—31 (34, 37, 40, 43, 45) sts rem for each front and 67 (73, 79, 85, 91, 95) sts rem for back. Do not break yarn.

Set aside.

Sleeves

With dpn and using the long-tail method, CO 32 (32, 34, 34, 36, 36) sts.

Distribute sts evenly over dpn and join in the rnd as foll:

Sl 1 pwise wyb, bring yarn to front between needles and return sl st to left needle, turn work. Pm for beg of rnd.

Note: *This makes purl bump of long-tail cast-on visible on RS.)*

[Knit 1 rnd, purl 1 rnd] 7 times.

Work in St st until piece measures 2½" from CO.

Inc rnd: K1, M1L, knit to last st, M1R, k1—2 sts inc'd.

Rep Inc rnd every 11 (10, 9, 8, 7, 7)th rnd 5 (5, 7, 6, 10, 5) more times, then every 9 (8, 7, 6, 5, 5)th rnd 4 (5, 4, 7, 4, 11) times—52 (54, 58, 62, 66, 70) sts.

Work even until piece measures 18½" from CO.

Place first and last 5 (6, 7, 8, 9, 11) sts of rnd on holder—42 (42, 44, 46, 48, 48) sts rem. Break yarn and place rem sts on separate holder.

Yoke

Joining row: (RS) Using yarn attached to body, work in patt across 31 (34, 37, 40, 43, 45) right front sts, pm for raglan, k42 (42, 44, 46, 48, 48) sleeve sts from holder, pm for raglan, work in patt across 67 (73, 79, 85, 91, 95) back sts, pm for raglan, k42 (42, 44, 46, 48, 48) sleeve sts from holder, pm for raglan, work in patt across 31 (34, 37, 40, 43, 45) left front sts—213 (225, 241, 257, 273, 281) sts total.

SHAPE RAGLAN ARMHOLES
SIZES 37 (41, 45, 49, 53)" ONLY

Next row: (WS) *Work to 1 st before raglan m, k1, sl m, k1; rep from * 3 more times, work to end. Body dec row (RS) *Work to 3 sts before raglan m, ssk, k1, sl m, knit to next raglan m, sl m, k1, k2tog; rep from * once more, work to end—4 sts dec'd.

Work 1 WS row.

Body and sleeve dec row: (RS) *Work to 3 sts before raglan m, ssk, k1, sl m, k1, k2tog; rep from * 3 more times, work to end—8 sts dec'd.

Rep last 4 rows 1 (1, 2, 2, 4) more time(s)—201 (217, 221, 237, 221) sts rem: 30 (33, 34, 37, 35) sts for each front, 38 (40, 40, 42, 38) sts for each sleeve, and 65 (71, 73, 79, 75) sts for back.

ALL SIZES

Next row: (WS) *Work to 1 st before raglan m, k1, sl m, k1; rep from * 3 more times, work to end.

Body and sleeve dec row: (RS) *Work to 3 sts before raglan m, ssk, k1, sl m, k1, k2tog; rep from * 3 more times, work to end—8 sts dec'd.

Rep last 2 rows 9 (7, 6, 6, 5, 4) more times—133 (137, 161, 165, 189, 181) sts rem: 21 (22, 26, 27, 31, 30) sts for each front, 22 (22, 26, 26, 30, 28) sts for each sleeve, and 47 (49, 57, 59, 67, 65) sts for back.

SHAPE NECK

Next row: (WS) BO 4 (5, 5, 6, 6, 7) sts, work in patt to end—129 (132, 156, 159, 183, 174) sts rem.

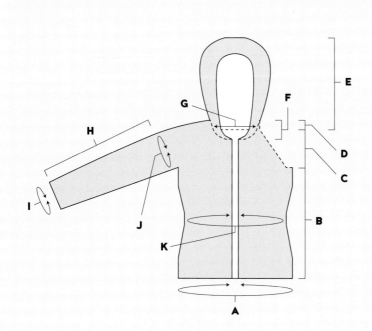

A: 32¼ (36¼, 40¼, 44¼, 48¼, 52¼)"

B: 16½"

C: 5 (5½, 6½, 7¼, 8¼, 8½)"

D: 1½"

E: 14¼ (14½, 14½, 14¾, 14¾, 15)"

F: 3 (3, 4½, 4½, 5¾, 5)

G: 6¾ (7¼, 7¼, 7¾, 7¾, 8¼)"

H: 18½"

I: 8 (8, 8½, 8½, 9, 9)"

J: 13 (13½, 14½, 15½, 16½, 17½)"

K: 28¼ (32¼, 36¼, 40¼, 44¼, 48¼)"

Next row: (RS) BO 4 (5, 5, 6, 6, 7) sts, *work to 3 sts before raglan m, ssk, k1, sl m, k1, k2tog; rep from * 3 more times, work to end—117 (119, 143, 145, 169, 159) sts rem: 16 (16, 20, 20, 24, 22) sts for each front, 20 (20, 24, 24, 28, 26) sts for each sleeve, and 45 (47, 55, 57, 65, 63) sts for back.

Neck dec row: (WS) P1, ssp, work to last 3 sts, p2tog, p1—2 sts dec'd.

Neck, body, and sleeve dec row: (RS) K1, k2tog, *work to 3 sts before raglan m, ssk, k1, sl m, k1, k2tog; rep from * 3 more times, work to last 3 sts, ssk, k1--10 sts dec'd.

Rep last 2 rows 3 more times—69 (71, 95, 97, 121, 111) sts rem: 4 (4, 8, 8, 12, 10) sts for each front, 12 (12, 16, 16, 20, 18) sts for each sleeve, and 37 (39, 47, 49, 57, 55) sts for back.

SIZES 41 (45, 49, 53)" ONLY

Body dec row: (WS) *Work to 3 sts before raglan m, p2tog, k1, sl m, k1, purl to 1 st before next raglan m, k1, sl m, k1, ssp; rep from * once more, work to end—4 sts dec'd.

Body and sleeve dec row: (RS) *Work to 3 sts before raglan m, ssk, k1, sl m, k1, k2tog; rep from * 3 more times, work to end—8 sts dec'd.

Rep last 2 rows 1 (1, 3, 2) more time(s)—71 (73, 73, 75) sts rem: 4 sts for each front, 12 sts for each sleeve, and 39 (41, 41, 43) sts for back.

ALL SIZES

▌ *Note:* On next row, sts are BO for stability, then picked up on the foll row.

Next row: (WS) Loosely BO all sts to first back cable m, remove m, work chart patt to next m, remove m, work in Garter Ridge patt to next cable m, remove m, work chart patt to next m, remove m, BO rem sts—33 (35, 35, 37, 37, 39) sts rem for back neck. Break yarn.

Hood

With cir needle and RS facing, beg at right front neck edge, pick up and knit 4 (5, 5, 6, 6, 7) sts evenly along front neck BO sts, 7 (7, 9, 9, 11, 11) sts along front neck edge, 3 sts along top of front BO sts, 12 sts along top of sleeve BO sts, then 2 sts along top of back to held sts, pm, work in patt as est across 33 (35, 35, 37, 37, 39) back neck sts, pm, then pick up and knit 2 sts along top of back, 12 sts along top of sleeve BO sts, 3 sts along top of front BO sts, 7 (7, 9, 9, 11, 11) sts along left front neck edge to BO sts, then 4 (5, 5, 6, 6, 7) sts along rem BO sts—89 (93, 97, 101, 105, 109) sts total.

Next row: (WS) Purl to m, sl m, work in patt as est to next m, sl m, purl to end.

Next row: (RS) Knit to m, sl m, work in patt as est to next m, sl m, knit to end.

Cont in patt as est until hood measures 1½" from pick-up row, ending with a WS row.

SHAPE HOOD

Inc row: (RS) Knit to 1 st before first m, M1L, k1, sl m, work in patt to next m, sl m, k1, M1R, knit to end—2 sts inc'd.

Rep Inc row every 12th row 2 more times—95 (99, 103, 107, 111, 115) sts.

Work even until hood measures 10" from pick-up row, ending with a WS row.

Dec row: (RS) Knit to 2 sts before m, ssk, sl m, work in patt to next m, sl m, k2tog, knit to end—2 sts dec'd.

Rep Dec row every RS row 2 more times—89 (93, 97, 101, 105, 109) sts rem: 33 (35, 35, 37, 37, 39) sts in center and 28 (29, 31, 32, 34, 35) sts at each side.

Work 1 WS row even.

Work short-rows as foll:

▌ *Note:* do not wrap sts at turns.

Short-row 1: (RS) Knit to first m, sl m, work in patt to next m, sl m, k2tog, turn—88 (92, 96, 100, 104, 108) sts rem.

Short-row 2: (WS) Sl 1 pwise wyf, sl m, work in patt to next m, sl m, ssp, turn—87 (91, 95, 99, 103, 107) sts rem.

Short-row 3: Sl 1 pwise wyb, sl m, work to m, sl m, k2tog, turn—1 st dec'd.

Short-row 4: Sl 1 pwise wyf, sl m, work to m, sl m, ssp, turn—1 st dec'd.

Rep last 2 short-rows 25 (26, 28, 29, 31, 32) more times—35 (37, 37, 39, 39, 41) sts rem; 1 st rem outside m at each side.

Place sts on holder.

Break yarn and set aside.

Finishing

Join underarms as foll:

Place 10 (12, 14, 16, 18, 22) held underarm sts on dpn, picking up 1 additional st at each end of each needle--12 (14, 16, 18, 20, 24) sts on each needle.

Hold needles parallel with RS tog and join sts using three-needle BO.

Block to measurements.

BUTTONBAND

With cir needle and RS facing, beg at lower edge of right front, pick up and knit 80 (83, 81, 84, 83, 87) sts evenly along right front edge to beg of hood, 44 sts along edge of hood to held sts, k35 (37, 37, 39, 39, 41) sts from holder, pick up and knit 44 sts along edge of hood, then 80 (83, 81, 84, 83, 87) sts along left front edge—283 (291, 287, 295, 293, 303) sts total.

Knit 1 WS row.

Buttonhole row: (RS) K3, [yo] 2 times, k2tog, *k10 (11, 10, 11, 11, 11), [yo] 2 times, k2tog; rep from * 5 more times, knit to end.

Next row: (WS) *Knit to double yo, knit into yo dropping extra wrap; rep from * 6 more times, knit to end.

Next row: (RS) *Knit to yo from previous row, knit into yo in row below; rep from * 6 more times, knit to end.

Knit 2 rows.

BO all sts kwise on WS.

Weave in ends.

Sew on buttons.

blue columbine cardigan

Mari Chiba

Finished Size

Bust circumference: 33½ (37, 41, 44¾, 48¼, 51¾, 55¼)".

Cardigan shown measures 37"; modeled with 4" of positive ease.

Yarn

DK weight (#3 light).

Shown here: Harrisville Designs Silk & Wool (50% silk, 50% wool; 175 yd [160 m]/1¾ oz [50 g]): #207 Veronica, 4 (5, 6, 7, 8, 8, 9) skeins.

Needles

Size U.S. 4 (3.5 mm): 32" circular (cir) and set of double-pointed (dpn).

Adjust needle size if necessary to obtain the correct gauge.

Notions

Markers (m); stitch holders or waste yarn; tapestry needle.

Gauge

23½ sts and 28 rows = 4" in St st.

7 sts = 4" in Lace patt.

Notes

- The body of this cardigan is worked back and forth in one piece to the underarms, then divided for working the fronts and back separately. Stitches for the sleeves are picked up around the armhole and the sleeves are knit from the top down with the sleeve caps shaped with short-rows.
- A circular needle is used to accommodate the large number of stitches.

STITCH GUIDE

Lace Pattern:
(even number of sts)

Row 1: (RS) *Ssk, yo; rep from * to last 2 sts, k2.

Row 2: (WS) Purl.

Row 3: K1, *yo, k2tog; rep from * to last st, k1.

Row 4: Purl.

Rep Rows 1–4 for patt.

Body

CO 166 (186, 206, 226, 246, 266, 286) sts. Do not join.

Knit 4 rows, ending with a RS row.

Next row: (WS) K44 (53, 59, 67, 76, 85, 95) sts for left front, place marker (pm), k78 (80, 88, 92, 94, 96, 96) sts for back, pm, k44 (53, 59, 67, 76, 85, 95) sts for right front.

Next row: (RS) Knit to m, sl m, work Lace patt (see Stitch Guide) to m, sl m, knit to end.

Next row: Purl.

Cont in patt as est until piece measures about 11¼ (11¼, 9¾, 9¾, 9¾, 11¼, 10¾)" from CO, ending with Row 4 of Lace patt.

SHAPE V-NECK

SIZES 48¼ (51¾, 55¼)" ONLY

Dec row: (RS) K2, [ssk] 2 times, work in patt to last 6 sts, [k2tog] 2 times, k2—4 sts dec'd.

Rep Dec row every other row 1 (7, 13) more time(s)—238 (234, 230) sts rem.

Work 1 WS row even.

SIZES 37 (41, 44¾, 48¼, 51¾)" ONLY

Dec row: (RS) K2, ssk, work in patt to last 4 sts, k2tog, k2—2 sts dec'd.

Rep Dec row every other row 1 (1, 3, 3, 1) more time(s)—182 (202, 218, 230, 230) sts rem.

Work 1 WS row even.

ALL SIZES

Next row: (RS) K2, [ssk] 0 (1, 1, 1, 1, 1, 1) time, knit to m, sl m, M1R, ssk, *ssk, yo; rep from * to 2 sts before m, k2tog, M1L, sl m, knit to last 2 (4, 4, 4, 4, 4, 4) sts, [k2tog] 0 (1, 1, 1, 1, 1, 1) time, k2—166 (180, 200, 216, 228, 228, 228) sts rem.

Next row: Purl.

Next row: K2, [ssk] 0 (1, 1, 1, 1, 1, 1) time, knit to m, sl m, k1, M1R, ssk, *yo, k2tog; rep from * to 3 sts before m, k2tog, M1L, k1, sl m, knit to last 2 (4, 4, 4, 4, 4, 4) sts, [k2tog] 0 (1, 1, 1, 1, 1, 1) time, k2—166 (178, 198, 214, 226, 226, 226) sts rem.

Next row: Purl.

Next row: K2, [ssk] 0 (1, 1, 1, 1, 1, 1) time, knit to m, sl m, k2, M1R, ssk, *ssk, yo; rep from * to 4 sts before m, k2tog, M1L, k2, sl m, knit to last 2 (4, 4, 4, 4, 4, 4) sts, [k2tog] 0 (1, 1, 1, 1, 1, 1) time, k2—166 (176, 196, 212, 224, 224, 224) sts rem.

Next row: Purl.

Next row: K2, [ssk] 0 (1, 1, 1, 1, 1, 1) time, knit to m, sl m, k3, M1R, ssk, *yo, k2tog; rep from * to 5 sts before m, k2tog, M1L, k3, sl m, knit to last 2 (4, 4, 4, 4, 4, 4) sts, [k2tog] 0 (1, 1, 1, 1, 1, 1) time, k2—166 (174, 194, 210, 222, 222, 222) sts rem.

Next row: Purl.

Next row: K2, ssk, knit to m, sl m, k4, M1R, ssk, *ssk, yo; rep from * to 6 sts before m, k2tog, M1L, k4, sl m, knit to last 4 sts, k2tog, k2—164 (172, 192, 208, 220, 220, 220) sts rem.

Next row: Purl.

Next row: K2, ssk, knit to m, sl m, k5, M1R, ssk, *yo, k2tog; rep from * to 7 sts before m, k2tog, M1L, k5, sl m, knit to last 4 sts, k2tog, k2—162 (170, 190, 206, 218, 218, 218) sts rem.

Next row: Purl.

Cont in back lace patt as est, working 2 fewer sts in lace patt and 2 more sts in St st every RS row, ***at the same time***, dec 1 neck st each side as est every RS row 12 (10, 16, 16, 14, 12, 10) more times—138 (150, 158, 174, 190, 194, 198) sts rem: 78 (80, 88, 92, 94, 96, 96) back sts and 30 (35, 35, 41, 48, 49, 51) sts for each front.

Purl 1 WS row—piece measures about 16½ (16½, 16½, 17, 17, 19¼, 19¼)" from CO.

DIVIDE FOR FRONTS AND BACK

Next row: (RS) K2, ssk, knit to 4 (4, 5, 5, 6, 7, 7) sts before m and place 25 (30, 29, 35, 41, 41, 43) sts just worked on holder for right front, place next 8 (8, 10, 10, 12, 14, 14) sts on holder for underarm, join new yarn and work in patt as est (working 2 fewer sts in lace patt and 2 more sts in St st) to 4 (4, 5, 5, 6, 7, 7) sts before m, place next 8 (8, 10, 10, 12, 14, 14) sts on holder for underarm, place rem 26 (31, 30, 36, 42, 42, 44) sts on holder for left front—70 (72, 78, 82, 82, 82, 82) sts rem for back.

Back

SHAPE ARMHOLES

Dec row: (WS) P2, p2tog, purl to last 4 sts, ssp, p2—68 (70, 76, 80, 80, 80, 80) sts rem.

Dec row: (RS) K2, ssk, work in patt to last 4 sts, k2tog, k2—66 (68, 74, 78, 78, 78, 78) sts rem.

SIZE 33½" ONLY

Next row: Purl.

SIZES 37 (41, 44¾, 48¼, 51¾, 55¼)" ONLY

Next row: P2, p2tog, purl to last 4 sts, ssp, p2—66 (72, 76, 76, 76, 76) sts rem.

ALL SIZES

Cont in lace patt as est until 4 sts rem between M1R and M1L (last RS row worked has only 1 yo).

Purl 1 WS row.

Next row: (RS) K31 (31, 34, 36, 36, 36, 36), M1R, ssk, k2tog, M1L, knit to end.

Work in St st over all sts until armhole measures 6¼ (6¾, 7½, 8, 8¼, 8¾, 9½)", ending with a WS row.

Shape shoulders using short-rows as foll:

Short-row 1: (RS) Knit to last 5 sts, wrap next st, turn.

Short-row 2: (WS) Purl to last 5 sts, wrap next st, turn.

Short-row 3: Knit to 5 sts before wrapped st, wrap next st, turn.

Short-row 4: Purl to 5 sts before wrapped st, wrap next st, turn.

Rep last 2 short-rows 0 (0, 1, 1, 2, 2, 3) more time(s).

Next row: (RS) Knit to end, working wraps tog with wrapped sts.

Next row: Purl to end, working wraps tog with wrapped sts.

Next row: Knit. Place sts on holder.

Right Front

Return 25 (30, 29, 35, 41, 41, 43) right front sts to needle and, with WS facing, rejoin yarn.

SHAPE ARMHOLE AND NECK

Dec row: (WS) P2, p2tog, purl to end—24 (29, 28, 34, 40, 40, 42) sts rem.

Dec row: (RS) K2, ssk, knit to last 4 sts, k2tog, k2—22 (27, 26, 32, 38, 38, 40) sts rem.

Next row: Purl.

Next row: K2, ssk, knit to end—1 st dec'd.

Next row: Purl. Rep last 2 rows 9 (14, 10, 14, 20, 20, 22) more times—12 (12, 15, 17, 17, 17, 17) sts rem.

Work even until armhole measures 6¼ (6¾, 7½, 8, 8¼, 8¾, 9½)", ending with a WS row.

Shape shoulder using short-rows as foll:

Short-row 1: (RS) Knit to last 5 sts, wrap next st, turn.

Short-row 2: (WS) Purl to end.

Short-row 3: Knit to 5 sts before wrapped st, wrap next st, turn.

Short-row 4: Purl to end.

Rep last 2 short-rows 0 (0, 1, 1, 2, 2, 3) more time(s).

Next row: (RS) Knit to end, working wraps tog with wrapped sts.

Work 2 rows even. Place sts on holder.

Left Front

Return 26 (31, 30, 36, 42, 42, 44) left front sts to needle and, with RS facing, rejoin yarn.

SHAPE ARMHOLE AND NECK

Dec row: (RS) Knit to last 4 sts, k2tog, k2—25 (30, 29, 35, 41, 41, 43) sts rem.

Dec row: (WS) Purl to last 4 sts, ssp, p2—24 (29, 28, 34, 40, 40, 42) sts rem.

Dec row: K2, ssk, knit to last 4 sts, k2tog, k2—22 (27, 26, 32, 38, 38, 40) sts rem.

Next row: Purl.

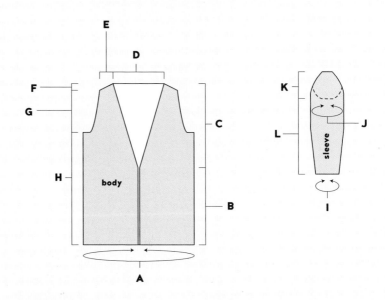

BODY

A: 33½ (37, 41, 44¾, 48¼, 51¾, 55¼)"

B: 1¼ (11¼, 9¾, 9¾, 9¾, 11¼, 10¾)"

C: 2½ (13, 15¼, 16½, 17¼, 18½, 19¾)"

D: 7¼"

E: 2 (2, 2½, 2¾, 2¾, 2¾, 2¾)"

F: ½ (½, ¾, ¾, 1¼, 1¼, 1½)"

G: 6¾ (7¼, 7¾, 8½, 8¾, 9¼, 9¾)"

H: 16½ (16½, 16½, 17, 17, 19¼, 19¼)"

SLEEVE

I: 7 (7¾, 8¼, 9, 9, 9, 9)"

J: 10¼ (10¾, 11¾, 12¾, 13¾, 14¾, 15¾)"

K: 4 (4¼, 4¼, 5, 5¼, 5½, 6)"

L: 11¼ (11¼, 12, 13, 13½, 15¾, 16)"

SLEEVE

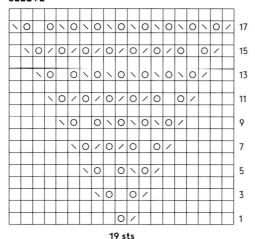

19 sts

knit

k2tog

ssk

yo

Next row: Knit to last 4 sts, k2tog, k2—1 st dec'd.

Next row: Purl.

Rep last 2 rows 9 (14, 10, 14, 20, 20, 22) more times—12 (12, 15, 17, 17, 17, 17) sts rem.

Work even until armhole measures 6¼ (6¾, 7½, 8, 8¼, 8¾, 9½)", ending with a RS row.

Shape shoulder, using short-rows as foll:

Short-row 1: (WS) Purl to last 5 sts, wrap next st, turn.

Short-row 2: (RS) Knit to end.

Short-row 3: Purl to 5 sts before wrapped st, wrap next st, turn.

Short-row 4: Knit to end.

Rep last 2 short-rows 0 (0, 1, 1, 2, 2, 3) more time(s).

Next row: (WS) Purl to end, working wraps tog with wrapped sts.

Work 1 row even. Place sts on holder.

Join shoulders, using three-needle BO—42 sts rem for back neck.

Sleeves

With dpn and RS facing, k4 (4, 5, 5, 6, 7, 7) sts from underarm holder, pm for beg-of-rnd, k4 (4, 5, 5, 6, 7, 7) sts from underarm holder, pick up and knit 52 (55, 59, 65, 69, 73, 79) sts evenly around armhole, knit to end—60 (63, 69, 75, 81, 87, 93) sts.

Shape cap using short-rows as foll:

Short-row 1: (RS) K40 (42, 46, 50, 54, 58, 62), wrap next st, turn.

Short-row 2: (WS) P20 (21, 23, 25, 27, 29, 31), wrap next st, turn.

Short-row 3: Knit to wrapped st, knit wrap tog with wrapped st, wrap next st, turn.

Short-row 4: Purl to wrapped st, purl wrap tog with wrapped st, wrap next st, turn.

Rep last 2 short-rows 14 (15, 16, 18, 19, 20, 22) more times.

Beg working in the rnd.

Next rnd: Knit, working wraps tog with wrapped sts. Work in St st until sleeve measures 3½" from underarm.

Dec rnd: K1, k2tog, knit to last 3 sts, ssk, k1—2 sts dec'd.

Rep Dec rnd every 7 (7, 7, 6, 6, 5)th rnd 6 (6, 7, 8, 10, 13, 16) more times—46 (49, 53, 57, 59, 59, 59) sts rem.

SIZE 33½" ONLY

Next rnd: K1, k2tog, knit to end—45 sts rem.

ALL SIZES

Next rnd: K13 (15, 17, 19, 20, 20, 20), pm, work Sleeve chart over 19 sts, pm, knit to end.

Cont working chart between m through Rnd 18, *at the same time*, cont to dec 2 sts every 7 (7, 7, 6, 6, 5)th rnd 2 (2, 2, 2, 3, 3, 3) times—41 (45, 49, 53, 53, 53, 53) sts rem.

BO all sts using the I-cord method.

Edging

With RS facing, pick up and knit 3 sts for every 4 rows along right front edge, k42 back neck sts from holder, pick up and knit 3 sts for every 4 rows along left front edge.

Next row: (WS) Purl.

BO all sts using the I-cord method.

Finishing

Weave in ends.

Block to measurements.

wilderness cardigan

Megan Nodecker

Finished Size

Bust circumference, excluding collar: 30¾ (38¼, 46, 53½, 61)".

Cardigan shown measures 38¼"; modeled with 5¼" of positive ease.

Yarn

DK weight (#3 light).

Shown here: The Fibre Co. Acadia (60% Merino wool, 20% baby alpaca, 20% silk; 145 yd [133 m]/1¾ oz [50 g]): sand, 7 (8, 10, 11, 13) skeins.

Needles

Size U.S. 8 (5 mm): 16" and 32" circular (cir).

Adjust needle size if necessary to obtain the correct gauge.

Notions

Markers (m); stitch holders or waste yarn; tapestry needle.

Gauge

17 sts and 25 rows = 4" in Wheat Lace patt.

Notes

■ The body of this cardigan is worked back and forth in one piece from the lower edge to the underarm, then the upper fronts and back are worked separately. The sleeves are picked up from the armholes and worked in the round.

■ A circular needle is used to accommodate the large number of stitches on the body and collar.

■ The Wheat Lace chart is worked both in rounds and back and forth in rows. When working in rounds, work every row as a right-side row.

Seed Stitch in Rows: (odd number of sts)

Row 1: (RS) K2, *p1, k1; rep from * to last st, k1.

Row 2: (WS) P2, *p1, k1; rep from * to last 3 sts, p3.

Rep Rows 1 and 2 for patt.

Seed Stitch in Rounds: (even number of sts)

Rnd 1: *K1, p1; rep from * to end.

Rnd 2: *P1, k1; rep from * to end.

Rep Rnds 1 and 2 for patt.

Body

With longer cir needle, CO 131 (163, 195, 227, 259) sts. Do not join.

Work Seed st in rows (see Stitch Guide) for 6 rows.

Work Wheat Lace chart until piece measures 20 (21¼, 21¼, 21¼, 22½)" from CO, ending with a WS row.

DIVIDE FOR FRONTS AND BACK

Next row: (RS) Work 33 (41, 49, 57, 65) sts in patt, place next 64 (80, 96, 112, 128) sts on holder for back, then place foll 34 (42, 50, 58, 66) sts on holder for left front—33 (41, 49, 57, 65) sts rem for right front.

Right Front

Next row: (WS) Using the backward-loop method, CO 2 sts, purl to end—35 (43, 51, 59, 67) sts.

Working chart over all sts, cont in patt until armhole measures 7½ (7½, 8½, 9½, 9½)", ending with a WS row.

Place sts on holder.

Back

Return 64 (80, 96, 112, 128) held back sts to needle and, with RS facing, rejoin yarn.

Next row: (RS) CO 1 st, work in patt to end—65 (81, 97, 113, 129) sts.

Next row: (WS) CO 2 sts, purl to end—67 (83, 99, 115, 131) sts.

Working chart over all sts, cont in patt until armhole measures 7½ (7½, 8½, 9½, 9½)", ending with a WS row.

JOIN RIGHT SHOULDER

Place sts from right front holder onto separate needle. With RS tog, join 34 (42, 50, 58, 66) shoulder sts using three-needle BO, then BO rem 1 right front st—33 (41, 49, 57, 65) sts rem for back.

Place back sts on holder.

Left Front

Return 34 (42, 50, 58, 66) held left front sts to needle and, with RS facing, rejoin yarn.

Next row: (RS) CO 1 st, work in patt to end—35 (43, 51, 59, 67) sts.

Working chart over all sts, cont in patt until armhole measures 7½ (7½, 8½, 9½, 9½)", ending with a WS row.

JOIN LEFT SHOULDER

Place sts from back holder onto separate needle. With RS tog, join 33 (41, 49, 57, 65) shoulder sts using three-needle BO, then BO rem 2 left front sts.

WHEAT LACE

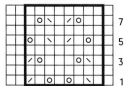

8-st rep

	k on RS; p on WS
o	yo
/	k2tog
\	ssk
	pattern repeat

Sleeves

With shorter cir needle and RS facing, beg at center of underarm, pick up and knit 64 (64, 72, 80, 80) sts evenly spaced around armhole edge. Place marker and join in the rnd.

Working 8-st rep of chart only, work Wheat Lace chart until piece measures 7¾ (7¾, 9, 9, 10¼)" from underarm, ending with an odd-numbered chart row.

Work Seed st in rnds (see Stitch Guide) for 6 rnds.

BO all sts in patt.

Finishing

Weave in ends.

Block to measurements.

COLLAR

With longer cir needle and RS facing, beg at right front lower edge, pick up and knit 221 (233, 243, 253, 265) sts evenly spaced up right front edge and down left front edge, ending at left front lower edge.

Beg with Row 2, work Seed st in rows for 4".

Loosely BO all sts in patt.

Sew any holes closed at the underarms and back of neck.

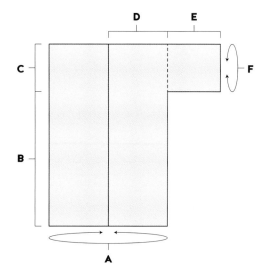

A: 30¾ (38¼, 46, 53½, 61)"

B: 20 (21¼, 21¼, 21¼, 22½)"

C: 7½ (7½, 8½, 9½, 9½)"

D: 7¾ (9½, 11½, 13¼, 15¼)"

E: 8½ (8½, 9¾, 9¾, 11)"

F: 15 (15, 17, 18¾, 18¾)"

two trees cardigan

Meghan Babin

Finished Size

Bust circumference: 30½ (36, 41½, 42½, 47½)", including a - (2½, 5, -, 2)" gap or ½ (-, -, 1, -)" overlap at center front.

Cardigan shown measures 36"; modeled with 4" of positive ease.

Yarn

DK weight (#3 light).

Shown here: Hudson Valley Fibers Moodna (60% USA wool, 40% New York State Romney wool; 260 yd [238 m]/3½ oz [100 g]): morel, 4 (5, 5, 6, 6) skeins.

Needles

Size U.S. 5 (3.75 mm): 32" circular (cir).

Adjust needle size if necessary to obtain the correct gauge.

Notions

Markers (m); cable needle (cn); spare needle in same size or smaller than working needle for three-needle BO; stitch holders or waste yarn; tapestry needle.

Gauge

23 sts and 32 rows = 4" in charted patt.

Notes

■ The body of this cardigan is worked back and forth in one piece from the lower edge to the underarm, then the upper fronts and back are worked separately. The sleeves are worked back and forth.

■ A circular needle is used to accommodate the large number of stitches.

STITCH GUIDE

1/2 RC: Sl 2 sts onto cn, hold in back, k1, k2 from cn.

1/2 LC: Sl 1 st onto cn, hold in front, k2, k1 from cn.

1/2 DecRC: Sl 2 sts onto cn, hold in back, k1, k1 from cn, transfer st from cn to left needle, ssk—1 st dec'd.

1/2 DecLC: Sl 1 pwise, sl 1 st onto cn, hold in front, transfer st from right needle to left needle, k2tog, k1, k1 from cn—1 st dec'd.

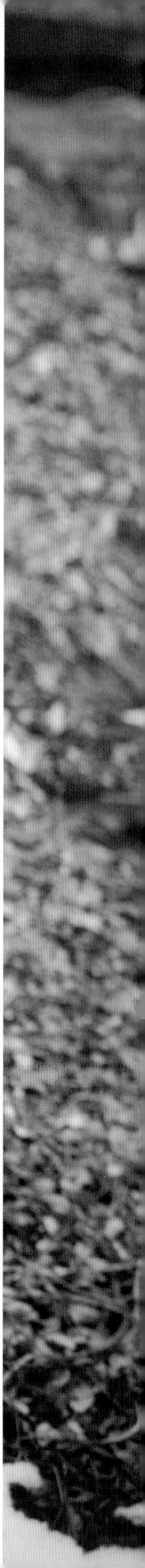

Body

Using the long-tail method, CO 176 (193, 210, 244, 261) sts. Do not join.

Next row: (WS) P6, knit to last 6 sts, p6.

Next row: (RS) 1/2 LC (see Stitch Guide), 1/2 RC (see Stitch Guide), knit to last 6 sts, 1/2 LC, 1/2 RC.

Rep last 2 rows 3 more times.

Beg with a WS row, work Rows 1–8 of Body chart once, then rep Rows 3–8 of chart until piece measures 15 (15, 15½, 15½, 16)" from CO, ending with Row 8.

DIVIDE FOR FRONTS AND BACK

Next row: (WS) Work 45 (45, 45, 62, 62) sts in patt, p1f&b, transfer 1 st from right needle to left needle, place 46 (46, 46, 63, 63) sts from right needle on holder for left front, sl 1 pwise wyb, work 84 (101, 118, 118, 135) sts in patt, p1f&b, transfer 1 st from right needle to left needle, place 86 (103, 120, 120, 137) sts from right needle on holder for back, sl 1 pwise wyb, work in patt to end—46 (46, 46, 63, 63) sts rem for right front.

Right Front

Work even until armhole measures 1", ending with a WS row.

SHAPE NECK

Note: *Shoulder shaping beg before neck shaping ends; read the foll section all the way through before proceeding.*

Dec row: (RS) 1/2 LC, 1/2 DecRC (see Stitch Guide), work in patt to end—1 st dec'd.

Rep Dec row every 4th (6th, 6th, 2nd, 4th) row 15 (10, 10, 22, 17) more times—30 (35, 35, 40, 45) sts rem. **At the same time**, when armhole measures 8 (8½, 8½, 8¾, 8¾)", ending with a WS row, shape shoulder using German short-rows as foll:

Short-row 1: (RS) Work in patt to last 6 (6, 6, 9, 11) sts, turn.

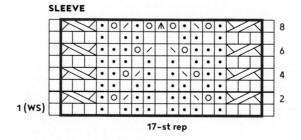

Short-row 2: (WS) Make double st, work in patt to end.

Short-row 3: Work in patt to 6 (6, 6, 9, 11) sts before double st, turn.

Short-row 4: Make double st, work in patt to end.

Short-rows 5 and 6: Rep Short-rows 3 and 4.

Next row: (RS) Work to end, working all double sts as single sts.

Place sts on holder.

Chart Legend

□	k on RS; p on WS	⋀	sl 2 as if to k2tog, k1, p2sso
•	p on RS; k on WS	□	pattern repeat
O	yo	⟋⟍	1/2 RC (see Stitch Guide)
⟋	k2tog	⟋⟍	1/2 LC (see Stitch Guide)
⟍	ssk		

Back

Return 86 (103, 120, 120, 137) held back sts to needle and, with RS facing, rejoin yarn.

Work even in patt until armhole measures 8 (8½, 8½, 8¾, 8¾)", ending with a WS row.

Shape shoulders and neck using short-rows as foll:

Short-row 1: (RS) Work in patt to last 6 (6, 6, 9, 11) sts, turn.

Short-row 2: (WS) Make double st, work in patt to last 6 (6, 6, 9, 11) sts, turn.

Short-row 3: Make double st, work 20 (25, 25, 27, 30) sts in patt, join new yarn and BO 32 (39, 56, 46, 53) sts, work to 6 (6, 6, 9, 11) sts before double st, turn—27 (32, 32, 37, 42) sts rem each side.

Short-row 4: Make double st, work to 2 sts before neck edge, ssp; p2tog, work to 6 (6, 6, 9, 11) sts before double st, turn—26 (31, 31, 36, 41) sts rem each side.

Short-row 5: Make double st, work to 2 sts before neck edge, k2tog; ssk, work to 6 (6, 6, 9, 11) sts before double st, turn—25 (30, 30, 35, 40) sts rem each side.

Short-row 6: Make double st, work to 2 sts before neck edge, ssp; p2tog, work to 6 (6, 6, 9, 11) sts before double st, turn—24 (29, 29, 34, 39) sts rem each side.

Short-row 7: Make double st, work to neck edge; work to end of left shoulder, working all double sts as single sts.

Place left shoulder sts on holder.

RIGHT SHOULDER
Next row: (WS) Work to end, working all double sts as single sts.

Place sts on holder.

Left Front

Return 46 (46, 46, 63, 63) held left front sts to needle and, with RS facing, rejoin yarn.

Work even until armhole measures 1", ending with a WS row.

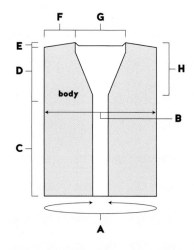

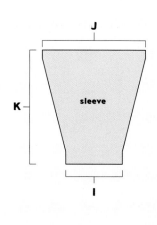

BODY

A: 30½ (33½, 36½, 42½, 45½)"

B: 15 (18, 20¾, 20¾, 23¾)"

C: 15 (15, 15½, 15½, 16)"

D: 6½ (7¾, 10¾, 9, 10¼)"

E: ¾"

F: 4¼ (5, 5, 6, 6¾)"

G: 8 (8½, 8½, 8¾, 8¾)"

H: 7¾ (8¼, 8¼, 8½, 8½)"

SLEEVE

I: 9¼"

J: 16¼ (16¾, 16¾, 17½, 17½)"

K: 18 (18, 18, 18½, 18½)"

SHAPE NECK

> **Note:** Shoulder shaping beg before neck shaping ends; read the foll section all the way through before proceeding.

Dec row: (RS) Work in patt to last 7 sts, 1/2 DecLC (see Stitch Guide), 1/2 RC—1 st dec'd.

Rep Dec row every 4th (6th, 6th, 2nd, 4th) row 15 (10, 10, 22, 17) more times—30 (35, 35, 40, 45) sts rem.

At the same time, when armhole measures 8 (8½, 8½, 8¾, 8¾)", ending with a RS row, shape shoulder using short-rows as foll:

Short-row 1: (WS) Work in patt to last 6 (6, 6, 9, 11) sts, turn.

Short-row 2: (RS) Make double st, work in patt to end.

Short-row 3: Work in patt to 6 (6, 6, 9, 11) sts before double st, turn.

Short-row 4: Make double st, work in patt to end.

Short-rows 5 and 6: Rep Short-rows 3 and 4.

Next row: (WS) Work to end, working all double sts as single sts.

Place sts on holder.

Sleeves

Using the long-tail method, CO 53 sts. Do not join.

Next row: (WS) P4, knit to last 4 sts, p4.

Next row: (RS) K1, 1/2 RC, knit to last 4 sts, 1/2 LC, k1.

Rep last 2 rows 3 more times.

> *Note: Sleeve shaping beg before first chart rep ends; read the foll section all the way through before proceeding.*

Beg with a WS row, work Rows 1-8 of Sleeve chart once, then rep Rows 3-8 as needed to end of sleeve.

At the same time, when piece measures 1" from CO, ending with a WS row, shape sleeve as foll:

Inc row: (RS) Work 4 sts in patt, M1L, work in patt to last 4 sts, M1R, work in patt to end—2 sts inc'd.

Rep Inc row every 6th row 19 (21, 21, 23, 23) more times, working new sts into patt—93 (97, 97, 101, 101) sts.

Work even until piece measures 18 (18, 18, 18½, 18½)" from CO. BO all sts.

Finishing

With RS tog, join 24 (29, 29, 34, 39) left shoulder sts using three-needle BO, leaving 6 cable sts at left front neck edge on holder.

Rep for right shoulder.

RIGHT NECKBAND

Return 6 held right front sts to needle and, with WS facing, rejoin yarn.

Next row: (WS) Purl.

Next row: (RS) 1/2 LC, 1/2 RC, pick up and knit 2 sts along back neck edge—8 sts.

Next row: (WS) Sl 1 pwise wyf, p7.

Next row :(RS) 1/2 LC, 1/2 RC, ssk, pick up and knit 1 st along back neck edge.

Rep last 2 rows until band reaches center back neck, ending with a RS row, but do not pick up a st on last row—7 sts rem.

Place sts on holder.

LEFT NECKBAND

Return 6 held left front sts to needle and, with RS facing, rejoin yarn.

Next row: (RS) 1/2 LC, 1/2 RC.

Next row: P6, pick up and purl 2 sts along back neck edge—8 sts.

Next row: K2, 1/2 LC, 1/2 RC.

Next row: P6, p2tog, pick up and purl 1 st along back neck edge.

Rep last 2 rows until band reaches center back neck, ending with a WS row, but do not pick up a st on last row—7 sts rem.

Place held 7 right neckband sts onto spare needle. With RS tog, join neckbands using three-needle BO.

Weave in ends.

Block pieces to measurements.

Sew sleeve seams using a ½-st seam allowance. Sew sleeves into armholes.

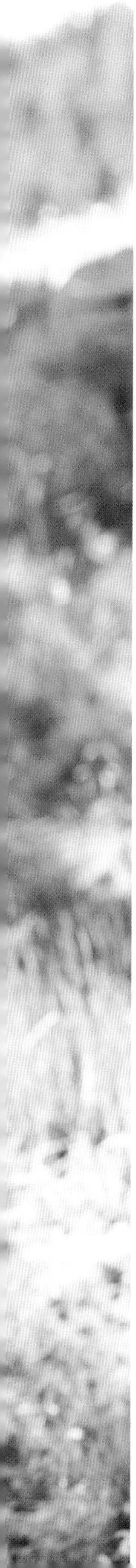

gyre cardigan

Norah Gaughan

Finished Size

Back width at sleeve opening:
16¼ (17, 17¾, 18½, 19½)".

Cardigan shown measures 17".

Yarn

DK weight (#3 light).

Shown here: Berroco Linus
(50% acrylic, 20% linen,
18% nylon, 12% viscose; 159
yd [145 m]/1¾ oz [50 g]):
#6834 charcoal, 7 (7, 7, 8, 8)
balls.

Needles

Size U.S. 7 (4.5 mm): 32"
circular (cir).

Size U.S. 8 (5 mm): 32" cir and
set of double-pointed (dpn).

*Adjust needle size if necessary
to obtain the correct gauge.*

Notions

Markers (m); removable m;
tapestry needle.

Gauge

20 sts and 28 rows = 4" in
St st on larger needle

Notes

■ This cardigan is worked back
and forth from the top down
as a ¾ circle, with openings
bound off and cast on for the
sleeves. Sleeves are picked up
and worked in the round from
the top down.

■ Eyelet increases, twisted
rib, and dropped stitches that
create a cobweb-like openness
alternate in concentric circles.
The fabric is very stretchy and
will accommodate a wide range
of sizes.

■ A circular needle is used
to accommodate the large
number of stitches.

Body

STOCKINETTE SECTION

With smaller needle, CO 8 sts. Do not join.

Row 1 and all WS rows: Purl.

Row 2: (RS) K2, [yo, k1] 5 times, k1—13 sts.

Row 4: K2, [yo, k1] 10 times, k1—23 sts.

Row 6: Knit.

Row 8: K2, [yo, k1] 20 times, k1—43 sts.

Rows 10 and 12: Knit.

Row 14: [K2, yo] 20 times, k3—63 sts.

Rows 16 and 18: Knit.

Row 20: K2, [yo, k3] 19 times, [yo, k2] 2 times—84 sts.

Rows 22 and 24: Knit.

Row 26: K2, [yo, k4] 20 times, yo, k2—105 sts.

Rows 28 and 30: Knit.

Row 31: Purl.

RIBBED SECTION

Next row: (RS) K2, *yo, k1; rep from * to last st, k1—207 sts.

Next row: P2, *k1, p1tbl; rep from * to last 3 sts, k1, p2.

Next row: K2, *p1, k1tbl; rep from * to last 3 sts, p1, k2.

Next row: P2, *k1, p1tbl; rep from * to last 3 sts, k1, p2.

Rep last 2 rows until ribbed section measures 4", ending with a WS row.

LACE SECTION

Place removable m at end of row.

Change to larger needle.

Next row: (RS) K2, p1, *k2tog tbl, yo, k1tbl, p1; rep from * to last 4 sts, k1tbl, p1, k2.

Next row: P2, *k1, p1tbl; rep from * to last 3 sts, k1, p2.

Next row: K2, *p1, k1tbl; rep from * to last 3 sts, p1, k2.

Next row: P2, *k1, p1tbl; rep from * to last 3 sts, k1, p2.

Rep last 2 rows until piece measures 1½ (2, 2½, 3, 3½)" from m, ending with a WS row.

ARMHOLE OPENING

Next row: (RS) K2, [p1, k1tbl] 18 times, *p1, k1tbl, pass 2nd st over first to BO 1 st, [drop next st *(caution: foll column down to make sure this is the column a yo made above marked row)* (yo, pass last st over yo) 3 times, (work 1 st, pass 2nd st over first to BO 1 st) 3 times] 7 times*, [p1, k1tbl] 35 times, rep from * to * once, [p1, k1tbl] 18 times, p1, k2—149 sts rem: 38 sts before first armhole, 71 sts between armholes, 40 sts after 2nd armhole.

Next row: (WS) P2, [k1, p1tbl] 19 times, turn work so RS is facing, using the knitted method, CO 36 (41, 41, 46, 46) sts, turn work so WS is facing, [p1tbl, k1] 35 times, p1tbl, turn, CO 36 (41, 46, 46) sts, turn, [p1tbl, k1] 18 times, p2—221 (231, 231, 241, 241) sts.

Next row: K2, [p1, k1tbl] 18 times, *p1, [k2tog tbl, yo, k2tog tbl, p1] 7 (8, 8, 9, 9) times*, [k1tbl, p1] 35 times, k1tbl, rep from * to * once, [k1tbl, p1] 19 times, k2—207 (215, 215, 223, 223) sts rem.

Next row: P2, *k1, p1tbl; rep from * to last 3 sts, k1, p2.

Next row: (RS) K2, *p1, k1tbl; rep from * to last 3 sts, p1, k2.

Next row: (WS) P2, *k1, p1tbl; rep from * to last 3 sts, k1, p2.

Rep last 2 rows until piece measures 7" from m, ending with a WS row.

Next row: (RS) *(Caution: When dropping st, foll column down to make sure dropped st is the column a yo made above marked row or above armhole)* K2, p1, k1tbl, *drop next st, yo, k1tbl, p1, k1tbl; rep from * to last 3 sts, p1, k2. Next row (WS) P3, *p3, (k1, p1, k1) into yo; rep from * to last 4 sts, p4—307 (319, 319, 331, 331) sts. Remove m.

STOCKINETTE SECTION

Work even in St st for 8 rows.

Next row: (RS) K3, *yo, k2tog, k2; rep from * to end.

Work even in St st for 5 rows.

Next row: (RS) K2 (4, 4, 1, 1), *yo, k2tog, k3; rep from * to end.

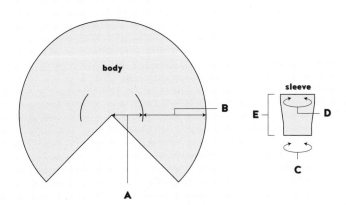

BODY
A: 10 (10½, 11, 11½, 12)"
B: 18"

SLEEVE
C: 9½ (10½, 11½, 12½, 13½)"
D: 11¼ (12, 13¼, 14, 15¼)"
E: 6½"

Work even in St st for 5 rows.

Next row: (RS) K5, *yo, k2tog, k4; rep from * to last 2 sts, k2.

Work even in St st for 5 rows.

RIBBED SECTION

Next row: (RS) K2, *yo, k2tog; rep from * to last st, k1.

Next row :P2, *k1, p1tbl; rep from * to last 3 sts, k1, p2.

Next row: (RS) K2, *p1, k1tbl; rep from * to last 3 sts, p1, k2.

Next row: (WS) P2, *k1, p1tbl; rep from * to last 3 sts, k1, p2.

Rep last 2 rows until ribbed section measures 3", ending with a WS row.

LACE SECTION

Place removable m at end of row.

Next row: (RS) K2, p1, *k2tog tbl, yo, k1tbl, p1; rep from * to last 4 sts, k1tbl, p1, k2.

Next row: P2, *k1, p1tbl; rep from * to last 3 sts, k1, p2.

Next row: K2, *p1, k1tbl; rep from * to last 3 sts, p1, k2.

Next row: P2, *k1, p1tbl; rep from * to last 3 sts, k1, p2.

Rep last 2 rows until piece measures 4½ (5, 5½, 6, 6½)" from m, ending with a WS row.

Next row: (RS) *(Caution: When dropping st, foll column down to make sure dropped st is the column a yo made above marked row)* K2, p1, k1tbl, *drop next st, yo, k1tbl, p1, k1tbl; rep from * to last 3 sts, p1, k2.

Next row: (WS) P3, *p3, (k1, p1, k1) into yo; rep from * to last 4 sts, p4—457 (475, 475, 493, 493) sts. Work even in St st for 4 rows.

Next row: (RS) K2, *yo, k2tog; rep from * to last st, k1.

With WS facing, BO all sts kwise.

Sleeves

With larger dpn, RS facing, and beg at center of armhole CO, pick up and knit 56 (60, 66, 70, 76) sts evenly spaced around armhole. Pm and join in the rnd.

Knit 8 rnds.

Dec rnd: (RS) K2, k2tog, knit to last 4 sts, ssk, k2—2 sts dec'd.

Rep Dec rnd every 8th rnd 3 more times—48 (52, 58, 62, 68) sts rem.

Work even until piece measures 6" from pick-up rnd.

Next rnd: *Yo, k2tog; rep from * around.

Knit 2 rnds.

BO all sts pwise.

Finishing

Weave in ends.

Steam or wet block.

agrotera pullover

Amanda Bell

Finished Size

Bust circumference: 35¼ (38¾, 43¼, 46¾, 49¼)".

Pullover shown measures 35¼", modeled with 1¼" of positive ease.

Yarn

Worsted weight (#4 medium).

Shown here: The Fibre Company Cumbria (60% wool, 30% masham wool, 10% mohair; 238 yd [218 m]/3½ oz [100 g]): #56 catbells, 4 (5, 5, 6, 7) skeins.

Needles

Size U.S. 6 (4 mm): 16" circular (cir) and set of double-pointed (dpn).

Size U.S. 7 (4.5 mm): 16", 24", and 32" cirs, and set of dpn.

Adjust needle size if necessary to obtain the correct gauge.

Notions

Markers (m); stitch holders; tapestry needle.

Gauge

20 sts and 26 rnds = 4" in St st on larger needle.

Notes

■ This pullover is worked in the round from the top down.

STITCH GUIDE

Twisted Rib
(even number of sts)

Rnd 1: *K1tbl, p1; rep from * to end.

Rep Rnd 1 for patt.

Inc 1

Using the backward-loop method, CO 1 st—1 st inc'd.

Yoke

With smaller cir needle, CO 88 (88, 88, 96, 96) sts. Place marker (pm) and join in the rnd. Work in Twisted Rib (see Stitch Guide) for 1".

Change to larger 16" cir needle.

Work Rows 1–39 (1–39, 1–45, 1–45, 1–45) of Chart A, changing to longer cir needle when necessary—220 (220, 264, 288, 288) sts.

Next rnd: Remove m, k1tbl, p4 (4, 5, 5, 5), pm for new beg-of-rnd.

Work Rows 1–6 of Chart B for your size—264 (264, 308, 336, 336) sts.

SIZE 35¼" ONLY

Inc rnd: K26, Inc 1 (see Stitch Guide), *k26, Inc 1, k27, Inc 1; rep from * 3 more times, k26, Inc 1—274 sts.

SIZE 38¼" ONLY

Inc rnd: *[K8, Inc 1 (see Stitch Guide)] 3 times, k9, Inc 1; rep from * 7 more times—296 sts.

SIZE 43¼" ONLY

Inc rnd: *K22, Inc 1 (see Stitch Guide); rep from * 13 more times—322 sts.

SIZE 46¼" ONLY

Inc rnd: *[K17, Inc 1 (see Stitch Guide)] 4 times, k16, Inc 1; rep from * 3 more times—356 sts.

SIZE 49¼" ONLY

Inc rnd: *K10, Inc 1 (see Stitch Guide), k11, Inc 1; rep from * 15 more times—368 sts.

ALL SIZES

Knit 1 rnd. Work short-rows as foll:

Short-row 1: (RS) K8 (9, 10, 11, 11), wrap next st, turn.

Short-row 2: (WS) Purl to m, sl m, p8 (9, 10, 11, 11), wrap next st, turn.

Short-row 3: Knit to m, sl m, k16 (18, 20, 22, 22), wrap next st, turn.

Short-row 4: Purl to m, sl m, p16 (18, 20, 22, 22), wrap next st, turn.

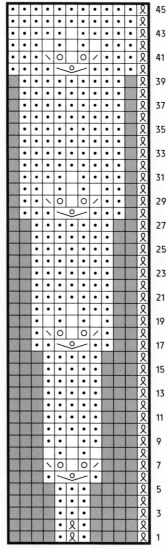

CHART A

4 st to 10 (10, 12, 12, 12) st repeat

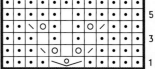

CHART B: SIZES 35¼" & 38¼"

10 st to 12 st repeat

CHART B: SIZES 43¼", 46¼" & 49¼"

12 st to 14 st repeat

 knit

 purl

k1tbl

yo

k2tog

ssk

no stitch

pattern repeat

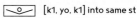 [k1, yo, k1] into same st

Short-row 5: Knit to m, sl m, k24 (27, 30, 33, 33), wrap next st, turn.

Short-row 6: Purl to m, sl m, p24 (27, 30, 33, 33), wrap next st, turn.

Short-row 7: Knit to m, sl m, k32 (36, 40, 44, 44), wrap next st, turn.

Short-row 8: Purl to m, sl m, p32 (36, 40, 44, 44), wrap next st, turn.

Short-row 9: Knit to m, sl m, k40 (45, 50, 55, 55), wrap next st, turn.

Short-row 10: Purl to m, sl m, p40 (45, 50, 55, 55), wrap next st, turn.

Knit 5 (8, 5, 8, 11) rnds, working wraps tog with wrapped sts.

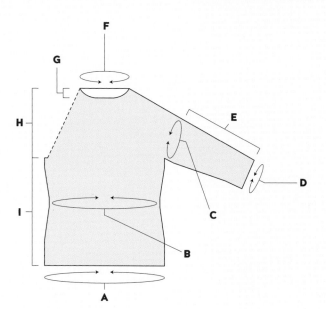

A: 35¼ (38¾, 43¼, 46¾, 49¼)"
B: 32 (35½, 40, 43½, 46)"
C: 12 (12½, 13½, 15¼, 46)"
D: 9½ (10, 10¾, 11¼, 11½)"
E: 13"
F: 17½, 17½, 17½, 19¼, 19¼)"
G: 1½"
H: 10½ (11, 11½, 12, 12½)"
I: 17 (17, 16¼, 16¼, 16)"

DIVIDE FOR BODY AND SLEEVES

Next rnd: K42 (46, 51, 55, 57) for half of back, place 54 (56, 60, 68, 71) sts on holder for right sleeve, using the backward-loop method, CO 2 (2, 3, 3, 5) sts, pm for side, CO 3 (3, 4, 4, 5) sts, k83 (92, 101, 110, 113) for front, place 54 (56, 60, 68, 71) sts on holder for left sleeve, CO 2 (2, 3, 3, 5) sts, pm for side, CO 3 (3, 4, 4, 5) sts, knit to end (rnd beg at center back)—176 (194, 216, 234, 246) body sts rem: 88 (97, 108, 117, 123) sts each for front and back.

Body

Knit 9 (9, 8, 8, 8) rnds.

SHAPE WAIST

Dec rnd: *Knit to 6 sts before m, ssk, k4, sl m, k4, k2tog; rep from * once more, knit to end—4 sts dec'd.

Rep Dec rnd every 10th rnd 3 more times—160 (178, 200, 218, 230) sts rem.

Work 9 (9, 8, 8, 8) rnds even.

Inc rnd: *Knit to 4 sts before m, M1L, k4, sl m, k4, M1R; rep from * once more, knit to end—4 sts inc'd.

Rep Inc rnd every 10th rnd 0 (0, 1, 1, 2) more time(s), then every 11th rnd 3 (3, 2, 2, 1) time(s)—176 (194, 216, 234, 246) sts.

Work even until piece measures 15 (15, 14¼, 14¼, 14)" from underarm.

Next rnd: Remove beg-of-rnd m, knit to first side m (this is new beg-of-rnd).

Change to smaller cir needle. Work in Twisted Rib for 2". BO all sts in patt.

Sleeves

Return held sleeve sts to larger dpn.

With RS facing, beg at center of underarm, pick up and knit 3 (3, 4, 4, 6) sts along underarm CO, k54 (56, 60, 68, 71) sleeve sts, pick up and knit 3 (3, 4, 4, 5) sts—60 (62, 68, 76, 82) sts.

Pm and join in the rnd.

Working in St st, work 9 (9, 8, 5, 4) rnds even.

Dec rnd: K3, k2tog, knit to last 5 sts, ssk, k3—2 sts dec'd.

Rep Dec rnd every 11 (11, 10, 7, 6)th rnd 5 (5, 2, 5, 5) more times, then every 0 (0, 9, 6, 5)th rnd 0 (0, 4, 4, 6) times—48 (50, 54, 56, 58) sts rem.

Work even until sleeve measures 10" from underarm.

Change to smaller dpn. Work in Twisted Rib for 3". BO all sts in patt.

Finishing

Block to measurements. Weave in ends.

tucker sweater

Amanda Scheuzger

Finished Size

Bust circumference:
36 (40, 44, 48, 52)".

Pullover shown measures 36",
modeled with 2" of positive
ease.

Yarn

Bulky weight (#5 bulky).

Shown here: HiKoo Kenz-
ington (60% New Zealand
Merino wool, 25% nylon, 10%
alpaca, 5% silk noils; 208
yd [190 m]/3½ oz [100 g]):
#1000 pavlova, 5 (5, 6, 7, 7)
skeins.

Needles

Size U.S. 8 (5 mm): 24" and
32" circular (cir) and set of
double-pointed (dpn).

Size U.S. 9 (5.5 mm): 24" and
32" cir and set of dpn.

*Adjust needle size if necessary
to obtain the correct gauge.*

Notions

Markers (m); 2 cable needles
(cn); stitch holders; tapestry
needle.

Gauge

16 sts and 24 rnds = 4" in St st
on larger needle.

Notes

▪ The body and sleeves of this
pullover are worked in the
round from the bottom up to
the yoke, then the pieces are
joined for working the circular
yoke.

▪ Slip stitches purlwise with
yarn in back, except where
indicated otherwise.

▪ In order to maintain a
continuous cable around the
yoke, the beginning of the
round must sometimes shift
to allow for cable crossings.
This is achieved by slipping
stitches at the beginning of
the round and moving the
marker to a new location.

In order to shift it back to its
original location, stop the
round a few stitches early
and move the marker again.
Instructions in the pattern
give specific information on
shifting the beginning of
round when it is necessary.

Centered Double Inc

Knit into back and front of
next st on left needle, then
insert the left needle behind
the vertical strand that runs
between the two sts just made
and knit the strand through its
back loop—2 sts inc'd.

5-to-1 Dec

[Sl 1 kwise wyb] 3 times, drop
yarn, *pass 2nd st on right
needle over first (center) st, sl
center st back to left needle,
pass 2nd st on left needle over
center st,* sl center st back to
right needle, rep from * to *
once, k1—4 sts dec'd.

Body

With smaller 32" cir needle, CO 144 (160, 176, 192, 208) sts. Place marker (pm) and join in the rnd.

[Purl 1 rnd, knit 1 rnd] 9 times.

Change to larger 32" cir needle. Work in St st until piece measures 4" from CO.

Next rnd: K20 (23, 25, 28, 31), pm for right back dart, k31 (33, 37, 39, 41), pm for left back dart, k41 (47, 51, 57, 63), pm for left front dart, k31 (33, 37, 39, 41), pm for right front dart, knit to end.

SHAPE WAIST

Dec rnd: *Knit to m, sl m, ssk, knit to 2 sts before m, k2tog, sl m; rep from * once more, knit to end—4 sts dec'd.

Rep Dec rnd every 6th rnd 3 more times— 128 (144, 160, 176, 192) sts rem.

Work even until piece measures 8½" from CO.

Inc rnd: *Knit to m, sl m, k1, M1L, knit to 1 st before m, M1R, k1, sl m; rep from * once more, knit to end—4 sts inc'd.

Rep Inc rnd every 8th rnd 3 more times— 144 (160, 176, 192, 208) sts.

Work even until piece measures 15½" from CO. Do not break yarn. Set aside.

Sleeves

With smaller dpn, CO 34 (36, 38, 40, 42) sts. Pm and join in the rnd.

[Purl 1 rnd, knit 1 rnd] 9 times. Change to larger dpn.

Work in St st until piece measures 3" from CO.

Inc rnd: M1L, knit to last st, M1R, k1—2 sts inc'd.

Rep Inc rnd every 10 (8, 8, 6, 6)th rnd 4 (9, 2, 7, 6) more times, then every 8 (6, 6, 4, 4)th rnd 5 (1, 10, 9, 11) time(s)—54 (58, 66, 74, 78) sts.

Work even until piece measures 17½ (17½, 18, 18, 18½)" from CO.

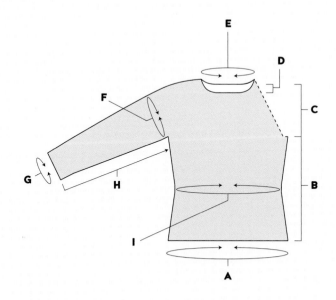

A: 36 (40, 44, 48, 52)"

B: 15½"

C: 7¾ (8¼, 8¾, 9¼, 9½)"

D: 1¼"

E: 19¾ (20, 22½, 22½, 25)"

F: 13½ (14½, 16½, 18½, 19½)"

G: 8½ (9, 9½, 10, 10½)"

H: 17½ (17½, 18, 18, 18½)"

I: 32 (36, 40, 44, 48)"

Next rnd: Remove m, k4 (5, 6, 6, 7), break yarn, leaving a 24" tail for grafting, place last 9 (11, 13, 13, 15) sts worked on holder for underarm—45 (47, 53, 61, 63) sts rem.

Place sts on holder.

Yoke

JOIN BODY AND SLEEVES

With cir needle and working yarn from body, k4 (5, 6, 6, 7) body sts, place last 9 (11, 13, 13, 15) sts worked on holder for right underarm (removing rnd m), k63 (69, 75, 83, 89) body sts for back, knit next 9 (11, 13, 13, 15) sts then place them on holder for left underarm, k45 (47, 53, 61, 63) sleeve sts, k63 (69, 75, 83, 89) body sts for front, k45 (47, 53, 61, 63) sleeve sts—216 (232, 256, 288, 304) sts.

Pm and join in the rnd.

Knit 5 (6, 9, 9, 10) rnds.

Shape neck using short-rows as foll:

Short-row 1: (RS) K129 (139, 153, 171, 181), wrap next st, turn.

Short-row 2: (WS) P195 (209, 231, 259, 273), wrap next st, turn.

Short-row 3: (RS) Knit to 7 (7, 8, 9, 9) sts before wrapped st, wrap next st, turn.

Short-row 4: (WS) Purl to 7 (7, 8, 9, 9) sts before wrapped st, wrap next st, turn.

Rep Short-rows 3 and 4 two more times.

Next rnd: Knit to end of rnd. Next rnd Knit to end, working wraps tog with wrapped sts.

SIZE 36" ONLY

Dec rnd : *K2tog, k1, k2tog, k2; rep from * to last 6 sts, [k2tog, k1] 2 times—154 sts rem.

SIZES 40 (50)" ONLY

Dec rnd: *[K2tog, k1, k2tog, k2] 7 (21) times, k9 (5); rep from * to end—176 (220) sts rem.

SIZES 44 (48)" ONLY

Dec rnd: *[K2tog, k1] 5 times, k1; rep from * to end—176 (198) sts rem.

ALL SIZES

Knit 1 rnd.

Remove rnd m, k6 (19, 20, 12, 4), replace rnd m.

Work Rnds 1-24 of Yoke chart, working marked rows as foll (see Notes) and changing to shorter cir needle when necessary—140 (160, 160, 180, 200) sts rem after chart is complete:

Rnds 6, 10, 14, and 18: Work to end, remove m, sl 2 sts to right needle, pm for new beg-of-rnd.

Rnds 8, 12, 16 and 20: Work to last 2 sts, sl 2 sts to right needle, remove m, sl 2 sts back to left needle, pm for new beg-of-rnd.

Dec rnd: *K2tog, k2; rep from * to end—105 (120, 120, 135, 150) sts rem.

Work 6 (8, 8, 11, 12) rnds even in St st.

SIZES 36 (44)" ONLY

Dec rnd: *K2tog, k2; rep from * to last 1 (0) st, k1 (0)—79 (90) sts rem.

SIZES 40 (48, 52)" ONLY

Dec rnd: *K2tog, k1; rep from * to end—80 (90, 100) sts rem.

ALL SIZES
NECKBAND

Change to smaller 24" cir needle. [Purl 1 rnd, knit 1 rnd] 3 times.

BO all sts pwise.

Finishing

Graft underarm sts using Kitchener st. Weave in ends. Block to measurements.

YOKE

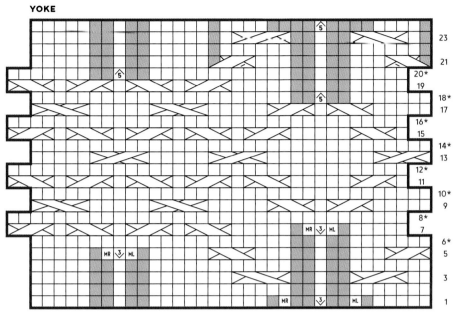

22 st to 34 st to 20 st repeat

* work as given in instructions

☐	knit
ML	M1L
MR	M1R
3	Centered Double Inc (see Stitch Guide)
5	5-to-1 Dec (see Stitch Guide)

sl 3 sts onto cn, hold in back, k2, k3 from cn

sl 2 sts onto cn, hold in front, k3, k2 from cn

sl 2 sts onto cn, hold in back, k2, k2 from cn

sl 2 sts onto cn, hold in front, k2, k2 from cn

sl 3 sts onto cn, hold in back, k2, sl leftmost st from cn back to left needle and knit it, k2 from cn

sl 2 sts onto first cn and hold in front, sl 1 st onto 2nd cn and hold in back, k2, k1 from 2nd cn, k2 from first cn

sl 2 sts onto cn, hold in back, k2, k2tog from cn–1 st dec'd

sl 2 sts onto cn, hold in front, ssk, k2 from cn–1 st dec'd

no stitch

pattern repeat

Finished Size

Bust circumference: 35 (37¾, 41½, 44¼, 48½, 51½)".

Pullover shown measures 37¾", modeled with ¼" of positive ease.

Yarn

Worsted weight (#4 medium).

Shown here: Schoppel Wolle Relikt (70% wool, 30% nylon; 137 yd [125 m]/1¾ oz [50 g]): #7693 mocha, 8 (8, 9, 10, 11, 11) balls.

Needles

Size U.S. 6 (4 mm): 32" circular (cir) and set of double-pointed (dpn).

Adjust needle size if necessary to obtain the correct gauge.

Notions

Markers (m); stitch holders; waste yarn for provisional CO; tapestry needle.

Gauge

21 sts and 28 rnds = 4" in St st.

23 sts and 30 rnds = 4" in Lace patt.

Notes

■ The body of this pullover is worked in the round from the lower edge to the underarms. The sleeves are worked separately in the round, then the sleeves and body are joined to work the yoke.

■ When increasing and decreasing in the lace pattern, work the stitches of partial repeats into the lace pattern when they are available; however, do not work a yarnover unless there are enough stitches to work its corresponding decrease.

brick lane pullover

Amanda Scheuzger

Body

With cir needle, CO 180 (192, 216, 228, 252, 264) sts. Place marker (pm) and join in the rnd.

Next rnd: *P1, k5; rep from * to end. Rep last rnd 4 more times.

Work Rows 1–9 of Lace Rib chart once.

Next rnd: Knit, inc 4 (6, 2, 4, 2, 6) sts evenly spaced—184 (198, 218, 232, 254, 270) sts.

Work in St st until piece measures 3 (3, 3, 3, 3½, 3½)" from CO.

Next rnd: K29 (31, 34, 36, 40, 43), pm for left front dart, k35 (38, 42, 45, 48, 50), pm for right front dart, k57 (61, 67, 71, 79, 85), pm for right back dart, k35 (38, 42, 45, 48, 50), pm for left back dart, knit to end.

SHAPE WAIST

Dec rnd: *Knit to m, sl m, ssk, knit to 2 sts before m, k2tog, sl m; rep from * once more, knit to end—4 sts dec'd.

Rep Dec rnd every 8th rnd 3 more times—168 (182, 202, 216, 238, 254) sts rem.

Work even until piece measures 7½ (7½, 7½, 7½, 8, 8)" from CO.

Inc rnd: *Knit to m, sl m, k1, M1L, knit to 1 st before m, M1R, k1, sl m; rep from * once more, knit to end—4 sts inc'd.

Rep Inc rnd every 12th rnd 3 more times—184 (198, 218, 232, 254, 270) sts.

Work even until piece measures 15½" from CO. Do not break yarn. Set aside.

Sleeves

With dpn, CO 54 (54, 60, 60, 66, 78) sts. Pm and join in the rnd.

Next rnd: *P1, k5; rep from * to end.

Rep last rnd 4 more times.

Work Rows 1–9 of Lace Rib chart once.

Knit 1 rnd.

Next rnd: K1, then using the backward-loop method, CO 1 st (counts as first st of Lace chart), beg with 2nd st of chart, work Row 1 of Lace chart over 53 (53, 59, 59, 65, 77) sts, CO 1 st (counts as last st of Lace chart)—56 (56, 62, 62, 68, 80) sts.

Keeping first st of rnd in St st and working all other sts according to chart, work 13 (9, 9, 7, 7, 9) rnds even.

Inc rnd: K1, CO 1 st, work in patt to end, CO 1 st—2 sts inc'd.

Rep Inc rnd every 14 (10, 10, 8, 8, 10)th rnd 1 (3, 3, 6, 6, 1) more time(s), then every 12 (8, 8, 6, 6, 8)th rnd 3 (3, 3, 1, 1, 5) time(s), working new sts into patt (see Notes)—66 (70, 76, 78, 84, 94) sts.

Work 14 (14, 14, 16, 16, 18) rnds even in patt, ending with Row 7 of chart.

Next rnd: Remove m, k6 (7, 8, 9, 11, 12), break yarn, leaving a 24" tail, place last 11 (13, 15, 17, 21, 23) sts worked on holder for underarm—55 (57, 61, 61, 63, 71) sts rem.

Place sts on holder.

LACE

6 st repeat

LACE RIB

6 st repeat

	k on RS; p on WS
·	p on RS; k on WS
O	yo
/	k2tog
\	ssk
⋏	sl 1, k2tog, psso
□	pattern repeat

Yoke

JOIN BODY AND SLEEVES

With cir needle and working yarn from body, k6 (7, 8, 9, 11, 12) body sts, place last 11 (13, 15, 17, 21, 23) body sts on holder for underarm, k81 (86, 94, 99, 106, 112) front sts, place next 11 (13, 15, 17, 21, 23) body sts on holder for underarm, pm, work 55 (57, 61, 61, 63, 71) right sleeve sts in patt, pm, k81 (86, 94, 99, 106, 112) back sts, pm, work 55 (57, 61, 61, 63, 71) left sleeve sts in patt—272 (286, 310, 320, 338, 366) sts total.

Pm and join in the rnd.

Work 2 rnds even in patt, working first and last st of each sleeve section in St st.

Raglan dec rnd: *Ssk, knit to 2 sts before m, k2tog, sl m, ssk, work in patt to 2 sts before m, k2tog, sl m; rep from * once more—8 sts dec'd.

Rep Raglan dec rnd every 4th rnd 3 (3, 1, 0, 0, 0) more time(s)—240 (254, 294, 312, 330, 358) sts rem: 73 (78, 90, 97, 104, 110) sts each for front and back, 47 (49, 57, 59, 61, 69) sts for each sleeve.

SIZES 37¾ (41½, 44¼, 48½, 51½)" ONLY

Work 1 rnd even.

Dec rnd: *Ssk, knit to 2 sts before m, k2tog, sl m, work in patt to m, sl m; rep from * once more—4 sts dec'd.

Work 1 rnd even.

Work Raglan dec rnd—8 sts dec'd.

Rep last 4 rnds 0 (1, 3, 3, 1) more time(s)—242 (270, 264, 282, 334) sts rem: 74 (82, 81, 88, 102) sts each for front and back, 47 (53, 51, 53, 65) sts for each sleeve.

ALL SIZES

Work 1 rnd even.

Rep Raglan dec rnd on next rnd, then every other rnd 10 (10, 13, 12, 13, 19) more times—152 (154, 158, 160, 170, 174) sts rem: 51 (52, 54, 55, 60, 62) sts each for front and back, 25 sts for each sleeve.

Work 1 rnd even.

SHAPE NECK

Next rnd: Ssk, k14 (14, 14, 14, 16, 16), BO 19 (20, 22, 23, 24, 26) sts, knit to 2 sts before m, k2tog, sl m, ssk, work in patt to 2 sts before m, k2tog, sl m, ssk, knit to 2 sts before m, k2tog, sl m, ssk, work in patt to 2 sts before m, k2tog, sl m, knit to BO sts—125 (126, 128, 129, 138, 140) sts rem: 15 (15, 15, 15, 17, 17) sts for each front, 23 sts for each sleeve, 49 (50, 52, 53, 58, 60) sts for back.

Work back and forth in rows.

Next row: (WS) BO 3 (3, 3, 3, 5, 5) sts, work in patt to end—122 (123, 125, 126, 133, 135) sts rem.

Dec row: (RS) BO 3 (3, 3, 3, 5, 5) sts, *knit to 2 sts before m, k2tog, sl m, ssk, work in patt to 2 sts before m, k2tog, sl m, ssk; rep from * once more, knit to end—111 (112, 114, 115, 120, 122) sts rem: 11 sts for each front, 21 sts for each sleeve, 47 (48, 50, 51, 56, 58) sts for back.

Neck dec row: (WS) P1, p2tog, work in patt to last 3 sts, ssp, p1—2 sts dec'd.

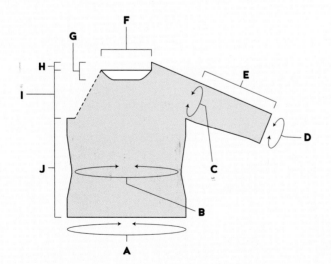

A: 35 (37¾, 41½, 44¼, 48½, 51½)"

B: 32 (34¾, 38½, 41¼, 45¼, 48½)"

C: 11½ (12¼, 13¼, 13½, 14½, 16¼)"

D: 9½ (9½, 10½, 10½, 11½, 13½)"

E: 12½"

F: 7¾ (8, 8½, 8½, 9½, 10)"

G: 2¾"

H: 1¼"

I: 7 (7½, 7¾, 8¼, 8½, 9)"

J: 15½"

Neck and raglan dec row: (RS) K1, ssk, *knit to 2 sts before m, k2tog, sl m, ssk, work in patt to 2 sts before m, k2tog, sl m, ssk; rep from * once more, knit to last 3 sts, k2tog, k1—10 sts dec'd.

Rep last 2 rows once more—87 (88, 90, 91, 96, 98) sts rem: 5 sts for each front, 17 sts for each sleeve, 43 (44, 46, 47, 52, 54) sts for back.

Work Neck dec row once more—85 (86, 88, 89, 94, 96) sts rem: 4 sts for each front, 17 sts for each sleeve, 43 (44, 46, 47, 52, 54) sts for back.

Next row: (RS) *Knit to 2 sts before m, k2tog, sl m, ssk, work in patt to 2 sts before m, k2tog, sl m, ssk; rep from * once more, knit to end—77 (78, 80, 81, 86, 88) sts rem: 3 sts each for front, 15 sts for each sleeve, 41 (42, 44, 45, 50, 52) sts for back.

Next row: (WS) Purl. Place sts on holder.

Finishing

Weave in ends. Block to measurements. Graft underarm sts using Kitchener st.

NECKBAND

With dpn and using a provisional method, CO 4 sts.

With RS facing, beg at back left raglan line, work I-cord BO across sleeve and front sts, work applied I-cord across front neck, then work I-cord BO across front, sleeve, and back sts, ending at back left raglan line.

Remove provisional CO and place sts on dpn.

Graft I-cord sts to CO sts using Kitchener st.

nevelson lace pullover

Amy Christoffers

Finished Size

Bust circumference: About 36¾ (39¾, 42½, 45½, 48¼)".

Pullover shown measures 39¾".

Yarn

Sport weight (#2 fine).

Shown here: Lorna's Laces Shepherd Sport (100% superwash Merino wool; 200 yd [183 m]/56 g): patina, 7 (7, 8, 8, 9) skeins.

Needles

Size U.S. 4 (3.5 mm): 24" circular (cir) and set of 4 or 5 double-pointed (dpn).

Size U.S. 2 (2.75 mm): 16" and 24" cir and set of 4 or 5 dpn.

Adjust needle sizes if necessary to obtain the correct gauge.

Notions

Stitch markers (m); stitch holders or waste yarn; tapestry needle.

Gauge

22 sts and 30 rnds = 4" in Lace chart, worked in rnds, on larger needles.

25 sts and 26 rnds = 4" in St st, worked in rnds, on larger needles.

Notes

■ When establishing the Lace chart, work the first stitch of the chart, then repeat the 4 stitches in the red box for the indicated number of repeats, then work the final 4 stitches to the marker; work the second half of the body in the same manner.

■ When shaping armholes, be careful to keep the stitch count accurate by working corresponding increase and decrease together. If there are not enough stitches to work both the increase and decrease, work them both in St st (knit on RS, purl on WS) instead. If only 1 yarnover is worked for the sl1-k2tog-psso stitch, work k2tog or ssk instead.

STITCH GUIDE

Twisted 1×1 Rib (multiple of 2 sts)

Rnd 1: *K1tbl, p1tbl; rep from *.

Rep Rnd 1 for patt.

Body

With smaller 24" cir, CO 202 (218, 234, 250, 266) sts. Place marker (pm) for beg of rnd and join for working in the rnd, being careful not to twist sts.

Work in twisted 1×1 rib until piece measures 1" from beg.

Change to larger cir.

Place marker for side: K101 (109, 117, 125, 133) sts, pm for side, k101 (109, 117, 125, 133) sts to end.

Est patt: *Work Lace chart to side m, working the 4-st red rep box 24 (26, 28, 30, 32) times, sl m; rep from * once more (see Notes).

Cont working Lace chart even as est until piece measures 16" from beg, ending last rnd 5 (6, 7, 8, 9) sts before beg of the rnd m.

DIVIDE FOR BACK AND FRONT

Next Rnd: BO next 10 (12, 14, 16, 18) sts, removing m, work front sts to 5 (6, 7, 8, 9) sts before m, BO next 10 (12, 14, 16, 18) sts, removing m, work back sts to end—91 (97, 103, 109, 115) sts rem for each back and front. Cont working back and forth on back sts only. Place sts for front onto st holder or waste yarn.

Back

SHAPE ARMHOLES

Work 1 WS row even.

Dec Row: (RS) K2, k2tog, work to last 4 sts, ssk, k2—2 sts dec'd.

Rep the last 2 rows 4 (5, 6, 7, 8) times—81 (85, 89, 93, 97) sts rem.

Work even as est until armholes measure 7¾ (8, 8½, 8¾, 9)" from divide, ending after a WS row.

LACE

	k on RS; p on WS
·	p on RS; k on WS
O	yo
/	k2tog
\	ssk
⅄	sl 1, k2tog, psso
☐	pattern repeat

Next Row: (WS) BO 4 sts, work to end—4 sts dec'd.

Work 1 RS row.

Rep the last 2 rows 1 (1, 1, 1, 2) times—20 (22, 24, 26, 24) sts rem.

Next Row: (WS) BO 2 sts, work to end—2 sts dec'd.

Work 1 RS row.

Rep the last 2 rows 1 (1, 2, 2, 1) times—16 (18, 18, 20, 20) sts rem.

Cont working even as est until armhole measures 7¾ (8, 8½, 8¾, 9)" from divide, ending after a WS row.

Place all sts onto st holders or waste yarn. Break yarn, leaving a tail at least 1 yd long.

SHAPE NECK

Next Row: (RS) Work 16 (18, 18, 20, 20) sts, then place these sts onto a st holder or waste yarn for shoulder, BO 49 (49, 53, 53, 57) sts, work rem 16 (18, 18, 20, 20) sts to end, then place them onto st holder or waste yarn for shoulder. Break yarn.

Front

Return 91 (97, 103, 109, 115) held front sts to larger needle and join yarn, preparing to work a WS row.

SHAPE ARMHOLES

Work 1 WS row even.

Dec Row: (RS) K2, k2tog, work to last 4 sts, ssk, k2—2 sts dec'd.

Rep the last 2 rows 4 (5, 6, 7, 8) times—81 (85, 89, 93, 97) sts rem.

Work even as est until armholes measure 5¾ (6, 6½, 6¾, 7)" from divide, ending after a WS row.

SHAPE NECK

Next Row: (RS) Work 36 (38, 40, 42, 44) sts as est for left front, BO the next 9 sts, work to end for right front—36 (38, 40, 42, 44) sts rem on each side. Cont working back and forth on right front sts only. Place sts for left front onto st holder or waste yarn.

Right Front

Work 1 WS row.

Next Row: (RS) BO 8 sts, work to end—28 (30, 32, 34, 36) sts rem.

Work 1 WS row.

Next Row: (RS) BO 4 sts, work to end—4 sts dec'd.

Rep the last 2 rows 1 (1, 1, 1, 2) times—20 (22, 24, 26, 24) sts rem.

Work 1 WS row.

Next Row: (RS) BO 2 sts, work to end—2 sts dec'd.

Rep the last 2 rows 1 (1, 2, 2, 1) times—16 (18, 18, 20, 20) sts rem.

Cont working even as est until armhole measures 7¾ (8, 8½, 8¾, 9)" from divide, ending after a WS row.

Place all sts onto st holders or waste yarn. Break yarn, leaving a tail at least 1 yd long.

Left Front

Return 36 (38, 40, 42, 44) held left front sts to larger needle and join yarn, preparing to work a WS row.

Next Row: (WS) BO 8 sts, work to end—28 (30, 32, 34, 36) sts rem.

Work 1 RS row.

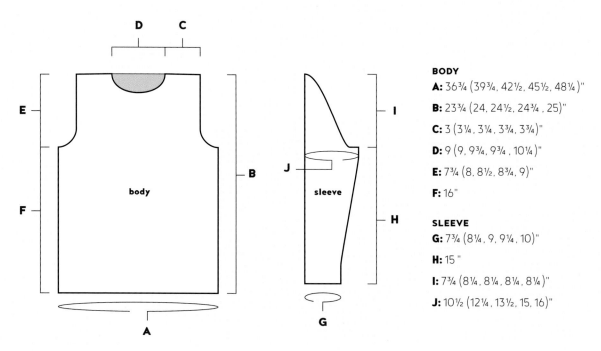

BODY

A: 36¾ (39¾, 42½, 45½, 48¼)"

B: 23¾ (24, 24½, 24¾, 25)"

C: 3 (3¼, 3¼, 3¾, 3¾)"

D: 9 (9, 9¾, 9¾, 10¼)"

E: 7¾ (8, 8½, 8¾, 9)"

F: 16"

SLEEVE

G: 7¾ (8¼, 9, 9¼, 10)"

H: 15 "

I: 7¾ (8¼, 8¼, 8¼, 8¼)"

J: 10½ (12¼, 13½, 15, 16)"

Sleeve

With smaller needle, CO 48 (52, 56, 58, 62) sts. Divide the sts evenly over 3 or 4 dpn. Pm for beg of rnd and join for working in the rnd, being careful not to twist sts.

Work in twisted 1×1 rib until piece measures 2½" from beg.

Change to larger needles. Work in St st (knit all sts, every rnd) until piece measures 4" from beg.

SHAPE SLEEVE

Inc Rnd: K1, M1L, knit to last st, M1R, k1—2 sts inc'd.

Knit 7 (5, 4, 3, 3) rnds even.

Rep the last 8 (6, 6, 4, 4) rnds 7 (10, 12, 16, 17) times, then work inc rnd once more—66 (76, 84, 94, 100) sts.

Work even in St st until piece measures 15" from beg, ending 5 (6, 7, 8, 9) sts before the beg of rnd m.

SHAPE CAP

Next Rnd: BO next 10 (12, 14, 16, 18) sts removing m, knit to end—56 (64, 70, 78, 82) sts rem. Cont working back and forth in rows.

Purl 1 WS row.

Dec Row: (RS) K2, k2tog, knit to last 4 sts, ssk, k2—2 sts dec'd.

Rep the last 2 rows 5 (6, 7, 8, 9) times—44 (50, 54, 60, 62) sts rem.

[Work 3 rows even, then rep Dec row] 4 (4, 3, 2, 1) times—36 (42, 48, 56, 60) sts rem.

[Purl 1 WS row, then rep Dec row] 9 (9, 10, 11, 12) times—18 (24, 28, 34, 36) sts rem.

Dec Row: (WS) P2, ssp, purl to last 4 sts, p2tog, p2—2 sts dec'd.

Rep Dec row on RS.

Rep the last 2 rows once more—10 (16, 20, 26, 28) sts rem.

BO rem sts.

Make a second sleeve the same as the first.

Finishing

Block pieces to measurements.

JOIN SHOULDERS

Return 16 (18, 18, 20, 20) held sts from left front and back shoulders onto larger needle and with RS facing each other, WS facing out, join the back and front shoulders together using the three-needle BO. Rep for right front and back shoulder. Set in sleeves, easing the cap into place.

NECKBAND

With 16" cir, beg at shoulder, pick up and knit 108 (108, 116, 116, 122) sts around neck edge. Pm for beg of rnd and join for working in the rnd. Work in twisted 1×1 rib for 5 rnds. BO all sts loosely in rib.

Weave in all ends. Block again if desired.

telluride aran

Amy Herzog

Finished Size

Bust circumference: 29½ (31, 34½, 36, 37½, 39, 42½, 44, 45½, 47, 50½, 53½)".

Pullover shown measures 36", modeled with 1" of positive ease.

Yarn

Worsted weight (#4 medium).

Shown here: Valley Yarns Northampton (100% wool; 247 yd [226 m]/3½ oz [100 g]): pacific teal, 4 (4, 5, 5, 5, 5, 6, 6, 7, 7, 8, 8) balls.

Needles

Size U.S. 7 (4.5 mm): straight and 16" circular (cir).

Adjust needle size if necessary to obtain the correct gauge.

Notions

Markers (m); cable needle (cn); stitch holders; tapestry needle.

Gauge

20 sts and 27 rows = 4" in St st.

31 sts and 27 rows = 4" in Aran Honeycomb patt.

Notes

■ This pullover is worked back and forth in pieces from the bottom up and seamed.

■ Despite the plethora of cables, this pullover is a snap to modify. Turn it into a fun warmer-weather pullover by shortening the sleeves: Cast on the final bicep stitch count, working in 2×2 ribbing for 1", stockinette for two rows, then follow the sleeve-cap shaping as written. Bump up the waist shaping on the back of the piece, and add more in the stockinette panels on the front, for a more curvaceous look.

Back

CO 74 (78, 86, 90, 94, 98, 106, 110, 114, 118, 126, 134) sts.

Next row: (RS) K1, *k2, p2; rep from * to last st, k1.

Next row: P1, *k2, p2; rep from * to last st, p1.

Cont in rib patt as est until piece measures 2¼" from CO, ending with a RS row.

Knit 1 WS row.

Change to St st and work 5 rows even, ending with a RS row.

Next row: (WS) P25 (26, 29, 30, 31, 33, 35, 37, 38, 39, 42, 45), place marker (pm), p24 (26, 28, 30, 32, 32, 36, 36, 38, 40, 42, 44), pm, p25 (26, 29, 30, 31, 33, 35, 37, 38, 39, 42, 45).

SHAPE WAIST

Dec row: (RS) Knit to 2 sts before m, ssk, sl m, knit to m, sl m, k2tog, knit to end—2 sts dec'd.

Rep Dec row every 10th row 3 more times—66 (70, 78, 82, 86, 90, 98, 102, 106, 110, 118, 126) sts rem.

Work even until piece measures 9" from CO, ending with a WS row.

Inc row: (RS) Knit to m, M1R, sl m, knit to m, sl m, M1L, knit to end—2 sts inc'd.

Rep Inc row every 8th row 3 more times—74 (78, 86, 90, 94, 98, 106, 110, 114, 118, 126, 134) sts.

Remove m. Work even until piece measures 14½ (14¾, 15, 15¼, 15½, 15¾, 16, 16, 16½, 16½, 16½, 16½)" from CO, ending with a WS row.

SHAPE ARMHOLES

BO 6 (6, 6, 6, 6, 6, 6, 8, 8, 10, 10) sts at beg of next 2 rows, then BO 0 (0, 2, 2, 2, 2, 4, 4, 4, 6, 8, 8) sts at beg of foll 2 rows—62 (66, 70, 74, 78, 82, 86, 90, 90, 90, 90, 98) sts rem.

Dec row: (RS) K1, k2tog, knit to last 3 sts, ssk, k1—2 sts dec'd.

Rep Dec row every RS row 1 (2, 2, 3, 3, 3, 4, 5, 5, 4, 4, 5) more time(s)—58 (60, 64, 66, 70, 74, 76, 78, 78, 80, 80, 86) sts rem.

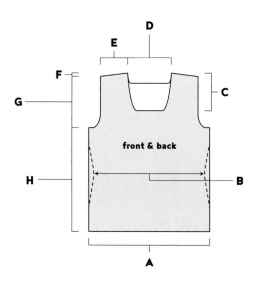

FRONT & BACK

A: 14¾ (15½, 17¼, 18, 18¾, 19½, 21¼, 22, 22¾, 23½, 25¼, 26¾)"

B: 13¼ (14, 15½, 16½, 17¼, 18, 19½, 20½, 21¼, 22, 23½, 25¼)"

C: 5½"

D: 5½ (6, 6½, 6½, 6¾, 7¼, 7½, 7½, 7½, 8, 8, 8½)"

E: 3 (3, 3¼, 3½, 3½, 3¾, 3¾, 4, 4, 4, 4, 4½)"

F: ½"

G: 6½ (7, 7¼, 7½, 8, 8¼, 8½, 9, 9¼, 9¾, 10, 10½)"

H: 14½ (14¾, 15, 15¼, 15½, 15¾, 16, 16, 16½, 16½, 16½, 16½)"

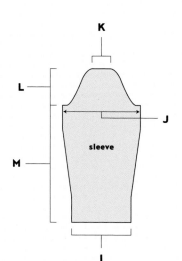

SLEEVE

I: 8¾ (8¾, 9½, 9½, 10½, 10½, 10½, 11¼, 11¼, 11¼, 12, 12)"

J: 11¼ (11½, 12, 12½, 12¾, 13¼, 14, 15¼, 16, 16¾, 18, 18¾)"

K: 2¾ (2¾, 2¾, 2¾, 2¾, 2¾, 2¾, 2¾, 3½, 3½, 3½, 3½)"

L: 4¼ (4¾, 5¼, 5¾, 6, 6¼, 6½, 6¾, 6½, 7, 7¾, 8)"

M: 18 (18, 18½, 18½, 19, 19, 19½, 19½, 20, 20, 20, 20)"

Work even until armhole measures 5½ (6, 6¼, 6½, 7, 7¼, 7½, 8, 8¼, 8¾, 9, 9½)", ending with a WS row.

SHAPE NECK

Next row: (RS) K17 (17, 18, 19, 20, 21, 21, 22, 22, 22, 22, 24) sts and place these sts on a holder for right shoulder, BO center 24 (26, 28, 28, 30, 32, 34, 34, 34, 36, 36, 38) sts, knit to end—17 (17, 18, 19, 20, 21, 21, 22, 22, 22, 22, 24) sts rem for left shoulder.

LEFT SHOULDER

Purl 1 WS row.

Dec row: (RS) K1, k2tog, knit to end—1 st dec'd.

Purl 1 WS row.

Rep last 2 rows once more--15 (15, 16, 17, 18, 19, 19, 20, 20, 20, 20, 22) sts rem.

Work 1 RS row even—armhole measures 6½ (7, 7¼, 7½, 8, 8¼, 8½, 9, 9¼, 9¾, 10, 10½)".

Shape shoulder

At beg of WS rows, BO 8 (8, 8, 9, 9, 10, 10, 10, 10, 10, 10, 11) sts once, then BO 7 (7, 8, 8, 9, 9, 9, 10, 10, 10, 10, 11) sts once—no sts rem.

RIGHT SHOULDER

Return held right shoulder sts to needle. With WS facing, rejoin yarn. Purl 1 WS row.

Dec row: (RS) Knit to last 3 sts, ssk, k1—1 st dec'd.

Purl 1 WS row.

Rep last 2 rows once more—15 (15, 16, 17, 18, 19, 19, 20, 20, 20, 20, 22) sts rem.

Shape shoulder

At beg of RS rows, BO 8 (8, 8, 9, 9, 10, 10, 10, 10, 10, 10, 11) sts once, then BO 7 (7, 8, 8, 9, 9, 9, 10, 10, 10, 10, 11) sts once—no sts rem.

Front

CO 88 (92, 100, 104, 116, 122, 130, 138, 142, 146, 154, 162) sts.

SIZES 29½ (31, 34½, 36)"

Next row: (RS) K3 (1, 1, 3), [p2, k2] 2 (3, 4, 4) times, pm, p3, k3, p1, k3, p3, pm, work Moss St Rib chart over 8 sts, pm, [p2, k4, p2] 3 times, pm, work Moss St Rib chart over 8 sts, pm, p3, k3, p1, k3, p3, pm, [k2, p2] 2 (3, 4, 4) times, k3 (1, 1, 3).

SIZES 37½ (39, 42½, 44, 45½, 47, 50½, 53½)" ONLY

Next row: (RS) K3 (2, 2, 2, 0, 2, 2, 2), [p2, k2] 3 (3, 4, 4, 5, 5, 6, 7) times, pm, work Little Plait Cable chart over 10 sts, pm, p3, k3, p1, k3, p3, pm, work Moss St Rib chart over 8 sts, pm, [p2, k4, p2] 3 (4, 4, 5, 5, 5, 5) times, pm, work Moss St Rib chart over 8 sts, pm, p3, k3, p1, k3, p3, pm, work Little Plait Cable chart over 10 sts, pm, [k2, p2] 3 (3, 4, 4, 5, 5, 6, 7) times, k3 (2, 2, 2, 0, 2, 2, 2).

ALL SIZES

Work in rib and cable patt as est until piece measures 2¼" from CO, ending with a RS row.

Next row: (WS) Knit to first m, sl m, work in patt as est to last m, sl m, knit to end.

SIZES 29½ (31, 34½, 36)"

Next row: (RS) Knit to first m, sl m, work Wheat Ear Cable chart over 13 sts, sl m, work Moss St Rib chart as est over 8 sts, sl m, work Aran Honeycomb chart over 24 sts, sl m, work Moss St Rib chart as est over 8 sts, sl m, work Wheat Ear Cable chart over 13 sts, sl m, knit to end.

SIZES 37½ (39, 42½, 44, 45½, 47, 50½, 53½)" ONLY

Next row: (RS) Knit to first m, sl m, work Little Plait Cable chart as est over 10 sts, sl m, work Wheat Ear Cable chart over 13 sts, sl m, work Moss St Rib chart as est over 8 sts, sl m, work Aran Honeycomb chart over 24 (32, 32, 40, 40, 40, 40, 40) sts, sl m, work Moss St Rib chart as est over 8 sts, sl m, work Wheat Ear Cable chart over 13 sts, sl m, work Little Plait Cable chart as est over 10 sts, sl m, knit to end.

ALL SIZES

Cont in patts as est until piece measures 14½ (14¾, 15, 15¼, 15½, 15¾, 16, 16, 16½, 16½, 16½, 16½)" from CO, ending with a WS row.

SHAPE ARMHOLES

BO 6 (6, 6, 6, 6, 6, 6, 8, 8, 10, 10) sts at beg of next 2 rows, then BO 0 (0, 2, 2, 2, 2, 4, 4, 6, 8, 8) sts at beg of foll 2 rows—76 (80, 84, 88, 100, 106, 110, 118, 118, 118, 118, 126) sts rem.

Dec row: (RS) K1, k2tog, work in patt to last 3 sts, ssk, k1—2 sts dec'd.

Rep Dec row every RS row 1 (2, 2, 3, 3, 3, 4, 5, 5, 4, 4, 5) more time(s)—72 (74, 78, 80, 92, 98, 100, 106, 106, 108, 108, 114) sts rem.

Work even until armhole measures 1½ (2, 2¼, 2½, 3, 3¼, 4, 4¼, 4¾, 5, 5½)", ending with a WS row.

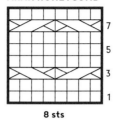

8 sts

ARAN HONEYCOMB

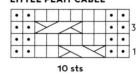

8 sts

LITTLE PLAIT CABLE

10 sts

WHEAT EAR CABLE

13 sts

 k on RS; p on WS

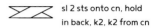 p on RS; k on WS

pattern repeat

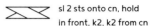 sl 2 sts onto cn, hold in back, k2, k2 from cn

sl 2 sts onto cn, hold in front, k2, k2 from cn

 sl 3 sts onto cn, hold in back, k3, k3 from cn

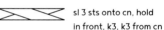 sl 3 sts onto cn, hold in front, k3, k3 from cn

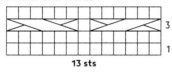

SHAPE NECK
Next row: (RS) Work 26 (26, 28, 29, 34, 36, 36, 38, 38, 39, 39, 41) sts in patt and place these sts on holder for left shoulder, BO center 20 (22, 22, 22, 24, 26, 28, 30, 30, 30, 30, 32) sts, work to end—26 (26, 28, 29, 34, 36, 36, 38, 38, 39, 39, 41) sts rem for right shoulder.

RIGHT SHOULDER
Dec row: (WS) Work in patt to last 3 sts, p2tog, p1—1 st dec'd.

Dec row: (RS) K1, k2tog, work in patt to end—1 st dec'd.

Rep last 2 rows 1 (1, 1, 1, 1, 2, 2, 2, 2, 2, 2) more time(s), then work RS Dec row only every other row 4 (4, 5, 5, 6, 5, 5, 6, 6, 6, 6, 6) times, then every 4th row 2 (2, 2, 2, 2, 2, 2, 2, 3, 3, 3) times—16 (16, 17, 18, 22, 23, 23, 24, 24, 24, 24, 26) sts rem.

Work even until armhole measures 6½ (7, 7¼, 7½, 8, 8¼, 8½, 9, 9¼, 9¾, 10, 10½)", ending with a RS row and dec 1 (1, 1, 1, 4, 4, 4, 4, 4, 4, 4, 4) st(s) across cables on last row—15 (15, 16, 17, 18, 19, 19, 20, 20, 20, 20, 22) sts rem.

Shape shoulder
At beg of WS rows, BO 8 (8, 8, 9, 9, 10, 10, 10, 10, 10, 10, 11) sts once, then BO 7 (7, 8, 8, 9, 9, 9, 10, 10, 10, 10, 11) sts once—no sts rem.

LEFT SHOULDER
Return 26 (26, 28, 29, 34, 36, 36, 38, 38, 39, 39, 41) held left shoulder sts to needle and with WS facing, rejoin yarn.

Dec row: (WS) P1, ssp, work in patt to end—1 st dec'd.

Dec row: (RS) Work in patt to last 3 sts, ssk, k1—1 st dec'd.

Rep last 2 rows 1 (1, 1, 1, 1, 2, 2, 2, 2, 2, 2) more time(s), then work RS Dec row only every other row 4 (4, 5, 5, 6, 5, 5, 6, 6, 6, 6, 6) times, then every 4th row 2 (2, 2, 2, 2, 2, 2, 2, 3, 3, 3) times—16 (16, 17, 18, 22, 23, 23, 24, 24, 24, 24, 26) sts rem.

Work even until armhole measures 6½ (7, 7¼, 7½, 8, 8¼, 8½, 9, 9¼, 9¾, 10, 10½)", ending with a WS row and Dec 1 (1, 1, 1, 4, 4, 4, 4, 4, 4, 4, 4) st(s) across cables on last row—15 (15, 16, 17, 18, 19, 19, 20, 20, 20, 20, 22) sts rem.

Shape shoulder
At beg of RS rows, BO 8 (8, 8, 9, 9, 10, 10, 10, 10, 10, 10, 11) sts once, then BO 7 (7, 8, 8, 9, 9, 9, 10, 10, 10, 10, 11) sts once—no sts rem.

Sleeves
CO 44 (44, 48, 48, 52, 52, 52, 56, 56, 56, 60, 60) sts.

Work in k2, p2 rib until piece measures 5" from CO, ending with a RS row.

Knit 1 WS row.

Inc row: (RS) K1, M1R, knit to last st, M1L, k1—2 sts inc'd.

Rep Inc row every 14 (12, 14, 12, 14, 12, 10, 10, 8, 6, 6, 6)th row 5 (6, 5, 6, 5, 6, 8, 9, 11, 13, 14, 16) more times—56 (58, 60, 62, 64, 66, 70, 76, 80, 84, 90, 94) sts.

Work even until piece measures 18 (18, 18½, 18½, 19, 19, 19½, 19½, 20, 20, 20, 20)" from CO, ending with a WS row.

Shape cap: BO 6 (6, 6, 6, 6, 6, 6, 6, 8, 8, 10, 10) sts at beg of next 2 rows, then BO 0 (0, 2, 2, 2, 4, 4, 4, 6, 7, 7) sts at beg of foll 2 rows—44 (46, 44, 46, 48, 50, 50, 56, 56, 56, 56, 60) sts rem.

Dec row: (RS) K1, k2tog, knit to last 3 sts, ssk, k1—2 sts dec'd.

Rep Dec row every 6th row 0 (0, 1, 1, 1, 1, 2, 1, 2, 3, 4, 4) more time(s), then every 4th row 0 (1, 1, 1, 1, 1, 0, 0, 1, 1, 1, 0) time, then every RS row 10 (10, 8, 9, 10, 11, 11, 15, 9, 8, 7, 10) times—22 (22, 22, 22, 22, 22, 22, 22, 30, 30, 30, 30) sts rem.

Work 1 row even. BO 2 (2, 2, 2, 2, 2, 2, 2, 3, 3, 3, 3) sts at beg of next 4 rows—14 (14, 14, 14, 14, 14, 14, 14, 18, 18, 18, 18) sts rem. BO all sts.

Finishing
Block pieces to measurements. Sew shoulder seams. Sew in sleeves. Sew side and sleeve seams.

NECKBAND
With RS facing, cir needle and beg at right shoulder seam, pick up and knit 100 (104, 108, 108, 112, 116, 116, 120, 120, 120, 120, 124) sts evenly around neck edge. Pm and join in the rnd.

Work in k2, p2 rib until neckband measures 1½".

BO all sts. Weave in ends.

feathernest raglan

Amy Miller

Finished Size

Bust circumference: 34 (38, 42½, 46½, 50½)".

Pullover shown measures 34", modeled with 1" of positive ease.

Yarn

Worsted weight (#4 medium).

Shown here: Harrisville Designs Watershed (100% wool; 110 yd [101 m]/1¾ oz [50 g]): #901 birchbark, 8 (9, 10, 11, 12) skeins.

Needles

Sizes U.S. 6 (4 mm): 16" and 29" circular (cir) and set of double-pointed (dpn).

Sizes U.S. 8 (5 mm): 16" and 29" cir and dpn.

Adjust needle size if necessary to obtain the correct gauge.

Notions

Markers (m); stitch holders; tapestry needle.

Gauge

16 sts and 25 rnds = 4" in Herringbone patt on larger needle.

Notes

■ This pullover is worked in the round from the top down with short-row shaping to lower the front neck.

■ Two stitches on each side of the raglan, side, and sleeve markers are kept in Stockinette stitch throughout, with new stitches being incorporated into the Herringbone pattern.

Neckband

With smaller cir needle, CO 108 (100, 106, 98, 102) sts. Place marker (pm) and join in the rnd. Working in k1, p1 rib, shape neck using short-rows as foll:

Short-row 1: (RS) Work 16 (12, 12, 8, 8) sts in patt, wrap next st, turn.

Short-row 2: (WS) Work 70 (62, 65, 57, 59) sts in patt, wrap next st, turn.

Short-row 3: Work to wrapped st, work wrap tog with wrapped st, work 3 sts, wrap next st, turn.

Rep Short-row 3 five more times—4 wrapped sts on each side of front.

Next row: (RS) Work to end of rnd. Work 4 rnds even in rib.

Yoke

Change to larger cir needle. Beg and ending as indicated for your size, work Row 1 of Herringbone chart as foll: K2, work Herringbone chart over 12 (8, 8, 4, 4) sts for right sleeve, k2, pm, k2, work Herringbone chart over 34 (34, 37, 37, 39) sts for front, k2, pm, k2, work Herringbone chart over 12 (8, 8, 4, 4) sts for left sleeve, k2, pm, k2, work Herringbone chart over 34 (34, 37, 37, 39) sts for back, k2.

Inc rnd: *K2, M1L, work in patt to 2 sts before m, M1R, k2; rep from * 3 more times—8 sts inc'd.

Rep Inc rnd every other rnd 0 (6, 9, 15, 18) more times, then every 3rd rnd 10 (8, 7, 5, 4) times, working new sts into patt—196 (220, 242, 266, 286) sts: 38 (42, 46, 50, 54) sts for each sleeve, 60 (68, 75, 83, 89) sts each for front and back.

DIVIDE FOR BODY AND SLEEVES

Next rnd: Remove m, place 38 (42, 46, 50, 54) sts on holder for right sleeve, remove m, using the backward-loop method, CO 4 (4, 5, 5, 6) sts for underarm, pm for new beg of rnd, CO 4 (4, 5, 5, 6) sts for underarm, work to m, remove m, place 38 (42, 46, 50, 54) sts on holder for left sleeve, remove m, CO 4 (4, 5, 5, 6) sts for underarm, pm for side, CO 4 (4, 5, 5, 6) sts for underarm, work to end—136 (152, 170, 186, 202) sts rem for body.

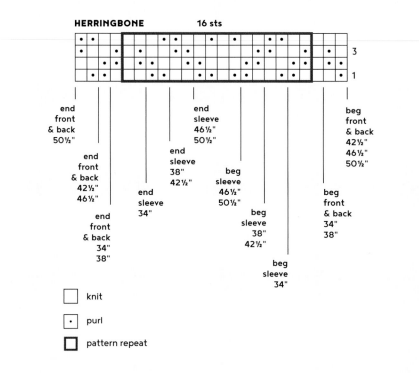

HERRINGBONE — 16 sts

knit

· purl

pattern repeat

end front & back 50½"

end front & back 42½" 46½"

end front & back 34" 38"

end sleeve 34"

end sleeve 38" 42½"

end sleeve 46½" 50½"

beg sleeve 46½" 50½"

beg sleeve 38" 42½"

beg sleeve 34"

beg front & back 34" 38"

beg front & back 42½" 46½" 50½"

Body

Work 14 rnds even in patt (see Notes).

SHAPE WAIST

Dec rnd: *K1, k2tog, work to 3 sts before m, ssk, k1; rep from * once more—4 sts dec'd.

Rep Dec rnd every 13th rnd once more—128 (144, 162, 178, 194) sts rem.

Work 18 rnds even.

Inc rnd: *K2, M1R, work to 2 sts before m, M1L, k2; rep from * once more—4 sts inc'd.

Rep Inc rnd every 13th rnd once more, working new sts into patt—136 (152, 170, 186, 202) sts.

Work even in patt until piece measures 13 (13, 13, 13½, 13½)" from underarm, or 3" less than desired finished length.

Change to smaller needle. Work in k1, p1 rib for 3". Loosely BO all sts in patt.

Sleeves

Transfer 38 (42, 46, 50, 54) sleeve sts to larger dpn. With RS facing and beg at center of underarm, pick up and knit 4 (4, 5, 5, 6) sts along underarm, work 38 (42, 46, 50, 54) sleeve sts in patt, pick up and knit 4 (4, 5, 5, 6) sts along underarm, pm and join in the rnd—46 (50, 56, 60, 66) sts.

Work even in patt for 2".

Dec rnd: K1, ssk, work to last 3 sts, k2tog, k1—2 sts dec'd.

Rep Dec rnd every 15 (11, 8, 7, 6)th rnd 5 (7, 9, 11, 13) more times—34 (34, 36, 36, 38) sts rem.

Work even until piece measures 17 (17, 17, 17½, 17½)" from underarm. Change to smaller dpn. Work in k1, p1 rib for 3". Loosely BO all sts in patt.

Finishing

Weave in ends. Block to measurements.

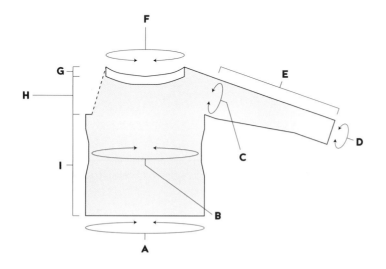

A: 34 (38, 42½, 46½, 50½)"

B: 32 (36, 40½, 44½, 48½)"

C: 11½ (12½, 14, 15, 16½)"

D: 8½ (8½, 9, 9, 9½)"

E: 20 (20, 20, 20½, 20½)"

F: 27 (25, 26½, 24½, 25½)"

G: 2 (1½, 1½, 1, 1)"

H: 5 (6, 6½, 7½, 8)"

I: 16 (16, 16, 16½, 16½)"

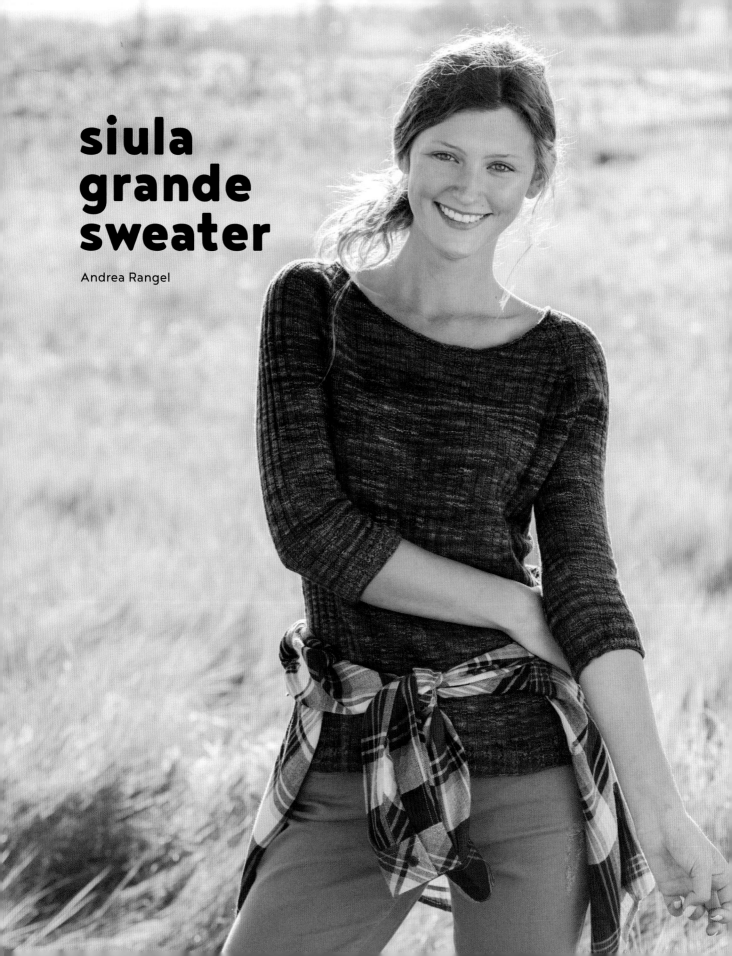

siula grande sweater

Andrea Rangel

Finished Size

Bust circumference: 34 (36½, 40¼, 42¾, 46½, 49)".

Shown in size 34", modeled with 2" of positive ease.

Yarn

Lace weight (#1 fine).

Shown here: Malabrigo Lace (100% Merino wool; 470 yd [430 m]/50 g): #LMBB062 marine, 4 (5, 5, 6, 6, 7) skeins.

Needles

Size U.S. 1 (2.25 mm): 16" and 32" circular (cir) and set of double-pointed (dpn).

Size U.S. 2 (2.75 mm): 16" cir.

Adjust needle size if necessary to obtain the correct gauge.

Notions

Stitch markers (m); stitch holders; tapestry needle.

Gauge

38 sts and 54 rnds = 4" in k3, p3 rib on smaller needle.

Notes

■ The body and sleeves of this pullover are worked in the round from the bottom up to the yoke, then the pieces are joined for working the circular yoke.

■ When working the yoke shaping, change to shorter circular needle when necessary.

■ The Lace Rib for Body and Lace Rib for Raglan charts are worked both in rounds and back and forth in rows. When working in rounds, work every chart row as a right-side row.

■ The sleeve decreases in the yoke are worked using the first and last knit stitches of each sleeve. Depending on the arrangement of the rib pattern for your size, there may be one or more purl stitches between these first and last knit stitches and the raglan markers. In this case, purl to the first knit stitch, ssk (first knit stitch with stitch after it), work in pattern to one stitch before the last knit stitch, k2tog (last knit stitch with stitch before it), then purl any stitches to the marker. If the first and last sleeve stitches for your size are knit stitches, simply work the first two sleeve stitches as ssk, work in pattern to the last two sleeve stitches, then k2tog.

■ During front neck shaping, the front raglan decreases are worked differently when only 11 stitches remain for each front. Work the right front as k1, ssk, work in pattern to the marker; and work the left front in pattern to the last 3 stitches, k2tog, k1. When only 2 stitches remain for each front, work the right front as ssk and the left front as k2tog. When decreasing in the lace pattern, do not work a yarnover unless there are enough stitches to work its corresponding decrease.

Body

With smaller 32" cir needle, CO 322 (346, 382, 406, 442, 466) sts. Place marker (pm) and join in the rnd.

Set-up rnd: K161 (173, 191, 203, 221, 233), pm for side, knit to end.

Next rnd: *Work Lace Rib for Body chart to m, sl m; rep from * once more.

Cont in patt as est until piece measures 1½ (1¾, 2, 2¼, 2½, 2¾)" from CO, ending with Rnd 1 or 3 of chart.

Next rnd: [K1, *p3, k3; rep from * to 4 sts before m, p3, k1, sl m] 2 times.

Rep last rnd until piece measures 3 (3¼, 3½, 3¾, 4, 4¼)" from CO.

SHAPE WAIST

Dec rnd 1: *K1, p2tog, work in patt to 3 sts before m, p2tog, k1, sl m; rep from * once more—4 sts dec'd.

Work 21 rnds even.

Rep Dec rnd 1—314 (338, 374, 398, 434, 458) sts rem: 157 (169, 187, 199, 217, 229) sts each for front and back.

Work 21 rnds even.

Dec rnd 2: *K1, k2tog, work in patt to 3 sts before m, k2tog, k1, sl m; rep from * once more—4 sts dec'd.

[Work 21 rnds even, then rep Dec rnd 2] 2 times—302 (326, 362, 386, 422, 446) sts rem: 151 (163, 181, 193, 211, 223) sts each for front and back.

Work 11 rnds even.

Inc rnd 1: *K1, M1, work in patt to 1 st before m, M1, k1, sl m; rep from * once more—4 sts inc'd.

Work 11 rnds even, working new sts in St st.

Rep Inc rnd 1—310 (334, 370, 394, 430, 454) sts: 155 (167, 185, 197, 215, 227) sts each for front and back.

Work 11 rnds even.

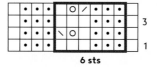

LACE RIB FOR BODY

6 sts

LACE RIB FOR SLEEVE

6 sts

LACE RIB FOR RAGLAN

9 sts

	k on RS; p on WS
•	p on RS; k on WS
O	yo
/	k2tog
\	ssk
	pattern repeat

Inc rnd 2: *K1, M1P, work in patt to 1 st before m, M1P, k1, sl m; rep from * once more—4 sts inc'd.

[Work 11 rnds even, then rep Inc rnd 2] 2 times, working new sts in rev St st—322 (346, 382, 406, 442, 466) sts: 161 (173, 191, 203, 221, 233) sts each for front and back.

Work even until piece measures 15¼ (15½, 15¾, 16, 16¼, 16½)" from CO. Do not break yarn. Set aside.

Sleeves

With dpn, CO 84 (90, 102, 114, 120, 126) sts. Pm and join in the rnd.

Knit 1 rnd.

Work Lace Rib for Sleeve chart until piece measures 1¼" from CO, ending with Rnd 1 or 3 of chart.

Next rnd: P1, k3, *p3, k3; rep from * to last 2 sts, p2.

Next rnd: M1P, work in rib patt to end—85 (91, 103, 115, 121, 127) sts.

Cont in rib patt as est, work 9 (7, 9, 9, 7, 5) rnds even.

Inc rnd: P1, M1 or M1P as needed to maintain patt, work to last st, M1 or M1P as needed to maintain patt, p1—2 sts inc'd.

Rep Inc rnd every 10 (8, 10, 10, 8, 6)th rnd 5 (9, 5, 5, 9, 18) more times, then every 8 (6, 8, 8, 6, 0)th rnd 7 (6, 7, 7, 6, 0) times—111 (123, 129, 141, 153, 165) sts.

Work even until piece measures 10¾" from CO.

Place first and last 7 (7, 10, 10, 13, 13) sts on holder for underarm—97 (109, 109, 121, 127, 139) sts rem. Place sts on separate holder. Break yarn.

Yoke

Joining rnd: With yarn attached to body, *work to 7 (7, 10, 10, 13, 13) sts before m, pm, place next 14 (14, 20, 20, 26, 26) sts on holder for underarm, removing side m, work 97 (109, 109, 121, 127, 139) sleeve sts*, pm, rep from * to * once more, pm for new beg of rnd—488 (536, 560, 608, 644, 692) sts: 147 (159, 171, 183, 195, 207) sts each for front and back, 97 (109, 109, 121, 127, 139) sts for each sleeve.

Next rnd: *Work Lace Rib for Raglan chart over 9 sts, work in rib patt as est to 9 sts before m, work Lace Rib for Raglan chart over 9 sts, sl m, work sleeve sts in rib patt as est to m, sl m; rep from * once more.

Rep last rnd 11 (9, 7, 11, 7, 11) more times.

Body dec rnd: *Work 9 sts in chart patt, ssk, work in patt to 11 sts before m, k2tog, work 9 sts in chart patt, sl m, work in patt to m, sl m; rep from * once more—4 sts dec'd; 2 sts each for front and back.

Rep Body dec rnd every other rnd 0 (1, 2, 0, 2, 0) more time(s)—484 (528, 548, 604, 632, 688) sts rem: 145 (155, 165, 181, 189, 205) sts each for front and back, 97 (109, 109, 121, 127, 139) sts for each sleeve.

Work 3 rnds even.

Body and sleeve dec rnd: *Work 9 sts in chart patt, ssk, work in patt to 11 sts before m, k2tog, work 9 sts in chart patt, sl m, work any purl sts until you reach the first knit st (see Notes), ssk, work in patt to 1 st before last knit st of sleeve section, k2tog, work any purl sts until you reach the m, sl m; rep from * once more—8 sts dec'd; 2 sts each for front, back, and both sleeves.

Rep Body and sleeve dec rnd every 4th rnd 8 (7, 8, 6, 9, 7) more times, then every other rnd 7 (12, 12, 20, 15, 21) times—356 (368, 380, 388, 432, 456) sts rem: 113 (115, 123, 127, 139, 147) sts each for front and back, 65 (69, 67, 67, 77, 81) sts for each sleeve.

Work 1 rnd even—yoke measures about 4¾ (5¼, 5½, 6¼, 6¼, 6½)".

SHAPE FRONT NECK

Next rnd: Work 9 sts in chart patt, ssk, work 35 (36, 39, 40, 46, 49) sts in patt, BO 21 (21, 23, 25, 25, 27) center front sts in patt, work in patt to 11 sts before m, k2tog, work 9 sts in chart patt, sl m, *purl any sts to first knit st, ssk, work in patt to last 2 knit sts, k2tog, purl any sts to m, sl m*, work 9 sts in chart patt, ssk, work in patt to 11 sts before m, k2tog, work 9 sts in chart patt, sl m, rep from * to * once more—327 (339, 349, 355, 399, 421) sts rem: 45 (46, 49, 50, 56, 59) sts for each front, 111 (113, 121, 125, 137, 145) back sts, 63 (67, 65, 65, 75, 79) sts for each sleeve.

Break yarn.

With RS facing, transfer 45 (46, 49, 50, 56, 59) left front sts to right needle without working them, ending at center front BO gap.

Beg working back and forth in rows (see Notes).

With WS facing, rejoin yarn at left front neck.

Work 1 WS row.

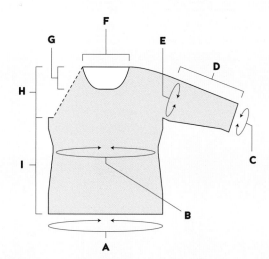

A: 34 (36½, 40¼, 42¾, 46½, 49)"

B: 31¾ (34¼, 38, 40¾, 44½, 47)"

C: 8¾ (9½, 10¾, 12, 12¾, 13¼)"

D: 10¾"

E: 11¾ (13, 13½, 14¾, 16, 17¼)"

F: 7¼ (7¼, 8, 8½, 9¼, 9¾)"

G: 3¼ (3½, 3¾, 3½, 4, 4)"

H: 8 (8¾, 9¼, 9¾, 10¼, 10½)"

I: 15¼ (15½, 15¾, 16, 16¼, 16½)"

Cont to work Body and sleeve dec row every RS row 21 (22, 23, 22, 25, 26) more times (see Notes), and *at the same time*, BO 3 sts at beg of next 6 (6, 6, 6, 10, 10) rows, BO 2 sts at beg of foll 4 (4, 4, 8, 4, 6) rows, then BO 1 st at beg of foll 20 (20, 24, 20, 22, 22) rows, then work neck edges even until raglan shaping has been completed—113 (117, 115, 125, 139, 149) sts rem: 1 st for each front, 69 (69, 75, 81, 87, 93) sts for back, 21 (23, 19, 21, 25, 27) sts for each sleeve.

Next row: (WS) P2tog, removing m between front and sleeve, work in patt to last 2 sts, ssp, removing m between front and sleeve—111 (115, 113, 123, 137, 147) sts rem; yoke measures about 8 (8¾, 9¼, 9¾, 10¼, 10½)".

BO all sts as foll: *Ssk, work 1 st in patt, pass first st over 2nd; rep from * to last 2 sts, k2tog, fasten off last st.

Finishing

NECK EDGING

With larger 16" cir needle and RS facing, beg at left back raglan, pick up and knit 1 st for every BO st along neck edge as foll: 21 (23, 19, 21, 25, 27) left sleeve sts, 23 (23, 25, 27, 30, 32) left neck sts, 21 (21, 23, 25, 25, 27) center front sts, 23 (23, 25, 27, 30, 32) right neck sts, 21 (23, 19, 21, 25, 27) right sleeve sts, and 69 (69, 75, 81, 87, 93) back sts—178 (182, 186, 202, 222, 238) sts total.

Pm and join in the rnd. Knit 5 rnds. BO all sts.

With tail threaded on a tapestry needle, graft underarm sts using Kitchener st.

Weave in ends. Block to measurements.

chamei pullover

Bristol Ivy

Finished Size

Bust circumference: 32 (35¾, 40¼, 44, 48½, 52)".

Pullover shown measures 40¼", modeled with 4¼" of positive ease.

Yarn

Worsted weight (#4 medium).

Shown here: Pigeonroof Studios American Twist Worsted (100% American Merino wool; 175 yd [160 m]/115 g): sagebrush, 6 (7, 8, 8, 9, 10) skeins.

Needles

Size U.S. 6 (4 mm): 32" circular (cir) and set of double-pointed (dpn).

Size U.S. 8 (5 mm): 32" cir and set of dpn.

Adjust needle size if necessary to obtain the correct gauge.

Notions

Markers (m); stitch holders; tapestry needle.

Gauge

17½ sts and 25 rnds = 4" in St st on larger needle.

Notes

■ The body of this pullover is worked in the round to the underarms, then divided for working the fronts and back separately. The twisted moss stitch pattern shifts across the front using increases and decreases, and continues after the shoulders are bound off to create the cowl, which is shaped with short rows. Stitches for the right shoulder are cast on at the end of the cowl, and the right front is worked down. The sleeves are worked in the round to the underarm, with the cap worked flat. The shoulders are seamed, the right front piece is seamed to the rest of the front, the bound-off edge of the cowl is seamed to the slanted side edge of the front/cowl to form a tube, and then the sleeves are sewn in.

■ While working the collar short-rows, if working a wrap together with a wrapped stitch on a twisted stitch, work the wrap together with the wrapped stitch through the back loop.

STITCH GUIDE

Twisted Moss Stitch in rnds (even number of sts)

Rnd 1: *K1tbl, p1; rep from * to end.

Rnds 2 and 3: *P1, k1tbl; rep from * to end.

Rnd 4: Rep Rnd 1.

Rep Rnds 1-4 for patt.

Twisted Moss Stitch in rows (even number of sts)

Row 1: (RS) *K1tbl, p1; rep from * to end.

Row 2: (WS) *P1tbl, k1; rep from * to end.

Row 3: *P1, k1tbl; rep from * to end.

Row 4: *K1, p1tbl; rep from * to end.

Rep Rows 1-4 for patt.

Twisted Moss Stitch in rows (odd number of sts)

Row 1: (RS) *K1tbl, p1; rep from * to last st, k1tbl.

Row 2: (WS) *K1, p1tbl; rep from * to last st, k1.

Row 3: *P1, k1tbl; rep from * to last st, p1.

Row 4: *P1tbl, k1; rep from * to last st, p1tbl.

Rep Rows 1-4 for patt.

Twisted Rib: (continued from Twisted Moss Stitch)

Set-up row: (WS) Knit the twisted purl sts and purl tbl the knit sts, as they appear.

Row 1: (RS) Knit tbl the twisted knit sts and purl the purl sts, as they appear.

Row 2: (WS) Purl tbl the twisted purl sts and knit the knit sts, as they appear.

Rep Rows 1 and 2 for patt.

Body

With smaller cir needle, CO 140 (156, 176, 192, 212, 228) sts. Place marker (pm) and join in the rnd.

Work in k1, p1 rib for 2". Change to larger cir needle.

Next rnd: K70 (78, 88, 96, 106, 114), pm for side, knit to end.

Next rnd: Knit to 2 sts before m, k2tog, pm, M1, sl m, knit to end.

Next rnd: Knit.

Shift rnd: Knit to 2 sts before m, k2tog, sl m, k1tbl, M1P, sl m, knit to end.

Next rnd: Knit to m, sl m, p1, k1tbl, sl m, knit to end.

Shift rnd: Knit to 2 sts before m, k2tog, sl m, k1tbl, p1, M1, sl m, knit to end.

Next rnd: Knit to m, sl m, p1, k1tbl, p1, sl m, knit to end.

Shift rnd: Knit to 2 sts before m, k2tog, sl m, work Twisted Moss st in rnds (see Stitch Guide) as est to m, M1 (or M1P to keep in patt), sl m, knit to end.

Next rnd: Knit to m, sl m, work in patt to m, sl m, knit to end.

Rep last 2 rnds 36 (40, 44, 45, 46, 49) more times, working new sts between m into Twisted Moss st, and ending 3 (3, 4, 4, 5, 5) sts before end of rnd on last rnd—30 (34, 40, 47, 56, 61) sts in St st between rnd m and patt m and 40 (44, 48, 49, 50, 53) sts in patt between patt m and side m; piece measures about 15 (16¼, 17½, 17¾, 18¼, 19)" from CO.

DIVIDE FOR FRONT AND BACK

Next rnd: BO 6 (6, 8, 8, 10, 10) sts, removing rnd m, knit to 2 sts before patt m, k2tog, sl m, work in patt to 3 (3, 4, 4, 5, 5) sts before side m, M1, place 64 (72, 80, 88, 96, 104) sts just worked on holder for front, BO 6 (6, 8, 8, 10, 10) sts, removing side m, knit to end—64 (72, 80, 88, 96, 104) sts rem for back.

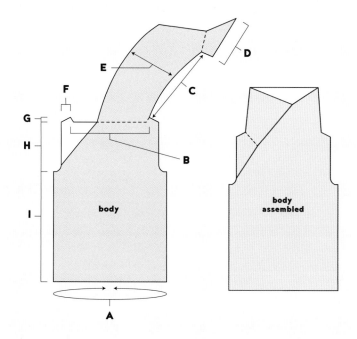

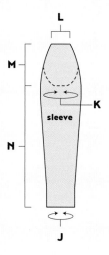

BODY

A: 32 (35¾, 40¼, 44, 48½, 52)"

B: 11½ (12¼, 12¾, 13¼, 12, 12¼)"

C: 14"

D: 6¾ (6¾, 7¼, 7, 7, 7)"

E: 8 (8¾, 9, 9¼, 9, 9½)"

F: 1½ (1½, 1¾, 1¾, 2¾, 2¾)"

G: ¾"

H: 7¼ (7¾, 8½, 9, 9¼, 10)"

I: 15 (16¼, 17½, 17¾, 18¼, 19)"

SLEEVE

J: 9½ (9½, 9½, 9½, 10½, 10½)"

K: 19 (19, 19, 19¼, 19¼, 19½)"

L: 12 (12¾, 13¾, 14¾, 16, 17¾)"

M: 5½ (6¼, 6½, 7¼, 7¼, 7½)"

N: 3¼ (3¼, 3¾, 3¾, 4, 4½)"

Back

Next row: (WS) Purl.

SHAPE ARMHOLES

SIZES 35¾ (40¼, 44, 48½, 52)" ONLY

Dec row: (RS) K1, ssk, knit to last 3 sts, k2tog, k1—2 sts dec'd.

Dec row: (WS) P1, p2tog, purl to last 3 sts, ssp, p1—2 sts dec'd.

Rep last 2 rows 0 (1, 1, 2, 3) more time(s)—68 (72, 80, 84, 88) sts rem.

SIZES 44 (48½, 52)" ONLY

Dec row: (RS) K1, ssk, knit to last 3 sts, k2tog, k1—2 sts dec'd.

Rep Dec row every RS row 2 (3, 4) more times—74 (76, 78) sts rem.

ALL SIZES

Work even until armhole measures 7¼ (7¾, 8½, 9, 9¼, 10)", ending with a WS row.

SHAPE NECK AND SHOULDERS

Next row: (RS) BO 2 (2, 2, 2, 4, 4) sts, k4 (4, 5, 5, 7, 7) (including last st from BO), k2tog, k1, place last 6 (6, 7, 7, 9, 9) sts worked on holder for right shoulder, BO 46 (50, 52, 54, 48, 50) sts, k1, ssk, knit to end—8 (8, 9, 9, 13, 13) sts rem for left shoulder.

Left shoulder

Next row: (WS) BO 2 (2, 2, 2, 4, 4) sts, purl to end—6 (6, 7, 7, 9, 9) sts rem.

Dec row: (RS) K1, ssk, knit to end—5 (5, 6, 6, 8, 8) sts rem.

Next row: (WS) BO 2 (2, 3, 3, 4, 4) sts, purl to end—3 (3, 3, 3, 4, 4) sts rem.

Knit 1 RS row. BO all sts.

Right shoulder

Return 6 (6, 7, 7, 9, 9) held right shoulder sts to needle and, with WS facing, rejoin yarn. Purl 1 WS row.

Dec row: (RS) BO 2 (2, 3, 3, 4, 4) sts, knit to last 3 sts, k2tog, k1—3 (3, 3, 3, 4, 4) sts rem.

Purl 1 WS row. BO all sts.

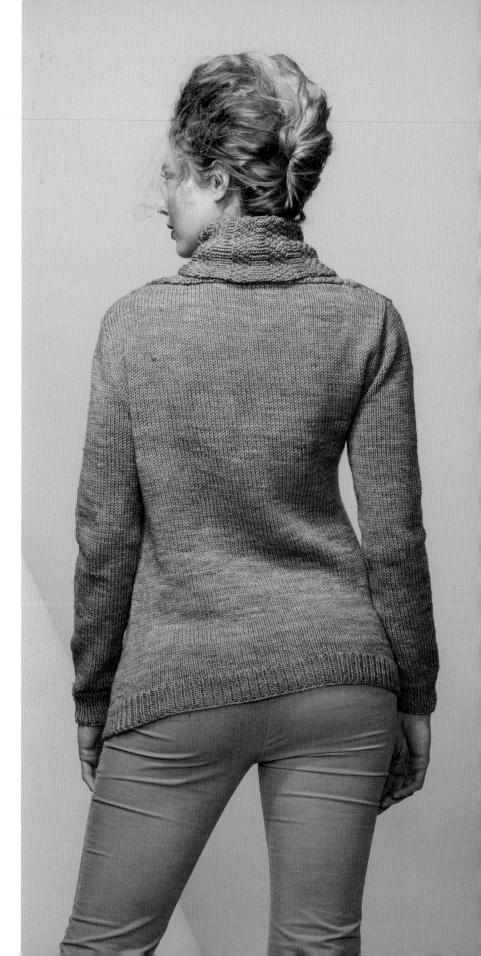

Front

Return 64 (72, 80, 88, 96, 104) held front sts to needle and, with WS facing, rejoin yarn—26 (30, 35, 42, 50, 55) sts in St st before m and 38 (42, 45, 46, 46, 49) sts in patt after m.

Next row: (WS) Work Twisted Moss st in rows (see Stitches) to m (working Row 2 or 4 to keep in patt), sl m, purl to end.

SHAPE ARMHOLES
SIZES 35¾ (40¼, 44, 48½, 52)" ONLY
Dec row: (RS) K1, ssk, knit to 2 sts before patt m, k2tog, sl m, work in patt to last 3 sts, M1 (or M1P to keep in patt), k2tog, k1—2 sts dec'd.

Dec row: (WS) P1, p2tog, work in patt to last 3 sts, ssp, p1—2 sts dec'd.

Rep last 2 rows 0 (1, 1, 2, 3) more time(s)--68 (72, 80, 84, 88) sts rem: 27 (29, 36, 41, 43) sts in St st before m and 41 (43, 44, 43, 45) sts in patt after m.

SIZES 44 (48½, 52)" ONLY
Dec row: (RS) K1, ssk, knit to 2 sts before patt m, k2tog, sl m, work in patt to end—2 sts dec'd (1 st at left armhole and 1 st at m).

Rep Dec row every RS row 2 (3, 4) more times—74 (76, 78) sts rem: 30 (33, 33) sts in St st before m and 44 (43, 45) sts in patt after m.

Work 1 WS row even.

ALL SIZES
Dec row: (RS) Knit to 2 sts before patt m, k2tog, sl m, work in patt to end—1 st dec'd.

Rep Dec row every RS row 18 (19, 20, 21, 20, 20) more times—45 (48, 51, 52, 55, 57) sts rem: 7 (7, 8, 8, 12, 12) sts in St st before m and 38 (41, 43, 44, 43, 45) sts in patt after m.

Work even in patt until armhole measures 7¼ (7¾, 8½, 9, 9¼, 10)", ending with a WS row.

SHAPE LEFT SHOULDER
At beg of RS rows, BO 2 (2, 2, 2, 4, 4) sts once, then BO 2 (2, 3, 3, 4, 4) sts once, then BO 3 (3, 3, 3, 4, 4) sts once—38 (41, 43, 44, 43, 45) sts rem.

Cowl

Work 9 rows even in patt, ending with a RS row. Shape collar using short-rows as foll:

> **Note:** Short-rows 1-6 are worked in Twisted Rib (see Stitch Guide) and Rows 8-15 are worked in Twisted Moss st.

Short-row 1: (WS) Work Set-up row of Twisted Rib over 14 sts, wrap next st, turn.

Short-row 2: (RS) Work in patt to end.

Short-row 3: Work 28 sts in patt, working wrap tog with wrapped st (see Notes), wrap next st, turn.

Short-row 4: Rep Short-row 2.

Short-row 5: Work 14 sts in patt, wrap next st, turn.

Short-row 6: Rep Short-row 2.

Row 7: Knit the twisted purl sts and purl tbl the knit sts, as they appear, working wraps tog with wrapped sts.

Row 8: Knit tbl the twisted knit sts and purl the purl sts, as they appear.

Rows 9-14: Rep Rows 7 and 8 three times.

Rep Short-rows/Rows 1-14 eight more times.

SHAPE RIGHT FRONT SHOULDER

Next row: (WS) Work in patt to end, pm, turn, then using the cable method, CO 3 (3, 3, 3, 4, 4) sts—41 (44, 46, 47, 47, 49) sts.

Next row: (RS) Knit to m, sl m, work in patt to end.

Next row: (WS) Work in patt to m, sl m, purl to end, turn, then CO 2 (2, 3, 3, 4, 4) sts—43 (46, 49, 50, 51, 53) sts.

Next row: (RS) Knit to m, sl m, work in patt to end.

Next row: (WS) Work in patt to m, sl m, purl to end, turn, then CO 2 (2, 2, 2, 4, 4) sts—45 (48, 51, 52, 55, 57) sts.

SIZES 44 (48½, 52)" ONLY

Inc row: (RS) Knit to 2 sts before m, M1L, k2, sl m, work in patt to end—1 st inc'd.

Inc row: (WS) Work in patt to m, sl m, p2, M1P, purl to end—1 st inc'd.

Rep last 2 rows once more—56 (59, 61) sts.

ALL SIZES

Inc row: (RS) Knit to 2 sts before m, M1L, k2, sl m, work in patt to end—1 st inc'd.

Rep Inc row every RS row 7 (7, 8, 6, 6, 6) more times—53 (56, 60, 63, 66, 68) sts.

Next row: (WS) BO 38 (41, 43, 44, 43, 45) sts pwise, purl to end—15 (15, 17, 19, 23, 23) sts rem.

Dec row: (RS) Knit to last 3 sts, k2tog, k1—1 st dec'd.

Rep Dec row every RS row 12 (12, 14, 10, 6, 6) more times—2 (2, 2, 8, 16, 16) sts rem.

SIZES 44 (48½, 52)" ONLY

Dec row: (WS) P1, p2tog, purl to end—1 st dec'd.

Dec row: (RS) Knit to last 3 sts, k2tog, k1—1 st dec'd.

Rep last 2 rows 2 (6, 6) more times—2 sts rem.

ALL SIZES

Work 2 (2, 0, 0, 0, 0) rows even. BO all sts.

Sleeves

With smaller dpn, CO 42 (42, 42, 42, 46, 46) sts. Pm and join in the rnd. Work in k1, p1 rib for 2".

Change to larger dpn and work in St st until piece measures 5¾ (4¾, 4, 3¾, 3½, 3)" from CO.

Inc rnd: K1, M1, knit to last st, M1, k1—2 sts inc'd.

Rep Inc rnd every 20 (14, 12, 10, 10, 8)th rnd 1 (4, 2, 4, 1, 2) more time(s), then every 18 (12, 10, 8, 8, 6)th rnd 3 (2, 6, 6, 10, 13) times—52 (56, 60, 64, 70, 78) sts.

Work even until piece measures 19 (19, 19, 19¼, 19¼, 19½)" from CO, ending 3 (3, 4, 4, 5, 5) sts before end of rnd on last rnd.

Next rnd: BO 6 (6, 8, 8, 10, 10) sts, removing m, knit to end—46 (50, 52, 56, 60, 68) sts rem.

Purl 1 WS row.

SHAPE CAP

SIZES 35¾ (40¼, 44, 48½, 52)" ONLY

Dec row: (RS) K1, ssk, knit to last 3 sts, k2tog, k1—2 sts dec'd.

Dec row: (WS) P1, p2tog, purl to last 3 sts, ssp, p1—2 sts dec'd.

Rep last 2 rows 0 (1, 1, 2, 3) more time(s)—46 (44, 48, 48, 52) sts rem.

SIZE 40¼" ONLY

Work 2 rows even.

ALL SIZES

Dec row: (RS) K1, ssk, knit to last 3 sts, k2tog, k1—2 sts dec'd.

Rep Dec row every RS row 4 (3, 0, 2, 3, 4) more times, then every 4th row 5 (6, 7, 6, 2, 3) times, then every 6th row 0 (0, 0, 1, 3, 2) time(s)—26 (26, 28, 28, 30, 32) sts rem.

BO 3 sts at beg of next 4 rows—14 (14, 16, 16, 18, 20) sts rem. BO all sts.

Finishing

Sew left shoulder seam. Sew CO shoulder sts of right front shoulder piece to BO sts of back right shoulder.

Beg at end of armhole shaping [about ¼ (¾, 1, 2, 2½, 3¼)" up from armhole BO] seam diagonal edge of St st insert to slanted side edge of front, then seam BO edge of collar to slanted side edge of front/collar, such that BO edge of collar shows on RS, and leaving about a 22" circumference open at top of collar for neck.

Sew in sleeves.

Seam collar to back neck, stretching slightly to fit.

Weave in ends. Block to measurements.

climbing rose henley

Cassie Castillo

Finished Size

Bust circumference: 36¼
(40¾, 44¼, 48, 52¼, 56¾)".

Pullover shown measures
36¼", modeled with 2¼" of
positive ease.

Yarn

DK weight (#3 light).

Shown here: Elsebeth
Lavold Silky Wool (45% wool,
35% silk, 20% nylon; 192 yd
[175 m]/1¾ oz [50 g]): #60
granite (MC), 6 (6, 7, 7, 8, 9)
skeins; #86 dark oak (CC1), 2
skeins; #96 magenta (CC2),
1 skein.

Needles

Size U.S. 4 (3.5 mm): 24"
circular (cir) and set of
double-pointed (dpn).

Size U.S. 5 (3.75 mm): 16" and
24" cir, and set of dpn.

*Adjust needle size if necessary
to obtain the correct gauge.*

Notions

Markers (m); tapestry needle;
sewing needle; two ¾" buttons.

Gauge

22 sts and 32 rnds= 4" in St st
on larger needle.

24 sts and 28 rnds= 4" in
charted patt on larger needle.

Notes

▪ This pullover is worked in
the round from the bottom
up. Steeks are used at the
armhole and neck openings.

▪ Stitches are picked up
around the armhole for the
sleeve and the cap is worked
with short-rows, then the
sleeve is worked in the round
to the cuff.

▪ If necessary, use a larger
needle for the charted pattern
in order to obtain gauge. At
pattern gauge, 47 chart rounds
will be worked. Chart shows
a full pattern repeat, in case
more rounds are required due
to a difference in row gauge.

▪ Use your favorite steeking
method to secure the steeks
at the front of the pullover and
the armholes before cutting.
For detailed steeking instructions, see *Knittingdaily.com/
steeking*.

Body

With CC1 and smaller cir needle, CO 198 (222, 243, 264, 288, 309) sts. Place marker (pm) and join in the rnd.

Work in k1, p2 rib for 2". Change to MC and larger 24" cir needle.

Knit 1 rnd.

SIZES 36¼ (40¾)" ONLY

Next rnd: RLI, k99 (111), LLI, knit to end—200 (224) sts.

SIZE 44¼" ONLY

Next rnd: RLI, knit to end—244 sts.

SIZE 56¾" ONLY

Next rnd: RLI, k154, LLI, knit to last st, RLI, k1—312 sts.

ALL SIZES

Work in St st until piece measures 3" from CO.

SHAPE WAIST

Set-up rnd: K33 (37, 41, 44, 48, 52), pm, k34 (38, 40, 44, 48, 52), pm, k66 (74, 82, 88, 96, 104), pm, k34 (38, 40, 44, 48, 52), pm, knit to end.

Dec rnd: *Knit to 2 sts before m, ssk, sl m, knit to m, sl m, k2tog; rep from * once more, knit to end—4 sts dec'd.

Rep Dec rnd every 8th rnd 5 more times—176 (200, 220, 240, 264, 288) sts rem.

Work even until piece measures 9¾" from CO.

Inc rnd: *Knit to m, RLI, sl m, knit to m, sl m, LLI; rep from * once more, knit to end—4 sts inc'd.

Rep Inc rnd every 8th rnd 5 more times—200 (224, 244, 264, 288, 312) sts.

Work even until piece measures 15½" from CO, removing all m on last rnd (except rnd m) and ending 6 (7, 9, 10, 12, 13) sts before end of rnd.

DIVIDE FOR FRONT AND BACK

Next rnd: BO 12 (14, 18, 20, 24, 26) sts, removing m, k88 (98, 104, 112, 120, 130) (including last st from BO), BO 12 (14, 18, 20, 24, 26) sts, knit to end—88 (98, 104, 112, 120, 130) sts rem each for front and back. Do not turn.

Set-up rnd: Pm for new beg of rnd, then using the backward-loop method, CO 6 sts for steek, pm, knit to gap, pm, CO 6 sts for steek, pm, knit to end (steek sts are not included in final st counts).

SHAPE ARMHOLES

Dec rnd: *K6 steek sts, sl m, ssk, knit to 2 sts before m, k2tog, sl m; rep from * once more—2 sts dec'd each for front and back.

Rep Dec rnd every rnd 3 (5, 5, 6, 8, 10) more times—80 (86, 92, 98, 102, 108) sts rem each for front and back.

Work even until armhole measures ¾ (1, 1½, 2, 2½, 3)". Change to CC1 and knit 1 rnd.

Next rnd: *K6 steek sts, sl m, purl to m, sl m; rep from * once more.

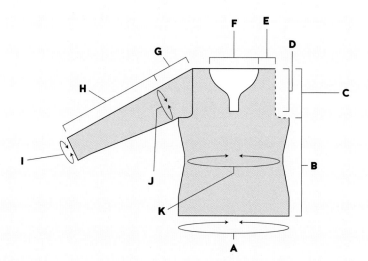

A: 36¼ (40¾, 44¼, 48,51¼, 56¾)"

B: 15½"

C: 7¾ (8, 8½, 9, 9½, 10)"

D: 6¾"

E: 2¾ (3¼, 3¾, 4¼, 4¼,4¾)"

F: 7¾ (7¾, 8, 8, 8¼, 8¼)"

G: 4¾ (5, 5, 5¼, 5½, 5¾)"

H: 17¼ (17½, 17¾, 17¾,17¾, 17¾)"

I: 7¼ (7¾, 8¼, 8¾, 9½,9¾)"

J: 13 (14¼, 15¾, 16¾,18¼, 19¼)"

K: 32 (36¼, 40, 43¾, 48,52¼)"

BEG STRANDED YOKE PATT AND DIVIDE FOR NECK

Next rnd: Work Steek chart over 6 sts, sl m, then beg and ending as indicated for left front for your size, work Yoke chart over 36 (39, 42, 45, 47, 50) sts, BO 8 sts for neck, beg and ending as indicated for right front for your size, work Yoke chart over 36 (39, 42, 45, 47, 50) sts (including last st from neck BO), sl m, work Steek chart over 6 sts, sl m, beg and ending as indicated for back for your size, work Yoke chart over 80 (86, 92, 98, 102, 108) sts.

Next rnd: Work in patt to neck BO, pm, CO 6 sts for steek, pm, work to end—36 (39, 42, 45, 47, 50) sts for each front and 80 (86, 92, 98, 102, 108) back sts rem.

Work even in patt until yoke measures 2" from CC1 ridge.

SHAPE FRONT NECK

Dec rnd: Work to 2 sts before 2nd m, k2tog, sl m, work to m, sl m, ssk, work to end—2 neck sts dec'd.

Rep Dec rnd every other rnd 4 more times, then every rnd 8 (8, 10, 10, 12, 12) times, then every other rnd 6 (6, 5, 5, 4, 4) times—17 (20, 22, 25, 26, 29) sts rem for each front, 80 (86, 92, 98, 102, 108) back sts.

Work even until armhole measures 7¾ (8, 8½, 9, 9½, 10)".

Break CC1 and CC2. BO all sts with MC. Secure and cut steeks for neck and armholes. Wet block body. With MC, sew shoulder seams.

> **Tip:** Working with three colors of yarn at the same time can be tricky; try holding one color over each of the first three fingers on your right hand, or holding two yarns in your right hand and one in your left hand. To trap long floats, insert the needle through the next stitch and scoop up the float from the row below and knit together; this method is easier and faster than twisting the yarns together as you go.

Sleeves

With MC, larger 16" cir needle and RS facing, beg at shoulder seam, pick up and knit 36 (39, 43, 46, 50, 53) sts evenly along armhole to center of armhole BO, pm, pick up and knit 36 (39, 43, 46, 50, 53) sts evenly along armhole to shoulder seam—72 (78, 86, 92, 100, 106) sts.

Pm and join in the rnd. Working back and forth, shape cap using short-rows as foll:

> **Note:** Do not work wraps tog with their sts.

Short-row 1: (RS) K12 (13, 15, 16, 17, 18), wrap next st, turn.

Short-row 2: (WS) Purl to m, sl m, p12 (13, 15, 16, 17, 18), wrap next st, turn.

Short-row 3: Knit to m, sl m, knit to wrapped st, knit wrap tog with wrapped st, wrap next st, turn.

Short-row 4: Purl to m, sl m, purl to wrapped st, purl wrap tog with wrapped st, wrap next st, turn.

YOKE

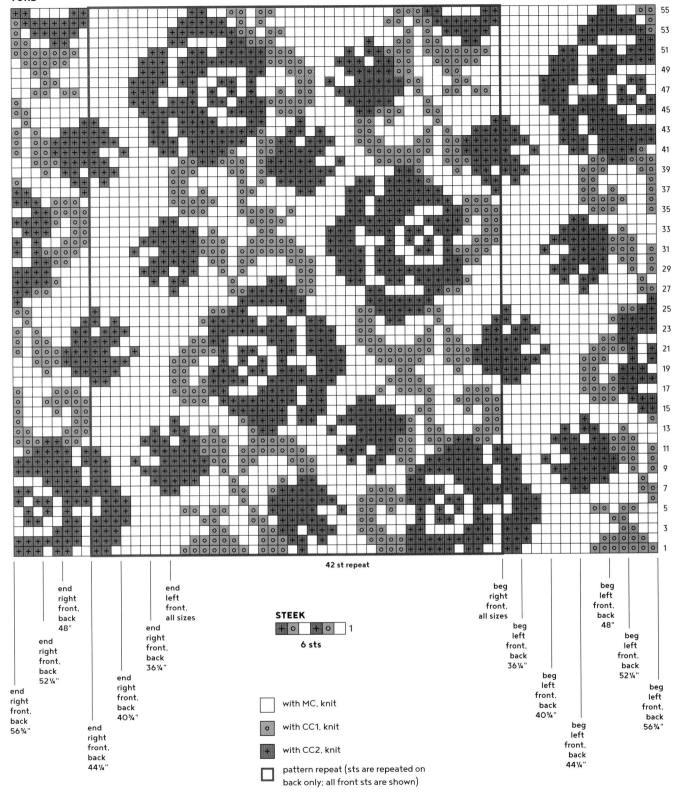

55
53
51
49
47
45
43
41
39
37
35
33
31
29
27
25
23
21
19
17
15
13
11
9
7
5
3
1

42 st repeat

end right front, back 56¾"

end right front, back 52¼"

end right front, back 48"

end right front, back 44¼"

end right front, back 40¾"

end right front, back 36¼"

end left front, all sizes

end right front, all sizes

beg right front, all sizes

beg left front, back 36¼"

beg left front, back 40¾"

beg left front, back 44¼"

beg left front, back 48"

beg left front, back 52¼"

beg left front, back 56¾"

STEEK

1

6 sts

☐ with MC, knit

▣ with CC1, knit

✚ with CC2, knit

☐ pattern repeat (sts are repeated on back only; all front sts are shown)

Rep last 2 short-rows 16 (17, 17, 18, 19, 20) more times—6 (7, 9, 10, 12, 13) sts rem unworked on each side of armhole m. Resume working in rnds.

Next rnd: Knit to shoulder m, remove m, knit to armhole m. This will now be beg-of-rnd m.

Work even in St st for 1".

Dec rnd: K1, k2tog, knit to last 3 sts, ssk, k1—2 sts dec'd.

Rep Dec rnd every 6 (4, 4, 4, 4, 4)th rnd 10 (0, 4, 9, 16, 22) more times, then every 8 (6, 6, 6, 6, 6)th rnd 5 (17, 15, 12, 7, 3) times, changing to dpn when necessary—40 (42, 46, 48, 52, 54) sts rem.

Work even until sleeve measures 15¼ (15½, 15¾, 15¾, 15¾, 15¾)" from underarm.

SIZES 36¼ (44¼, 52¼)" ONLY

K1, k2tog, knit to end—39 (45, 51) sts rem.

ALL SIZES

Change to CC1 and smaller dpn. Knit 1 rnd. Work in k1, p2 rib for 1½".

RUFFLE

Rnd 1: *[K1, yo, k1] in same st, p2; rep from * to end—65 (70, 75, 80, 85, 90) sts.

Rnd 2: *K3, p2; rep from * to end.

Rnd 3: *[K1, M1] 2 times, k1, p2; rep from * to end—91 (98, 105, 112, 119, 126) sts.

Rnds 4-6: *K5, p2; rep from * to end.

BO all sts in patt.

Finishing

NECKBAND

With CC1, smaller cir needle and RS facing, pick up and knit 38 (38, 39, 39, 38, 38) sts along right front neck to shoulder, 46 (46, 48, 48, 52, 52) sts along back neck to shoulder, and 39 sts along left front neck—123 (123, 126, 126, 129, 129) sts.

Next row: (WS) *K2, p1; rep from * to end.

Ruffle

Row 1: (RS) *[K1, yo, k1] in same st, p2; rep from * to end—205 (205, 210, 210, 215, 215) sts.

Row 2: (WS) *K2, p3; rep from * to end.

Row 3: *[K1, M1] 2 times, k1, p2; rep from * to end—287 (287, 294, 294, 301, 301) sts.

Row 4: *K2, p5; rep from * to end.

Row 5: *K5, p2; rep from * to end.

Row 6: *K2, p5; rep from * to end.

BO all sts. Sew ends of ruffle to BO edge at center front neck.

BUTTON LOOPS (MAKE 2)

With CC1 and smaller dpns, work 2-st I-cord for 2". Break yarn and draw through both sts.

Sew ends of one button loop to WS of ruffle on right front placket ¾" up from garter ridge.

Sew ends of 2nd button loop 1¾" up from garter ridge.

Sew buttons on left front placket opposite button loops.

Whipstitch edges of steeks neatly to WS of body. Weave in ends. Block to measurements.

trail
henley

Cassie Castillo

Finished Size

Bust circumference: 31¼
(35½, 39¾, 43¾, 48, 52¼)".

Pullover shown measures
31¼", modeled with ¾" of
negative ease.

Yarn

DK weight (#3 light).

Shown here: Elsebeth Lavold
Silky Wool (45% wool,
35% silk, 20% nylon; 192 yd
[175 m]/1¾ oz [50 g]): #145
tangelo orange, 6 (7, 8, 9, 10,
11) skeins.

Needles

Sizes U.S. 4 (3.5 mm): 24
or 32" circular (cir) and set
double-pointed (dpn).

Size U.S. 5 (3.75 mm): 24 or
32" cir and set of dpn.

*Adjust needle size if necessary
to obtain the correct gauge.*

Notions

Markers (m); stitch holders;
tapestry needle; five ⅝"
buttons.

Gauge

23 sts and 35 rnds = 4" in
charted patt on larger needle.

Notes

■ The body of this pullover is
worked in the round to the
underarm, then the front and
back are worked separately
back and forth. The sleeves
are worked in the round, with
the sleeve cap worked flat.

■ The chart is worked both in
rounds and back and forth
in rows. When working in
rounds, work every chart row
as a right-side row.

■ During shaping, if there
are not enough stitches to
work each decrease with its
companion yarnover, knit the
remaining stitch instead.

Body

With smaller cir needle, CO 180 (204,
228, 252, 276, 300) sts. Place marker
(pm) and join in the rnd.

Next rnd: P1, *k1, p2; rep from * to last
2 sts, k1, p1. Rep last rnd until ribbing
measures 2". Change to larger cir needle.

Work Eyelet chart until piece measures 14
(14½, 15, 15, 15, 15)" from CO, ending with
an even-numbered chart rnd.

DIVIDE FOR FRONT NECK

Next rnd: BO 6 sts for front neck, work
in patt to end—174 (198, 222, 246, 270,
294) sts rem.

Beg working back and forth in rows
(see Notes).

Next row: (WS) P1, work in patt to last
st, p1.

Keeping 1 st each side in St st for
selvedge, work until piece measures 2"
from neck BO, ending with a WS row.

DIVIDE FOR FRONTS AND BACK

Next row: (RS) Work 38 (42, 47, 51, 56, 60)
sts in patt and place these sts on holder
for right front, BO 8 (12, 14, 18, 20, 24)
underarm sts, work until there are 82 (90,
100, 108, 118, 126) sts for back and place
these sts on holder, BO 8 (12, 14, 18, 20,
24) underarm sts, work in patt to end—38
(42, 47, 51, 56, 60) sts rem for left front.

Left Front

Next row: (WS) P1, work in patt to last st, p1.

> **Note:** *Armhole and neck shaping
> occur simultaneously; read the foll
> section all the way through before
> proceeding.*

Dec row: (RS) Ssk, work in patt to last 2
sts, k2tog—2 sts dec'd.

Cont to dec 1 st at armhole edge at beg of
every RS row 1 (2, 4, 5, 7, 8) more time(s),
at the same time, dec 1 st at neck edge at
end of every RS row 19 (21, 21, 22, 22, 20)
more times, then every 4th row 3 (3, 4, 5,

6, 8) times—13 (14, 16, 17, 19, 22) sts rem when all shaping is complete.

Work even until armhole measures 7 (7½, 8, 8½, 9, 9½)", ending with a WS row.

SHAPE SHOULDER

At beg of RS rows, BO 4 (5, 5, 6, 6, 7) sts 2 times, then BO 5 (4, 6, 5, 7, 8) sts once—no sts rem.

Right Front

Return 38 (42, 47, 51, 56, 60) held right front sts to needle and, with WS facing, rejoin yarn.

Next row: (WS) P1, work in patt to last st, p1.

> *Note: Armhole and neck shaping occur simultaneously; read the foll section all the way through before proceeding.*

Dec row: (RS) Ssk, work in patt to last 2 sts, k2tog—2 sts dec'd.

Cont to dec 1 st at neck edge at beg of every RS row 19 (21, 21, 22, 22, 20) more times, then every 4th row 3 (3, 4, 5, 6, 8) times, **at the same time**, dec 1 st at armhole edge at end of every RS row 1 (2, 4, 5, 7, 8) more time(s)—13 (14, 16, 17, 19, 22) sts rem when all shaping is complete.

Work even until armhole measures 7 (7½, 8, 8½, 9, 9½)", ending with a RS row.

SHAPE SHOULDER

At beg of WS rows, BO 4 (5, 5, 6, 6, 7) sts 2 times, then BO 5 (4, 6, 5, 7, 8) sts once—no sts rem.

Back

Return 82 (90, 100, 108, 118, 126) held back sts to needle and, with WS facing, rejoin yarn.

Next row: (WS) P1, work in patt to last st, p1.

SHAPE ARMHOLES

Dec row: (RS) Ssk, work in patt to last 2 sts, k2tog—2 sts dec'd.

Rep Dec row every RS row 1 (2, 4, 5, 7, 8) more time(s)—78 (84, 90, 96, 102, 108) sts rem.

Work even until armhole measures 6½ (7, 7½, 8, 8½, 9)", ending with a WS row.

SHAPE NECK

Next row: (RS) Work 15 (16, 18, 19, 21, 24) sts in patt and place these sts on holder for right shoulder, BO 48 (52, 54, 58, 60, 60) sts, work in patt to end—15 (16, 18, 19, 21, 24) sts rem for left shoulder.

LEFT SHOULDER

Next row: (WS) P1, work in patt to last st, p1.

Dec row: (RS) Ssk, work in patt to last st, k1—1 st dec'd.

Rep last 2 rows once more—13 (14, 16, 17, 19, 22) sts rem.

Shape shoulder

At beg of WS rows, BO 4 (5, 5, 6, 6, 7) sts 2 times, then BO 5 (4, 6, 5, 7, 8) sts once—no sts rem.

RIGHT SHOULDER

Return 15 (16, 18, 19, 21, 24) held sts to needle and, with WS facing, rejoin yarn.

Next row: (WS) P1, work in patt to last st, p1.

Dec row: (RS) K1, work in patt to last 2 sts, k2tog—1 st dec'd.

Rep last 2 rows once more—13 (14, 16, 17, 19, 22) sts rem.

Work 1 WS row even.

Shape shoulder

At beg of RS rows, BO 4 (5, 5, 6, 6, 7) sts 2 times, then BO 5 (4, 6, 5, 7, 8) sts once—no sts rem.

Sleeves

With smaller dpn, CO 54 (60, 72, 78, 84, 96) sts. Pm and join in the rnd.

Next rnd: P1, *k1, p2; rep from * to last 2 sts, k1, p1.

Rep last rnd until ribbing measures 2". Change to larger dpn.

EYELET

6-st rep

□ k on RS; p on WS

· p on RS; k on WS

○ yo

╱ k2tog

╲ ssk

□ pattern repeat

Work Eyelet chart until piece measures 12¾ (12¾, 13, 13¼, 13¼, 13½)" from CO, ending with an even-numbered chart rnd and ending 4 (6, 7, 9, 10, 12) sts before end of rnd on last rnd.

Beg working back and forth in rows.

SHAPE CAP

Next row: (RS) BO 8 (12, 14, 18, 20, 24) sts, work in patt to end—46 (48, 58, 60, 64, 72) sts rem.

Next row: (WS) P1, work in patt to last st, p1.

Dec row: (RS) Ssk, work in patt to last 2 sts, k2tog—2 sts dec'd.

Rep Dec row every RS row 4 (3, 8, 7, 8, 10) more times, then every 4th row 9 (10, 8, 9, 9, 9) times—18 (20, 24, 26, 28, 32) sts rem. BO all sts.

Finishing

Block pieces to measurements. Sew shoulder seams.

NECKBAND

With smaller cir needle and RS facing, beg at lower corner of right front neck, pick up and knit 58 (62, 64, 69, 73, 76) sts evenly along right front neck to shoulder, 64 (68, 70, 72, 76, 76) sts along back neck, and

58 (62, 64, 69, 73, 76) sts along left front neck to lower corner—180 (192, 198, 210, 222, 228) sts total.

Next row: (WS) K1, p1, *k2, p1; rep from * to last st, k1.

Next row: (RS) P1, *k1, p2; rep from * to last 2 sts, k1, p1.

Rep last 2 rows once more, then work WS row again.

Buttonhole row: (RS) Work 2 sts in patt, work 3-st one-row buttonhole, work 3 sts in patt, work 3-st one-row buttonhole, work to end.

Work 3 more rows in patt.

BO all sts in patt.

Overlap neckband ends and sew to front neck BO. Sew on 2 buttons opposite buttonholes, and sew rem 3 buttons evenly spaced along neckband.

Sew sleeves into armholes. Weave in ends.

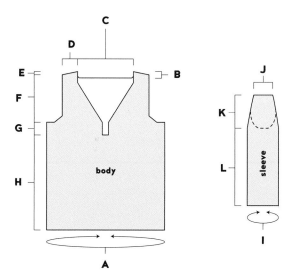

BODY

A: 31¼ (35½, 39¾, 43¾, 48, 52¼)"

B: 1"

C: 9 (9¾, 10, 10¾, 11¼, 11¼)"

D: 2¼ (2½, 2¾, 3, 3¼, 3¾)"

E: ½"

F: 7 (7½, 8, 8½, 9, 9½)"

G: 2"

H: 14 (14½, 15, 15, 15, 15)"

SLEEVE

I: 9¼ (10½, 12½, 13½, 14½, 16¾)"

J: 3¼ (3½, 4¼, 4½)"

K: 5¼ (5½, 5¾, 6, 6¼, 6½)"

L: 12¾ (12¾, 13, 13¼, 13¼, 13½)"

charlestown pullover

Cheryl Chow

Finished Size

Bust circumference: 36¼
(40¼, 44¼, 47¾, 51¾, 55)".

Pullover shown measures
36¼", modeled with 2¼" of
positive ease.

Yarn

Worsted weight (#4 medium).

Shown here: Brown Sheep
Company Nature Spun
Worsted (100% wool; 245
yd [224 m]/3½ oz [100 g]):
#720W ash, 5 (6, 7, 8, 9, 9)
balls.

Needles

Size U.S. 6 (4 mm): 32"
circular (cir) and set of
double-pointed (dpn).

Size U.S. 7 (4.5 mm): 32" cir
and set of dpn.

*Adjust needle size if necessary
to obtain the correct gauge.*

Notions

Markers (m); removable m;
cable needle (cn); stitch
holders; tapestry needle.

Gauge

24 sts and 26 rows = 4" in
Texture patt on larger needles.

15 sts of Zigzag chart = 2¼"
wide on larger needles.

18 (24, 24, 30, 30, 30) sts of
Body Cable chart = 2½ (3¼,
3¼, 4¼, 4¼, 4¼)" wide on
larger needles.

Notes

▪ This pullover is worked from
the top down. The saddle
shoulders are worked back
and forth, then stitches for
the front and back are picked
up along the edges of the
saddles, with stitches cast on
for the neck, and worked back
and forth. Stitches for the
sleeves are picked up around
the armhole and the sleeves
are worked in the round from
the top down, with short-rows
to shape the cap.

▪ The charts are worked both
in rounds and back and forth
in rows. When working in
rounds, work every chart row
as a right-side row.

▪ When working Right or Left
Texture or Right or Left Zigzag
charts, if you do not have
enough stitches to complete
the three-stitch maneuver or
a cable, knit or purl the extra
stitches as they are worked in
the background of the chart
(refer to the row above).

Saddle (make 2)

With larger cir needle, CO 20 sts. Do not join.

Work Sleeve Cable chart until piece measures 3½ (3½, 4, 4½, 5, 5)" from CO, ending with a RS row. Break yarn. Place sts on holder for sleeve.

Back

With larger cir needle and RS facing, and beg next to live saddle sts, pick up and knit 22 (22, 25, 28, 32, 32) sts along saddle edge ending next to CO edge, using the cable method CO 40 (42, 46, 48, 48, 52) sts for back neck, with RS of 2nd saddle facing and beg next to CO edge, pick up and knit 22 (22, 25, 28, 32, 32) sts along 2nd saddle edge—84 (86, 96, 104, 112, 116) sts total.

Knit 1 WS row.

Set-up row: (RS) Beg as indicated for your size, work Right Texture chart over 4 (2, 7, 8, 12, 14) sts (see Notes), work Column chart over 7 sts beg and ending as indicated for back, work Right Zigzag chart over 15 sts, work Column chart over 7 sts, work Body Cable chart over 18 (24, 24, 30, 30, 30) sts, work Column chart over 7 sts beg and ending as indicated for back, work Left Zigzag chart over 15 sts, work Column chart over 7 sts, work Left Texture chart over 4 (2, 7, 8, 12, 14) sts, ending as indicated for your size.

Cont in patt as est until piece measures 5¼ (5, 5, 5¾, 6, 6)" from pick-up row, ending with a WS row.

SHAPE ARMHOLES

Inc row: (RS) K1f&b, work in patt to last st, k1f&b—2 sts inc'd.

Rep Inc row every other row 0 (2, 3, 3, 4, 4) more times, working new sts into Right or Left Texture patt—86 (92, 104, 112, 122, 126) sts.

Work 1 WS row even. CO 2 sts at beg of next 2 (4, 4, 4, 4, 6) rows, working new sts into Right or Left Texture patt—90 (100, 112, 120, 130, 138) sts.

Break yarn and place sts on holder.

COLUMN

7 sts

SLEEVE TEXTURE

4-st rep

BODY CABLE

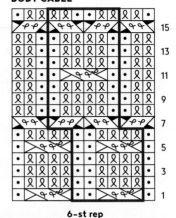

6-st rep

SLEEVE CABLE

20 sts

☐ k on RS; p on WS		⟋φφ sl 2 sts onto cn, hold in front, p1, [k1tbl] 2 times from cn
• p on RS; k on WS		⟋ sl 2 sts onto cn, hold in front, [k1tbl] 2 times, [k1tbl] 2 times from cn
℞ k1tbl on RS; p1tbl on WS		⟋φφ sl 2 sts onto cn, hold in back, [k1tbl] 3 times, [p1, k1] from cn
☐ pattern repeat		
⟝○⟞ pass 3rd st on left needle over first 2 sts and off needle, k1, yo, k1		⟋φφφ sl 3 sts onto cn, hold in front, k1, p1, [k1tbl] 3 times from cn
φφ⟍ sl 1 st onto cn, hold in back, [k1tbl] 2 times, p1 from cn		

LEFT ZIGZAG

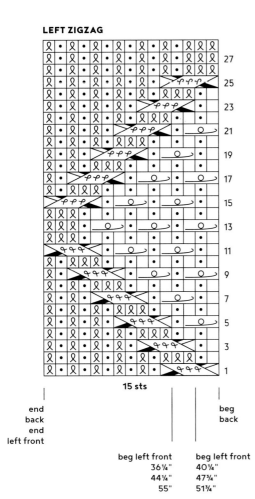

15 sts

end
back
end
left front

beg left front
36¼"
44¼"
55"

beg left front
40¼"
47¾"
51¾"

beg
back

RIGHT ZIGZAG

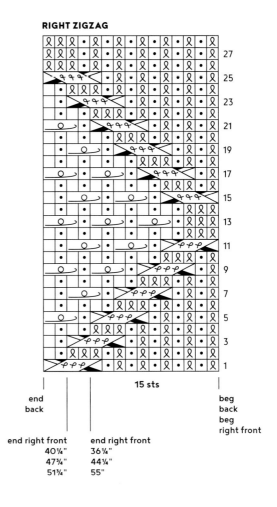

15 sts

end
back

end right front
40¼"
47¾"
51¾"

end right front
36¼"
44¼"
55"

beg
back
beg
right front

RIGHT TEXTURE

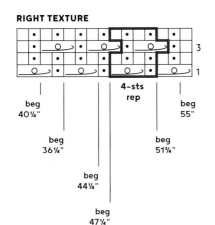

4-sts
rep

beg
40¼"

beg
36¼"

beg
44¼"

beg
47¼"

beg
51¾"

beg
55"

LEFT TEXTURE

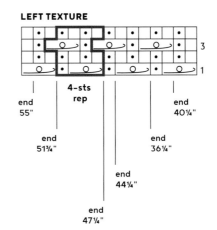

4-sts
rep

end
55"

end
51¾"

end
44¼"

end
47¼"

end
36¼"

end
40¼"

RIGHT FRONT

With larger cir needle and RS facing, pick up and knit 22 (22, 25, 28, 32, 32) sts along right saddle edge.

Knit 1 WS row.

Set-up row: (RS) Beg as indicated for your size, work Right Texture chart over 4 (2, 7, 8, 12, 14) sts, work Column chart over 7 sts, work Right Zigzag chart over rem 11 (13, 11, 13, 13, 11) sts, ending as indicated for right front for your size.

Cont in patt as est until piece measures 1½ (2, 2, 2½, 2½, 2½)" from pick-up row, ending with a WS row.

Shape neck

Inc row: (RS) Work to last st, k1f&b—1 st inc'd.

Rep Inc row every RS row 3 more times, working 4 (2, 4, 2, 2, 4) new sts into Right Zigzag patt and foll 0 (2, 0, 2, 2, 0) sts in Column patt—26 (26, 29, 32, 36, 36) sts.

Work 2 rows even.

At beg of WS rows, CO 2 sts 2 times, working new sts in Column patt—30 (30, 33, 36, 40, 40) sts.

Place sts on holder. Do not break yarn.

LEFT FRONT

With 2nd ball of yarn, larger cir needle, and RS facing, pick up and knit 22 (22, 25, 28, 32, 32) sts along left saddle edge.

Knit 1 WS row.

Set-up row: (RS) Beg as indicated for your size, work Left Zigzag chart over 11 (13, 11, 13, 13, 11) sts, work Column chart over 7 sts, work Left Texture chart over 4 (2, 7, 8, 12, 14) sts, ending as indicated for left front for your size.

Cont in patt as est until piece measures 1½ (2, 2, 2½, 2½, 2½)" from pick-up row, ending with a WS row.

Shape neck

Inc row: (RS) K1f&b, work to end.

Rep Inc row every other row 3 more times, working 4 (2, 4, 2, 2, 4) new sts into Right Zigzag patt and foll 0 (2, 0, 2, 2, 0) sts in Column chart patt—26 (26, 29, 32, 36, 36) sts.

Work 1 WS row even.

At beg of RS rows, CO 2 sts 2 times, working new sts in Column patt—30 (30, 33, 36, 40, 40) sts.

Work 1 WS row even. Break yarn.

Front

Joining row: (RS) Work 30 (30, 33, 36, 40, 40) held right front sts from holder, CO 24 (26, 30, 32, 32, 36) sts for neck, work 30 (30, 33, 36, 40, 40) left front sts—84 (86, 96, 104, 112, 116) sts total.

Next row: (WS) Work in est patt over 26 (24, 29, 30, 34, 36) sts, work Column chart over 7 sts, k1, [p4, k2] 2 (3, 3, 4, 4, 4) times, p4, k1, work Column chart over 7 sts, work in est patt to end.

Next row: (RS) Work 33 (31, 36, 37, 41, 43) sts in patt, work Body Cable chart over 18 (24, 24, 30, 30, 30) sts, work in patt to end.

Work even until piece measures 5¼ (5, 5, 5¾, 6, 6)" from pick-up row, ending with a WS row.

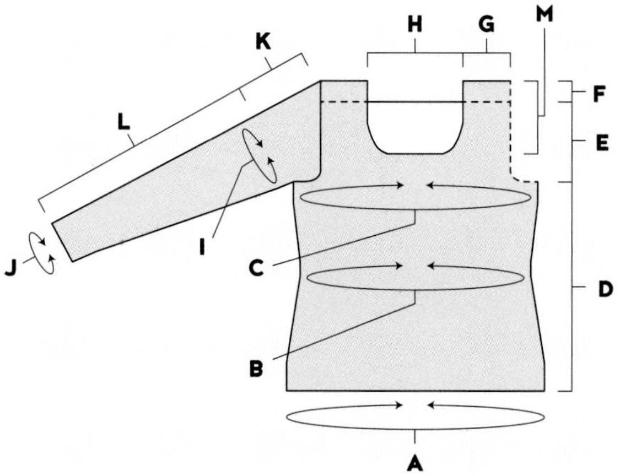

A: 37¾ (41¾, 45, 48¼, 52¼, 55¾)"

B: 34¼ (38¼, 42¼, 45¾, 50¼, 53¾)"

C: 36¼ (40¼, 44¼, 47¾, 51¾, 55)"

D: 15 (15, 15½, 15½, 16, 16)"

E: 5¾ (6½, 6¾, 7½, 8¼, 8½)"

F: 1½"

G: 3½ (3½, 4, 4½, 5, 5)"

H: 6¾ (7, 7¾, 8, 8, 8¾)"

I: 12½ (12¾, 13½, 14¾, 15¾, 17¼)"

J: 7¼ (7½, 7¾, 8½, 8½, 8¾)"

K: 3½ (3½, 3¾, 4¼, 4½, 5¼)"

L: 17 (17, 17¼, 17¼, 17½, 17½)"

M: 5¼ (5¾, 5¾, 6¼, 6¼, 6¼)"

SHAPE ARMHOLES

Inc row: (RS) K1f&b, work in patt to last st, k1f&b—2 sts inc'd.

Rep Inc row every RS row 0 (2, 3, 3, 4, 4) more times, working new sts into Right or Left Texture patt—86 (92, 104, 112, 122, 126) sts.

Work 1 WS row even.

CO 2 sts at beg of next 2 (4, 4, 4, 4, 6) rows, working new sts into Right or Left Texture patt—90 (100, 112, 120, 130, 138) sts.

Joining rnd: Work 90 (100, 112, 120, 130, 138) front sts in patt, CO 10 (11, 11, 12, 13, 14) sts, place marker (pm), CO 9 (10, 10, 11, 12, 13) sts, work 90 (100, 112, 120, 130, 138) back sts in patt, CO 9 (10, 10, 11, 12, 13) sts, pm, CO 10 (11, 11, 12, 13, 14) sts—218 (242, 266, 286, 310, 330) sts total.

Pm and join in the rnd.

Body

Next rnd: Work to 1 st before m, working new sts into Left Texture patt, k1, sl m, work to m, working new sts into Right or Left Texture patt.

> **Note:** This is new beg of rnd.

Next rnd: K1, work to 1 st before side m (removing old beg-of-rnd m and working new sts into Right Texture patt), k1, sl m, work in patt to end.

Work even until piece measures 1½" from underarm.

SHAPE WAIST

Dec rnd: K1, k2tog, work to 3 sts before m, ssk, k1, sl m, k2tog, work to last 2 sts, ssk—4 sts dec'd.

Rep Dec rnd every 13th (13th, 14th, 14th, 22nd, 22nd) rnd 2 (2, 2, 2, 1, 1) more time(s)—206 (230, 254, 274, 302, 322) sts rem.

Work 7 rnds even.

Inc rnd: K1, M1L, work to 1 st before m, M1R, k1, sl m, M1L, work to m, M1R—4 sts inc'd.

chart sts dec 3 (3, 3, 5, 5, 5) sts evenly as you go and ending with k1tbl, [p1, k1tbl] 22 (23, 26, 27, 30, 32) times, [p1] 1 (0, 1, 1, 1, 0) time, [p2tog] 0 (1, 0, 0, 0, 1) time**, k1tbl, rep from * to ** once more—220 (240, 264, 280, 304, 320) sts rem.

Next rnd: *K1tbl, p1; rep from * to end.

Rep last rnd for 2". BO all sts in patt.

Sleeves

With larger dpn and RS facing, beg at center of underarm, pick up and knit 10 (11, 11, 12, 13, 14) sts along underarm CO sts, 18 (18, 20, 23, 25, 28) sts to saddle, work 20 held saddle sts in patt, pick up and knit 18 (18, 20, 23, 25, 28) sts to underarm, and 9 (10, 10, 11, 12, 13) sts along underarm CO—75 (77, 81, 89, 95, 103) sts total.

Pm and join in the rnd. Using the German method, shape cap using short-rows as foll:

Short-row 1: (RS) K2 (1, 1, 1, 2, 2), [p1, k1] 13 (14, 15, 17, 18, 20) times, pm, work Sleeve Cable chart over 20 sts, pm, k2, turn.

Short-row 2: (WS) Make double st, p1, sl m, work Sleeve Cable chart over 20 sts, sl m, p2, turn.

Short-row 3: Make double st, k1, sl m, work in patt to m, sl m, k1, knit double st as single st, k2, turn.

Short-row 4: Make double st, p1, k1, p1, sl m, work in patt to m, sl m, p1, purl double st as single st, p2, turn.

Short-row 5: Make double st, pass 3rd st on left needle over first 2 sts and off needle, k1, yo, k1, sl m, work in patt to m, sl m, pass 3rd st on left needle over first 2 sts and off needle, k1, yo, k1, knit double st as single st, k2, turn.

Short-row 6: Make double st, [k1, p1] 2 times, sl m, work in patt to m, sl m, p1, k1, p1, purl double st as single st, p2, turn.

Short-row 7: Make double st, pass 3rd st on left needle over first 2 sts and off needle, k1, yo, k1, p1, k1, sl m, work in patt to m, sl m, k1, p1, pass 3rd st on left needle over first 2 sts and off needle, k1, yo, knit double st as single st, k1, turn.

Rep Inc rnd every 8 (8, 10, 10, 14, 14)th rnd 4 (4, 3, 3, 2, 2) more times, working new sts into Right or Left Texture patt—226 (250, 270, 290, 314, 334) sts.

Work even until piece measures 13 (13, 13½, 13½, 14, 14)" from underarm. Change to smaller cir needle.

Next rnd: K1tbl, *[p2tog] 0 (1, 0, 0, 0, 1) time, [p1] 1 (0, 1, 1, 1, 0) time, [k1tbl, p1] 22 (23, 26, 27, 30, 32) times, work in k1tbl, p1 rib over 18 (24, 24, 30, 30, 30) Body

Short-row 8: Make double st, [p1, k1] 2 times, p1, sl m, work in patt to m, sl m, p1, [k1, p1] 2 times, purl double st as single st, p2, turn.

Short-row 9: Make double st, work Row 1 of Sleeve Texture chart to m, sl m, work in patt to m, sl m, work Row 1 of Sleeve Texture chart to double st, knit double st as single st, k2, turn.

Short-row 10: Make double st, p1, k1, work Row 2 of Sleeve Texture chart to m, sl m, work in patt to m, sl m, work Row 2 of Sleeve Texture chart to double st, purl double st as single st, p2, turn.

Short-row 11: Make double st, k1, p1, [work in patt to m, sl m] 2 times, work in patt to double st, knit double st as single st, k2, turn.

Short-row 12: Make double st, p1, k1, [work in patt to m, sl m] 2 times, work in patt to double st, purl double st as single st, p2, turn.

Rep last 2 short-rows 4 (4, 5, 7, 8, 10) more times, working new sts on each side into Sleeve Texture patt as they become available.

Next row: (RS) Work to double st, knit double st as single st, *p1, k1; rep from * to last 1 (0, 0, 0, 1, 1) st, k1 (0, 0, 0, 1, 1).

Next rnd: K1, work in Sleeve Texture patt to double st, knit double st as single st, work in Sleeve Texture patt to end.

Work 4 rnds even in patt.

Dec rnd: K1, k2tog, work in patt to last 2 sts, ssk—2 sts dec'd.

Rep Dec rnd every 6 (6, 6, 5, 4, 4)th rnd 15 (15, 15, 10, 18, 21, 18) more times then every 0 (0, 5th, 0, 0, 3rd) rnd 0 (0, 6, 0, 0, 6) times—43 (45, 47, 51, 51, 53) sts rem.

Work even until piece measures 15 (15, 15¼, 15¼, 15½, 15½)" from underarm.

Next rnd: K2tog, work to end—42 (44, 46, 50, 50, 52) sts rem. Change to smaller dpn.

Next rnd: *K1tbl, p1; rep from * to end. Rep last rnd for 2". BO all sts in patt.

Finishing

NECKBAND

With smaller dpn and RS facing, beg at right saddle, pick up and knit 18 sts along saddle edge, 33 (34, 38, 39, 39, 43) sts along back neck edge, 18 sts along left saddle edge, 16 (18, 18, 20, 20, 20) sts along front edge to CO sts, 21 (22, 26, 27, 27, 31) sts along front neck CO sts, 16 (18, 18, 20, 20, 20) sts up front to saddle—122 (128, 136, 142, 142, 150) sts total.

Pm and join in the rnd.

Next rnd: *K1tbl, p1; rep from * to end.

Rep last rnd for 1".

BO all sts in patt. Weave in ends. Block to measurements.

eastbound sweater

Courtney Kelley

Finished Sizes

Waist circumference: 38 (41, 45, 48, 55)".

Sweater shown measures 38", modeled with 4½" of positive ease.

Yarn

Worsted weight (#4 medium).

Shown here: The Fibre Company Organik (70% Merino wool, 15% baby alpaca, 15% silk; 98 yd [90 m]/1¾ oz [50 g]): night sky, 10 (11, 13, 15, 18) skeins.

Needles

Size U.S. 8 (5 mm): and 16", 24", and 32" circulars (cir).

Size U.S. 9 (5.5 mm): 16", 24", and 32" cir.

Adjust needle size if necessary to obtain the correct gauge.

Notions

Markers (m); stitch holders.

Gauge

16 sts and 25 rows = 4" in St st on larger needle.

Notes

■ The body of this pullover is worked in the round from the bottom up to the underarm, then the front and back are worked separately back and forth. The front and back shoulders are joined with a saddle shoulder strip. The sleeves are picked up and worked in the round from the top down.

■ The underarm gusset shaping begins just after the ribbing.

■ The saddle shoulders are worked from the shoulder edge to the neck edge, back and forth beginning with saddle cast-on stitches. The shoulder stitches are held to each side, and one stitch of the reserved shoulder stitches is decreased at the end of each row until all of the shoulder stitches have been joined to the saddle in this manner.

S2kp2: Sl 2 sts as if to k2tog, k1, pass 2 sl sts over—2 sts dec'd.

1/1 RT: Knit 2nd st on left needle in front of first st, then knit first st; slip both sts off needle.

1/1 LT: Skip first st on left needle, knit 2nd st through back loop, knit first st; slip both sts off needle.

Left Twist Pattern: (over 3 sts)

Row 1: (WS) P2, k1.

Row 2: P1, 1/1 LT.

Rep Rows 1 and 2 for patt.

Right Twist Pattern: (over 3 sts)

Row 1: (WS) K1, p2.

Row 2: 1/1 RT, p1.

Rep Rows 1 and 2 for patt.

Body

With smaller 32" needle, CO 152 (160, 176, 192, 216) sts. Place marker (pm) and join in the rnd.

Next rnd: K76 (80, 88, 96, 108), pm for side, knit to end.

Knit 2 rnds.

Next rnd: *P2, k2; rep from * to end. Cont in rib patt as est until piece measures 2¼" from CO.

SIZES 38 (48)" ONLY

Next rnd: *P2, pm for gusset, work in patt to m, sl m; rep from * once more.

SIZES 41 (45, 55)" ONLY

Next rnd: *P2, pm for gusset, k1, M1L, work in patt to 1 st before m, M1R, k1, sl m; rep from * once more—164 (180, 220) sts.

ALL SIZES

Change to larger 32" needle.

Inc rnd: *P1, M1L, p1, sl m, knit to m, sl m; rep from * once more—154 (166, 182, 194, 222) sts.

Rnds 1–3: *P1, knit to 1 st before m, p1, sl m, knit to m, sl m; rep from * once more.

Rnd 4: *P1, M1R, knit to 1 st before m, M1L, p1, sl m, knit to m, sl m; rep from * once more—4 sts inc'd.

Rep last 4 rnds 14 (15, 15, 17, 19) more times—214 (230, 246, 266, 302) sts: 33 (35, 35, 39, 43) gusset sts each side and 74 (80, 88, 94, 108) sts each for front and back.

Work even until piece measures 12½ (12¾, 13½, 14¾, 15¾)" from CO.

DIVIDE FOR FRONT AND BACK

Remove m, p1, place next 31 (33, 33, 37, 41) sts on holder for left underarm gusset, place next 76 (82, 90, 96, 110) sts on separate holder for front, place next 31 (33, 33, 37, 41) sts on separate holder for right underarm gusset—76 (82, 90, 96, 110) sts rem for back.

LARGE PINECONE & DIAMOND

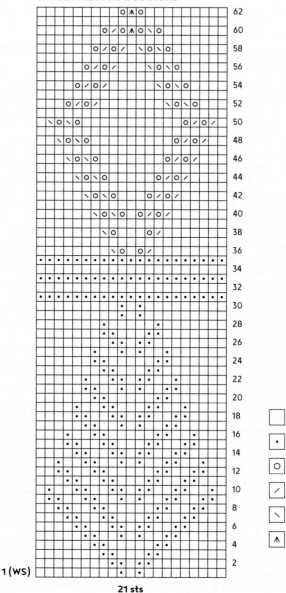

knit
· purl
O yo
╱ k2tog
╲ ssk
⋀ s2kp2 (see Stitch Guide)

21 sts

Back

Next row: (WS) M1L, knit to end—77 (83, 91, 97, 111) sts. Purl 1 RS row. Beg yoke patt:

SIZE 38" ONLY

Set-up row: (WS) P1, pm, work Arrow Flag A chart over 7 sts, pm, work Zigzag A chart over 10 sts, pm, work Arrow Flag A chart over 7 sts, pm, work Left Twist patt (see Stitch Guide) over 3 sts, pm, work Small Pinecone and Diamond chart over 21 sts, pm, work Right Twist patt (see Stitch Guide) over 3 sts, pm, work Arrow Flag B chart over 7 sts, pm, work Zigzag B chart over 10 sts, pm, work Arrow Flag B chart over 7 sts, pm, p1.

MEDIUM PINECONE & DIAMOND

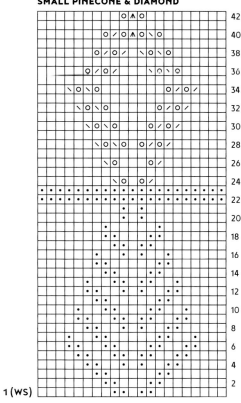

21 sts

SMALL PINECONE & DIAMOND

21 sts

ZIGZAG A

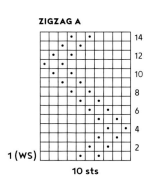

10 sts

ZIGZAG B

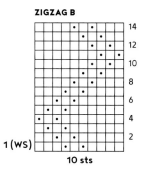

10 sts

ARROW FLAG A

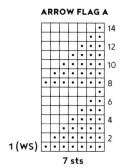

7 sts

ARROW FLAG B

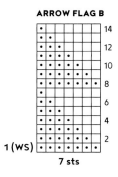

7 sts

SADDLE SHOULDER A

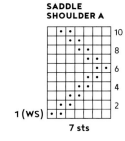

7 sts

SADDLE SHOULDER B

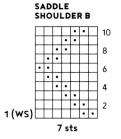

7 sts

SIZE 41" ONLY

Set-up row: (WS) P1, pm, work Left Twist patt (see Stitch Guide) over 3 sts, pm, work Arrow Flag A chart over 7 sts, pm, work Zigzag A chart over 10 sts, pm, work Arrow Flag A chart over 7 sts, pm, work Left Twist patt over 3 sts, pm, work Small Pinecone and Diamond chart over 21 sts, pm, work Right Twist patt (see Stitch Guide) over 3 sts, pm, work Arrow Flag B chart over 7 sts, pm, work Zigzag B chart over 10 sts, pm, work Arrow Flag B chart over 7 sts, pm, work Right Twist patt over 3 sts, pm, p1.

SIZE 45" ONLY

Set-up row: (WS) P1, pm, work Arrow Flag A chart over 14 sts, pm, work Zigzag A chart over 10 sts, pm, work Arrow Flag A chart over 7 sts, pm, work Left Twist patt (see Stitch Guide) over 3 sts, pm, work Medium Pinecone and Diamond chart over 21 sts, pm, work Right Twist patt (see Stitch Guide) over 3 sts, pm, work Arrow Flag B chart over 7 sts, pm, work Zigzag B chart over 10 sts, pm, work Arrow Flag B chart over 14 sts, pm, p1.

SIZE 48" ONLY

Set-up row: (WS) P1, pm, [work Zigzag A chart over 10 sts, pm, work Arrow Flag A chart over 7 sts, pm] 2 times, work Left Twist patt (see Stitch Guide) over 3 sts, pm, work Medium Pinecone and Diamond chart over 21 sts, pm, work Right Twist patt (see Stitch Guide) over 3 sts, pm, [work Arrow Flag B chart over 7 sts, pm, work Zigzag B chart over 10 sts, pm] 2 times, pm, p1.

SIZE 55" ONLY

Set-up row: (WS) P1, [work Arrow Flag A chart over 7 sts, pm, work Zigzag A chart over 10 sts, pm] 2 times, work Arrow Flag A chart over 7 sts, pm, work Left Twist patt (see Stitch Guide) over 3 sts, pm, work Large Pinecone and Diamond chart over 21 sts, pm, work Right Twist patt (see Stitch Guide) over 3 sts, pm, work Arrow Flag B chart over 7 sts, pm, [work Zigzag B chart over 10 sts, pm, Arrow Flag B chart over 7 sts, pm] 2 times, p1.

ALL SIZES

Cont in patts as est through Row 42 (42, 56, 56, 62) of Pinecone and Diamond chart.

Knit 1 row.

Purl 1 row.

Place sts on holder. Leave yarn attached. Set aside.

Front

Return 76 (82, 90, 96, 110) front sts to needle and with WS facing, join new yarn. Work as for back.

Saddle Shoulder

Starting at armhole edge, sl first 18 (21, 25, 27, 32) left front sts onto larger 24" needle, then sl 18 (21, 25, 27, 32) left back sts onto larger 16" needle.

With WS facing, using yarn attached to back sts, and the backward-loop method, CO 7 sts onto right end of 16" needle, turn, ssk first 2 sts from 24" needle (see Notes).

Turn, and cont working back and forth on 9 sts as foll:

Row 1: (WS) Sl 1 pwise wyf, work Saddle Shoulder A chart over 7 sts, p2tog (worked on back shoulder sts), turn.

Row 2: (RS) Sl 1 pwise wyb, work chart over 7 sts, ssk (worked on front shoulder sts), turn.

Rep last 2 rows 15 (18, 22, 24, 29) more times, then work WS row once more—9 sts rem: 7 saddle sts and 1 shoulder st on each side.

Place sts on holder. Rep for other shoulder, using yarn attached to front to CO saddle sts, placing right back sts on 24" needle and right front sts on 16" needle, and substituting Saddle Shoulder B chart.

Sleeves

Return 31 (33, 33, 37, 41) held gusset sts to larger 16" (or 24") needle and with RS facing, join yarn.

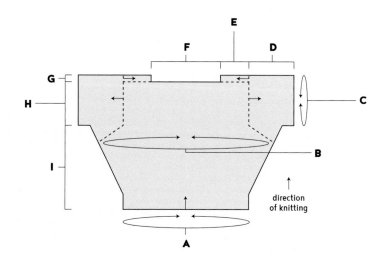

A: 38 (41, 45, 48, 55)"

B: 53½ (57½, 61½, 66½, 75½)"

C: 15 (16, 20, 20, 21)"

D: 6¾ (7, 7, 7¾, 8¼)"

E: 4½ (5¼, 6¼, 6¾, 8)"

F: 10¼ (10¼, 10¼, 10¾, 11¾)"

G: 1"

H: 7¼ (7¼, 9½, 9½, 10½)"

I: 12½ (12¾, 13½, 14¾, 15¾)"

Next rnd: Pick up and knit 1 st from the purl st between body and gusset, k31 (33, 33, 37, 41), pick up and knit 1 st from purl st between body and gusset, pm, pick up and knit 26 (28, 36, 36, 39) sts evenly along front armhole edge, pick up and knit 7 sts from CO saddle shoulder sts, pick up and knit 26 (28, 36, 36, 39) evenly along back armhole edge—92 (98, 114, 120, 128) sts. Pm and join in the rnd.

Rnd 1: P1, ssk, knit to 3 sts before m, k2tog, p1, sl m, purl to end—2 gusset sts dec'd.

Rnd 2: P1, knit to 1 st before m, p1, sl m, purl to end.

Rnd 3: P1, ssk, knit to 3 sts before m, k2tog, p1, sl m, knit to end—2 gusset sts dec'd.

Rnd 4 :P1, knit to 1 st before m, p1, sl m, knit to end.

Rep last 2 rnds 12 (13, 13, 15, 17) more times—64 (68, 84, 84, 90) sts rem: 5 gusset sts between m and 59 (63, 79, 79, 85) sleeve sts.

Next rnd: P1, s2kp2, p1, remove m, knit to end—62 (66, 82, 82, 88) sts rem.

Next rnd: P2tog, p1, knit to end and dec 1 (1, 1, 1, 3) st(s) evenly—60 (64, 80, 80, 84) sts rem.

CUFF

Change to smaller 16" needle.

Next rnd: *P2, k2; rep from * around.

Cont in rib patt as est for 1¼".

Knit 3 rnds. BO all sts.

Finishing

NECKBAND

With smaller 24" needle and RS facing, k41 (41, 41, 43, 47) neck sts from holder, knit 9 saddle sts from holder, k41 (41, 41, 43, 47) neck sts from holder, knit 9 saddle sts from holder—100 (100, 100, 104, 112) sts.

Work in k2, p2 rib for 1¼".

Knit 3 rnds. BO all sts.

Weave in ends. Block to measurements.

summer lace pullover

Courtney Spainhower

Finished Size

Bust circumference: about 33½ (35¾, 37½, 38½, 41, 44¼)".

Pullover shown measures 35¾".

Yarn

DK weight (#3 light).

Shown here: Classic Elite Firefly (75% viscose, 25% linen; 155 yd [142 m]/¾ oz [50 g]): #7706 linum (A), 2 (2, 2, 3, 3, 3) skeins; #7750 leopard's bane (B), 4 (5, 5, 5, 6, 6) skeins.

Needles

Size U.S. 5 (3.75 mm): 16" and 32" circular (cir) and set of 4 or 5 double-pointed (dpn).

Adjust needle size if necessary to obtain the correct gauge.

Notions

Markers (m); stitch holders or waste yarn; tapestry needle.

Gauge

23 sts and 30 rnds = 4" in stockinette stitch, worked in rnds.

21 sts and 32 rows = 4" in Little Diamond Lace chart, worked in rows.

24 sts and 37 rows = 4" in garter stitch, worked in rows.

Notes

■ For this pullover, stitches are cast on at the neckline, then the left saddle tab is worked, stitches are picked up along the back side of the left tab, the back neckline stitches are knit, then the right saddle tab is worked. Stitches are picked up along the front side of the right tab, the front neckline stitches are knit, then stitches are picked up along the front side of the left tab. The front of the pullover is worked to the underarm then held while the back is worked. The front and back pieces are joined and worked in the round,

and finished simply in 2 × 2 rib. Pleats are worked at the underarms when working the armbands.

■ Schematic shows the bust measurements while blocking. The pleats worked while knitting the armbands decrease stitches, which results in the finished bust circumference given under Finished Size.

STITCH GUIDE

Sskpo

Ssk, then place the st back on the left needle, lift the second st on the left needle over the ssk loop, then return the ssk loop to the right needle.

1×1 Rib (multiple of 2 sts)

Rnd 1: *K1, p1 rep from *.

Rep Rnd 1 for patt.

2×2 Rib (multiple of 4 sts)

Rnd 1: *K2, p2; rep from*.

Rep Rnd 1 for patt.

Neckband

Using color A and shorter cir needle, CO 104 (110, 114, 118, 120, 124). Place marker (pm) for beg of rnd and join for working in the rnd, being careful not to twist sts.

Work in 1×1 rib until piece measures 1" from CO edge.

Saddle tabs

LEFT TAB

Next row: K12, turn.

Work in garter st (knit all sts, every row) over these 12 sts only for 36 (36, 36, 38, 38, 42) rows, ending after a RS row.

Place these 12 saddle tab sts onto st holder or waste yarn.

RIGHT TAB

With RS facing, rotate work 90° clockwise, pick up and knit 18 (18, 18, 19, 19, 21) sts (one in each "valley" between garter bumps) along the saddle tab, k39 (40, 41, 43, 44, 46) back sts, k12, turn.

Work in garter st over the last 12 sts only for 36 (36, 36, 38, 38, 42) rows, ending after a RS row.

Place the 12 saddle tab sts onto st holder or waste yarn.

With RS facing, rotate work 90° clockwise, pick up and knit 18 (18, 18, 19, 19, 21) sts (one in each "valley" between garter bumps) along the saddle tab, k41 (46, 49, 51, 52, 54) across front, pick up and knit 18 (18, 18, 19, 19, 21) sts (one in each "valley" between garter bumps) along the left saddle tab—81 (82, 85, 89, 90, 96) sts for front; 57 (58, 59, 62, 63, 67) sts for back.

Place back sts onto st holder or waste yarn and cont working back and forth in rows on front sts only.

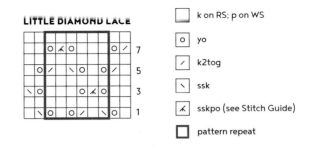

LITTLE DIAMOND LACE

	k on RS; p on WS
o	yo
/	k2tog
\	ssk
⋏	sskpo (see Stitch Guide)
	pattern repeat

Front

SIZES 33½ (38½)" ONLY

Dec row: (WS) P2tog, purl to end—76 (88) sts.

SIZES 41 (44¼)" ONLY

Dec row: (WS) P2tog, purl to last 2 sts, p2tog—88 (94) sts.

SIZE 35¾" ONLY

Purl 1 WS row.

SIZE 37½" ONLY

Inc row: (WS) P1, M1P, p41, M1P, purl to last st, M1P, p1—88 sts.

ALL SIZES

Work Rows 1-8 of Little Diamond Lace chart 4 (4, 4, 5, 5, 5) times.

RIGHT BUST SHAPING

Shape bust darts with no-wrap short-rows as foll:

Short-row 1: (RS) K24 (26, 28, 30, 30, 32), turn so WS is facing; (WS) sl 1 st purlwise with yarn in front (pwise wyf), purl to end.

Short-row 2: K22 (24, 26, 28, 28, 30), turn so WS is facing; (WS) sl 1 st pwise wyf, purl to end.

Short-row 3: Knit to 2 sts before gap, turn so WS is facing; (WS) sl 1 st pwise wyf, purl to end.

Rep the last short-row 9 (10, 11, 12, 12, 13) more times—2 sts rem unwrapped at armhole edge.

Next row: (RS) Knit to end, closing gaps as you come to them.

LEFT BUST SHAPING

Shape bust darts with no-turn short-rows as foll:

Short-row 1: (WS) P24 (26, 28, 30, 30, 32), turn so RS is facing; (RS) sl 1 st pwise with yarn in back (wyb), knit to end.

Short-row 2: P22 (24, 26, 28, 28, 30), turn so RS is facing; (RS) sl 1 st pwise wyb, knit to end.

Short-row 3: Purl to 2 sts before gap, turn so RS is facing; (RS) sl 1 st pwise wyb, knit to end.

Rep the last short-row 9 (10, 11, 12, 12, 13) more times—2 sts rem unwrapped at armhole edge.

Next row: (WS) Purl to end, closing gaps as you come to them. Break color A.

Change to color B.

Knit 2 rows, ending after a WS row.

Place sts onto st holder or waste yarn and set aside. Break yarn.

Back

Return 57 (58, 59, 62, 63, 67) held back sts to longer cir needle and join color A preparing to work a RS row. Knit to end, then pick up and knit 18 (18, 18, 19, 19, 21) sts in each "valley" between garter bumps along right saddle tab—75 (76, 77, 81, 82, 88) sts.

SIZES 33½ (38½)" ONLY

Inc row: (WS) P1, M1P, purl to end—76 (82) sts.

SIZES 35¾ (41, 44¼)" ONLY

Purl 1 WS row.

SIZE 37½" ONLY

Dec row: (WS) P2tog, purl to end—76 sts.

ALL SIZES

Work Rows 1-8 of Little Diamond Lace chart 7 (7, 7, 8, 8, 9) times.

Work even in St st (knit on RS, purl on WS) for ¼ (½, ¾, 1, 1, ¼)", ending after a WS row. Break color A.

Change to color B.

Knit 2 rows, ending after a WS row.

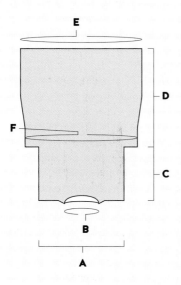

A: Front: 14½ (15½, 16¾, 16¾, 16¾, 18)"
Back: 14½ (14½, 14½, 15½, 15½, 16¾)"

B: 18 (19¼, 19¾, 20½, 20¾, 21½)"

C: 8½ (8¾, 9, 10¼, 10¼, 10½)"

D: 16 (16, 16½, 17, 17, 17½)"

E: 41 (43½, 45¼, 46¼, 49¾, 51¾)"

F: 37½ (40, 41¾, 42¾, 46¼, 48¼)"

Body

Joining rnd: (RS) K76 (76, 76, 82, 82, 88) back sts, turn so WS is facing, then use the cable method to CO 16 (18, 19, 19, 24, 24), pm for side, then CO another 16 (18, 19, 19, 24, 24) sts, turn so RS is facing, return 76 (82, 88, 88, 88, 94) held front sts to empty end of needle and knit across, turn so WS is facing, then use the cable method to CO 16 (18, 19, 19, 24, 24), pm for beg of rnd, then CO another 16 (18, 19, 19, 24, 24) sts—216 (230, 240, 246, 266, 278) sts.

Turn so RS is facing and join to work in the rnd.

Work even in St st (knit all sts, every rnd) until piece measures 3" from joining rnd.

SHAPE SIDES

Inc rnd: K1, *M1R, knit to 1 st before m, M1L, k1, sl m; rep from * once more—4 sts inc'd.

Knit 7 rnds even.

Rep the last 8 rnds 4 more times—236 (250, 260, 266, 286, 298) sts.

Work even in St st until piece measures 14 (14, 14½, 15, 15, 15½)" from joining rnd.

SIZES 35¾ (38½, 41, 44¼)" ONLY

Dec rnd: K1, k2tog, knit to m, slm, k2tog, knit to end—234 (248, 260, 284) sts.

SIZES 33½ (37½)" ONLY

Knit 1 rnd.

ALL SIZES

Work in 2×2 rib for 2".

BO all sts in patt.

Finishing

Block piece to measurements.

ARMBANDS

With RS facing, using color A and dpn, beg at center of underarm CO sts, pick up and knit 16 (18, 19, 19, 24, 24) sts along CO sts, 20 (20, 24, 28, 28, 30) sts evenly along selvedge edge to held saddle tab sts, return 12 saddle tab sts to empty end of needle and knit across, pick up and knit 20 (20, 24, 28, 28, 30) sts evenly along selvedge edge to CO sts, then pick up and knit 16 (18, 19, 19, 24, 24) sts in rem CO sts—84 (88, 98, 106, 116, 120) sts.

Pm for beg of rnd and join to work in the rnd.

Purl 1 rnd.

SHAPE PLEATS

Pleat rnd: Place 6 sts onto a dpn and hold to the back, place next 6 sts onto a second dpn and hold to the back. Hold the 2 dpn in the back of the work so the first dpn is in the back, the second dpn is in the center, and the working needle is in the front (like a Z). [Knit through first st on each needle, knitting them together] 6 times, knit to last 18 sts, place next 6 sts onto a dpn and hold to the front, place next 6 sts onto a second dpn and hold to the front. Hold the 2 dpn in the front of the work so the first dpn is in the front, the second dpn is in the center, and the working needle is in the back (like a Z). [Knit through first st on each needle, knitting them together] 6 times—60 (64, 74, 82, 92, 96) sts rem.

[Purl 1 rnd, knit 1 rnd] 3 times.

BO all sts loosely.

Work second armband the same as the first.

Using tapestry needle, weave in all ends neatly. Block again if desired.

pinewood pullover

Ela Torrente

Finished Size

Bust circumference: 34 (37¾, 41¾, 46, 50½, 55)".

Pullover shown measures 34", modeled with 2" of positive ease.

Yarn

DK weight (#3 light).

Shown here: Rowan Felted Tweed DK (50% wool, 25% alpaca, 25% viscose; 191 yd [175 m]/1¾ oz [50 g]): #184 celadon, 4 (5, 5, 6, 7, 7) skeins.

Needles

Size U.S. 5 (3.75 mm): 24" circular (cir) and set of double-pointed (dpn).

Size U.S. 6 (4 mm): 24" cir and set of dpn.

Adjust needle size if necessary to obtain the correct gauge.

Notions

Markers (m); stitch holders; tapestry needle.

Gauge

21½ sts and 30 rnds = 4" in Rev st st on larger needle.

21 sts and 30 rnds = 4" in charted patt on larger needle.

Notes

▪ This pullover is worked in the round from the top down with raglan shaping.

Neckband

With smaller cir needle, CO 114 (128, 134, 148, 154, 168) sts. Place marker (pm) and join in the rnd.

Work in k1, p1 rib for 5 rnds.

Yoke

Change to larger cir needle.

Next rnd: P20 (22, 25, 27, 30, 32) for right back, pm, p14 for right sleeve, pm, k45 (55, 55, 65, 65, 75) for front, p14 for left sleeve, pm, purl to end for left back.

Shape back using short-rows as foll:

Short-row 1: (RS) Purl to 1 st before m, M1RP, p1, sl m, p1, M1LP, p2, wrap next st, turn—2 sts inc'd.

Short-row 2: (WS) Knit to beg-of-rnd m, sl m, knit to m, sl m, k2, wrap next st, turn.

Short-row 3: Purl to 1 st before m, M1RP, p1, sl m, p1, M1LP, purl to beg-of-rnd m, sl m, purl to 1 st before m, M1RP, p1, sl m, p1, M1LP, purl to wrapped st, purl wrap tog with wrapped st, p2, wrap next st, turn—4 sts inc'd.

Short-row 4: Knit to beg-of-rnd m, sl m, knit to wrapped st, knit wrap tog with wrapped st, k2, wrap next st, turn.

Short-rows 5–8: Rep Short-rows 3 and 4 two times—128 (142, 148, 162, 168, 182) sts.

Short-row 9: Purl to 1 st before m, M1RP, p1, sl m, p1, M1LP, purl to beg-of-rnd m, sl m, purl to 1 st before m, M1RP, p1, sl m, p1, M1LP, purl to wrapped st, purl wrap tog with wrapped st, M1RP, p1, sl m, k1, M1L, k1, wrap next st, turn—6 sts inc'd.

Short-row 10: Purl to m, sl m, knit to wrapped st, knit wrap tog with wrapped st, k1, sl m, p2, wrap next st, turn.

Short-row 11: Knit to 1 st before m, M1R, k1, sl m, p1, M1LP, purl to 1 st before m, M1RP, p1, sl m, p1, M1LP, purl to beg-of-rnd m, sl m, purl to 1 st before m, M1RP, p1, sl m, p1, M1LP, purl to 1 st before m, M1RP, p1, sl m, k1, M1L, knit to wrapped st, knit wrap tog with wrapped st, k2, wrap next st, turn—8 sts inc'd.

Short-row 12: Purl to m, sl m, [knit to m, sl m] 4 times, purl to wrapped st, purl wrap tog with wrapped st, p2, wrap next st, turn.

Short-rows 13–16: Rep Short-rows 11 and 12 two times—158 (172, 178, 192, 198, 212) sts.

Next row: (RS) Knit to 1 st before m, M1R, k1, sl m, p1, M1LP, purl to 1 st before m, M1RP, p1, sl m, p1, M1LP, purl to beg-of-rnd m—162 (176, 182, 196, 202, 216) sts: 57 (61, 67, 71, 77, 81) sts for back, 26 sts for each sleeve, 53 (63, 63, 73, 73, 83) sts for front.

Next rnd: *Purl to m, sl m; rep from * once more, knit to m, working rem wraps tog with wrapped sts, sl m, purl to m, sl m, purl to end.

Inc rnd: Purl to 1 st before m, M1RP, p1, sl m, p1, M1LP, purl to 1 st before m, M1RP, p1, sl m, k1, M1L, work Yoke chart to 1 st before m, M1R, k1, sl m, p1, M1LP, purl to 1 st before m, M1RP, p1, sl m, p1, M1LP, purl to end—8 sts inc'd.

Rep Inc rnd every other rnd 12 (14, 14, 18, 20, 22) more times, working new sts into patt on front as illustrated on chart and into rev St st on back and sleeves, and ending with Rnd 1, 5, 9, 13, or 17 of chart—266 (296, 302, 348, 370, 400) sts: 83 (91, 97, 109, 119, 127) sts for back, 52 (56, 56, 64, 68, 72) sts for each sleeve, 79 (93, 93, 111, 115, 129) sts for front.

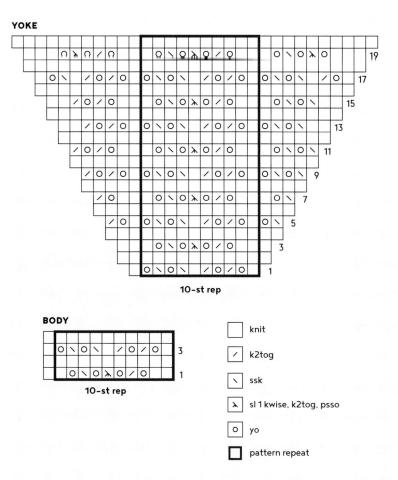

YOKE

10-st rep

BODY

10-st rep

□ knit

✓ k2tog

\ ssk

⋏ sl 1 kwise, k2tog, psso

○ yo

▭ pattern repeat

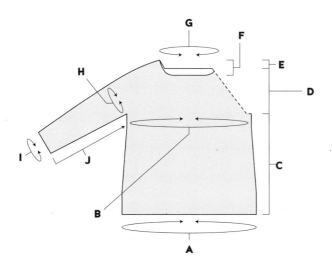

A: 37½ (41½, 45½, 49½, 54¼, 58¾)"

B: 34 (37¾, 41¾, 46, 50½, 55)"

C: 15"

D: 6¼ (6¾, 7¼, 7¾, 8½, 9)"

E: 1¼ "

F: 2¼ "

G: 21¼ (23¾, 25, 27½, 28¾, 31¼)"

H: 11¼ (12, 12¾, 14¼, 15¾, 16¾)"

I: 9 (10, 10¾, 12¼, 13¼, 14¼)"

J: 12"

SIZE 41¾" ONLY

Work 1 rnd even in patt.

Inc rnd: Purl to 1 st before m, M1RP, p1, sl m, purl to m, sl m, k1, M1L, work in patt to 1 st before m, M1R, k1, sl m, purl to m, sl m, p1, M1LP, purl to end—4 sts inc'd.

Rep last 2 rnds once more—310 sts: 101 sts for back, 56 sts for each sleeve, 97 sts for front.

ALL SIZES

Divide for body and sleeves: Purl to m, remove m, place 52 (56, 56, 64, 68, 72) sts on holder for right sleeve, remove m, using the backward-loop method, CO 3 (4, 10, 12, 9, 12) sts, pm, CO 6 (4, 2, 0, 8, 6) sts, work in patt as est to m, remove m, place next 52 (56, 56, 64, 68, 72) sts on holder for left sleeve, remove m, CO 6 (4, 2, 0, 8, 6) sts, pm, CO 3 (4, 10, 12, 9, 12) sts, purl to end—180 (200, 222, 244, 268, 292) sts rem for body.

Body

Next rnd: Purl to m, sl m, work Body chart to m, sl m, purl to end.

Cont in patt as est until piece measures 2" from underarm.

SHAPE WAIST

Inc rnd: Purl to 1 st before m, M1RP, p1, sl m, work in patt to m, sl m, p1, M1LP, purl to end—2 sts inc'd.

Rep Inc rnd every 8th rnd 9 more times—200 (220, 242, 264, 288, 312) sts.

Work even until piece measures 14" from underarm. Change to smaller cir needle.

Work in k1, p1 rib for 1". BO all sts in patt.

Sleeves

Place 52 (56, 56, 64, 68, 72) sleeve sts on larger dpn.

With RS facing, beg at center of underarm, pick up and knit 5 (4, 6, 6, 9, 9) sts along underarm CO, p52 (56, 56, 64, 68, 72) sleeve sts, pick up and knit 4 (4, 6, 6, 8, 9) more sts along underarm CO—61 (64, 68, 76, 85, 90) sts. Pm and join in the rnd.

Purl 15 rnds.

Dec rnd: P1, p2tog, purl to last 3 sts, ssp, p1—2 sts dec'd.

Rep Dec rnd every 10 (10, 10, 10, 8, 8)th rnd 5 (4, 4, 4, 6, 6) more times—49 (54, 58, 66, 71, 76) sts rem.

Work even until piece measures 11" from underarm.

SIZES 34 (50½)" ONLY

Next rnd: P1, p2tog, purl to end—48 (70) sts rem.

ALL SIZES

Change to smaller dpn. Work in k1, p1 rib for 1". BO all sts in patt.

Finishing

Weave in ends. Block.

harvey
pullover

Hannah Baker

Finished Size

Bust circumference: 36 (40, 44, 48, 52)".

Pullover shown measures 36", modeled with 2" of positive ease.

Yarn

Worsted weight (#4 medium).

Shown here: Cascade Yarns Cascade 220 Heathers (100% Peruvian highland wool; 220 yd [200 m]/3½ oz [100 g]): #8012 doeskin heather, 5 (6, 6, 7, 8) skeins.

Needles

Size U.S. 7 (4.5 mm): 16" and 32" circular (cir) and set of double-pointed (dpn).

Adjust needle size if necessary to obtain the correct gauge.

Notions

Markers (m); stitch holders; tapestry needle.

Gauge

20 sts and 28 rows = 4" in St st.

16 sts and 34 rows = 4" in Textured Brioche St.

Notes

■ This pullover is worked in the round from the bottom edge to the underarms, then the front and back are worked separately back and forth. Stitches for the sleeves are picked up around the armhole and the sleeves are worked in the round from the top down.

■ In Textured Brioche Stitch, when counting stitches, each slipped stitch with its companion yarnover counts as one stitch.

■ When decreasing for the front neck, if there are not enough stitches to complete the last Textured Brioche Stitch repeat, knit the remaining stitches in the row on both right-side and wrong-side rows. When one of the stitches to be decreased has a companion yarnover, work the yarnover into the decrease as well.

STITCH GUIDE

Brioche knit (brk): Knit st tog with its companion yo.

Yfsl1yo: Yarn forward between needles, sl next st pwise wyf, yarn over needle to back.

Sl1yof: Sl next st pwise wyf, yarn over needle to the back, then between needles to front.

Textured Brioche Stitch in Rnds (even number of sts)

Rnd 1: *P1, sl1yof; rep from * to end.

Rnd 2: *K1, brk; rep from * to end.

Rnd 3: *Sl1yof, p1; rep from * to end.

Rnd 4: *Brk, k1; rep from * to end.

Rep Rnds 1–4 for patt.

Textured Brioche Stitch in Rows (even number of sts)

Row 1: (WS) *Yfsl1yo, k1; rep from * to end.

Row 2: (RS) *K1, brk; rep from * to end.

Row 3: *K1, yfsl1yo; rep from * to end.

Row 4: *Brk, k1; rep from * to end.

Rep Rows 1–4 for patt.

Body

With longer cir needle, CO 164 (180, 200, 216, 236) sts. Place marker (pm) and join in the rnd.

Work in k2, p2 rib for 2¼", dec 2 (0, 2, 0, 2) sts on last rnd—162 (180, 198, 216, 234) sts rem.

Next rnd: Work Textured Brioche St in Rnds (see Stitch Guide) over 72 (80, 88, 96, 104) sts, pm, knit to end.

Cont in patt as est until piece measures 16 (16½, 17, 17½, 18)" from CO measured at center back, and 13½ (14, 14½, 14¾, 15¼)" measured at center front, ending with Rnd 4 of patt.

DIVIDE FOR FRONT AND BACK

Place first 72 (80, 88, 96, 104) sts on holder for front—90 (100, 110, 120, 130) sts rem for back. Beg working back and forth in rows.

Back

Beg with a purl row, work in St st until armhole measures 7 (7½, 8, 8½, 9)", ending with a WS row.

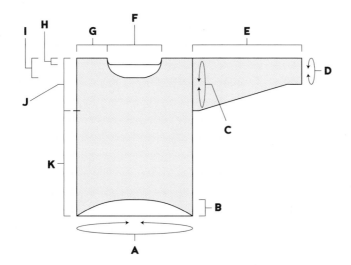

A: 36 (40, 44, 48, 52)"

B: 2½ (2½, 2½, 2¾, 2¾)"

C: 16 (17, 18, 19, 20)"

D: 8 (8¼, 8¾, 9, 9½)"

E: 17"

F: 8½ (9¼, 9¼, 10, 10)"

G: 4¾ (5½, 6½, 7, 8)"

H: 1"

I: 3"

J: 8 (8½, 9, 9½, 10)"

K: 16 (16½, 17, 17½, 18)"

SHAPE NECK

Next row: (RS) K26 (29, 34, 37, 42) and place these sts on holder for right shoulder, BO 38 (42, 42, 46, 46) sts, knit to end—26 (29, 34, 37, 42) sts rem for left shoulder.

LEFT SHOULDER

Next row: (WS) Purl.

Dec row: (RS) Ssk, knit to end—1 st dec'd.

Rep last 2 rows once more—24 (27, 32, 35, 40) sts rem.

Work even until armhole measures 8 (8½, 9, 9½, 10)". BO all sts.

RIGHT SHOULDER

Return 26 (29, 34, 37, 42) right shoulder sts to needle and, with WS facing, rejoin yarn.

Next row: (WS) Purl.

Dec row: (RS) Knit to last 2 sts, k2tog—1 st dec'd.

Rep last 2 rows once more—24 (27, 32, 35, 40) sts rem.

Work even until armhole measures 8 (8½, 9, 9½, 10)". BO all sts.

Front

Return 72 (80, 88, 96, 104) front sts to needle and, with WS facing, rejoin yarn.

Next row: (WS) M1 (in gap between front and back) for selvedge, work Row 1 of Textured Brioche St in Rows (see Stitch Guide) to end, M1 (in gap between front and back) for selvedge—74 (82, 90, 98, 106) sts.

Next row: Sl 1 kwise wyb, work in patt to last st, p1.

Cont in patt as est, sl first st of every row kwise wyb and purling last st, until armhole measures 5 (5½, 6, 6½, 7)", ending with Row 2 or 4 of patt.

SHAPE NECK

Next row: (WS) Work in patt for 31 (34, 38, 41, 45) sts and place these sts on holder for right shoulder, BO 12 (14, 14, 16, 16) sts pwise, work in patt to end—31 (34, 38, 41, 45) sts rem for left shoulder.

LEFT SHOULDER

Dec row: (RS) Sl 1 kwise wyb, work in patt to last 2 sts, p2tog (see Notes)—1 st dec'd.

Next row: (WS) Sl 1 kwise wyb, work in patt to last st, p1. Rep last 2 rows 10 (10, 10, 11, 11) more times—20 (23, 27, 29, 33) sts rem.

Work even until armhole measures 8 (8½, 9, 9½, 10)", ending with a RS row.

BO all sts pwise.

RIGHT SHOULDER

Return 31 (34, 38, 41, 45) right shoulder sts to needle and, with RS facing, rejoin yarn.

Next row: (RS) Sl 1 kwise wyb, work in patt to last st, p1.

Dec row: (WS) Sl 1 kwise wyb, work in patt to last 2 sts, p2tog—1 st dec'd.

Rep last 2 rows 10 (10, 10, 11, 11) more times—20 (23, 27, 29, 33) sts rem.

Work even until armhole measures 8 (8½, 9, 9½, 10)", ending with a RS row. BO all sts pwise. Sew shoulder seams.

Sleeves

With RS facing and dpn, beg at center of underarm, pick up and knit 80 (85, 90, 95, 100) sts evenly around armhole edge. Pm and join in the rnd. Work in St st for 1".

Dec rnd: K1, k2tog, knit to last 3 sts, ssk, k1—2 sts dec'd.

Rep Dec rnd every 4th (3rd, 3rd, 3rd, 3rd) rnd 13 (2, 4, 10, 14) more times, then every 5 (4, 4, 4, 4)th rnd 6 (19, 18, 14, 11) times—40 (41, 44, 45, 48) sts rem.

Work even until piece measures 14¾" from underarm, dec 0 (1, 0, 1, 0) st on last rnd—40 (40, 44, 44, 48) sts rem. Work in k2, p2 rib for 2¼". BO all sts in patt.

Finishing

Block to measurements.

NECKBAND

With shorter cir needle and RS facing, beg at left shoulder seam, pick up and knit 96 (100, 100, 104, 104) sts evenly around neck edge. Pm and join in the rnd. Work in k1, p1 rib for 1".

BO all sts in patt. Weave in ends.

Finished Size

Bust circumference: about 33¾ (36½, 41, 45¼, 49¾)".

Sweater shown measures 36½".

Yarn

Worsted weight (#4 medium).

Shown here: Cascade Yarns Longwood (100% superwash extrafine Merino wool; 191 yd [175 m]/100 g): #09 mustard, 7 (7, 8, 9, 9) balls.

Needles

Size U.S. 8 (5 mm): 24" circular (cir) and set of 4 or 5 double-pointed (dpn).

Adjust needle size if necessary to obtain the correct gauge.

Notions

5 markers (m); stitch holders or waste yarn; tapestry needle.

Gauge

18 sts and 24 rnds = 4" in St st worked in rnds.

22 sts and 36 rnds = 4" in slip-stitch patt worked in rnds.

cowl-neck raglan

Isabell Kraemer

Slip-Stitch Pattern 1 (mult of 2 sts + 1)

Row 1: (RS) *K1, sl 1 purlwise with yarn in back (pwise wyb); rep from * to last st, k1.

Row 2: (WS) *K1, sl 1 purlwise with yarn in front (pwise wyf); rep from * to last st, k1.

Row 3: (RS) Knit.

Row 4: (WS) Purl.

Rep Rows 1-4 for patt.

Slip-Stitch Pattern 2 (mult of 2 sts + 1)

Rnd 1: *K1, sl 1 purlwise with yarn in back (pwise wyb); rep from * to last st, k1.

Rnd 2: *P1, sl 1 pwise wyb; rep from * to last st, p1.

Rnds 3 and 4: Knit.

Rep Rnds 1-4 for patt.

Slip-Stitch Pattern 3 (mult of 2 sts)

Rnd 1: *K1, sl 1 purlwise with yarn in back (pwise wyb); rep from *.

Rnd 2: *P1, sl 1 pwise wyb; rep from *.

Rnds 3 and 4: Knit.

Rep Rnds 1-4 for patt.

Bodice

With cir needle and using the long-tail method, CO 65 (67, 71, 73, 75) sts.

Row 1: (WS) P2, place marker (pm), p13 (13, 15, 15, 15), pm, p35 (37, 37, 39, 41), pm, p13 (13, 15, 15, 15), pm, p2.

Row 2: (RS) [Knit to 1 st before m, M1R, k1, sl m, k1, M1L, work Row 1 of slip-st patt 1 (see Stitch Guide) to next m, M1R, k1, sl m, k1, M1L] 2 times, knit to end—8 sts inc'd.

Row 3 and all rem WS rows: [Purl to m, sl m, p2, work Row 2 of slip-st patt 1 to 2 sts before next m, p2, sl m] 2 times, purl to end.

Row 4: [Knit to 1 st before m, M1R, k1, sl m, k1, M1L, work Row 3 of slip-st pattern 1 to 1 st before next m, M1R, k1, sl m, k1, M1L] 2 times, knit to end—8 sts inc'd.

Rows 6 and 8: Rep Row 4—97 (99, 103, 105, 107) sts.

SHAPE NECK

Inc row: (RS) K2, M1L, [knit to 1 st before m, M1R, k1, sl m, k1, M1L, work slip-st patt 1 to 1 st before next m, M1R, k1, sl m, k1, M1L] 2 times, knit to 2 sts before end, M1R, k2—10 sts inc'd: 8 raglan incs and 2 neck incs.

Next row: (WS) [Purl to m, sl m, p2, work slip-st patt 1 to 2 sts before next m, p2, sl m] 2 times, purl to end.

Rep the last 2 rows once more—117 (119, 123, 125, 127) sts.

Next row: With RS facing, use the backward-loop method to CO 2 (3, 3, 3, 3) sts onto left needle tip, knit these newly CO sts, then [knit to 1 st before next m, M1R, k1, sl m, k1, M1L, work slip-st patt 1 to 1 st before m, M1R, k1, sl m, k1 M1L] 2 times, knit to end, use the backward-loop method to CO 2 (3, 3, 3, 3) sts onto right needle tip—12 (14, 14, 14, 14) sts inc'd.

Next row: (WS) [Purl to m, sl m, p2, work slip-st patt 1 to 2 sts before next m, p2, sl m] 2 times, purl to end.

Rep the last 2 rows once more—141 (147, 151, 153, 155) sts.

Joining row: With RS facing, use the backward-loop method to CO 19 (17, 17, 19, 21) sts onto left needle tip, knit these newly CO sts, [knit to 1 st before next m, M1R, k1, sl m, k1, M1L, work slip-st patt 1 to 1 st before next m, M1R, k1, sl m, k1, M1L] 2 times, knit to end, pm for beg of rnd (use a unique marker)—168 (172, 176, 180, 184) sts.

Cont working in rnds as foll:

Rnd 1: [Knit to next m, sl m, k2, work Rnd 2 of slip-st patt 2 to 2 sts before next m, k2, sl m] 2 times, knit to end.

Rnd 2: [Knit to 1 st before next m, M1R, k1, sl m, k1, M1L, work slip-st patt 2 to 1 st before next m, M1R, k1, sl m, k1, M1L] 2 times, knit to end—8 sts inc'd.

Rnd 3: [Knit to next m, sl m, k2, work slip-st patt 2 to 2 sts before next m, k2, sl m] 2 times, knit to end.

Rep the last 2 rnds 8 (10, 12, 15, 19) more times—240 (260, 280, 308, 344) sts.

Cont for your size as foll:

SIZES 41 (45¼ 49¾)" ONLY

Next rnd: [Knit to 1 st before next m, M1R, k1, sl m, k1, work slip-st patt 2 to 1 st before next m, k1, sl m, k1, M1L] 2 times, knit to end—8 sts inc'd.

Next rnd: [Knit to next m, sl m, k1, work slip-st patt 2 to 1 st before next m, k1, sl m] 2 times, knit to end.

Rep the last 2 rnds 1 (2, 2) more time(s)—296 (332, 368) sts.

ALL SIZES

Next rnd: [Knit to next m, sl m, k1, work slip-st patt 2 to 1 st before next m, k1, sl m] 2 times, knit to end.

Rep last rnd 3 (3, 3, 1, 1) more time(s).

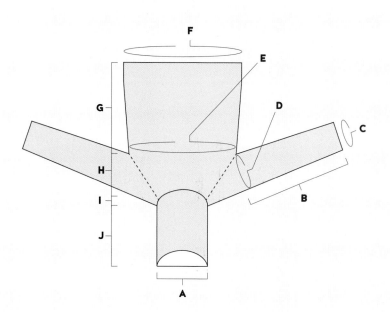

A: 7¾ (8¼, 8¼, 8¾, 9)"

B: 18½"

C: 8¾ (9½, 10¼, 11, 12¼)"

D: 9¾ (10½, 12¾, 14¼, 15¾)"

E: 33¾ (36½, 41, 45¼, 49¾)"

F: 37¼ (40, 44½, 49, 53¼)"

G: 15"

H: 6¾ (7½, 8¾, 9¾, 11¼)"

I: 1¼ (1¼, 1½, 1½, 1½)"

J: 10"

DIVIDE FOR BODY AND SLEEVES

Knit to m, remove m, place next 49 (53, 63, 71, 79) sts onto holder for sleeve, remove m, use the backward-loop method to CO 2 (2, 3, 3, 3) sts, pm, CO 3 (3, 4, 4, 4) more sts as before, knit to next m, remove m, place next 49 (53, 63, 71, 79) sts onto holder for sleeve, remove m, use the backward-loop method to CO 2 (2, 3, 3, 3) sts, pm, CO 3 (3, 4, 4, 4) more sts as before, knit to end, remove m, knit to next m—152 (164, 184, 204, 224) sts rem.

Lower body

Next rnd: [P1, knit to next m, sl m] 2 times.

Rep the last rnd until piece measures 2" from dividing rnd.

Inc rnd: [P1, k1, M1L, knit to 1 st before next m, M1R, k1, sl m] 2 times, knit to end—4 sts inc'd.

Work 3" even.

Rep Inc rnd on next rnd, then every 3" 2 more times—168 (180, 200, 220, 240) sts.

Cont even until piece measures 12" from dividing rnd.

RIBBING

Work in k2, p2 rib until piece measures 15" from dividing rnd.

Loosely BO all sts in patt.

Sleeves

Place 49 (53, 63, 71, 79) held sleeve sts onto dpn.

With RS facing and beg at the center of underarm, pick up and knit 3 sts, work 49 (53, 63, 71, 79) sleeve sts as foll: K1, work 47 (51, 61, 69, 77) sts in slip-st patt 2 as est, k1, pick up and knit 2 (2, 4, 4, 4) sts, pm, and join for working in rnds—54 (58, 70, 78, 86) sts total.

Work Rnds 1-4 of slip-st patt 3 (see Stitch Guide) until piece measures 3" from pick-up rnd.

Dec rnd: K2tog, work slip-st patt 3 as est to 2 sts before m, ssk—2 sts dec'd.

Work 29 (29, 15, 11, 11) rnds even.

Rep the last 30 (30, 16, 12, 12) rnds 2 (2, 6, 8, 8) more times—48 (52, 56, 60, 68) sts rem.

Work even in patt until piece measures 17" from pick-up rnd.

CUFF

Work in p2, k2 rib until piece measures 18½" from pick-up rnd.

Loosely BO all sts in patt.

Finishing

COWL

With cir needle, RS facing, and beg at the left back raglan, pick up and knit 116 (120, 120, 124, 124) sts evenly spaced around neck opening. Pm and join for working in rnds.

Work in k2, p2 rib until piece measures 10" from pick-up rnd.

Loosely BO all sts in patt.

Weave in loose ends.

Block to measurements.

mount robson pullover

Jessie McKitrick

Finished Size

Chest circumference: 34½ (38, 42, 45½, 49½, 52½)".

Pullover shown measures 38", modeled with 2" of negative ease.

Yarn

Fingering weight (#1 light).

Shown here: Cascade Yarns Cascade 220 Fingering (100% Peruvian highland wool; 273 yd [250 m]/1¾ oz [50 g]): #9429 mossy rock, 9 (10, 11, 12, 13, 14) skeins.

Needles

Size U.S. 2 (2.75 mm): 16" circular (cir).

Size U.S. 2½ (3 mm): 32" cir.

Adjust needle size if necessary to obtain the correct gauge.

Notions

Marker (m); removable m; tapestry needle.

Gauge

39 sts and 64 rows = 4" in Cartridge Rib patt on larger needle.

31 sts and 44 rows = 4" in St st on larger needle.

Notes

■ This pullover is worked back and forth in separate pieces and seamed. Sleeves with saddle shoulder extensions are worked flat and sewn in.

■ When picking up stitches around the neckline, pick up about 3 stitches in each repeat of the Cartridge Rib Pattern to maintain pattern gauge and texture.

■ The sleeves are designed to be worn cuffed, which accommodates both differences in arm length and wearing preference.

■ A circular needle is used to accommodate the large number of stitches.

STITCH GUIDE

Cartridge Rib Pattern: (multiple of 4 sts + 1)

Row 1: (RS) Sl 1 pwise wyb, *k3, sl 1 pwise wyf; rep from * to last 4 sts, k4.

Row 2: (WS) Sl 1 pwise wyb, k1, *sl 1 pwise wyf, k3; rep from * to last 3 sts, sl 1 pwise wyf, k2.

Rep Rows 1-2 for patt.

Back

With larger needle, CO 169 (185, 205, 221, 241, 257) sts. Do not join.

Work in Cartridge Rib patt (see Stitch Guide) until piece measures 15 (16, 16, 16½, 16½, 16½)" from CO, ending with a WS row.

SHAPE ARMHOLES

BO 5 (7, 9, 12, 15, 16) sts at beg of next 2 rows, then BO 3 sts at beg of next 2 (2, 2, 4, 6, 8) rows—153 (165, 181, 185, 193, 201) sts rem.

Dec row: (RS) K1, ssk, work to last 3 sts, k2tog, k1—2 sts dec'd.

Rep Dec row every RS row 1 (3, 5, 5, 7, 7) more time(s)—149 (157, 169, 173, 177, 185) sts rem.

Work even until armhole measures 4½ (5, 5½, 6, 6½, 7)", ending with a WS row.

SHAPE SADDLE SHOULDERS

BO 45 (48, 50, 52, 52, 54) sts at beg of next 2 rows—59 (61, 69, 69, 73, 77) sts rem.

Work even until piece measures 4" from saddle shoulder BO. BO all sts in patt.

Front

Work as for back until piece measures 1½ (1¼, 1, 1, 1, 1)" above saddle shoulder BO, ending with a WS row—59 (61, 69, 69, 73, 77) sts rem.

SHAPE NECK

Next row: (RS) Work 14 (15, 17, 17, 18, 18) sts for left shoulder and place rem 45 (46, 52, 52, 55, 59) sts on holder.

LEFT SHOULDER

At beg of WS rows, BO 3 sts once, then BO 2 sts once—9 (10, 12, 12, 13, 13) sts rem.

Dec row: (RS) Work to last 3 sts, k2tog, k1—1 st dec'd.

Rep Dec row every RS row 6 (7, 9, 9, 10, 10) more times—2 sts rem.

BO all sts. Return 45 (46, 52, 52, 55, 59) held sts to needle and, with RS facing, rejoin yarn.

Next row: (RS) BO 31 (31, 35, 35, 37, 41) sts, work to end—14 (15, 17, 17, 18, 18) sts rem for right shoulder.

RIGHT SHOULDER

Work 1 WS row even.

At beg of RS rows, BO 3 sts once, then BO 2 sts once—9 (10, 12, 12, 13, 13) sts rem.

Work 1 WS row even.

Dec row: (RS) K1, ssk, work to end—1 st dec'd.

Rep Dec row every RS row 6 (7, 9, 9, 10, 10) more times—2 sts rem. BO all sts.

Sleeves

With larger needle, CO 81 (85, 89, 93, 101, 105) sts. Do not join.

Work in Cartridge Rib patt until piece measures 6¼ (6¼, 6¼, 6½, 6½, 6½)" from CO, ending with a WS row.

Inc row: (RS) K1, M1, work to last st, M1, k1—2 sts inc'd.

Rep Inc row every 12 (12, 10, 8, 8, 8)th row 14 (12, 5, 16, 20, 17) more times, then every 10 (10, 8, 6, 6, 6)th row 5 (9, 24, 17, 18, 13) times, working new sts into rib patt—121 (129, 149, 161, 169, 177) sts.

Work even until sleeve measures 21¾ (22¾, 23¼, 23½, 24¼, 24½)" from CO, ending with a WS row.

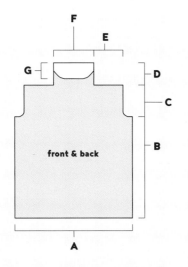

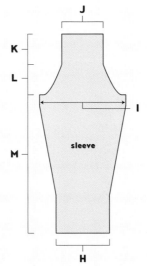

FRONT & BACK

A: 17¼ (19, 21, 22¾, 24¾, 26¼)"

B: 15 (16, 16, 16½, 16½, 16½)"

C: 4½ (5, 5½, 6, 6½, 7)"

D: 4"

E: 4½ (5, 5¼, 5¼, 5¼, 5½)"

F: 6 (6¼, 7, 7, 7½, 8)"

G: 2½ (2¾, 3, 3, 3, 3)"

SLEEVE

H: 8¼ (8¾, 9¼, 9½, 10¼, 10¾)"

I: 21¾ (22¾, 23¼, 23½, 24¼, 24½)"

J: 4½ (5, 5½, 6, 6½, 7)

K: 4½ (5, 5¼, 5¼, 5¼, 5½)"

L: 8¼"

M: 12½ (13¼, 15¼, 16½, 17¼, 18¼)"

SHAPE CAP

BO 5 (7, 9, 12, 15, 16) sts at beg of next 2 rows, then BO 3 sts at beg of foll 2 (2, 2, 4, 6, 8) rows—105 (109, 125, 125, 125, 129) sts rem.

Dec row: (RS) K1, ssk, work to last 3 sts, k2tog, k1—2 sts dec'd.

Rep Dec row every 4th row 14 (16, 12, 16, 19, 21) more times, then every RS row 5 (5, 17, 13, 10, 10) times—65 sts rem.

SADDLE SHOULDER EXTENSION

Work in St st for 4½ (5, 5¼, 5¼, 5¼, 5½)", ending with a WS row. BO all sts.

Finishing

Weave in ends. Block pieces to measurements.

Place removable m in center st of BO on sleeve. Sew selvedge of saddle extension to CO sts on back shoulder.

Cont sewing BO sts of saddle shoulder extensions to selvedge of center back section, easing as necessary so that neck edge of back is at m.

Sew selvedge of saddle extension to CO sts on front shoulder. Cont sewing BO sts of saddle shoulder extensions to selvedge of center front section, easing so that about 1½" rem between m and end of front shoulder seam.

Sew sleeve seams. Sew side and underarm seams.

NECKBAND

With smaller needle and RS facing, beg at right shoulder, pick up and knit 46 (46, 52, 52, 54, 56) sts along back neck BO, 11 sts along St st on left saddle shoulder, 10 (11, 14, 14, 16, 16) sts along left front neck edge, 30 (30, 32, 32, 34, 34) sts in BO sts on front neck, 10 (11, 14, 14, 16, 16) sts along right front neck edge, and 11 sts along St st on right saddle shoulder—118 (120, 134, 134, 142, 144) sts. Pm and join in the rnd.

Work in k1, p1 rib for 1". BO all sts in patt.

meltwater pullover

Kate Gagnon Osborn

Finished Size

Bust circumference: 32¾ (37, 40¾, 45, 48¾, 53)".

Sweater shown measures 37", modeled with 2½" of positive ease.

Yarn

Sport weight (#2 fine).

Shown here: The Fibre Company Savannah (50% wool, 20% cotton, 15% linen, 15% soya; 160 yd [146 m]/1¾ oz [50 g]): natural (MC), 5 (6, 6, 7, 7, 8) skeins; denim (CC1), 2 (3, 3, 3, 3, 3) skeins; seafoam (CC2), 1 (1, 2, 2, 2, 2) skein(s).

Needles

Size U.S. 4 (3.5 mm): 24" circular (cir) and set of double-pointed (dpn).

Size U.S. 6 (4 mm): 24" and 40" cir and set of dpn.

Adjust needle size if necessary to obtain the correct gauge.

Notions

Markers (m); stitch holders; tapestry needle.

Gauge

22 sts and 31 rnds = 4" in St st on larger needle.

Notes

■ This pullover is worked in the round from the lower edge to the underarms. The sleeves are worked separately in the round, then the sleeves and body are joined to work the yoke.

Body

With CC1 and smaller cir needle, CO 180 (204, 224, 248, 268, 292) sts. Place marker (pm) and join in the rnd.

Work in k2, p2 rib for 2¼".

Change to larger cir needle. Work Rows 1–15 of Band chart once.

Change to MC. Work in St st until piece measures 16" from CO. Do not break yarn. Set aside.

Sleeves

With CC1 and smaller dpn, CO 44 (44, 48, 48, 48, 48) sts. Pm and join in the rnd.

Work in k2, p2 rib for 2¼". Change to larger dpn.

Inc rnd: [K11 (11, 12, 12, 6, 6), M1] 4 (4, 4, 4, 8, 8) times—48 (48, 52, 52, 56, 56) sts.

Work Rows 1–15 of Band chart once. Change to MC.

Inc rnd: K1, M1L, knit to end, M1R—2 sts inc'd.

Rep Inc rnd every 10 (10, 9, 9, 8, 7)th rnd 8 (8, 9, 9, 10, 12) more times—66 (66, 72, 72, 78, 82) sts.

Work even until piece measures 18" from CO, ending 4 (4, 5, 5, 6, 6) sts before end of rnd on last rnd. Place first and last 4 (4, 5, 5, 6, 6) sts of rnd on holder, removing m—58 (58, 62, 62, 66, 70) sts rem. Place sts on holder.

Yoke

JOIN BODY AND SLEEVES

With MC attached to body, k4 (4, 5, 5, 6, 6) body sts and place these sts on holder for underarm, k82 (94, 102, 114, 122, 134) for back, place next 8 (8, 10, 10, 12, 12) body sts on holder for underarm, pm, k58 (58, 62, 62, 66, 70) sleeve sts, pm, k82 (94, 102, 114, 122, 134) for front, place next 4 (4, 5, 5, 6, 6) body sts on holder for underarm, pm, k58 (58, 62, 62, 66, 70) sleeve sts—280 (304, 328, 352, 376, 408) sts total.

Pm and join in the rnd.

Dec rnd: *K1, k2tog, knit to 3 sts before m, ssk, k1, sl m; rep from * 3 more times—8 sts dec'd.

Rep Dec rnd every other rnd 0 (1, 2, 3, 2, 2) more time(s)—272 (288, 304, 320, 352, 384) sts rem.

Next rnd: Knit to m, remove m, k15, pm, *knit to m, remove m; rep from * once more, knit to last 15 sts, pm, knit to end.

Shape back using short-rows as foll:

Short-row 1: (RS) Knit to 1 st before m, wrap next st, turn.

Short-row 2: (WS) Purl to beg of rnd, sl m, purl to 1 st before m, wrap next st, turn.

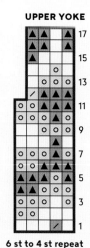

UPPER YOKE

6 st to 4 st repeat

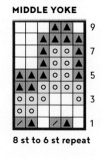

MIDDLE YOKE

8 st to 6 st repeat

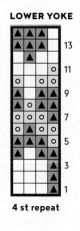

LOWER YOKE

4 st repeat

BAND

4 st repeat

	MC
	CC1
	CC2
	k2tog with CC1
	k2tog with CC2
	pattern repeat

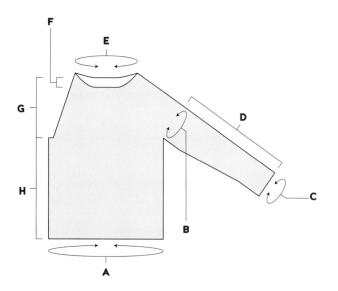

A: 32¾ (37, 40¾, 45, 48¾, 53)"

B: 12 (12, 13, 13, 14¼, 15)"

C: 8¾ (8¾, 9½, 9½, 10¼, 10¼)"

D: 18"

E: 18¼ (19¾, 20¼, 21¾, 21¾, 24)"

F: 1½"

G: 9¼ (9½, 9¾, 10½, 10¾, 10¾)"

H: 16"

Short-row 3: Knit to 10 sts before wrapped st, wrap next st, turn.

Short-row 4: Purl to 10 sts before wrapped st, wrap next st, turn.

Rep last 2 short-rows 4 more times—6 wrapped sts at each side of back.

Next row: (RS) Knit to end, working wraps tog with wrapped sts.

Resume working in the rnd. With MC, knit 1 (1, 2, 6, 10, 10) rnd(s) even, working rem wraps.

Work Rows 1–14 of Lower Yoke chart once.

Work Rows 1–9 of Middle Yoke chart once—204 (216, 228, 240, 264, 288) sts rem.

Work Rows 1–17 of Upper Yoke chart once—136 (144, 152, 160, 176, 192) sts rem.

Next rnd: Remove m, k1 with CC1, pm for new beg of rnd, *with MC, k1, with CC1, k1, k2tog; rep from * to end—102 (108, 114, 120, 132, 144) sts rem.

SIZES 32¾ (40¾)" ONLY

Dec rnd: With CC1, *k48 (54), k2tog; rep from * once more, k2—100 (112) sts rem.

SIZES 37 (45)" ONLY

With CC1, knit 1 rnd.

SIZES 48¾ (53)" ONLY

Dec rnd: With CC1, *k9 (10), k2tog; rep from * to end—120 (132) sts rem.

ALL SIZES

Rib: Change to smaller needle. With CC1, work in k2, p2 rib for 7 rnds. BO all sts in patt.

Finishing

Using Kitchener st, graft sts at underarm. Weave in ends. Soak in cool water and woolwash and block to measurements.

biscotti sweater

Kiyomi Burgin

Finished Size

Bust circumference: 37¼ (41¼, 45¼, 49¼, 52, 56)".

Pullover shown measures 37¼", modeled with 5¼" of positive ease.

Yarn

Bulky weight (#5 bulky).

Shown here: Cascade Yarns Nevado (39% llama, 38% wool, 23% nylon; 164 yd [150 m]/3½ oz [100 g]): #06 charcoal (MC), 4 (5, 5, 5, 6, 6) skeins; #02 almond (CC) 1 (1, 2, 2, 2, 2) skein(s).

Needles

Size U.S.10½ (6.5 mm): 16" and 32" circular (cir) and set of double-pointed (dpn).

Size U.S. 11 (8 mm): 32" cir and set of dpn.

Adjust needle size if necessary to obtain the correct gauge.

Notions

Markers (m); stitch holders; tapestry needle.

Gauge

12 sts and 18 rnds = 4" in St st on larger needle.

Notes

■ This pullover is worked from the top down with raglan shaping. The yoke begins by working back and forth in rows to shape the back neck, then stitches are added at the center front and joined in the round for working the rest of the body.

■ When working the stranded two-color pattern, the color that is carried underneath the other color into working position becomes dominant and its stitches will appear larger. The sample shown was knit with the main color (MC) yarn carried underneath the contrast color (CC) yarn at the color changes so the MC vertical stripes appear slightly thicker than the CC stripes.

■ When working with two colors, keep the floats loose to avoid puckering. If necessary, use a needle one to two sizes larger to maintain the correct gauge.

STITCH GUIDE

Vertical Stripe Pattern (even number of sts)

Rnd 1: *With CC, k1, with MC, k1; rep from * to end.

Rep Rnd 1 for patt.

Corrugated Rib (even number of sts)

Rnd 1: *Bring both yarns to back, k1 with CC, bring MC to front, p1 with MC; rep from * to end.

Rep Rnd 1 for patt.

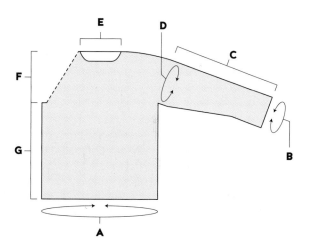

A: 37¼ (41¼, 45¼, 49¼, 52, 56)"

B: 10 (10¾, 11¼, 11¼, 12, 12)"

C: 17 (17, 17½, 17½, 18, 18)"

D: 14¾ (16, 16¾, 18, 18¾, 20)"

E: 6¾ (7¼, 8, 8¾, 9¼, 10)"

F: 8 (8½, 9, 9½, 10, 10¾)"

G: 15 (15, 15½, 15½, 16, 16)"

Yoke

With MC and larger cir needle, CO 40 (42, 44, 46, 48, 50) sts. Do not join.

Set-up row: (WS) P2 for right front, place marker (pm), p8 for right sleeve, pm, p20 (22, 24, 26, 28, 30) for back, pm, p8 for left sleeve, pm, p2 for left front.

Next row: (RS) [Knit to 1 st before m, RLI, k1, sl m, k1, LLI] 4 times, knit to end—48 (50, 52, 54, 56, 58) sts: 10 sts each sleeve, 22 (24, 26, 28, 30, 32) back sts, and 3 sts each front.

Purl 1 WS row.

Raglan and neck inc row: (RS) K1, M1L, [knit to 1 st before m, RLI, k1, sl m, k1, LLI] 4 times, knit to last st, M1R, k1—10 sts inc'd; 2 sts each for sleeves, back, and fronts.

Rep raglan and neck inc row every other row 2 more times—78 (80, 82, 84, 86, 88) sts: 16 sts each sleeve, 28 (30, 32, 34, 36, 38) back sts, and 9 sts each front; piece measures 1¾" from CO at center back. Do not turn.

Next rnd: With RS still facing and using the backward-loop method, CO 10 (12, 14, 16, 18, 20) sts onto right needle for center front neck—88 (92, 96, 100, 104, 108) sts: 16 sts each sleeve, and 28 (30, 32, 34, 36, 38) sts each for front and back.

Pm and join in the rnd. Knit 1 rnd.

Raglan inc rnd: [Knit to 1 st before m, RLI, k1, sl m, k1, LLI] 4 times, knit to

end—8 sts inc'd; 2 sts each sleeve, 2 sts each for front and back.

Rep raglan inc rnd every other rnd 10 (12, 13, 15, 16, 18) more times—176 (196, 208, 228, 240, 260) sts: 38 (42, 44, 48, 50, 54) sts each sleeve, 50 (56, 60, 66, 70, 76) sts each for front and back.

Work 5 (3, 3, 2, 2, 1) rnd(s) even—yoke measures about 8 (8½, 9, 9½, 10, 10¾)" at center back.

DIVIDE FOR BODY AND SLEEVES

Next rnd: Removing old m as you come to them, knit to first raglan m, place next 38 (42, 44, 48, 50, 54) sts on holder for left sleeve, use the backward-loop method to CO 3 (3, 4, 4, 4, 4) sts, pm for new beg of rnd, CO 3 (3, 4, 4, 4, 4) sts, k50 (56, 60, 66, 70, 76) back sts, place next 38 (42, 44, 48, 50, 54) sts on holder for right sleeve, CO 6 (6, 8, 8, 8, 8) sts, knit to new beg-of-rnd m—112 (124, 136, 148, 156, 168) body sts rem.

Body

Work even until piece measures 10 (10, 10½, 10½, 11, 11)" from underarm.

Join CC and work in Vertical Stripe patt (see Stitch Guide) for 3". Break MC.

With CC, knit 1 rnd.

Change to smaller 32" cir needle. Work in k1, p1 rib until piece measures 15 (15, 15½, 15½, 16, 16)" from underarm.

BO all sts in patt.

Sleeves

With MC, larger dpn, and RS facing, beg at center of underarm, pick up and knit 3 sts along underarm CO, k38 (42, 44, 48, 50, 54) sleeve sts from holder, pick up and knit 3 sts along underarm CO—44 (48, 50, 54, 56, 60) sts.

Pm and join in the rnd. Knit 6 (5, 5, 4, 4, 3) rnds.

Dec rnd: K1, k2tog, knit to last 3 sts, ssk, k1—2 sts dec'd.

Rep Dec rnd every 7 (6, 6, 5, 5, 4)th rnd 6 (7, 7, 9, 9, 11) more times—30 (32, 34, 34, 36, 36) sts rem.

Work even until piece measures 11 (11, 11½, 11½, 12, 12)" from underarm. Join CC and work in Vertical Stripe patt for 3". Break MC.

With CC, knit 1 rnd.

Change to smaller dpn. Work in k1, p1 rib until piece measures 17 (17, 17½, 17½, 18, 18)" from underarm. BO all sts in patt.

Finishing

Weave in ends. Block to measurements.

NECKBAND

With MC, 16" cir needle, and RS facing, beg at left back raglan, pick up and knit 8 sts across top of left sleeve, 7 sts down side of left neck, 10 (12, 14, 16, 18, 20) sts across center front, 7 sts up side of right neck, 8 sts across top of right sleeve, and 20 (22, 24, 26, 28, 30) sts across back—60 (64, 68, 72, 76, 80) sts.

Pm and join in the rnd. Join CC and work in Corrugated Rib (see Stitch Guide) for 1¼". BO all sts with CC.

zigzag wanderer

Laura Grutzeck

Finished Size

Bust circumference: 36½ (39, 42, 46, 50½, 54½)".

Pullover shown measures 39", modeled with 5" of positive ease.

Yarn

Sport weight (#2 fine).

Shown here: Classic Elite Yarns Mohawk Wool (60% Merino wool, 30% romney wool, 10% nylon; 375 yd [343 m]/3½ oz [100 g]); 3-ply: #3306 oatmeal, 4 (5, 5, 5, 6, 6) skeins.

Needles

Size U.S. 5 (3.75 mm): straight and 16" circular (cir).

Adjust needle size if necessary to obtain the correct gauge.

Notions

Markers (m); stitch holders; tapestry needle.

Gauge

23 sts and 39 rows = 4" in Zigzag Lace patt.

Notes

- This pullover is worked back and forth in separate pieces and seamed. Sleeves with saddle shoulders are worked flat and sewn in.
- As sleeve stitches are increased, do not work added stitches into pattern. The underarm is stockinette stitch with a garter stitch selvedge.
- When shaping the sleeve saddle shoulder in the lace pattern, do not work a yarnover unless there are enough stitches to work its corresponding decrease.

STITCH GUIDE

Seed Stitch (odd number of sts)

Row 1: K1, *p1, k1; rep from * to end.

Rep Row 1 for patt.

Front

With straight needles, CO 105 (113, 121, 133, 145, 157) sts. Work in Seed st (see Stitch Guide) for 6 rows.

Next row: (WS) K1, purl to last st, k1. Work Zigzag Lace chart until piece measures about 21½ (22, 22, 22½, 23, 23)" from CO, ending with Row 4 or 8 of chart.

Next row: (RS) BO 25 (29, 31, 37, 41, 45) sts, k55 (55, 59, 59, 63, 67) and place these sts on holder, BO rem sts—55 (55, 59, 59, 63, 67) neck sts rem.

Back

Work as for front.

Sleeves

With straight needles, CO 53 (53, 53, 53, 61, 61) sts. Work in Seed st for 6 rows.

Next row: (WS) K1, purl to last st, k1.

Work Zigzag Lace chart for 6 rows, ending with a WS row.

Inc row: (RS) K1, M1R, work in patt as est to last st, M1L, k1—2 sts inc'd.

Rep Inc row every 16 (12, 10, 6, 6, 6)th row 8 (3, 13, 6, 9, 21) more times, then every 0 (14, 0, 8, 8, 0)th row 0 (7, 0, 12, 9, 0) times, working new sts in St st (see Notes)—71 (75, 81, 91, 99, 105) sts.

Work even until piece measures about 17 (17, 16½, 16, 15½, 15)" from CO, ending with Row 2 or Row 6 of chart.

SHAPE SADDLE SHOULDER

Next row: (RS) BO 25 (27, 30, 35, 39, 42) sts, work in patt to end—46 (48, 51, 56, 60, 63) sts rem.

> **Note:** As the lace pattern cont in the saddle shoulder, reestablish the 9 sts outside the chart repeat to include the selvedge sts each side.

Next row: (WS) BO 25 (27, 30, 35, 39, 42) sts, work Row 4 or Row 8 of Zigzag Lace chart over 21 sts.

Work even until saddle shoulder measures about 4¼ (5, 5½, 6½, 7, 7¾)", ending with Row 4 or 8 of chart.

Next row: (RS) Knit. Place sts on holder.

Finishing

Block pieces to measurements. Sew selvedge of saddle extensions of sleeves to BO sts at shoulders.

NECKBAND

Place live sts for neckband on cir needle as foll: beg at left shoulder, place 21 saddle sts on needle, place marker (pm), place 55 (55, 59, 59, 63, 67) front neck sts on needle, pm, place 21 saddle sts on needle, pm, place 55 (55, 59, 59, 63, 67) back neck sts on needle—152 (152, 160, 160, 168, 176) sts. Pm and join in the rnd. With RS facing, join yarn.

ZIGZAG LACE

k on RS; p on WS			
k on WS			
yo			
k2tog on RS; p2tog on WS			
ssk on RS; ssp on WS			
pattern repeat			

4 st repeat

Rnd 1: [Ssk, *k1, p1; rep from * to 3 sts before m, k1, k2tog, sl m] 4 times—8 sts dec'd.

Rnd 2: [*K1, p1; rep from * to 1 st before m, k1, sl m] 4 times.

Rnd 3: [Ssk, *p1, k1; rep from * to 3 sts before m, p1, k2tog, sl m] 4 times—136 (136, 144, 144, 152, 160) sts rem.

Rnd 4: [K1, *k1, p1; rep from * to 2 sts before m, k2, sl m] 4 times.

Rnd 5: Rep Rnd 1—128 (128, 136, 136, 144, 152) sts rem.

Rnd 6: Rep Rnd 2.

BO all sts in patt. Sew shoulder and side seams. Weave in ends.

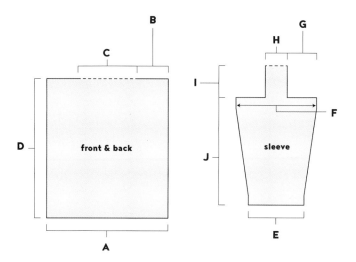

FRONT & BACK

A: 18¼ (19½, 21, 23, 25¼, 27¼)"

B: 4¼ (5, 5½, 6½, 7, 7¾)"

C: 9½ (9½, 10¼, 10¼, 11, 11¾)"

D: 21½ (22, 22, 22½, 23, 23)"

SLEEVE

E: 9¼ (9¼, 9¼, 9¼, 10½, 10½)"

F: 12¼ (13, 14, 15¾, 17¼, 18¼)"

G: 4¼ (4¾, 5¼, 6, 6¾, 7¼)"

H: 3¾"

I: 4¼ (5, 5½, 6½, 7, 7¾)"

J: 17 (17, 16½, 16, 15½, 15)"

coldfield pullover

Meghan Babin

Finished Size

Bust circumference: 36¼ (40, 43¾, 47½, 51½)".

Pullover shown measures 36¼", modeled with 2¼" of positive ease.

Yarn

Sport weight (#2 fine).

Shown here: Harrisville Designs flyWHEEL (100% wool; 170 yd [155 m]/1¾ oz [50 g]): monarch, 8 (9, 9, 10, 11) skeins.

Needles

Size U.S. 3 (3.25 mm): 16" and 32" circular (cir) and set of double-pointed (dpn).

Size U.S. 5 (3.75 mm): 16" and 32" cir and set of dpn.

Adjust needle size if necessary to obtain the correct gauge.

Notions

Markers (m); stitch holders; waste yarn for provisional CO; Size U.S. F/5 (3.75 mm) crochet hook; tapestry needle.

Gauge

21 sts and 36 rnds = 4" in Garter Rib on larger needle.

Notes

■ This pullover is worked in the round from the top down with raglan shaping. The sleeves are worked in the round from the top down.

STITCH GUIDE

**Garter Rib
(even number of sts)**

Rnd/Row 1: (RS) Knit.

Rnd/Row 2: *K1, p1; rep from * to end.

Rep Rnds/Rows 1 and 2 for patt.

Yoke

With smaller 16" cir needle, CO 96 (96, 96, 106, 106) sts. Place marker (pm) and join in the rnd.

Work in k1, p1 rib for ¾". Change to larger 16" cir needle.

Set-up rnd: K5 for left front raglan, pm, [p1, k1] 2 times, pm, k5 for left back raglan, pm, [k1, p1] 17 (17, 17, 19, 19) times, k0 (0, 0, 1, 1), pm, k5 for right back raglan, pm, [p1, k1] 2 times, pm, k5 for right front raglan, pm, [p1, k1] 17 (17, 17, 19, 19) times, p0 (0, 0, 1, 1).

Using the German method, shape front neck using short-rows as foll:

> **Note:** First inc on Short-row 1 is worked before beg-of-rnd m.

Short-row 1: (RS) *M1R, sl m, work Row 1 of Raglan chart over 5 sts, sl m, M1L, knit to m; rep from * 2 more times, M1R, sl m, work Row 1 of Raglan chart over 5 sts, sl m, M1L, k1, turn—8 sts inc'd.

Short-row 2: (WS) Make double st, p1, sl m, work chart to m, sl m, work Row 2 of Garter Rib (see Stitch Guide) to m, sl m, work chart to m, sl m, p1 (1, 1, 0, 0), work Row 2 of Garter Rib to m, sl m, work chart to m, sl m, work Row 2 of Garter Rib to m, sl m, work chart to m, sl m, k1 (k1, k1, p1, p1), p1 (p1, p1, k1, k1), turn.

Short-row 3: Make double st, *work in Garter Rib as est to m, M1R, sl m, work chart to m, sl m, M1L; rep from * 3 more times, work in Garter Rib as est to double st, work double st, work 1 st, turn—8 sts inc'd.

Short-row 4: Make double st, *work in Garter Rib to m, work chart to m; rep from * 3 more times, work in Garter Rib to double st, work double st, work 1 st, turn.

Rep last 2 short-rows 10 (10, 10, 11, 11) more times—192 (192, 192, 210, 210) sts: 58 (58, 58, 65, 65) sts each for front and back, 28 (28, 28, 30, 30) sts for each sleeve, 20 raglan sts.

BODY

10 st repeat

RAGLAN

5 sts

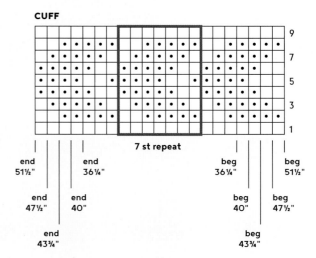

CUFF

7 st repeat

end 51½"
end 36¼"
beg 36¼"
beg 51½"

end 47½"
end 40"
beg 40"
beg 47½"

end 43¾"
beg 43¾"

SIZES 36¼ (40, 43¾)" ONLY

Short-row 5: Make double st, *work in Garter Rib to m, work chart to m; rep from * 3 more times, work in Garter Rib to double st, work double st, work 1 st, turn.

Short-row 6: Rep Short-row 4.

ALL SIZES

Break yarn. With RS facing, sl sts to 2nd m, then rejoin yarn—beg of rnd is at beg of left sleeve (after chart). Resume working in the rnd.

SIZE 51½" ONLY

Inc rnd: *M1L, work in Garter Rib to m, M1R, sl m, work chart to m, sl m; rep from * 3 more times—8 sts inc'd.

Next rnd: *Work in Garter Rib to m, work chart to m; rep from * 3 more times. Rep last 2 rnds once more—226 sts: 69 sts each for front and back, 34 sts for each sleeve, 20 raglan sts.

ALL SIZES

Inc rnd: *M1L, work to m, M1R, sl m, work chart to m, sl m; rep from * 3 more times—8 sts inc'd.

SLEEVE

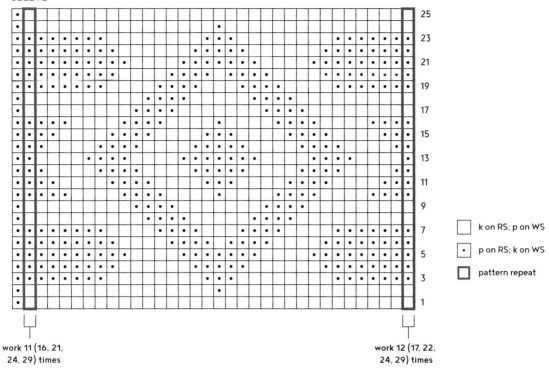

work 11 (16, 21, 24, 29) times

work 12 (17, 22, 24, 29) times

☐ k on RS; p on WS

⊡ p on RS; k on WS

☐ pattern repeat

Rep Inc rnd every 4th rnd 8 (9, 10, 10, 10) more times, then every other rnd 4 (4, 4, 6, 6) times, working new sts into Garter Rib—296 (304, 312, 346, 362) sts: 84 (86, 88, 99, 103) sts each for front and back, 54 (56, 58, 64, 68) sts for each sleeve, 20 raglan sts.

Work 1 rnd even.

DIVIDE FOR BODY AND SLEEVES

Next rnd: *Place 54 (56, 58, 64, 68) sleeve sts on holder, remove m, using the crochet chain provisional method, CO 1 (9, 17, 16, 22) st(s) onto left needle*, work in Garter Rib over 1 (4, 9, 7, 11) CO st(s), pm for new beg of rnd, cont in Garter Rib over 0 (5, 8, 9, 11) CO sts, [work in Garter Rib to m, remove m] 3 times; rep from * to * once, [work in Garter Rib to m, remove m] 3 times, work in Garter Rib to end—190 (210, 230, 250, 270) sts.

Body

Work in Garter Rib until piece measures 12" from underarm. Change to smaller cir needle.

[Knit 1 rnd, purl 1 rnd] 2 times.

Work Rows 1–15 of Body chart. [Purl 1 rnd, knit 1 rnd] 2 times.

Work in k1, p1 rib until piece measures 15½" from underarm.

Loosely BO all sts in patt.

Sleeves

Place 54 (56, 58, 64, 68) held sleeve sts onto smaller dpn. Remove waste yarn from provisional CO and place 0 (5, 8, 9, 11) live sts onto dpn, pm for beg of rnd, place 1 (4, 9, 7, 11) live st(s) onto dpn—55 (65, 75, 80, 90) sts total.

Join in the rnd.

Next rnd: Knit to last st, p1.

Next rnd: Purl.

Rep last 2 rnds once more.

Work Rows 1–25 of Sleeve chart, working reps as shown on chart.

Next rnd: Purl.

Next rnd: Knit to last st, p1.

Rep last 2 rnds once more. Change to larger dpn and Garter Rib.

Dec rnd: K2tog, work in patt to last 3 sts, ssk, p1 (seam st)—2 sts dec'd.

Rep Dec rnd every 18 (10, 7, 6, 4)th rnd 5 (9, 13, 15, 19) more times, maintaining purl seam st—43 (45, 47, 48, 50) sts rem. Work even until piece measures 14" from underarm, ending with Rnd 2 of patt.

SIZES 36¼ (40, 43¾)" ONLY

Dec rnd: K2tog, knit to last st, p1—42 (44, 46) sts rem.

ALL SIZES

Change to smaller dpn.

Next rnd: Knit to last st, p1.

Next rnd: Purl.

Rep last 2 rnds once more.

Beg and ending as indicated for your size, work Cuff chart to last st, p1. Cont in patt through Row 9 of chart.

Next rnd: Purl.

Next rnd: Knit to last st, p1.

Rep last 2 rnds once more.

Work in k1, p1 rib until piece measures 18" from underarm. Loosely BO all sts in patt.

Finishing

Weave in ends. Block to measurements.

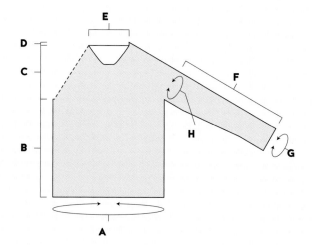

A: 36¼ (40, 43¾, 47½, 51½)"

B: 15½"

C: 8½ (8¾, 9¼, 9¾, 10¼)"

D: ½"

E: 6½ (6½, 6½, 7½, 7½)"

F: 18"

G: 8¼ (8½, 9, 9¼, 9½)"

H: 10½ (12½, 14¼, 15¼, 17¼)"

macgowan pullover

Quenna Lee

Finished Size

Bust circumference: 33 (34½, 37¾, 41, 44¼, 49, 52¼)".

Pullover shown measures 34½", modeled with 2½" of positive ease.

Yarn

Light worsted weight (#3 light).

Shown here: The Fibre Company Knightsbridge (65% baby llama, 25% Merino wool, 10% silk; 120 yd [110 m]/1¾ oz [50 g]): barley, 9 (9, 10, 10, 11, 12, 13) skeins.

Needles

Size U.S. 5 (3.75 mm): 16" and 29" circulars (cir) and set of double-pointed (dpn).

Size U.S. 6 (4 mm): 29" cir and set of dpn.

Adjust needle size if necessary to obtain the correct gauge.

Notions

Markers (m); cable needle (cn); stitch holders; tapestry needle.

Gauge

20 sts and 28 rnds = 4" in St st on larger needle.

20 sts and 32 = 4" rnds in Moss st on larger needle.

29-st Front Lace chart = 5¼" wide on larger needle.

25-st Back Lace chart = 4½" wide on larger needle.

Notes

■ The body of this pullover is worked in the round to the underarm, then the front and back are worked separately back and forth. After the shoulders are seamed, sleeve stitches are picked up and the sleeve cap is shaped with short rows. The sleeve is then worked in the round from the top down.

■ The charts are worked both in rounds and back and forth in rows. When working in rounds, work every chart row as a right-side row.

STITCH GUIDE

Front Rib in rnds (worked over 29 sts)

Rnd 1: P2, k3, p2, k2, p3, k2, p1, k2, p3, k2, p2, k3, p2.

Rep Rnd 1 for patt.

Front Rib in rows (worked over 29 sts)

Row 1: (WS) K2, p3, k2, p2, k3, p2, k1, p2, k3, p2, k2, p3, k2.

Row 2: (RS) P2, k3, p2, k2, p3, k2, p1, k2, p3, k2, p2, k3, p2.

Rep Rows 1 and 2 for patt.

Back Rib (worked over 25 sts)

Rnd 1: [P2, k3, p2, k2] 2 times, p2, k3, p2.

Rep Rnd 1 for patt.

Moss Stitch in rnds (even number of sts)

Rnds 1 and 2: *K1, p1; rep from * to end.

Rnds 3 and 4: *P1, k1; rep from * to end.

Rep Rnds 1–4 for patt.

Moss Stitch in rows (even number of sts)

Row 1: (RS) *K1, p1; rep from * to end.

Row 2: (WS) *K1, p1; rep from * to end.

Rows 3 and 4: *P1, k1; rep from * to end.

Rep Rows 1–4 for patt.

Body

With smaller, longer cir needle, CO 170 (178, 194, 210, 226, 250, 266) sts as foll: CO 28 (30, 34, 38, 42, 48, 52) sts, place marker (pm), CO 29 sts, pm, CO 28 (30, 34, 38, 42, 48, 52) sts, pm, CO 30 (32, 36, 40, 44, 50, 54) sts, pm, CO 25 sts, pm, CO 30 (32, 36, 40, 44, 50, 54) sts. Pm and join in the rnd.

Next rnd: K0 (2, 2, 2, 2, 0, 0), [p2, k2] 7 (7, 8, 9, 10, 12, 13) times, sl m, work Front Rib in rnds (see Stitch Guide) to m, sl m, [k2, p2] 7 (7, 8, 9, 10, 12, 13) times, k0 (2, 2, 2, 2, 0, 0), sl m, k2 (0, 0, 0, 0, 2, 2), [p2, k2] 7 (8, 9, 10, 11, 12, 13) times, sl m, work Back Rib (see Stitch Guide) to m, sl m, [k2, p2] 7 (8, 9, 10, 11, 12, 13) times, k2 (0, 0, 0, 0, 2, 2).

Cont in patt as est until rib measures 1½ (1½, 1½, 2, 2, 2, 2)" from CO. Change to larger cir needle.

Set-up rnd: Work Moss st in rnds (see Stitch Guide) to m, sl m, work Front Lace chart over 29 sts, sl m, [work Moss st to m, sl m] 2 times, work Back Lace chart over 25 sts, sl m, work Moss st to end.

Cont in patt until piece measures 15 (14¾, 14½, 15, 14½, 14¼, 14)" from CO, ending with an even-numbered rnd of charts.

DIVIDE FOR FRONTS AND BACK

Place last 85 (89, 97, 105, 113, 125, 133) sts worked on holder for back—85 (89, 97, 105, 113, 125, 133) sts rem for front. Beg working back and forth in rows.

Front

SHAPE ARMHOLES

BO 4 (4, 5, 5, 5, 7, 7) sts at beg of next 2 rows, then BO 0 (0, 0, 3, 2, 2, 2) sts at beg of foll 0 (0, 0, 2, 4, 4, 4) rows—77 (81, 87, 89, 95, 103, 111) sts rem.

SIZES 41 (44¼, 49, 52¼)" ONLY

Dec row: (RS) K2, ssk, work in patt to last 4 sts, k2tog, k2—2 sts dec'd.

Next row: (WS) K1, p2, work in patt to last 3 sts, p2, k1.

Rep last 2 rows 0 (1, 4, 4) more time(s)—87 (91, 93, 101) sts rem.

ALL SIZES

Dec row: (RS) K2, ssk, work in patt to last 4 sts, k2tog, k2—2 sts dec'd.

Next row: (WS) K1, p2, work in patt to last 3 sts, p2, k1.

Next row: (RS) K3, work in patt to last 3 sts, k3.

Next row: (WS) K1, p2, work in patt to last 3 sts, p2, k1.

Rep last 4 rows 2 (3, 4, 4, 4, 3, 4) more times—71 (73, 77, 77, 81, 85, 91) sts rem.

Rep Dec row once more—69 (71, 75, 75, 79, 83, 89) sts rem.

Work even until armhole measures about 4¾ (5, 5¼, 5¼, 5¾, 6, 6¼)", ending with Row 1 of Front Lace chart.

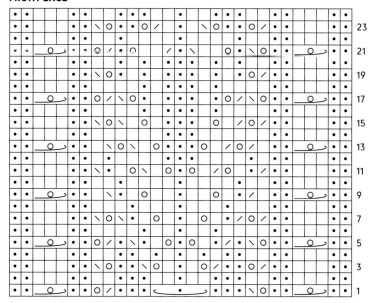

FRONT LACE

29 sts

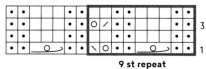

BACK LACE

9 st repeat

MOCK CABLE

5 sts

☐ k on RS; p on WS

• p on RS; k on WS

O yo

╱ k2tog

╲ ssk

☐ pattern repeat

⟨—O—⟩ pass 3rd st on left needle over first 2 sts, k1, yo, k1

⟨—•—⟩ k2, p1, k2, sl first 5 sts on right needle onto cn, wrap yarn counter-clockwise 2 times around these sts, sl sts back to right needle

Next row: (WS) Work in patt to m, sl m, work Front Rib in rows (see Stitch Guide) to m, sl m, work in patt to end.

Work 2 more rows in patt as est.

SHAPE NECK

Next row: (RS) Work in patt over 21 (22, 23, 23, 23, 25, 27) sts, place these sts on holder for left front (do not break yarn), join 2nd ball of yarn and BO 27 (27, 29, 29, 33, 33, 35) sts, work in patt to end—21 (22, 23, 23, 23, 25, 27) sts rem for right shoulder.

RIGHT SHOULDER

Work 1 WS row in patt.

Dec row: (RS) K1, ssk, work in patt to end—1 st dec'd.

Next row: (WS) Work in patt to last 2 sts, p2.

Rep last 2 rows once more—19 (20, 21, 21, 21, 23, 25) sts rem.

Work even until armhole measures 7 (7¼, 7½, 7¾, 8¼, 8½, 9)", ending with a WS row.

Shape shoulder using short-rows as foll:

Short-row 1: (RS) Work 14 (15, 15, 15, 15, 17, 18) sts in patt, wrap next st, turn.

Short-row 2: (WS) Work in patt to end.

Short-row 3: Work 10 (11, 11, 11, 11, 12, 13) sts in patt, wrap next st, turn.

Short-row 4: Work in patt to end.

Short-row 5: Work 5 (5, 5, 5, 5, 6, 6) sts in patt, wrap next st, turn.

Short-row 6: Work in patt to end.

Next row: (RS) Knit to end, working wraps tog with wrapped sts. Place sts on holder. Break yarn, leaving a 30" tail.

LEFT SHOULDER

Return 21 (22, 23, 23, 23, 25, 27) left shoulder sts to needle and resume with attached yarn.

Work 1 WS row in patt.

Dec row: (RS) Work in patt to last 3 sts, k2tog, k1—1 st dec'd.

Next row: (WS) P2, work in patt to end. Rep last 2 rows once more—19 (20, 21, 21, 21, 23, 25) sts rem.

Work even until armhole measures 7 (7¼, 7½, 7¾, 8¼, 8½, 9)", ending with a RS row.

Shape shoulder using short-rows as foll:

Short-row 1: (WS) Work 14 (15, 15, 15, 15, 17, 18) sts in patt, wrap next st, turn.

Short-row 2: (RS) Work in patt to end.

Short-row 3: Work 10 (11, 11, 11, 11, 12, 13) sts in patt, wrap next st, turn.

Short-row 4: Work in patt to end.

Short-row 5: Work 5 (5, 5, 5, 5, 6, 6) sts in patt, wrap next st, turn.

Short-row 6: Work in patt to end.

Next row: (WS) Purl to end, working wraps tog with wrapped sts. Place sts on holder. Break yarn, leaving a 30" tail.

Back

Return 85 (89, 97, 105, 113, 125, 133) back sts to needle and, with RS facing, rejoin yarn.

Shape armholes as for front—69 (71, 75, 75, 79, 83, 89) sts rem.

Work even until armhole measures 6¼ (6½, 6¾, 7, 7½, 7¾, 8¼)", ending with a WS row.

SHAPE NECK

Next row: (RS) Work 21 (22, 23, 23, 23, 25, 27) sts in patt and place these sts on holder for right shoulder (do not break yarn), join 2nd ball of yarn and BO 27 (27, 29, 29, 33, 33, 35) sts, work in patt to end—21 (22, 23, 23, 23, 25, 27) sts rem for left shoulder.

LEFT SHOULDER

Work 1 WS row in patt.

Dec row: (RS) K1, ssk, work in patt to end—1 st dec'd.

Next row: (WS) Work in patt to last 2 sts, p2.

Rep last 2 rows once more—19 (20, 21, 21, 21, 23, 25) sts rem; armhole measures about 7 (7¼, 7½, 7¾, 8¼, 8½, 9)".

Shape shoulder using short-rows as foll:

Short-row 1: (RS) Work 14 (15, 15, 15, 15, 17, 18) sts in patt, wrap next st, turn.

Short-row 2: (WS) Work in patt to end.

Short-row 3: Work 10 (11, 11, 11, 11, 12, 13) sts in patt, wrap next st, turn.

Short-row 4: Work in patt to end.

Short-row 5: Work 5 (5, 5, 5, 5, 6, 6) sts in patt, wrap next st, turn.

Short-row 6: Work in patt to end.

Next row: (RS) Knit to end, working wraps tog with wrapped sts. Place sts on holder. Break yarn, leaving a 30" tail.

RIGHT SHOULDER

Return 21 (22, 23, 23, 23, 25, 27) right shoulder sts to needle and resume with attached yarn.

Work 1 WS row in patt.

Dec row: (RS) Work in patt to last 3 sts, k2tog, k1—1 st dec'd.

Next row: (WS) P2, work in patt to end. Rep last 2 rows once more—19 (20, 21, 21, 21, 23, 25) sts rem.

Work 1 RS row in patt—armhole measures about 7 (7¼, 7½, 7¾, 8¼, 8½, 9)".

Shape shoulder using short-rows as foll:

Short-row 1: (WS) Work 14 (15, 15, 15, 15, 17, 18) sts in patt, wrap next st, turn.

Short-row 2: (RS) Work in patt to end.

Short-row 3: Work 10 (11, 11, 11, 11, 12, 13) sts in patt, wrap next st, turn.

Short-row 4: Work in patt to end.

Short-row 5: Work 5 (5, 5, 5, 5, 6, 6) sts in patt, wrap next st, turn.

Short-row 6: Work in patt to end.

Next row: (WS) Purl to end, working wraps tog with wrapped sts. Break yarn, leaving a 30" tail. Join shoulders using three-needle BO.

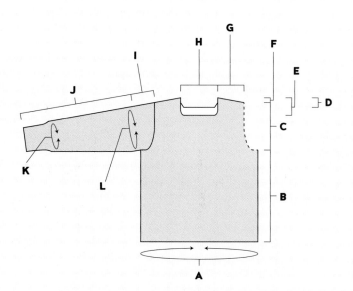

A: 33 (34½, 37¾, 41, 44¼, 49, 52¼)"

B: 15 (14¾, 14½, 15, 14½, 14¼, 14)"

C: 7 (7¼, 7½, 7¾, 8¼, 8½, 9)"

D: 1½"

E: 2¾ (2¾, 2¾, 3, 3, 3, 3¼)"

F: ¾"

G: 3¾ (4, 4¼, 4¼, 4¼, 4½, 5)"

H: 5¾ (5¾, 6, 6, 7, 7, 7¼)"

I: 3¼ (3¾, 3¾, 4, 4, 4½, 4¾)"

J: 18 (18, 18½, 18¾, 19, 19½, 20)"

K: 10 (10, 10, 10¾, 10¾, 10¾, 11½)"

L: 12¾ (13½, 14½, 14¾, 15½, 16¾, 18¾)"

Short-row 8: Work in patt to wrapped st, work wrap tog with wrapped st, wrap next st, turn.

Rep last 2 short-rows 6 (8, 8, 9, 9, 11, 12) more times.

Next row: (RS) Work in patt to end, working wrap tog with wrapped st.

Next rnd: Work in patt to end, working last wrap tog with wrapped st. Work 5 rnds even in patt.

Dec rnd: K1, ssk, work in patt to last 3 sts, k2tog, k1—2 sts dec'd.

Rep Dec rnd every 14 (10, 8, 9, 8, 6, 5)th rnd 6 (8, 10, 9, 11, 14, 17) more times—50 (50, 50, 54, 54, 54, 58) sts rem.

Work even until piece measures 14 (14, 14½, 14¾, 15, 15½, 16)" from underarm, ending with an even-numbered rnd of chart. Change to smaller dpn.

CUFF

Next rnd: Remove m, k17 (17, 17, 19, 19, 19, 21), pm for new beg-of-rnd, work chart over 5 sts, k2, p2, k2, work chart over 5 sts, k2, *p2, k2; rep from * to end.

Cont in patt until cuff measures 3¾", ending with Rnd 2 of chart.

Next rnd: K7, p2, k9, *p2, k2; rep from * to end.

Next rnd: P1, k3, p1, k2, p2, k2, p1, k3, p1, work in rib patt as est to end. BO all sts in patt.

Finishing

Block to measurements.

NECKBAND

With smaller, shorter cir needle and RS facing, beg at back neck BO, pick up and knit 27 (27, 29, 29, 33, 33, 35) sts along BO sts, 24 (24, 24, 25, 25, 25, 26) sts evenly along left neck edge, 27 (27, 29, 29, 33, 33, 35) sts along front neck BO, and 24 (24, 24, 25, 25, 25, 26) sts along right neck edge—102 (102, 106, 108, 116, 116, 122) sts. Pm and join in the rnd.

Work in k1, p1 rib for 7 rnds. BO all sts in patt. Weave in ends.

Sleeves

With larger dpn and RS facing, beg at center of underarm and pick up and knit 64 (68, 72, 74, 78, 84, 94) sts evenly spaced around armhole edge, being sure to pick up 32 (34, 36, 37, 39, 42, 47) sts on each side of shoulder seam. Pm and join in the rnd.

Next rnd: K24 (26, 28, 29, 31, 34, 39), pm, p1, k3, p1, k6, p1, k3, p1, pm, knit to end.

Shape sleeve cap using short-rows as foll:

Short-row 1: (RS) Knit to m, remove m, work Mock Cable chart over 5 sts, k6, work Mock Cable chart over 5 sts, sl m, k1 (1, 2, 2, 3, 3, 5), wrap next st, turn.

Short-row 2: (WS) Purl to m, remove m, work chart over 5 sts, p6, work chart over 5 sts, p1 (1, 2, 2, 3, 3, 5), wrap next st, turn. Cont in St st and chart as est.

Short-row 3: Work in patt to wrapped st, work wrap tog with wrapped st, k1, wrap next st, turn.

Short-row 4: Work in patt to wrapped st, work wrap tog with wrapped st, p1, wrap next st, turn.

Short-rows 5 and 6: Rep Short-rows 3 and 4.

Short-row 7: Work in patt to wrapped st, work wrap tog with wrapped st, wrap next st, turn.

rau
sweater

Quenna Lee

Finished Size

Bust circumference: 35¾ (37¾, 39¾, 42¼, 45¾, 49¾, 53¾)".

Pullover shown measures 37¾", modeled with ¼" of positive ease.

Yarn

Fingering weight (#1 super fine).

Shown here: Spud & Chloë Fine Sock (80% superwash wool, 20% silk; 248 yd [227 m]/2⅓ oz [65 g]): #7822 sidewalk, 5 (5, 5, 5, 6, 6, 7) skeins.

Needles

Size U.S. 5 (3.75 mm): 16" and 29" circular (cir) and set of double-pointed (dpn).

Adjust needle size if necessary to obtain the correct gauge.

Notions

Markers (m); stitch holders; tapestry needle.

Gauge

24 sts and 32 rnds = 4" in St st.

23 sts and 36 rows = 4" in garter st.

Notes

■ The hem of this pullover is worked flat in two pieces, then the pieces are joined and the rest of the body is worked in the round to the underarm. The upper front and back are worked separately back and forth. Stitches for the sleeves are picked up around the armhole and the sleeves are worked from the top down in the round.

Split hem

With longer cir needle, CO 107 (113, 119, 127, 137, 149, 161) sts, then with 2nd ball of yarn, CO 107 (113, 119, 127, 137, 149, 161) sts. Do not join.

Working both pieces *at the same time* with separate balls of yarn, work as foll:

Next row: (RS) Sl 1 pwise wyf, knit to end of first piece; with 2nd ball of yarn, sl 1 pwise wyf, knit to end.

Next row: (WS) Sl 1 pwise wyf, *k1, p1; rep from * to last 2 sts of first piece, k2; with 2nd ball of yarn, sl 1 pwise wyf, *k1, p1; rep from * to last 2 sts, k2.

Rep last 2 rows 7 more times—pieces measure 1½".

JOIN HEMS

Next row: (RS) Knit to end of first piece, place marker (pm), then with same yarn, knit to end of 2nd piece—214 (226, 238, 254, 274, 298, 322) sts. Do not turn.

Place marker (pm) and join in the rnd. Break other ball of yarn.

Work in St st until piece measures 15" from CO.

SHAPE GUSSET

Knit 1 rnd.

Purl 1 rnd.

Inc rnd: *K1, M1L, knit to 1 st before m, M1R, k1, sl m; rep from * once more—4 sts inc'd.

Purl 1 rnd.

Rep last 2 rnds 5 more times—238 (250, 262, 278, 298, 322, 346) sts; piece measures 16½" from CO.

DIVIDE FOR FRONT AND BACK

Place last 119 (125, 131, 139, 149, 161, 173) sts worked on holder for back, removing m—119 (125, 131, 139, 149, 161, 173) sts rem for front.

Beg working back and forth.

LEFT LEAF

19

17

15

13

11

9

7

5

3

1

19 sts

RIGHT LEAF

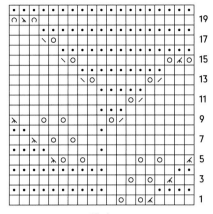

19

17

15

13

11

9

7

5

3

1

19 sts

CENTER LEAF

15

13

11

9

7

5

3

1

19 sts

	k on RS; p on WS
·	p on RS; k on WS
o	yo
∕	k2tog
∖	ssk
⋏	k3tog
⅄	sl 1, k2tog, psso

Front

Work in garter st (knit every row) for 0 (0, 2, 2, 4, 6, 8) rows.

Next row: (RS) K50 (53, 56, 60, 65, 71, 77), pm, work Center Leaf Chart over 19 sts, pm, knit to end.

Keeping sts between m in chart patt and rem sts in garter st, work through Row 16 of chart. Remove m.

Work in garter st for 4 (4, 6, 8, 8, 8, 12) rows.

Next row: (RS) K19 (22, 24, 28, 31, 36, 41), pm, work Left Leaf Chart over 19 sts, pm, k43 (43, 45, 45, 49, 51, 53), pm, work Right Leaf Chart over 19 sts, pm, knit to end.

Keeping sts between m in chart patt and rem sts in garter st, work through Row 20 of charts. Remove m.

Work in garter st until armhole measures 5½ (5¾, 6¼, 6½, 6¾, 7½, 8½)", ending with a WS row.

SHAPE NECK

Next row: (RS) K40 (43, 46, 50, 53, 58, 64) and place these sts on holder for left shoulder, k39 (39, 39, 39, 43, 45, 45) and place these sts on holder for neck—40 (43, 46, 50, 53, 58, 64) sts rem unworked for right shoulder.

RIGHT SHOULDER

Shape shoulder using short-rows as foll:

Short-row 1: (RS) Knit to last 4 (4, 5, 5, 5, 6, 7) sts, wrap next st, turn.

Short-row 2 and all WS short-rows: Knit to end.

Short-rows 3, 5, and 7: Knit to 4 (4, 5, 5, 5, 6, 7) sts before wrapped st, wrap next st, turn.

Short-rows 9, 11, 13, and 15: Knit to 4 (5, 5, 5, 6, 6, 7) sts before wrapped st, wrap next st, turn.

Short-row 16: Knit to end.

Next row: (RS) Knit to end, working wraps tog with wrapped sts. Place sts on holder.

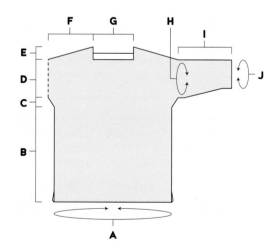

A: 35¾ (37¾, 39¾, 42¼, 45¾, 49¾. 53¾)"

B: 15"

C: 1½"

D: 5½ (5¾, 6¼, 6½, 6¾, 7½, 8½)"

E: 2"

F: 7 (7½, 8, 8¾, 9¼, 10, 11¼)"

G: 6¾ (6¾, 6¾, 6¾, 7½, 7¾, 7¾)"

H: 11 (11¾, 12¼, 13, 13¾, 15, 17)"

I: 8¾ (8¾, 8¾, 8½, 8¼, 8¼, 8¼)"

J: 8¼ (9, 9¾, 9¾, 9¾, 10¼, 10¼)"

LEFT SHOULDER

Return 40 (43, 46, 50, 53, 58, 64) left shoulder sts to needle and, with WS facing, rejoin yarn.

Shape shoulder using short-rows as foll:

Short-row 1: (WS) Knit to last 4 (4, 5, 5, 6, 7) sts, wrap next st, turn.

Short-row 2 and all RS short-rows: Knit to end.

Short-rows 3, 5, and 7: Knit to 4 (4, 5, 5, 5, 6, 7) sts before wrapped st, wrap next st, turn.

Short-rows 9, 11, 13, and 15: Knit to 4 (5, 5, 5, 6, 6, 7) sts before wrapped st, wrap next st, turn.

Next row: (WS) Knit to end, working wraps tog with wrapped sts. Knit 1 RS row. Place sts on holder.

Back

Return 119 (125, 131, 139, 149, 161, 173) back sts to needle and, with RS facing, rejoin yarn.

Work in garter st until armhole measures 5½ (5¾, 6¼, 6½, 6¾, 7½, 8½)", ending with a WS row. Mark center 39 (39, 39, 39, 43, 45, 45) sts for neck.

Shape shoulders using short-rows as foll:

Short-rows 1 and 2: Knit to last 4 (4, 5, 5, 5, 6, 7) sts, wrap next st, turn.

Short-rows 3–8: Knit to 4 (4, 5, 5, 5, 6, 7) sts before wrapped st, wrap next st, turn.

Shape neck and cont working short-rows as foll:

Short-row 9: (RS) Knit to m, remove m, place 40 (43, 46, 50, 53, 58, 64) right shoulder sts on holder, join 2nd ball of yarn and knit to m, remove m, place 39 (39, 39, 39, 43, 45, 45) sts just worked on holder for neck, knit to last 4 (5, 5, 5, 6, 6, 7) sts, wrap next st, turn—40 (43, 46, 50, 53, 58, 64) sts rem for left shoulder.

LEFT SHOULDER

Short-rows 10, 12, 14, and 16: (WS) Knit to end.

Short-rows 11, 13, and 15: Knit to last 4 (5, 5, 5, 6, 6, 7) sts, wrap next st, turn.

Short-row 17: Knit to end, working wraps tog with wrapped sts. Place sts on holder.

RIGHT SHOULDER

Return 40 (43, 46, 50, 53, 58, 64) held right shoulder sts to needle and, with WS facing, rejoin yarn.

Short-rows 10, 12, 14, and 16: (WS) Knit to last 4 (5, 5, 5, 6, 6, 7) sts, wrap next st, turn.

Short-rows 11, 13, 15, and 17: (RS) Knit to end.

Next row: (WS) Knit to end, working wraps tog with wrapped sts. Join shoulders using three-needle BO.

Sleeves

With dpn and RS facing, beg at center of underarm, pick up and knit 66 (70, 74, 78, 82, 90, 102) sts evenly spaced around armhole edge. Pm and join in the rnd.

Knit 7 rnds.

Dec rnd: K1, ssk, knit to last 3 sts, k2tog, k1—2 sts dec'd.

Rep Dec rnd every 7th (7th, 7th, 5th, 4th, 3rd, 2nd) rnd 7 (7, 7, 9, 11, 13, 19) more times—50 (54, 58, 58, 58, 62, 62) sts rem.

Work even until piece measures 8 (8, 8, 7¾, 7½, 7½, 7½)" from underarm.

Next rnd: *K1, p1; rep from * to end.

Next rnd: Knit.

Rep last 2 rnds 3 more times—piece measures 8¾ (8¾, 8¾, 8½, 8¼, 8¼, 8¼)" from underarm.

Loosely BO all sts in patt.

Finishing

Block to measurements.

NECKBAND

With shorter cir needle and RS facing, k39 (39, 39, 39, 43, 45, 45) back sts from holder, pick up and knit 6 sts along left back neck and 10 sts along left front neck, k39 (39, 39, 39, 43, 45, 45) front sts from holder, then pick up and knit 10 sts along right front neck and 6 sts along right back neck—110 (110, 110, 110, 118, 122, 122) sts.

Pm and join in the rnd. Knit 1 rnd.

Neck I–cord BO

CO 2 sts and return both sts to left needle. Working loosely, *k1, ssk, return 2 sts to left needle; rep from * to last 2 sts, BO rem sts. Seam I-cord ends tog. Weave in ends.

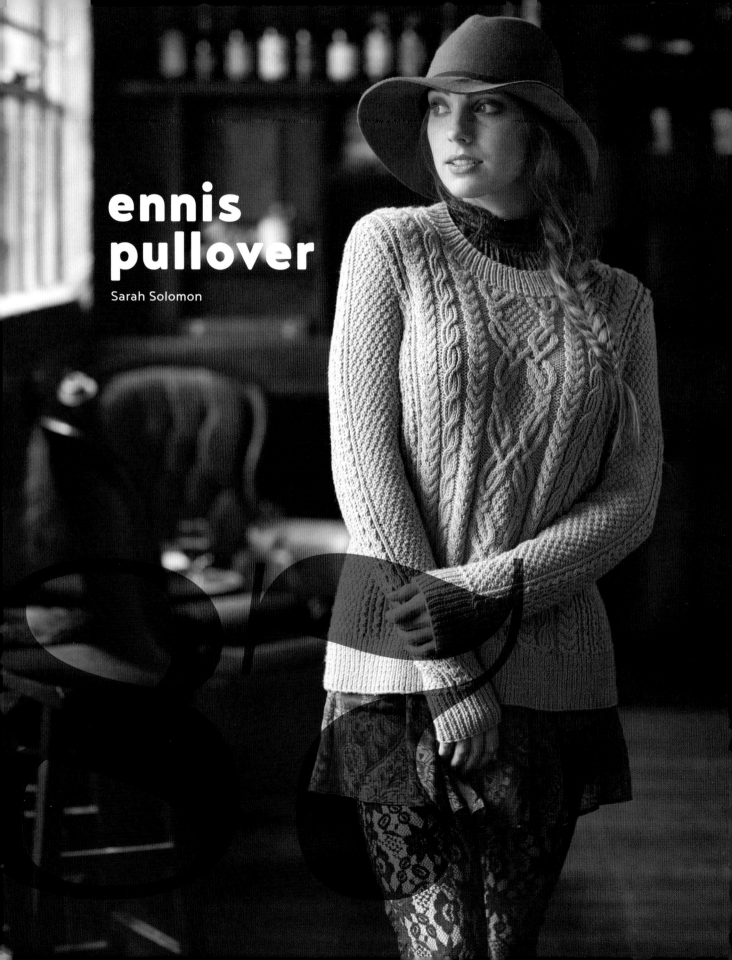

ennis
pullover

Sarah Solomon

Finished Size

Bust circumference: 34½ (36, 39, 42½, 45½, 49)".

Pullover shown measures 39", modeled with 5" of positive ease.

Yarn

DK weight (#3 light).

Shown here: Sublime Baby Cashmere Merino wool, Silk DK (75% extra fine Merino wool, 20% silk, 5% cashmere; 127 yd [116 m]/1¾ oz [50 g]): #006 pebble, 11 (12, 12, 14, 15, 16) skeins.

Needles

Size U.S. 4 (3.5 mm): straight and 24" circular.

Size U.S. 6 (4 mm): straight.

Adjust needle size if necessary to obtain the correct gauge.

Notions

Markers (m); cable needle (cn); stitch holder; tapestry needle.

Gauge

20 sts and 30 rows = 4" in Moss st on larger needles.

Chart B = 3½" wide.

Notes

■ This pullover is worked back and forth in pieces and seamed.

■ Keep one stitch at each edge in stockinette stitch for selvedge.

■ When working neck shaping, if you do not have enough stitches to complete a cable, work these stitches in est pattern instead.

STITCH GUIDE

Moss Stitch A (even number of sts)

Row 1: (RS) *K1, p1; rep from * to end.

Row 2: (WS) Rep Row 1.

Row 3: *P1, k1; rep from * to end.

Row 4: Rep Row 3.

Rep Rows 1-4 for patt.

Moss Stitch B (even number of sts)

Row 1: (RS) *P1, k1; rep from * to end.

Row 2: (WS) Rep Row 1.

Row 3: *K1, p1; rep from * to end.

Row 4: Rep Row 3.

Rep Rows 1-4 for patt.

Moss Stitch C (odd number of sts)

Row 1: (RS) *K1, p1; rep from * to last st, k1.

Row 2: (WS) *P1, k1; rep from * to last st, p1.

Row 3: Rep Row 2.

Row 4: Rep Row 1.

Rep Rows 1-4 for patt.

Fancy Columns (multiple of 5 sts + 3)

Row 1: (RS) *P1, k1tbl, p1, sl 1 st onto cn, hold in back, k1, k1 from cn; rep from * to last 3 sts, p1, k1tbl, p1.

Row 2: (WS) *K1, p1tbl, k1, p2; rep from * to last 3 sts, k1, p1tbl, k1.

Row 3: *P1, k1tbl, p1, sl 1 st onto cn, hold in front, k1, k1 from cn; rep from * to last 3 sts, p1, k1tbl, p1.

Row 4: Rep Row 2.

Rep Rows 1-4 for patt.

Back

With smaller straight needles, CO 126 (130, 138, 146, 154, 162) sts. Work in k1, p1 rib for 2¾", ending with a RS row. Change to larger needles.

Next row: (WS) P1, k2tog, k48 (50, 54, 58, 62, 66), place marker (pm), k4, p4, k2, p5, k2, p4, k4, pm, knit to last st, p1—125 (129, 137, 145, 153, 161) sts rem.

Next row: (RS) K1, work Moss st A (see Stitch Guide) over 2 (4, 8, 12, 16, 20) sts, pm, work Fancy Columns patt (see Stitch Guide) over 18 sts, pm, work Chart A over 27 sts, pm, p2, sl m, work Chart B over 25 sts, sl m, p2, pm, work Chart A over 27 sts, pm, work Fancy Columns patt over 18 sts, pm, work Moss st B (see Stitch Guide) over 2 (4, 8, 12, 16, 20) sts, k1.

Next row: (WS) P1, work Moss st B over 2 (4, 8, 12, 16, 20) sts, sl m, work Fancy Columns patt over 18 sts, sl m, work Chart A over 27 sts, sl m, k2, sl m, work Chart B over 25 sts, sl m, k2, sl m, work Chart A over 27 sts, sl m, work Fancy Columns patt over 18 sts, sl m, work Moss st A over 2 (4, 8, 12, 16, 20) sts, p1.

Cont in patts as est until piece measures 16 (16, 16, 17, 17, 17)" from CO, ending with a WS row.

SHAPE ARMHOLES

BO 6 (6, 6, 6, 8, 8) sts in patt at beg of next 2 rows, then BO 2 sts at beg of foll 6 (4, 8, 8, 8, 8) rows, then BO 1 st at beg of foll 10 (12, 12, 12, 12, 12) rows—91 (97, 97, 105, 109, 117) sts rem.

Work even in patt until armhole measures 7 (7¼, 7½, 8, 8½, 9)", ending with a WS row.

SHAPE SHOULDERS

BO 6 (7, 7, 7, 8, 9) sts in patt at beg of next 8 (6, 6, 6, 6, 6) rows, then BO 0 (6, 6, 8, 7, 8) sts at beg of foll 0 (2, 2, 2, 2, 2) rows—43 (43, 43, 47, 47, 47) sts rem.

BO all sts in patt.

CHART A

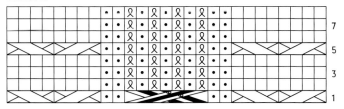

27 sts

CHART B

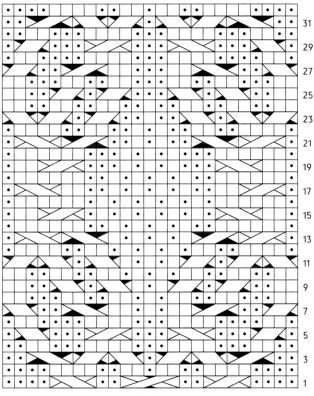

25 sts

	k on RS; p on WS
•	p on RS; k on WS
Ω	k1tbl on RS; p1tbl on WS

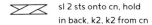 sl 2 sts onto cn, hold in back, k2, k2 from cn

sl 2 sts onto cn, hold in front, k2, k2 from cn

sl 2 sts onto cn, hold in back, k2, p2 from cn

sl 2 sts onto cn, hold in front, p2, k2 from cn

sl 1 st onto cn, hold in back, k2, p1 from cn

sl 2 sts onto cn, hold in front, p1, k2 from cn

sl 3 sts onto cn, hold in back, k2, then [p1, k2] from cn

sl 4 sts onto cn, hold in back, k1tbl, p1, k1tbl, then [p1, k1tbl] 2 times from cn

sl 1 st onto cn, hold in back, k1, k1 from cn

sl 1 st onto cn, hold in front, k1, k1 from cn

CHART C

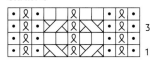

11 sts

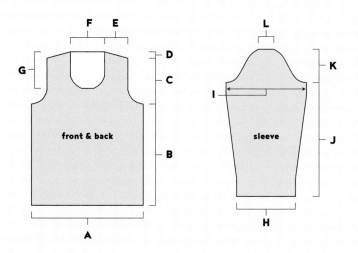

FRONT & BACK

A: 17¼ (18, 19½, 21¼, 22¾, 24½)"

B: 16 (16, 16, 17, 17, 17)"

C: 7 (7¼, 7½, 8, 8½, 9)"

D: 1"

E: 3¼ (3¾, 3¾, 4, 4¼, 4¾)"

F: 5¾ (5¾, 5¾, 6¼, 6¼, 6¼)"

G: 5½ (5¾, 5½, 5¾, 6½, 7)"

H: 9¾ (9¾, 9¾, 10½, 10½, 11¼)"

SLEEVE

I: 12½ (13, 13¾, 15¼, 16¼, 17)"

J: 18"

K: 5¼ (5¼, 5¾, 6¼, 6½, 6½)"

L: 2½ (2½, 2½, 3, 3, 3¼)"

Front

Work as for back until armhole measures 2½ (2½, 3, 3¼, 3, 3)", ending with a WS row—91 (97, 97, 105, 109, 117) sts rem.

SHAPE NECK

Next row: (RS) Work 38 (41, 41, 44, 46, 50) sts in patt and place these sts on holder for left shoulder, BO 15 (15, 15, 17, 17, 17) sts in patt, work in patt to end—38 (41, 41, 44, 46, 50) sts rem for right shoulder.

RIGHT SHOULDER

Work 1 WS row.

At beg of RS rows, BO 4 sts once, then BO 3 sts once, then BO 2 sts 2 times, then BO 1 st 3 (3, 3, 4, 4, 4) times—24 (27, 27, 29, 31, 35) sts rem.

Work even until armhole measures 7 (7¼, 7½, 8, 8½, 9)", ending with a RS row.

Shape shoulder

At beg of WS rows, BO 6 (7, 7, 7, 8, 9) sts in patt 4 (3, 3, 3, 3, 3) times, then BO 0 (6, 6, 8, 7, 8) sts 0 (1, 1, 1, 1, 1) time—no sts rem.

LEFT SHOULDER

Return 38 (41, 41, 44, 46, 50) left shoulder sts to needle and, with WS facing, rejoin yarn.

At beg of WS rows, BO 4 sts once, then BO 3 sts once, then BO 2 sts 2 times, then BO 1 st 3 (3, 3, 4, 4, 4) times—24 (27, 27, 29, 31, 35) sts rem.

Work even until armhole measures 7 (7¼, 7½, 8, 8½, 9)", ending with a WS row.

Shape shoulder

At beg of RS rows, BO 6 (7, 7, 7, 8, 9) sts in patt 4 (3, 3, 3, 3, 3) times, then BO 0 (6, 6, 8, 7, 8) sts in patt 0 (1, 1, 1, 1, 1) time—no sts rem.

Sleeves

With smaller straight needles, CO 52 (52, 52, 56, 56, 60) sts.

Work in k1, p1 rib for 2½", ending with a RS row. Change to larger needles.

Next row: (WS) P1, k2tog, knit to last st, p1—51 (51, 51, 55, 55, 59) sts rem.

Next row: (RS) K1, work Moss st C (see Stitch Guide) over 19 (19, 19, 21, 21, 23) sts, pm, work Chart C over 11 sts, pm, work Moss st C over 19 (19, 19, 21, 21, 23) sts, k1.

Keeping 1 st each side in St st, work 13 (11, 9, 7, 7, 7) rows even, ending with a WS row.

Inc row: (RS) K1, M1 or M1P as needed to maintain patt, work in patt to last st, M1 or M1P as needed to maintain patt, k1—2 sts inc'd.

Rep Inc row every 14 (12, 10, 8, 8, 8)th row 6 (7, 9, 11, 8, 8) more times, then every 0 (0, 0, 0, 6, 6)th row 0 (0, 0, 0, 5, 5) times, working new sts into Moss st—65 (67, 71, 79, 83, 87) sts.

Work even until piece measures 18" from CO, ending with a WS row.

SHAPE CAP

BO 6 (6, 6, 6, 8, 8) sts in patt at beg of next 2 rows, then BO 2 sts at beg of next 4 (4, 4, 6, 6, 6) rows, then BO 1 st at beg of next 8 (12, 16, 14, 12, 22) rows—37 (35, 35, 41, 43, 37) sts rem.

[Work 2 rows in patt, then BO 1 st at beg of next 2 rows] 4 (3, 3, 3, 4, 2) times—29 (29, 29, 35, 35, 33) sts rem.

BO 1 st at beg of next 6 rows, then BO 2 sts at beg of next 4 (4, 4, 6, 6, 4) rows—15 (15, 15, 17, 17, 19) sts rem. BO all sts.

Finishing

Block pieces to measurements. Sew shoulder seams. Sew sleeve and side seams. Sew sleeves into armholes.

NECKBAND

With cir needle and RS facing, beg at right shoulder seam, pick up and knit 43 (43, 43, 47, 47, 47) sts evenly along back neck, 31 (31, 31, 34, 36, 38) sts along left front neck, 15 (15, 15, 17, 17, 17) sts along center front neck, and 31 (31, 31, 34, 36, 38) sts along right front neck—120 (120, 120, 132, 136, 140) sts. Pm and join in the rnd.

Purl 1 rnd.

Work in k1, p1 rib for 1½".

BO all sts in patt.

Weave in ends.

hitch pullover

Vanessa Ewing

Finished Size

Bust circumference: 36 (37¾, 41¾, 45¾, 49¾)".

Pullover shown measures 36", modeled with 3" of positive ease.

Yarn

Worsted weight (#4 medium).

Shown here: HiKoo Simplinatural (40% baby alpaca, 40% fine Merino wool, 20% mulberry silk; 183 yd [167 m]/ 3½ oz [100 g]): #100 slate grey, 6 (7, 8, 8, 9) skeins.

Needles

Size U.S. 8 (5 mm): 16" and 32" circulars (cir) and set of double-pointed (dpn).

Adjust needle size if necessary to obtain the correct gauge.

Notions

Markers (m); cable needle (cn); stitch holder; tapestry needle; three 1" buttons.

Gauge

18 sts and 26 rows = 4" in St st.

22 sts and 26 rows = 4" in Twisted rib patt.

26-st cable panel measures about 4¼" wide.

Notes

■ This pullover is worked in the round to the underarm, then the front and back are worked separately back and forth. The sleeves are worked separately in the round with the sleeve cap and saddle shoulder worked flat.

■ The Cable chart is worked both in rounds and back and forth in rows. When working in rounds, work every chart row as a right-side row.

STITCH GUIDE

Twisted Rib in rnds (multiple of 4 sts)

Rnd 1: *[K1tbl] 2 times, p2; rep from * around.

Rep Rnd 1 for patt.

Twisted Rib in rows (multiple of 4 sts + 2)

Row 1: (WS) *[P1tbl] 2 times, k2; rep from * to last 2 sts, [p1tbl] 2 times.

Row 2: (RS) *[K1tbl] 2 times, p2; rep from * to last 2 sts, [k1tbl] 2 times.

Rep Rows 1 and 2 for patt.

Body

With longer cir needle, CO 192 (208, 232, 256, 280) sts. Place marker (pm) and join in the rnd.

Work Twisted Rib in rnds (see Stitch Guide) for 2½".

Next rnd: Work 22 sts, pm, work 74 (82, 94, 106, 118) sts, pm, work 22 sts, pm, work to end.

Next rnd: *Work in rib patt to m, sl m, k3, k2tog, [k5 (4, 3, 3, 3) k2tog] 3 (2, 8, 9, 9) times, [k4 (3, 4, 2, 2) k2tog] 4 (10, 1, 2, 5) time(s), [k5 (4, 3, 3, 3), k2tog] 3 (2, 8, 9, 9) times, k3, sl m; rep from * once more—170 (178, 196, 214, 232) sts rem: 22 rib sts each side and 63 (67, 76, 85, 94) sts between m on front and back.

Next rnd: *Work in rib patt to m, sl m, knit to m, sl m; rep from * once more.

Rep last rnd until piece measures 15½" from CO.

DIVIDE FOR FRONT AND BACK:

Remove rnd m, work 11 sts in rib and place last 85 (89, 98, 107, 116) sts worked on holder for front—85 (89, 98, 107, 116) sts rem for back.

Back

Work in St st, removing all m when you come to them.

SHAPE ARMHOLES

BO 6 (6, 7, 8, 9) sts at beg of next 2 rows—73 (77, 84, 91, 98) sts rem.

Dec row: (RS) K2, ssk, knit to last 4 sts, k2tog, k2—2 sts dec'd.

Rep dec row every RS row 5 (6, 7, 9, 10) more times—61 (63, 68, 71, 76) sts rem.

Work even until armhole measures 5½ (6, 6½, 7, 7½)", ending with a WS row.

SHAPE SHOULDERS

BO 19 (19, 21, 22, 24) sts at beg of next 2 rows—23 (25, 26, 27, 28) sts rem.

Work even for 1". Place all sts on holder.

CABLE

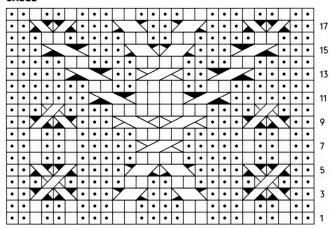

26 sts

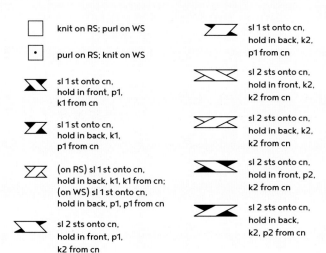

| | knit on RS; purl on WS |
| | purl on RS; knit on WS |

sl 1 st onto cn, hold in front, p1, k1 from cn

sl 1 st onto cn, hold in back, k1, p1 from cn

(on RS) sl 1 st onto cn, hold in back, k1, k1 from cn; (on WS) sl 1 st onto cn, hold in back, p1, p1 from cn

sl 2 sts onto cn, hold in front, p1, k2 from cn

sl 1 st onto cn, hold in back, k2, p1 from cn

sl 2 sts onto cn, hold in front, k2, k2 from cn

sl 2 sts onto cn, hold in back, k2, k2 from cn

sl 2 sts onto cn, hold in front, p2, k2 from cn

sl 2 sts onto cn, hold in back, k2, p2 from cn

Front

Return 85 (89, 98, 107, 116) held front sts to needle and with RS facing, rejoin yarn.

SHAPE ARMHOLES AND PLACKET

BO 6 (6, 7, 8, 9) sts at beg of next 2 rows—73 (77, 84, 91, 98) sts rem.

Next row: (RS) K2, ssk, k30 (32, 35, 39, 42), join 2nd ball of yarn and BO center 5 (5, 6, 5, 6) sts, knit to last 4 sts, k2tog, k2—33 (35, 38, 42, 45) sts rem each side.

Working both sides **at the same time**, dec 1 st at each armhole edge every RS row 5 (6, 7, 9, 10) times—28 (29, 31, 33, 35) sts rem each side.

Work even until armhole measures 4½ (5, 5½, 6, 6½)", ending with a WS row.

SHAPE NECK

At each neck edge, BO 4 (4, 4, 5, 5) sts once, then BO 3 (4, 4, 4, 4) sts once, then BO 2 sts once—19 (19, 21, 22, 24) sts rem each side. BO all sts.

Sleeves

With dpn, CO 48 (48, 48, 52, 52) sts. Pm and join in the rnd.

Work Twisted Rib in rnds for 2½".

Set-up rnd: K11 (11, 11, 13, 13), pm, work Cable chart over 26 sts, pm, k11 (11, 11, 13, 13).

Next rnd: Knit to m, sl m, work Cable chart over 26 sts, sl m, knit to end.

Cont in patt as est until sleeve measures 3½" from CO.

Inc rnd: K1, M1, work to last st, M1, k1—2 sts inc'd.

Rep Inc rnd every 16 (12, 8, 8, 7)th rnd 5 (7, 10, 10, 12) more times, changing to shorter cir needle when necessary—60 (64, 70, 74, 78) sts.

Work even until piece measures 18½" from CO, ending with an even-numbered chart rnd.

Work back and forth in rows as foll:

SHAPE CAP

BO 6 (7, 8, 9, 10) sts at beg of next 2 rows—48 (50, 54, 56, 58) sts rem.

Dec row: (RS) K2, ssk, work to last 4 sts, k2tog, k2—2 sts dec'd.

Rep Dec row every RS row 6 (4, 5, 5, 6) more times, then every 4th row 1 (4, 5, 6, 6) time(s)—32 sts rem.

Next row: (WS) P3, work to last 3 sts, removing m, p3.

Next row: (RS) K2, p2tog, work to last 4 sts, p2tog, k2—30 sts rem.

Next row: (WS) P2, work to last 2 sts, p2.

Next row: (RS) K1, p2tog, work to last 3 sts, p2tog, k1—28 sts rem.

Next row: (WS) P1, work to last st, p1.

Next row: (RS) P2tog, work to last 2 sts, p2tog—26 sts rem.

Work even until shoulder extension measures 4¼ (4¼, 4¾, 5, 5¼)", ending with a WS row.

Next row: (RS) BO all sts as foll: K2, pass first st on right needle over 2nd st (pfso), *k2tog, pfso, [k1, pfso] 2 times; rep from * to end, fasten off last st.

Finishing

Weave in ends. Block pieces to measurements. Sew shoulder extensions to front and back shoulders of body. Sew 1" back extension to first 1" of BO edges of sleeve shoulder extensions. Set in sleeves.

BUTTONHOLE BAND

With shorter cir needle and RS facing, pick up and knit 24 (28, 32, 32, 32) sts along right front placket edge up to first neck BO.

Next row: (WS) P1tbl, work Twisted Rib in rows (see Stitch Guide) to last st, p1tbl.

Next row: (RS) K1tbl, work in rib patt to last st, k1tbl. Buttonhole row P1tbl, work 2 sts in patt, [BO next 2 sts, work in patt until there are 5 (7, 9, 9, 9) sts on left

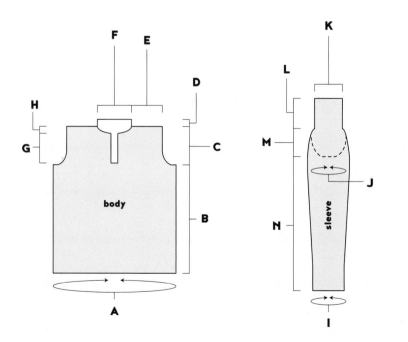

BODY

A: 36 (37¾, 41¾, 45¾, 49¾)"

B: 15½"

C: 5½ (6, 6½, 7, 7½)"

D: 1"

E: 4¼ (4¼, 4¾, 5, 5¼)"

F: 5 (5½, 5¾, 6, 6¼)"

G: 4¼ (4¾, 5¼, 5¾, 6)"

H: 1"

SLEEVE

I: 8¾ (8¾, 8¾, 9½, 9½)"

J: 12 (12¾, 14, 15, 16)"

K: 4¼"

L: 4¼ (4¼, 4¾, 5, 5¼)"

M: 4 (5¼, 6¼, 6¾, 7)"

N: 18½"

needle after last buttonhole] 2 times, BO next 2 sts, work in patt to last st, p1tbl—18 (22, 26, 26, 26) sts rem.

Next row: K1tbl, [work to BO sts, CO 2 sts using the backward-loop method] 3 times, work to last st, k1tbl—24 (28, 32, 32, 32) sts.

Work 2 rows in patt. BO all sts in patt.

BUTTONBAND

With shorter cir needle and RS facing, beg at first neck BO and pick up and knit 24 (28, 32, 32, 32) sts along left front placket edge.

Next row: (WS) P1tbl, work Twisted Rib in rows to last st, p1tbl.

Next row: (RS) K1tbl, work in rib patt to last st, k1tbl.

Rep last 2 rows 2 more times.

BO all sts in patt.

Sew side edge of placket down to center front BO, overlapping right front over left front.

COLLAR

> **Note:** Collar will beg with held sts at back neck, and additional sts will be picked up at beg and end of each RS row to shape collar.

Pick up 1 st in each row or st as you work.

Read instructions carefully for picking up sts at beg of rows; after picking up sts, the row is worked across new sts first, then across sts previously on needle.

Pick up sts at end of rows in normal manner, using right needle. Slip 23 (25, 26, 27, 28) sts from back neck onto shorter cir needle. Rejoin yarn ready to work a WS row.

Next row: (WS) Purl, inc 3 (1, 0, 3, 2) st(s) evenly spaced—26 (26, 26, 30, 30) sts.

Next row: (RS) Pick up 4 sts at beg of row as foll: [insert left needle tip into next sleeve extension BO st adjacent to needle tip and pick up a loop of working yarn] 4 times, [k1tbl] 2 times, *[p1tbl] 2 times, [k1tbl] 2 times; rep from * across all sts, pick up and knit 4 sts from sleeve extension BO edge—34 (34, 34, 38, 38) sts.

Next row: (WS) [P1tbl] 2 times, *[k1tbl] 2 times, [p1tbl] 2 times; rep from * to end.

Rep last 2 rows 3 more times (16 sts have been picked up from each sleeve extension edge; front neck edge has been reached)—58 (58, 58, 62, 62) sts.

Next row: (RS) Pick up and knit 1 st at beg of row as foll: insert left needle tip into next row or st of right front neck edge adjacent to needle tip and pick up a loop of working yarn, p1tbl, [k1tbl] 2 times, *[p1tbl] 2 times, [k1tbl] 2 times; rep from * across all sts, pick up and knit 1 st from left front neck edge—60 (60, 60, 64, 64) sts.

Next row: K1tbl, *[p1tbl] 2 times, [k1tbl] 2 times; rep from * to last 3 sts, [p1tbl] 2 times, k1tbl.

Next row: (RS) Pick up and knit 1 st at beg of row from right front neck edge (as before). [p1tbl] 2 times, *[k1tbl] 2 times, [p1tbl] 2 times; rep from * to last 3 sts, [k1tbl] 2 times, p1tbl, pick up and knit 1 st from left front neck edge—62 (62, 62, 66, 66) sts.

Next row: [K1tbl] 2 times, *[p1tbl] 2 times, [k1tbl] 2 times; rep from * to end.

Next row: (RS) Pick up and knit 1 st at beg of row from right front neck edge (as before). k1tbl, *[p1tbl] 2 times, [k1tbl] 2 times; rep from * to last 2 sts, [p1tbl] 2 times, pick up and knit 1 st from left front neck edge—64 (64, 64, 68, 68) sts.

Next row: P1tbl, *[k1tbl] 2 times, [p1tbl] 2 times; rep from * to last 3 sts, [k1tbl] 2 times, p1tbl.

Next row: (RS) Pick up and knit 1 st at beg of row from right front neck edge (as before), [k1tbl] 2 times, *[p1tbl] 2 times, [k1tbl] 2 times; rep from * to last 3 sts, [p1tbl] 2 times, k1tbl, pick up and knit 1 st from left front neck edge—66 (66, 66, 70, 70) sts.

Next row: [P1tbl] 2 times, *[k1tbl] 2 times, [p1tbl] 2 times; rep from * to end.

Rep last 8 rows until all BO neck sts and rows have been picked up—about 12 (13, 13, 14, 14) sts on each neck edge—82 (84, 84, 90, 90) sts.

Cont in this manner of picking up sts along buttonband edges and working new sts into patt—94 (96, 96, 102, 102) sts.

Collar measures about 6¼ (6½, 6½, 6¾, 6¾)" from back neck edge. BO all sts in patt.

Sew buttons to band opposite buttonholes.

Weave in ends.

kayleen pullover

Cassie Castillo

Finished Size

Bust circumference: 32½ (34¾, 38, 40½, 43½, 46)".

Pullover shown measures 32½", modeled with 3" of negative ease.

Yarn

Worsted weight (#4 medium).

Shown here: Juniper Moon Farm Sabine (40% cotton, 30% royal llama, 30% Merino wool; 218 yd [199 m]/3½ oz [100 g]): #014 muscadine, 3 (3, 4, 4, 4, 5) skeins.

Needles

Body and sleeves: size U.S. 6 (4 mm): 24" circular (cir).

Applied I-cord: size U.S. 5 (3.75 mm): two double-pointed (dpn).

Adjust needle size if necessary to obtain the correct gauge.

Notions

Markers (m); cable needle (cn); stitch holders or waste yarn; tapestry needle.

Gauge

20 sts and 30 rnds = 4" in St st on larger needle.

Notes

■ This pullover is worked in the round from the lower edge to the underarm, then the front and back are worked separately back and forth. Each sleeve begins as two separate pieces which are joined together. The sleeves are worked flat and sewn to the body.

■ The back section is worked in stockinette stitch and the front section is worked in reverse stockinette stitch.

Body

HEM

With larger cir needle and using the backward-loop method, CO 182 (194, 210, 222, 238, 250) sts. Place marker (pm) and join in the rnd.

Knit 6 rnds.

Purl 1 rnd for turning ridge.

Knit 6 rnds.

Fold hem to WS at turning ridge.

Joining rnd: *Insert right needle into next st on left needle and 1 st on CO edge and k2tog; rep from * to end.

Next rnd: P1, k89 (95, 103, 109, 117, 123), p1, pm for side, k1, purl to last st, k1.

Cont in patt until piece measures 1¾" from turning ridge.

Dec rnd: P1, ssk, knit to 3 sts before m, k2tog, p1, sl m, k1, ssp, purl to last 3 sts, p2tog, k1—4 sts dec'd.

Rep Dec rnd every 16 (16, 18, 18, 18, 20) th rnd 2 (4, 1, 4, 4, 1) more time(s), then every 14 (0, 16, 0, 0, 18) th rnd 2 (0, 3, 0, 0, 3) times—162 (174, 190, 202, 218, 230) sts rem: 81 (87, 95, 101, 109, 115) sts each for front and back.

Work even until piece measures 13 (13½, 13¾, 13¾, 14, 14)" from turning ridge.

Next rnd: Work in patt to m, sl m, work 18 (21, 25, 28, 32, 35) sts in patt, pm, work Row 1 of Front chart over 45 sts (inc'd to 49 sts), pm, work in patt to end.

Cont in patt through Row 16 of chart—166 (178, 194, 206, 222, 234) sts: 81 (87, 95, 101, 109, 115) sts for back, 85 (91, 99, 105, 113, 119) sts for front.

Cont in patt, work Rows 1-6 (1-2, 1-2, 1-2, 1-2, 1-2) of Front Neck chart between m, ending 5 (5, 7, 7, 9, 10) sts before end of rnd on last rnd—piece measures about 16 (16, 16¼, 16¼, 16½, 16½)" from turning ridge.

k on RS; p on WS	sl 2 sts onto cn, hold in front, p1, k2 from cn
p on RS; k on WS	sl 2 sts onto cn, hold in back, k2, k2 from cn
M1	sl 2 sts onto cn, hold in front, k2, k2 from cn
(k1, yo, k1) in same st	sl 2 sts onto cn, hold in back, k2, p2 from cn
[sl 1 kwise] 2 times, k3tog, p2sso	sl 2 sts onto cn, hold in front, p2, k2 from cn
bind off 1 st	sl 3 sts onto cn, hold in back, k2, p3 from cn
st rem on right needle after last BO st	sl 2 sts onto cn, hold in front, p3, k2 from cn
no stitch	sl 3 sts onto cn, hold in back, k2, (p1, k2) from cn
sl 1 st onto cn, hold in back, k2, k1 from cn	sl 2 sts onto cn, hold in front, k2, p1, k2 from cn
sl 2 sts onto cn, hold in front, k1, k2 from cn	
sl 1 st onto cn, hold in back, k2, p1 from cn	

FRONT

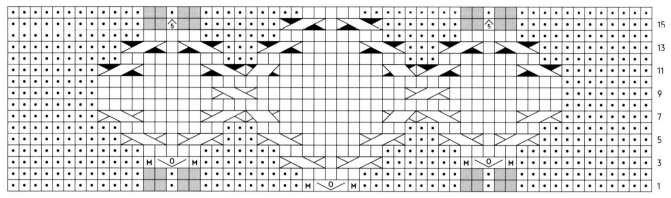

45 sts to 57 sts to 49 sts

FRONT NECK

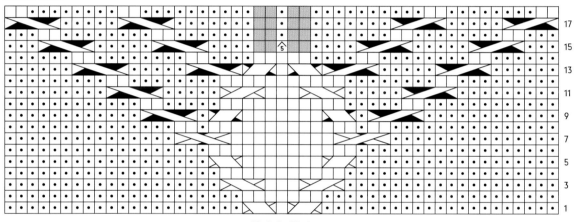

49 sts to 45 sts

RIGHT FRONT

rep as
needed

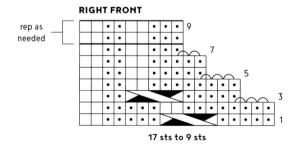

17 sts to 9 sts

LEFT FRONT

rep as
needed

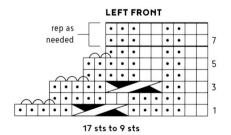

17 sts to 9 sts

DIVIDE FOR FRONT AND BACK

Next rnd: BO 10 (10, 14, 14, 18, 20) sts, removing m, work to 5 (5, 7, 7, 9, 10) sts before side m and place these 71 (77, 81, 87, 91, 95) sts on holder for back, BO 10 (10, 14, 14, 18, 20) sts, removing m, work in patt to end—75 (81, 85, 91, 95, 99) sts rem for front.

FRONT

Work back and forth in rows as foll:

Shape armholes

Dec row: (WS) P1, k2tog, work to last 3 sts, ssk, p1—2 sts dec'd.

Dec row: (RS) K1, ssp, work to last 3 sts, p2tog, k1—2 sts dec'd.

Rep last 2 rows 0 (0, 0, 1, 1, 1) more time, then rep RS Dec row every RS row 1 (2, 2, 2, 2, 2) time(s)—69 (73, 77, 79, 83, 87) sts rem.

Keeping 1 st at each edge in St st for selvedge, work even through Row 18 of chart—65 (69, 73, 75, 79, 83) sts rem.

Shape neck

Next row: (RS) Work to m, sl m, work Left Front chart over 17 sts and place 27 (29, 31, 32, 34, 36) sts just worked on holder for left front, BO 11 sts, work Right Front chart over 17 sts (last BO st counts as first st of chart), sl m, work to end—27 (29, 31, 32, 34, 36) sts rem for right front.

Right front

Work 1 WS row.

At beg of RS rows as shown on chart, BO 3 sts pwise 2 times, then BO 2 sts pwise once—19 (21, 23, 24, 26, 28) sts rem.

Work 1 WS row.

Dec row: (RS) Work in patt to m, sl m, ssp, work to end—1 st dec'd.

Rep Dec row every RS row 2 (2, 3, 3, 4, 4) more times—16 (18, 19, 20, 21, 23) sts rem.

Work even until armhole measures 6¼ (6¾, 7, 7¼, 7¾, 8)", ending with a WS row.

Shape shoulder using short-rows as foll:

Short-row 1: (RS) Work 12 (13, 14, 15, 16, 17) sts in patt, wrap next st, turn.

Short-row 2: (WS) Work to end.

Short-row 3: Work 8 (8, 10, 10, 10, 12) sts in patt, wrap next st, turn.

Short-row 4: Work to end.

Short-row 5: Work 4 (4, 5, 5, 5, 6) sts in patt, wrap next st, turn.

Short-row 6: Work to end.

Next row: (RS) Work in patt to end, working wraps tog with wrapped sts. BO all sts.

Left front

Return held left front sts to needle and, with WS facing, rejoin yarn.

At beg of WS rows as shown on chart, BO 3 sts kwise 2 times, then BO 2 sts kwise once—19 (21, 23, 24, 26, 28) sts rem.

Work 2 rows even.

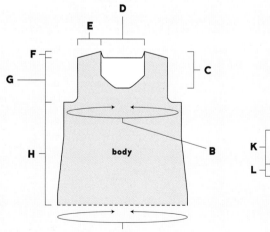

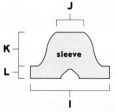

BODY

A: 36½ (38¾, 42, 44½, 47½, 50)"

B: 32½ (34¾, 38, 40½, 43½, 46)"

C: 5¾ (5½, 5¾, 6, 6½, 6¾)"

D: 6½ (6½, 7, 7, 7½, 7½)"

E: 3¼ (3½, 3¾, 4, 4¼, 4½)"

F: 1"

G: 6¼ (6¾, 7, 7¼, 7¾, 8)"

H: 16 (16, 16¼, 16¼, 16½, 16½)"

Note: *Hem is not included in length measurement.*

SLEEVE

I: 11¼ (12, 13¼, 13½, 14½, 15½)"

J: 4 (4, 4½, 4¾, 4¾, 5¼)"

K: 5¼ (5½, 5½, 5¾, 6, 6¼)"

L: 2"

Dec row: (RS) Work to 2 sts before m, p2tog, sl m, work to end—1 st dec'd.

Rep Dec row every RS row 2 (2, 3, 3, 4, 4) more times 16 (18, 19, 20, 21, 23) sts rem.

Work even until armhole measures 6¼ (6¾, 7, 7¼, 7¾, 8)", ending with a RS row.

Shape shoulder using short-rows as foll:

Short-row 1: (WS) Work 12 (13, 14, 15, 16, 17) sts in patt, wrap next st, turn.

Short-row 2: (RS) Work to end.

Short-row 3: Work 8 (8, 10, 10, 10, 12) sts in patt, wrap next st, turn.

Short-row 4: Work to end.

Short-row 5: Work 4 (4, 5, 5, 5, 6) sts in patt, wrap next st, turn.

Short-row 6: Work to end.

Next row: (WS) Work in patt to end, working wraps tog with wrapped sts. BO all sts.

BACK
Return 71 (77, 81, 87, 91, 95) held back sts to needle and, with WS facing, rejoin yarn.

Shape armholes
Dec row: (WS) P1, p2tog, purl to last 3 sts, ssp, p1—2 sts dec'd.

Dec row: (RS) K1, ssk, knit to last 3 sts, k2tog, k1—2 sts dec'd.

Rep last 2 rows 0 (0, 0, 1, 1, 1) more time, then rep RS Dec row every RS row 1 (2, 2, 2, 2, 2) time(s)—65 (69, 73, 75, 79, 83) sts rem.

Work even until armhole measures 5¼ (5¾, 6, 6¼, 6¾, 7)", ending with a WS row.

Shape neck
Next row: (RS) K19 (21, 22, 23, 24, 26) and place these sts on holder for right back, BO 27 (27, 29, 29, 31, 31) sts, knit to end—19 (21, 22, 23, 24, 26) sts rem for left back.

Left back

Next row: (WS) Purl.

Dec row: (RS) K1, ssk, knit to end—1 st dec'd.

Rep Dec row every RS row 2 more times—16 (18, 19, 20, 21, 23) sts rem.

Next row: (WS) Purl.

Shape shoulder using short-rows as foll:

Short-row 1: (RS) K12 (13, 14, 15, 16, 17), wrap next st, turn.

Short-row 2: (WS) Purl to end.

Short-row 3: K8 (8, 10, 10, 10, 12), wrap next st, turn.

Short-row 4: Purl to end.

Short-row 5: K4 (4, 5, 5, 5, 6), wrap next st, turn.

Short-row 6: Purl to end.

Next row: (RS) Knit to end, working wraps tog with wrapped sts.

BO all sts.

Right back

Return held right back sts to needle and, with WS facing, rejoin yarn.

Next row: (WS) Purl.

Dec row: (RS) Knit to last 3 sts, k2tog, k1—1 st dec'd.

Rep Dec row every RS row 2 more times—16 (18, 19, 20, 21, 23) sts rem.

Shape shoulder using short-rows as foll:

Short-row 1: (WS) P12 (13, 14, 15, 16, 17), wrap next st, turn.

Short-row 2: (RS) Knit to end.

Short-row 3: P8 (8, 10, 10, 10, 12), wrap next st, turn.

Short-row 4: Knit to end.

Short-row 5: P4 (4, 5, 5, 5, 6), wrap next st, turn.

Short-row 6: Knit to end.

Next row: (WS) Purl to end, working wraps tog with wrapped sts.

Next row: (RS) Knit.

BO all sts.

Sleeves

LEFT SIDE

With cir needle, CO 20 (22, 25, 26, 28, 31) sts. Do not join.

Knit 1 row.

Purl 1 row.

Next row: (RS) Using the knitted method, CO 2 sts, knit to end—2 sts inc'd.

Next row: (WS) Purl.

Rep last 2 rows once more—24 (26, 29, 30, 32, 35) sts.

Inc row: (RS) K1, RLI, knit to end—1 st inc'd.

Rep Inc row every RS row 2 more times—27 (29, 32, 33, 35, 38) sts.

Next row: (WS) Purl to end, turn, CO 2 sts—29 (31, 34, 35, 37, 40) sts. Place sts on holder.

RIGHT SIDE

With cir needle, CO 20 (22, 25, 26, 28, 31) sts. Do not join.

Knit 1 row.

Purl 1 row.

Knit 1 row.

Next row: (WS) CO 2 sts, purl to end—2 sts inc'd.

Rep last 2 rows once more—24 (26, 29, 30, 32, 35) sts.

Inc row: (RS) Knit to last st, LLI, k1—1 st inc'd.

Rep Inc row every RS row 2 more times—27 (29, 32, 33, 35, 38) sts.

Next row: (WS) Purl. Do not break yarn.

JOIN SIDES

Next row: (RS) K27 (29, 32, 33, 35, 38) sts of right side, then, with same yarn, k29 (31, 34, 35, 37, 40) held left side sts—56 (60, 66, 68, 72, 78) sts.

Purl 1 row.

SHAPE CAP

BO 5 (5, 7, 7, 9, 10) sts at beg of next 2 rows—46 (50, 52, 54, 54, 58) sts rem.

Dec row: (RS) K1, ssk, knit to last 3 sts, k2tog, k1—2 sts dec'd.

Rep Dec row every 4th row 6 (5, 5, 6, 7, 7) more times, then every RS row 6 (9, 9, 8, 7, 8) times—20 (20, 22, 24, 24, 26) sts rem.

BO all sts.

Finishing

Weave in ends. Block pieces to measurements.

Sew shoulder seams. Sew sleeve seams.

SLEEVE EDGING

With dpn and RS facing, work 3-st applied I-cord along bottom edge of sleeve.

Sew ends of I-cord tog. Sew in sleeves.

NECKBAND

With dpn and RS facing, beg at right shoulder seam, work 3-st applied I-cord along neck edge.

Sew ends of I-cord tog.

manzanita tee

Romi Hill

Finished Size

Bust circumference: about
31¼ (34½, 38¼, 41, 44¾)".

Tee shown measures 31¼".

Yarn

Sport weight (#2 fine).

Shown here: The Fibre
Company Road to China
Light (65% baby alpaca, 15%
silk, 10% cashmere, 10%
camel; 159 yd [145 m]/50 g):
carnelian, 5 (6, 7, 8, 9) skeins.

Needles

Body and sleeves: size U.S. 5
(3.75 mm): 24" or 32" circular
(cir), and 16" cir or set of 4 or 5
double-pointed (dpn).

Hem facings: size U.S. 4
(3.5 mm): 24" or 32" cir, and
16" cir or set of 4 or 5 dpn.

I-Cord BO: size U.S. 7
(4.5 mm): 1 dpn; size U.S. 2
(2.75 mm): 24" or 32" cir.

*Adjust needle size if necessary
to obtain the correct gauge.*

Notions

Stitch markers (m); waste
yarn; tapestry needle; blocking
wires.

Gauge

22 sts and 32 rnds = 4" in St
st, worked in rounds on body
needles.

Notes

■ To minimize the chance of
twisting the stitches, the first
yoke row is knitted before
being joined for working in
rounds. The small opening
created by the first row will be
concealed when the collar is
applied.

■ The loops picked up from
the provisional cast-on lie
between actual stitches,
so there will be one fewer
than the number of stitches
required. To make up the one-
loop deficit, create an extra
loop at one side by slipping
the needle under one leg of
an edge stitch from the first
knit row.

Yoke

With waste yarn and longer body cir needle, use a provisional method to CO 144 (160, 176, 192, 208) sts.

Change to working yarn and knit 1 row.

With knit side still facing, place marker (pm) and join for working in rnds, being careful not to twist sts.

Work Rnds 1–8 of Chart A, inc in Rnd 7 as shown—216 (240, 264, 288, 312) sts.

Work Rnds 1–4 of Chart B 2 (2, 3, 3, 4) times.

Work Rnds 1–4 of Chart C, inc in Rnd 4 as shown—252 (280, 308, 336, 364) sts.

Work Rnds 1–10 of Chart D—30 (30, 34, 34, 38) lace rnds total; piece measures about 3¾ (3¾, 4¼, 4¼, 4¾)" from CO.

Work even in St st (knit every rnd) until piece measures (4, 4½, 5¼, 5½, 6)" from CO.

DIVIDE FOR BODY AND SLEEVES

K76 (85, 93, 101, 109) front sts, place next 50 (55, 61, 67, 73) sts onto holder for left sleeve, use the backward-loop method to CO 5 (5, 6, 6, 7) sts, pm for left side "seam," CO 5 (5, 6, 6, 7) sts as before, k76 (85, 93, 101, 109) back sts, place next 50 (55, 61, 67, 73) sts onto another holder for right sleeve, CO 5 (5, 6, 6, 7) sts, pm for right side "seam" and beg of rnd, then CO 5 (5, 6, 6, 7) more sts—172 (190, 210, 226, 246) sts total; 86 (95, 105, 113, 123) sts each for front and back; rnds beg at marker in center of right underarm CO sts.

Lower Body

Work even in St st until piece measures 3¼ (4, 4½, 4½, 5)" from dividing rnd.

SHAPE WAIST

Dec rnd: K2, ssk, knit to 4 sts before side-seam m, k2tog, k2, sl m, k2, ssk, knit to last 4 sts, k2tog, k2—4 sts dec'd; 2 sts each from back and front.

[Knit 9 rnds even, then rep Dec rnd] 2 times—160 (178, 198, 214, 234) sts rem; 80 (89, 99,107, 117) sts each for back and front.

CHART A

work **18 (20, 22, 24, 26) times**

CHART B

work 2 (2, 3, 3, 4) times

work **18 (20, 22, 24, 26) times**

CHART C

work **18 (20, 22, 24, 26) times**

CHART D

work **18 (20, 22, 24, 26) times**

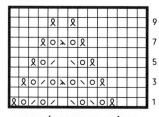

	knit
╱	k2tog
╲	ssk
ℓ	knit 1 through back loop (k1tbl)
⅄	sl 1, k2tog, psso
○	yo
▓	no stitch
▢	pattern repeat
⌣	work [k1, yo, k1] in same st

Work even for 2 (2½, 2¾, 3, 3¼)".

Inc rnd: K3, M1L, knit to 3 sts before m, M1R, k3, sl m, k3, M1L, knit to 3 sts before m, M1R, k3—4 sts inc'd; 2 sts each for back and front.

[Knit 7 rnds even, then rep Inc rnd] 2 times—172 (190, 210, 226, 246) sts; 86 (95, 105, 113, 123) sts each for front and back.

Work even until piece measures 14 (15, 15½, 16, 16½)" from dividing rnd.

HEM

Picot rnd: *K2tog, yo; rep from *.

Change to hem facing longer cir needle and knit 8 rnds.

BO as foll: K2, *return 2 sts onto left needle tip, k2tog through back loop (tbl), k1; rep from * until 2 sts rem on right needle, return 2 sts onto left needle tip, k2togtbl—1 st rem. Fasten off rem st.

Sleeves

With shorter body cir needle or dpn and beg at center of underarm, pick up and knit 6 (5, 6, 6, 7) sts along CO edge, k50 (55, 61, 67, 73) held sleeve sts, then pick up and knit 6 (7, 8, 8, 9) sts to end at center of underarm—62 (67, 75, 81, 89) sts total. Pm and join for working in rnds.

Next rnd: Knit to last 2 sts, k2 (k2tog, k2tog, k2tog, k2tog)—62 (66, 74, 80, 88) sts rem.

Work even in St st for 1 (1½, 1¾, 2, 2¼)".

Dec rnd: K2, ssk, knit to last 4 sts, k2tog, k2—2 sts dec'd.

[Knit 7 rnds even, then rep Dec rnd] 6 (6, 6, 7, 8) more times—48 (52, 60, 64, 70) sts rem.

Work even in St st until sleeve measures 9 (9¾, 10¼, 10¾, 11¼)" from pick-up rnd.

HEM

Picot rnd: *K2tog, yo; rep from *.

Change to hem facing shorter cir needle or dpn and knit 8 rnds.

BO as for body.

Finishing

COLLAR

Remove waste yarn from provisional CO and place exposed sts onto longer body cir needle (see Notes)—144 (160, 176, 192, 208) sts.

Turn garment inside out. The collar is worked with the WS of the sweater facing so the RS of the collar will show when folded over.

Pm and join for working in rnds.

Cont for your size as foll:

SIZE 31¼" ONLY

Inc rnd: P1, [yo, p4] 35 times to last 3 sts, yo, p3—180 sts.

SIZE 34½" ONLY

Inc rnd: P4, [yo, p6] 12 times, yo, p8, [yo, p6] 12 times, yo, p4—186 sts.

SIZE 38¼" ONLY

Inc rnd: P8, [yo, p12] 6 times, yo, p16, [yo, p12] 6 times, yo, p8—190 sts.

SIZE 41" ONLY

Inc rnd: P24, [yo, p48] 3 times, yo, p24—196 sts.

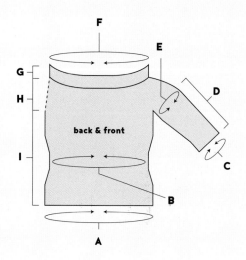

A: 31¼ (34½, 38¼, 41, 44¾)"

B: 29 (32¼, 36, 39, 42½)"

C: 8¾ (9½, 11, 11¾, 12¾)"

D: 9 (9¾, 10¼, 10¾, 11¼)"

E: 11¼ (12, 13½, 14½, 16)"

F: 32¾ (33¾, 34½, 35¾, 36¼)"

G: 2 (2, 2, 3, 3)"

H: 4 (4½, 5¼, 5½, 6)"

I: 14 (15, 15½, 16, 16½)"

SIZE 44¾" ONLY

Dec rnd: [P1, p2tog] 2 times, p92, p2tog, p1, p2tog, p2, p2tog, p1, p2tog, p92, [p2tog, p1] 2 times—200 sts.

Cut a length of waste yarn about 48" long and thread on a tapestry needle. Draw waste yarn through the 180 (186, 190, 196, 200) live sts on needle; this marks the rnd at base of collar for joining later.

Work in St st (knit all collar rnds with WS of garment still facing) for 4 (4, 4, 6, 6)".

Insert empty hem facing cir needle along path of waste yarn without removing waste yarn—180 (186, 190, 196, 200) sts from marked rnd.

Fold collar in half with its knit side on the outside to bring the two cir needles parallel, with the needle holding live collar sts below the needle holding marked sts.

With size U.S. 2 (2.75 mm) cir needle, join the sts on the two parallel needles, without knitting any sts, as foll:

*Sl 1 collar st knitwise from bottom needle, sl 1 marked rnd st purlwise from top needle, then lift the first st on right needle tip over the second and off the needle; rep from * to end—180 (186, 190, 196, 200) sts rem on size U.S. 2 (2.75 mm) cir needle.

With body dpn, use the knitted method to CO 2 sts onto left needle tip.

Change to size U.S. 7 (4.5 mm) dpn, and work 3-st I-cord BO as foll: K3 (2 new sts and 1 collar st), return 3 sts onto left needle tip while holding the yarn in back (wyb), *k2, k2togtbl (last I-cord st tog with 1 collar st), return 3 sts onto left needle tip wyb; rep from * until 3 I-cord sts rem; all collar sts have been BO.

Cut yarn, leaving a 10" tail. Use the Kitchener st to graft last 3 I-cord sts to base of I-cord CO.

HEMS

Fold body and sleeve hems to WS along picot rounds. With yarn threaded on a tapestry needle, sew in place on WS as invisibly as possible.

Wash in wool wash. Insert blocking wires along sides of neck to ensure it dries straight. Lay flat and allow to air-dry thoroughly before removing wires.

Weave in loose ends.

venice top

Amy Gunderson

Finished Size

Bust circumference: 30 (33½, 37, 40½, 44, 47½)".

Pullover shown measures 30", modeled with 4" of negative ease.

Yarn

Sport weight (#2 fine).

Shown here: Fibra Natura Cotton True Sport (100% Pima cotton; 197 yd [180 m]/1¾ oz [50 g]): #115 frappe, 5 (5, 6, 7, 7, 8) balls.

Needles

Size U.S. 2 (2.75 mm): straight, 16" circular (cir), and set of double-pointed (dpn).

Adjust needle size if necessary to obtain the correct gauge.

Notions

Markers (m); cable needle (cn); stitch holders; tapestry needle.

Gauge

27 sts and 34 rows = 4" in Back Twisted Chevron patt.

21 sts and 28 rows = 4" in Lace Rib patt.

Notes

■ This tank is worked back and forth in separate pieces and seamed.

■ When working the Back Twisted Chevron chart, if you do not have enough stitches to complete a cable, work the extra stitch as a purl stitch on the right side then knit the same stitch on the wrong side.

Lace Rib (multiple of 3 sts)

Row 1: (RS) K1, p1, *yo, ssk, p1; rep from * to last st, k1.

Row 2: (WS) P1, *k1, yo, p2tog; rep from * to last 2 sts, k1, p1.

Rep Rows 1 and 2 for patt.

I-cord BO: *K2 (first two I-cord sts), k2tog tbl (one I-cord st tog with one live st), transfer 3 sts from right needle back to left needle; rep from * until required number of sts has been bound off.

Back

With straight needles, CO 147 (165, 183, 201, 219, 237) sts.

Set-up row: (WS) P1, *k1, p2; rep from * to last 2 sts, k1, p1.

Work in Lace Rib (see Stitch Guide) until piece measures 15½" from CO, ending with a RS row.

Next row: (WS) P1, *k1, p2tog; rep from * to last 2 sts, k1, p1—99 (111, 123, 135, 147, 159) sts rem.

Next row: (RS) Using the knitted method, CO 3 sts, then, using the I-cord method (see Stitch Guide) BO all sts—3 I-cord sts rem.

BO 2 I-cord sts, leaving last st on needle, turn.

With WS facing and working through innermost I-cord st (so that 2 sts show on RS), pick up and purl 0 (13, 5, 4, 3, 2) sts along cord, place marker (pm), [pick up and purl 14 sts along cord, pm] 7 (6, 8, 9, 10, 11) times, pick up and purl 1 (14, 6, 5, 4, 3) st(s) along cord—100 (112, 124, 136, 148, 160) sts total.

SHAPE ARMHOLES

Note: *Remove m as you come to them. Maintain sts in patt as much as possible (see Notes).*

Next row: (RS) BO 5 (5, 7, 7, 9, 9) sts, k1tbl, beg and ending as indicated for your size, work Back Twisted Chevron chart over 86 (98, 106, 118, 126, 138) sts, k1tbl, p6 (6, 8, 8, 10, 10)—95 (107, 117, 129, 139, 151) sts.

Next row: (WS) BO 5 (5, 7, 7, 9, 9) sts, p1tbl, work in patt to last 2 sts, p1tbl, p1—90 (102, 110, 122, 130, 142) sts rem.

Dec row: (RS) K1, k1tbl, ssp, work in patt to last 4 sts, p2tog, k1tbl, k1—2 sts dec'd.

Dec row: (WS) P1, p1tbl, k2tog, work in patt to last 4 sts, ssk, p1tbl, p1—2 sts dec'd.

Rep Dec row every row 0 (2, 0, 2, 4, 8) more times, then every RS row 4 (6, 8, 10, 10, 10) times—78 (82, 90, 94, 98, 102) sts rem.

Work even until armhole measures 5¼ (5¾, 6¼, 6¾, 7¼, 7¾)", ending with a WS row.

SHAPE NECK

Next row: (RS) Work 27 (29, 33, 35, 37, 39) sts in patt and place these sts on holder for right shoulder, BO 24 sts, work to end—27 (29, 33, 35, 37, 39) sts rem for left shoulder.

LEFT SHOULDER

Work 1 WS row even.

At beg of RS rows, BO 4 sts once, then BO 3 sts once—20 (22, 26, 28, 30, 32) sts rem.

Work 1 WS row even.

Dec row: (RS) P1, p2tog, work in patt to end—1 st dec'd.

Rep Dec row every RS row 2 more times—17 (19, 23, 25, 27, 29) sts rem.

Work even until armhole measures 7 (7½, 8, 8½, 9, 9½)", ending with a WS row. BO all sts in patt.

RIGHT SHOULDER

Return 27 (29, 33, 35, 37, 39) held right shoulder sts to needle and, with WS facing, rejoin yarn.

At beg of WS rows, BO 4 sts once, then BO 3 sts once—20 (22, 26, 28, 30, 32) sts rem.

Dec row: (RS) Work in patt to last 3 sts, ssp, p1—1 st dec'd.

Rep Dec row every RS row 2 more times—17 (19, 23, 25, 27, 29) sts rem.

Work even until armhole measures 7 (7½, 8, 8½, 9, 9½)", ending with a WS row.

BO all sts in patt.

Front

Work as for back until piece measures 13¾" from CO, ending with a WS row.

Next row: (RS) Work in patt over 68 (77, 86, 95, 104, 113) sts, pm, work Row 1 of Lower Yoke chart over 11 sts, pm, work in patt to end.

Work 1 WS row in patt as est.

Next row: (RS) Work in patt to m, sl m, work chart over 11 sts, sl m, work in patt to m—2 sts dec'd.

Next row: (WS) Work in patt to 3 sts before m, pm, work in chart patt to end of chart row, removing m in center of first and last cables, pm, work in patt to end—2 sts dec'd.

Work in this manner through Row 15 of chart—120 (138, 156, 174, 192, 210) sts rem: 56 sts between m and 32 (41, 50, 59, 68, 77) sts on each side.

Note: *1 st has been dec'd in center of chart on Row 15.*

Next row: (WS) P1, [k1, p2tog] 9 (12, 15, 18, 21, 24) times, k1, pm, work Row 16 of chart to end of chart row, removing m in center of first and last cables, pm, [k1, p2tog] 9 (12, 15, 18, 21, 24) times, k1, p1—101 (113, 125, 137, 149, 161) sts rem: 61 sts between m and 20 (26, 32, 38, 44, 50) sts on each side.

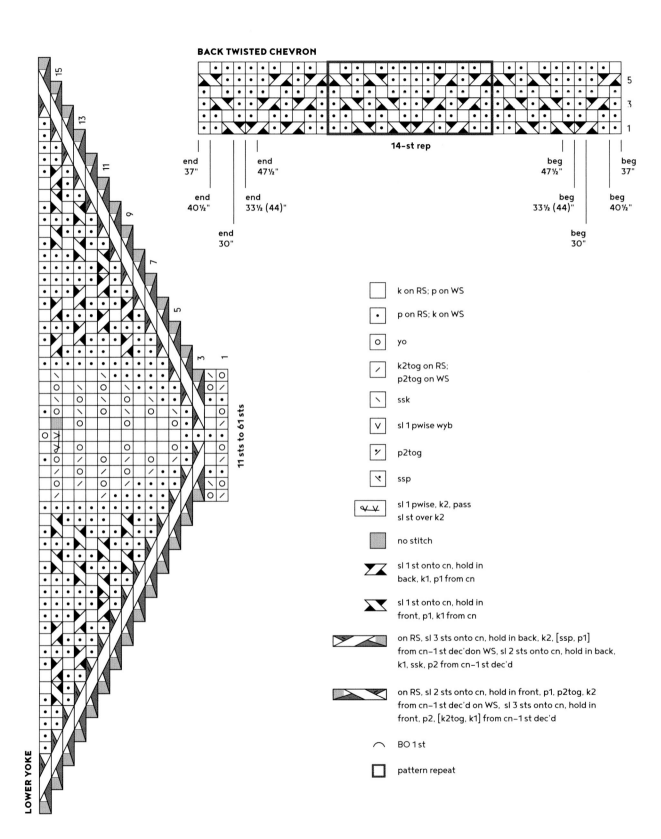

BACK TWISTED CHEVRON

14-st rep

end 37"
end 40½"
end 30"
end 47½"
end 33½ (44)"

beg 47½"
beg 33½ (44)"
beg 30"
beg 37"
beg 40½"

5
3
1

LOWER YOKE

11 sts to 61 sts

15
13
11
9
7
5
3
1

☐ k on RS; p on WS

• p on RS; k on WS

○ yo

╱ k2tog on RS;
p2tog on WS

╲ ssk

V sl 1 pwise wyb

⟍ p2tog

⟍ ssp

sl 1 pwise, k2, pass
sl st over k2

▨ no stitch

sl 1 st onto cn, hold in
back, k1, p1 from cn

sl 1 st onto cn, hold in
front, p1, k1 from cn

on RS, sl 3 sts onto cn, hold in back, k2, [ssp, p1]
from cn—1 st dec'd on WS, sl 2 sts onto cn, hold in back,
k1, ssk, p2 from cn—1 st dec'd

on RS, sl 2 sts onto cn, hold in front, p1, p2tog, k2
from cn—1 st dec'd on WS, sl 3 sts onto cn, hold in
front, p2, [k2tog, k1] from cn—1 st dec'd

⌒ BO 1 st

☐ pattern repeat

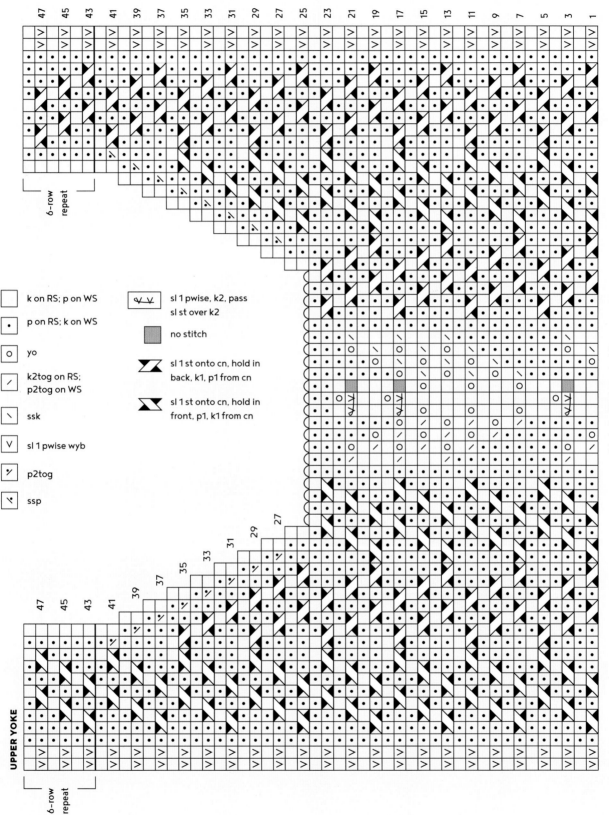

k on RS; p on WS

p on RS; k on WS

o yo

k2tog on RS;
p2tog on WS

ssk

sl 1 pwise wyb

p2tog

ssp

sl 1 pwise, k2, pass
sl st over k2

no stitch

sl 1 st onto cn, hold in
back, k1, p1 from cn

sl 1 st onto cn, hold in
front, p1, k1 from cn

61 sts to 12 sts each side

6-row
repeat

UPPER YOKE

6-row
repeat

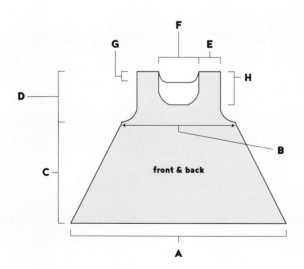

A: 28 (31½, 34¾, 38¼, 41¾, 45¼)"

B: 15 (16¾, 18½, 20¼, 22, 23¾)"

C: 16"

D: 7 (7½, 8, 8½, 9, 9½)"

E: 2½ (2¾, 3½, 3¾, 4, 4¼)"

F: 6½"

G: 1¾"

H: 4¼ (4¾, 5¼, 5¾, 6¼, 6¾)"

front & back

SHAPE ARMHOLES

Next row: (RS) BO 5 (5, 7, 7, 9, 9) sts, [k1tbl, p1] 7 (10, 12, 15, 17, 20) times, sl m, work Row 1 of Upper Yoke chart to m, sl m, [p1, k1tbl] 9 (12, 15, 18, 21, 24) times, p1, k1—96 (108, 118, 130, 140, 152) sts rem.

Next row: (WS) BO 5 (5, 7, 7, 9, 9) sts, [p1tbl, k1] 7 (10, 12, 15, 17, 20) times, sl m, work Row 2 of Upper Yoke chart to m, sl m, [k1, p1tbl] 7 (10, 12, 15, 17, 20) times, p1—91 (103, 111, 123, 131, 143) sts rem.

Dec row: (RS) K1, k1tbl, ssp, work in rib patt as est to m, sl m, work in patt to m, sl m, work in rib patt as est to last 4 sts, p2tog, k1tbl, k1—2 sts dec'd.

Dec row: (WS) P1, p1tbl, k2tog, work in patt to last 4 sts, ssk, p1tbl, p1—2 sts dec'd.

Rep Dec row every row 0 (2, 0, 2, 4, 8) more times, then every RS row 4 (6, 8, 10, 10, 10) times—79 (83, 91, 95, 99, 103) sts rem: 61 sts between m and 9 (11, 15, 17, 19, 21) sts on each side.

Work even in patt through Row 24 of Upper Yoke chart—armhole measures about 2¾".

SHAPE NECK

Next row: (RS) Work 29 (31, 35, 37, 39, 41) sts and place these sts on holder for left front, BO 21 sts, work to end—29 (31, 35, 37, 39, 41) sts rem for right front.

RIGHT FRONT

Work Rows 26-42 of chart, dec 1 st at neck edge as charted on every RS row—21 (23, 27, 29, 31, 33) sts rem.

Rep Rows 43-48 of chart until armhole measures 7 (7½, 8, 8½, 9, 9½)", ending with a WS row.

BO all sts in patt.

LEFT FRONT

Return 29 (31, 35, 37, 39, 41) held left front sts to needle and, with WS facing, rejoin yarn.

Work Rows 26-42 of chart, dec 1 st at neck edge as charted on every RS row—21 (23, 27, 29, 31, 33) sts rem.

Rep Rows 43-48 of chart until armhole measures 7 (7½, 8, 8½, 9, 9½)", ending with a WS row.

BO all sts in patt.

Finishing

Block pieces to measurements. Sew shoulder seams, easing front ribbed sections to fit back shoulders. Sew side seams.

ARMHOLE EDGING

With dpn and RS facing, beg at center of underarm and pick up and knit 96 (102, 112, 118, 124, 132) sts evenly around armhole edge.

BO all sts pwise.

NECK EDGING

With cir needle and RS facing, beg at right shoulder and pick up and knit 17 sts along right back neck, 24 sts along center back BO edge, 17 sts along left back neck, 27 (30, 33, 35, 38, 41) sts along left front neck, 21 sts along center front BO edge, and 27 (30, 33, 35, 38, 41) sts along right front neck—133 (139, 145, 149, 155, 161) sts total.

Pm and join in the rnd.

Next rnd: Using the knitted method, CO 3 sts next to first st on left needle, then, using the I-cord method, BO all sts—3 I-cord sts rem.

BO I-cord sts and sew end of cord neatly to beg of cord.

Weave in ends. Block again if desired.

western slope tee

Quenna Lee

Finished Size

Bust circumference: 38½ (40¾, 43, 45¾, 48¾, 52¼, 56¾)".

Top shown measures 38½", modeled with 5" of positive ease.

Yarn

Fingering weight (#1 super fine).

Shown here: Knit Picks Lindy Chain (70% linen, 30% pima cotton; 180 yd [164 m]/1¾ oz [50 g]): #U252 urchin, 4 (5, 5, 5, 6, 6) balls.

Needles

Size U.S. 6 (4 mm): 32" circular (cir) and one double-pointed (dpn).

Adjust needle size if necessary to obtain the correct gauge.

Notions

Markers (m); stitch holders; tapestry needle.

Gauge

22 sts and 32 rows = 4" in St st.

22 sts and 41 rows in garter st.

Notes

■ This top is worked in the round from the bottom up to the underarms, then the front and back are worked separately back and forth.

■ The Eyelet Rib chart is worked both in rounds and back and forth in rows. When working in rounds, work every chart row as a right-side row.

Right Mock Pleat (over 6 sts)

Sl 3 sts onto dpn and hold in back of next 3 sts on left needle, [k2tog (1 st from left needle, 1 st from dpn)] 3 times—3 sts dec'd.

Left Mock Pleat (over 6 sts)

Sl 3 sts onto dpn and hold in front of next 3 sts on left needle, [k2tog (1 st from dpn, 1 st from left needle)] 3 times—3 sts dec'd.

Body

With cir needle, CO 224 (236, 248, 264, 280, 300, 324) sts.

Place marker (pm) and join in the rnd.

Set-up rnd: K10 (12, 12, 18, 18, 20, 28), pm for front, k102 (106, 112, 114, 122, 130, 134), pm for side, k10 (12, 12, 18, 18, 20, 28), pm for back, knit to end.

Next rnd: Purl.

Cont in garter st (knit 1 rnd, purl 1 rnd) for 6 more rnds.

Dec rnd: *K2tog, knit to 2 sts before m, ssk, sl m, knit to m, sl m; rep from * once more—220 (232, 244, 260, 276, 296, 320) sts rem.

Next rnd: *Purl to m, sl m, knit to m, sl m; rep from * once more.

Work even in patt, working garter st over side panels and St st over front and back as est, until piece measures 5¼ (5½, 5¾, 6, 6¾, 6¾, 6½)" from CO, ending with a purl rnd in side panels.

Next rnd: K2tog, knit to 2 sts before m, ssk, sl m, k49 (51, 54, 55, 59, 63, 65), pm, work Rnd 1 of Eyelet Rib chart (see Notes) over 5 sts, knit to m, sl m, k2tog, knit to 2 sts before m, ssk, sl m, knit to end—216 (228, 240, 256, 272, 292, 316) sts rem.

Work even in patt through Rnd 4 of chart, then work Rnds 1-4 two more times.

Next rnd: Work to 5 sts before 2nd m, pm, work Rnd 1 of Eyelet Rib chart over 15 sts, removing m, work to end.

Cont in patt through Rnd 4 of chart, then rep Rnds 1-4 two more times.

Next rnd: Work to 5 sts before 2nd m, pm, work Rnd 1 of Eyelet Rib chart over 25 sts, removing m, work to end.

Cont in patt through Rnd 4 of chart, then rep Rnds 1-4 until piece measures 12 (12, 12, 12, 12½, 12½, 12½)" from CO, ending with an even-numbered rnd of chart.

Dec rnd: *K2tog, knit to 2 sts before m, ssk, sl m, work to side m, sl m; rep from * once more—212 (224, 236, 252, 268, 288, 312) sts rem.

Work even until piece measures 14 (14, 14, 14, 14½, 14½, 14½)" from CO, ending with an even-numbered rnd of chart.

DIVIDE FOR ARMHOLES

Remove beg-of-rnd m and k2 (3, 3, 6, 6, 7, 11), place last 106 (112, 118, 126, 134, 144, 156) sts worked on holder for back, removing back m—106 (112, 118, 126, 134, 144, 156) sts rem for front.

Beg working back and forth in rows.

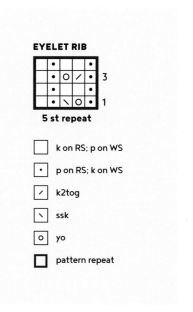

EYELET RIB

5 st repeat

	k on RS; p on WS
	p on RS; k on WS
	k2tog
	ssk
	yo
	pattern repeat

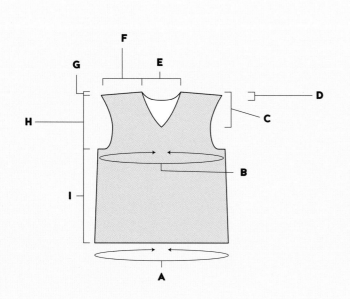

A: 40¾ (43, 45, 48, 51, 54½, 59)"

B: 38½ (40¾, 43, 45¾, 48¾, 52¼, 56¾)"

C: 5½ (5½, 5½, 5¾, 5¾, 5¾, 6¼)"

D: 1¼"

E: 5¾ (5¾, 5¾, 6¼, 7, 7, 7¼)"

F: 6¼ (6½, 7, 7, 7½, 8¼, 8¼)"

G: ½"

H: 8 (8¼, 8½, 8¾, 9¼, 9½, 10)"

I: 14 (14, 14, 14, 14½, 14½, 14½)"

Front

SHAPE ARMHOLES

Removing front and side m as you come to them, leaving Eyelet Rib m in place, cont in patt and BO 3 (4, 4, 6, 6, 7, 9) sts at beg of next 2 rows, then BO 2 (2, 2, 3, 3, 3, 5) sts at beg of foll 2 rows—96 (100, 106, 108, 116, 124, 128) sts rem.

Next row: (RS) Sl 1 pwise wyb, work to end.

Next row: (WS) Sl 1 pwise wyf, work to end.

Rep last 2 rows 2 (3, 4, 4, 6, 7, 7) more times.

Inc row: (RS) Sl 1 pwise wyb, k1, M1L, work to last 2 sts, M1R, k2—2 sts inc'd.

Rep Inc row every 4th row 3 more times—104 (108, 114, 116, 124, 132, 136) sts.

Work 1 WS row even.

Pleat row: (RS) Sl 1 pwise wyb, k11 (13, 16, 17, 19, 23, 23), [work Right Mock Pleat (see Stitch Guide) over 6 sts, k2] 2 times, work Right Mock Pleat over 6 sts, knit to m, remove m, work chart over 25 sts, k5 (5, 5, 5, 7, 7, 9), [work Left Mock Pleat (see Stitch Guide) over 6 sts, k2] 2 times, work Left Mock Pleat over 6 sts, knit to end—86 (90, 96, 98, 106, 114, 118) sts rem; armhole measures about 3¼ (3½, 3¾, 3¾, 4¼, 4½, 4½)".

Next row: (WS) Sl 1 pwise wyf, work 42 (44, 47, 48, 52, 56, 58) sts and place these sts on holder for right front, work to end—43 (45, 48, 49, 53, 57, 59) sts rem for left front.

> **Note:** Armhole and neck shaping occur simultaneously; read the foll section all the way through before proceeding.

LEFT FRONT

Beg working in garter st (knit every row) and slip first st of every row pwise wyf.

Armhole inc row: (RS) Sl 1 pwise wyf, k1, M1L, knit to end—1 armhole st inc'd.

Rep Armhole inc row every 4th row 6 more times.

At the same time, shape neck as foll:

Neck dec row: (RS) Work to last 4 sts, k2tog, k2—1 neck st dec'd. Rep Neck dec row every RS row 15 (15, 15, 16, 18, 18, 19) more times—34 (36, 39, 39, 41, 45, 46) sts rem.

Work even until armhole measures 8 (8¼, 8½, 8¾, 9¼, 9½, 10)", ending with a RS row.

Shape left shoulder using short-rows as foll:

Short-row 1: (WS) Sl 1 pwise wyf, k24 (26, 28, 27, 29, 32, 33), wrap next st, turn.

Short-row 2: (RS) Knit to end.

Short-row 3: Sl 1 pwise wyf, k16 (17, 18, 18, 19, 21, 22), wrap next st, turn.

Short-row 4: Knit to end.

Short-row 5: Sl 1 pwise wyf, k7 (8, 8, 8, 9, 10, 10), wrap next st, turn.

Short-row 6: Knit to end.

Next row: (WS) Sl 1 pwise wyf, knit to end, working wraps tog with wrapped sts. Place sts on holder, leaving a 1 yd tail for seaming.

RIGHT FRONT

Return held sts to needle and with RS facing, rejoin yarn.

Beg working in garter st and slip first st of every row pwise wyf.

Armhole inc row: (RS) Sl 1 pwise wyf, knit to last 2 sts, M1R, k2—1 armhole st inc'd.

Rep Armhole inc row every 4th row 6 more times.

At the same time, shape neck as foll:

Neck dec row: (RS) Sl 1 pwise wyf, k1, ssk, work to end—1 neck st dec'd.

Rep Neck dec row every RS row 15 (15, 15, 16, 18, 18, 19) more times—34 (36, 39, 39, 41, 45, 46) sts rem.

Work even until armhole measures 8 (8¼, 8½, 8¾, 9¼, 9½, 10)", ending with a WS row.

Shape right shoulder using short-rows as foll:

Short-row 1: (RS) Sl 1 pwise wyf, K24 (26, 28, 28, 29, 32, 33), wrap next st, turn.

Short-row 2: Knit to end.

Short-row 3: Sl 1 pwise wyf, K16 (17, 18, 18, 19, 21, 22), wrap next st, turn.

Short-row 4: Knit to end.

Short-row 5: Sl 1 pwise wyf, k7 (8, 8, 8, 9, 10, 10), wrap next st, turn.

Short-row 6: Knit to end.

Next row: (RS) Sl 1 pwise wyf, knit to end, working wraps tog with wrapped sts. Place sts on holder, leaving a 1 yd tail for seaming.

Back

Return 106 (112, 118, 126, 134, 144, 156) held back sts to needle and with RS facing, rejoin yarn.

SHAPE ARMHOLES

BO 3 (4, 4, 6, 6, 7, 9) sts at beg of next 2 rows, then BO 2 (2, 2, 3, 3, 3, 5) sts at beg of foll 2 rows—96 (100, 106, 108, 116, 124, 128) sts rem.

Next row: (RS) Sl 1 pwise wyb, work to end.

Next row: (WS) Sl 1 pwise wyf, work to end.

Rep last 2 rows 2 (3, 4, 4, 6, 7, 7) more times.

Next row: (RS) Sl 1 pwise wyb, k24 (26, 29, 30, 34, 38, 40), [work Right Mock Pleat over 6 sts, k2] 3 times, [work Left Mock Pleat over 6 sts, k2] 3 times, knit to end—78 (82, 88, 90, 98, 106, 110) sts rem.

Next row: Sl 1 pwise wyf, purl to end—armhole measures about 1½ (1¾, 2, 2, 2½, 2¾, 2¾)".

Beg working in garter st, and slip first st of every row pwise wyf.

Armhole inc row: (RS) Sl 1 pwise wyf, k1, M1L, knit to last 2 sts, M1R, k2—2 sts inc'd.

Rep Armhole inc row every 4th row 10 more times—100 (104, 110, 112, 120, 128, 132) sts.

Work even until armhole measures 7½ (7¾, 8, 8¼, 8¾, 9, 9½)", ending with a WS row.

SHAPE NECK

Next row: (RS) Sl 1 pwise wyf, k35 (37, 40, 40, 42, 46, 47) and place these sts on holder for right shoulder, BO 28 (28, 28, 30, 34, 34, 36) sts, knit to end—36 (38, 41, 41, 43, 47, 48) sts rem for left shoulder.

LEFT SHOULDER

Work 1 WS row.

Dec row: (RS) Sl 1 pwise wyf, k1, ssk, knit to end—1 st dec'd.

Work 1 WS row.

Rep last 2 rows once more—34 (36, 39, 39, 41, 45, 46) sts rem; armhole measures 8 (8¼, 8½, 8¾, 9¼, 9½, 10)".

Shape shoulder as for front right shoulder. Place sts on holder.

RIGHT SHOULDER

Return 36 (38, 41, 41, 43, 47, 48) held right shoulder sts to needle and with WS facing, rejoin yarn.

Work 1 WS row.

Dec row: (RS) Work to last 3 sts, k2tog, k1—1 st dec'd.

Rep last 2 rows once more—34 (36, 39, 39, 41, 45, 46) sts rem; armhole measures 8 (8¼, 8½, 8¾, 9¼, 9½, 10)".

Shape shoulder as for front left shoulder.

Finishing

Join shoulder seams using three-needle BO. Weave in ends. Block to measurements.

seiche tank

Yoko Johnston

Finished size

Bust circumference: 31¼ (34¼, 37¾, 40¾, 44¼)".

Tank shown measures 34¼", modeled with 2¼" of positive ease.

Yarn

DK weight (#3 light).

Shown here: Elsebeth Lavold Hempathy (41% cotton, 34% hemp, 25% rayon; 153 yd [140 m]/50 g): #61 kingfisher blue, 5 (5, 6, 6, 7) balls.

Gauge

22 sts and 30 rows = 4" in St st.

Needles

Size U.S. 4 (3.5 mm): 24" circular (cir).

Adjust needle size if necessary to obtain the correct gauge.

Notions

Markers (m); removable m; stitch holders; tapestry needle; size U.S. E/4 (3.5 mm) crochet hook

Notes

■ This tank is worked from the top down in one piece with short-row shoulder shaping. The upper fronts and back are worked flat until they are joined at the base of the armholes, then the lower body is worked in the round.

■ The lace chart is worked both back and forth in rows and in the round. When working in the round, work every chart row as a right-side row.

Yoke

Using the long-tail method, CO 49 (53, 57, 61, 65) sts. Do not join.

Next row: (RS) Knit.

Next row: (WS) P1, p1f&b, place marker (pm), p1f&b, purl to last 3 sts, p1f&b, pm, p1f&b, p1—53 (57, 61, 65, 69) sts: 3 front sts outside m at each side and 47 (51, 55, 59, 63) back sts in center.

Shape left shoulder using short-rows as foll:

Short-row 1: (RS) K2, yo, k1, sl m, k1, yo, k4 (5, 6, 7, 8), wrap next st, turn—2 sts inc'd.

Short-row 2: (WS) Purl to 2 sts before m, p1f&b, p1, sl m, p1, p1f&b, p2—2 sts inc'd.

Short-row 3: K2, p1, k1, yo, k1, sl m, k1, yo, knit to wrapped st, knit wrap tog with wrapped st, k1, wrap next st, turn—2 sts inc'd.

Short-row 4: Purl to 2 sts before m, p1f&b, p1, sl m, p1, p1f&b, wrap next st, turn—2 sts inc'd.

Short-row 5: K2, yo, k1, sl m, k1, yo, knit to wrapped st, knit wrap tog with wrapped st, k1, wrap next st, turn—2 sts inc'd.

Rep last 2 short-rows 1 (1, 1, 2, 2) more time(s)—67 (71, 75, 83, 87) sts.

Rep Short-row 4 once more—69 (73, 77, 85, 89) sts; with RS facing, 11 (11, 11, 13, 13) left front sts before first m, 55 (59, 63, 69, 73) back sts between m, and 3 right front sts after second m.

Next row: (RS) K2, yo, k1, sl m, k1, yo, knit to wrapped st, knit wrap tog with wrapped st, knit to 1 st before m, yo, k1, sl m, k1, yo, k2—73 (77, 81, 89, 93) sts: 12 (12, 12, 14, 14) left front sts, 57 (61, 65, 71, 75) back sts, 4 right front sts.

Shape right shoulder using short-rows as foll:

Short-row 1: (WS) P2, p1f&b, p1, sl m, p1, p1f&b, p4 (5, 6, 7, 8), wrap next st, turn—2 sts inc'd.

Short-row 2: (RS) Knit to 1 st before m, yo, k1, sl m, k1, yo, wrap next st, turn—2 sts inc'd.

Short-row 3: P1f&b, p1, sl m, p1, p1f&b, purl to wrapped st, purl wrap tog with wrapped st, p1, wrap next st, turn—2 sts inc'd.

Rep last 2 short-rows 2 (2, 2, 3, 3) more times—87 (91, 95, 107, 111) sts.

Next row: (RS) Knit to 1 st before m, yo, k1, sl m, k1, yo, k2, [knit wrap tog with wrapped st, k1] 2 (2, 2, 3, 3) times, knit wrap tog with wrapped st, p1, k2—89 (93, 97, 109, 113) sts: 12 (12, 12, 14, 14) front sts outside m at each side and 65 (69, 73, 81, 85) back sts in center.

Next row: (WS) Purl to 2 sts before m, p2tog, sl m, p1, p1f&b, purl to wrapped st, purl wrap tog with wrapped st, purl to 2 sts before m, p1f&b, p1, remove m, place 12 (12, 12, 14, 14) rem left front sts on holder—78 (82, 86, 96, 100) sts rem: 11 (11, 11, 13, 13) right front sts and 67 (71, 75, 83, 87) back sts.

Next row: (RS) K2, p1, knit to 3 sts before m, p1, k2, remove m, place 11 (11, 11, 13, 13) rem right front sts on holder—67 (71, 75, 83, 87) back sts rem; back measures ¾" from CO in center, and 1½ (1½, 1½, 1¾, 1¾)" from needle to CO edge at deepest point, measured straight up along a single column of sts.

Mark each end of last row completed with removable m to indicate top of armhole.

> **Note:** At this point there will be two k2 columns flanked by yos extending from CO to each end of back sts on needle; these columns are shoulder lines of garment that reach from neck edge to armhole edge.

Back

Next row: (WS) Purl. Next row (RS) K2, p1, knit to last 3 sts, p1, k2.

Next row: (WS) Purl.

Rep last 2 rows 17 (16, 15, 16, 17) more times—armhole measures 5 (4¾, 4½, 4¾, 5)" from removable m.

Inc row: (RS) K2, p1, M1L, knit to last 3 sts, M1R, p1, k2—2 sts inc'd.

Rep Inc row every RS row 7 (9, 11, 11, 13) more times—83 (91, 99, 107, 115) sts.

Purl 1 WS row—armhole measures 7¼ (7½, 7¾, 8, 8¾)".

Break yarn. Place sts on holder.

LEFT FRONT STRAP

Return 12 (12, 12, 14, 14) held left front sts to needle and, with WS facing, rejoin yarn.

Next row: (WS) P2tog, purl to end, working wraps tog with wrapped sts—11 (11, 11, 13, 13) sts rem.

Next row: (RS) K2, p1, knit to last 3 sts, p1, k2.

Next row: Purl.

Rep last 2 rows 15 (13, 12, 10, 9) more times.

Inc row: (RS) K2, p1, M1L, knit to last 3 sts, p1, k2—1 st inc'd at neck edge.

Rep Inc row every RS row 1 (3, 3, 6, 7) more time(s)—13 (15, 15, 20, 21) sts.

SIZE 31¼" ONLY

Next row: (WS) Purl to last 4 sts, k1, p3.

Next row: (RS) K2, p1, M1L, p1, knit to last 3 sts, p1, k2—14 sts.

SIZE 34¼" ONLY

Next row: (WS) Purl to last 4 sts, k1, p3.

Next row: (RS) K2, p1, M1L, p1, knit to last 3 sts, M1R, p1, k2—17 sts.

LACE

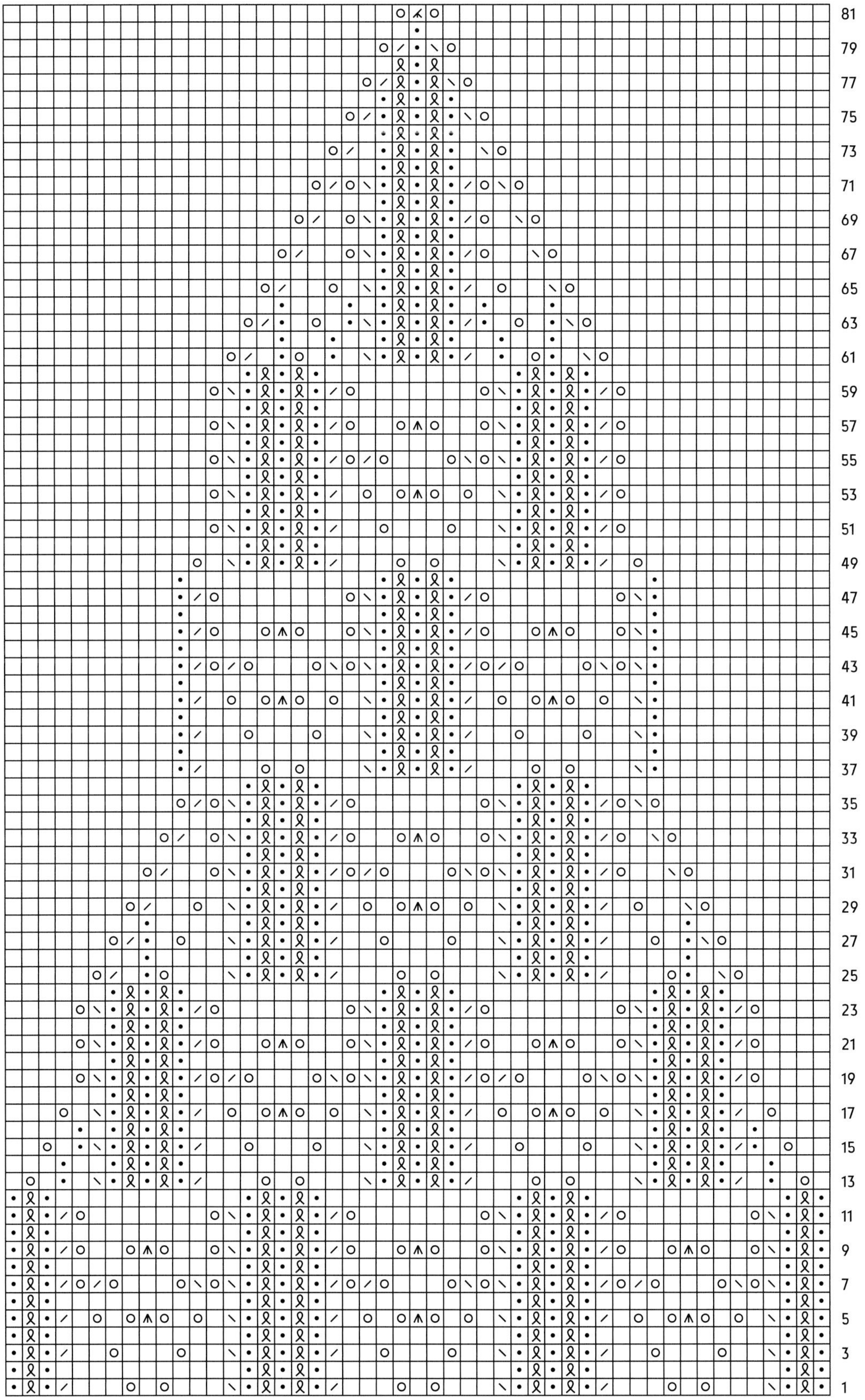

81
79
77
75
73
71
69
67
65
63
61
59
57
55
53
51
49
47
45
43
41
39
37
35
33
31
29
27
25
23
21
19
17
15
13
11
9
7
5
3
1

49 sts

Legend:

- ☐ k on RS; p on WS
- • p on RS; k on WS
- ℒ k1tbl on RS; p1tbl on WS
- ╱ k2tog
- ╲ ssk
- ○ yo
- ⋀ sl 2 as if to k2tog, k1, p2sso
- ⋌ k3tog

SIZE 37¾" ONLY

Next row :(WS) Purl.

Next row: (RS) K2, p1, M1L, knit to last 3 sts, M1R, p1, k2—2 sts inc'd, 1 st each at neck and armhole edges.

Rep last 2 rows once more—19 sts.

Next row: (WS) Purl to last 4 sts, k1, p3.

Next row: (RS) K2, p1, M1L, p1, knit to last 3 sts, M1R, p1, k2—21 sts.

SIZES 40¾ (44¼)" ONLY

Next row: (WS) Purl.

Next row: (RS) K2, p1, M1L, knit to last 3 sts, M1R, p1, k2—2 sts inc'd; 1 st each at neck and armhole edges.

Next row : Purl to last 4 sts, k1, p3. Next row K2, p1, M1L, p1, knit to last 3 sts, M1R, p1, k2—24 (25) sts.

ALL SIZES

Next row: (WS) Purl to last 5 sts, k1, p1tbl, p3.

Next row: (RS) K2, p1, M1L, k1tbl, p1, knit to last 3 sts, M1R, p1, k2—16 (19, 23, 26, 27) sts.

Next row: Purl to last 6 sts, k1, p1tbl, k1, p3— armhole measures 5½ (5½, 5¾, 5¾, 5¾)".

Break yarn. Place sts on holder.

RIGHT FRONT STRAP

Return 11 (11, 11, 13, 13) held right front sts to needle and, with RS facing, rejoin yarn.

Next row: (RS) K2, p1, knit to last 3 sts, p1, k2.

Next row: (WS) Purl.

Rep last 2 rows 15 (13, 12, 10, 9) more times.

Inc row: (RS) K2, p1, knit to last 3 sts, M1R, p1, k2—1 st inc'd at neck edge.

Rep Inc row every RS row 1 (3, 3, 6, 7) more time(s)—13 (15, 15, 20, 21) sts.

SIZE 31¼" ONLY

Next row: (WS) P3, k1, purl to end.

Next row: (RS) K2, p1, knit to last 4 sts, p1, M1R, p1, k2—14 sts.

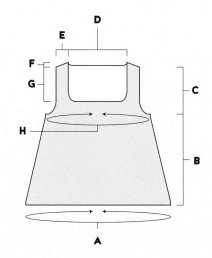

A: 43¾ (46½, 51, 53¾, 56¾)"

B: 14½ (14½, 15½, 15½, 14½)"

C: 7¼ (7½, 7¾, 8, 8¾)"

D: 8½ (9¼, 10, 10¾, 11½)"

E: 2 (2, 2, 2¼, 2¼)"

F: ¾ (¾, ¾, 1, 1)"

G: 5½ (5½, 5¾, 5¾, 5¾)"

H: 31¼ (34¼, 37¾, 40¾, 44¼)"

SIZE 34¼" ONLY

Next row: (WS) P3, k1, purl to end.

Next row: (RS) K2, p1, M1L, knit to last 4 sts, p1, M1R, p1, k2—17 sts.

SIZE 37¾" ONLY

Next row: (WS) Purl.

Next row: (RS) K2, p1, M1L, knit to last 3 sts, M1R, p1, k2—2 sts inc'd.

Rep last 2 rows once more—19 sts.

Next row: (WS) P3, k1, purl to end.

Next row: (RS) K2, p1, M1L, knit to last 4 sts, p1, M1R, p1, k2—21 sts.

SIZES 40¾ (44¼)" ONLY

Next row: (WS) Purl.

Next row: (RS) K2, p1, M1L, knit to last 3 sts, M1R, p1, k2—2 sts inc'd.

Next row: P3, k1, purl to end.

Next row: K2, p1, M1L, knit to last 4 sts, p1, M1R, p1, k2—24 (25) sts.

ALL SIZES

Next row: (WS) P3, p1tbl, k1, purl to end.

Next row: (RS) K2, p1, M1L, knit to last 5 sts, p1, k1tbl, M1R, p1, k2—16 (19, 23, 26, 27) sts.

Next row: P3, k1, p1tbl, k1, purl to end— armhole measures 5½ (5½, 5¾, 5¾, 5¾)".

Leave sts on needle.

JOIN FRONTS

Next row: (RS) K2, p1, M1L, knit to last 6 sts, pm, p1, k1tbl, p1, k3, then using the knitted method, CO 37 sts, place left front sts on needle and k3, p1, k1tbl, p1, pm, knit to last 3 sts, M1R, p1, k2—71 (77, 85, 91, 93) sts total; 49 center sts between m.

Next row: (WS) Purl to m, sl m, k1, p1tbl, k1, purl to 3 sts before m, k1, p1tbl, k1, sl m, purl to end.

Next row: (RS) K2, p1, M1L, knit to m, sl m, work Lace chart over 49 sts, sl m, knit to last 3 sts, M1R, p1, k2—2 sts inc'd.

Next row: Purl to m, sl m, work chart to m, sl m, purl to end.

Rep last 2 rows 5 (6, 6, 7, 10) more times— 83 (91, 99, 107, 115) sts; armhole measures about 7¼ (7½, 7¾, 8, 8¾)".

Body

JOIN FRONT AND BACK

Next row: (RS) K2, p1, knit to m, sl m, work chart to m, sl m, knit to last 3 sts, p1, k2, pm, CO 3 (3, 5, 5, 7) sts, pm, return 83 (91, 99, 107, 115) back sts to needle, k2, p1, knit to last 3 sts, p1, k2, pm, CO 3 (3, 5, 5, 7) sts—172 (188, 208, 224, 244) sts: 83 (91, 99, 107, 115) sts each for front and back and 3 (3, 5, 5, 7) sts in each marked side section.

Pm and join in the rnd.

Next rnd: Knit to m, sl m, work chart to m, sl m, knit to end. Rep last rnd 2 more times. Cont chart patt as est, work slipstitch columns and body shaping inside marked side sections as foll:

Rnds 1–4: Knit to m, sl m, work chart to m, sl m, *knit to m, sl m, sl 1 pwise wyb, knit to 1 st before m, sl 1 pwise wyb, sl m; rep from * once more.

Rnd 5: (Inc rnd) Knit to m, sl m, work chart to m, sl m, *knit to m, sl m, k1, M1L, knit to 1 st before m, M1R, k1, sl m; rep from * once more—4 sts inc'd, 2 sts in each side section.

Rnd 6: Knit to m, sl m, work chart to m, sl m, *knit to m, sl m, k1tbl, knit to 1 st before m, k1tbl, sl m; rep from * once more.

Rep last 6 rnds 16 (16, 17, 17, 16) more times, removing m on each side of center 49 front sts and working these sts in St st when chart is complete—240 (256, 280, 296, 312) sts; 83 (91, 99, 107, 115) sts each for front and back and 37 (37, 41, 41, 41) sts in each marked side section; body measures 14 (14, 15, 15, 14)" from underarm.

BORDER

Next rnd: *P3, [k1tbl, p3] 20 (22, 24, 26, 28) times, remove m, k1tbl, [p3, k1tbl] 9 (9, 10, 10, 10) times,* remove m; rep from * to * once more, leaving end-of-rnd m in place.

Next rnd: *K3, k1tbl; rep from * to end.

Next rnd: *P3, k1tbl; rep from * to end.

Next rnd: *k3, k1tbl; rep from * to end—body measures 14½ (14½, 15½, 15½, 14½)".

Loosely BO all sts.

Finishing

NECK EDGING

With RS facing and crochet hook, join yarn at center back and work 1 rnd of single crochet (sc) as foll: work 1 sc in every st along back neck, 3 sc for every 4 rows down left front neck, 1 sc for every st for CO st along center front, 3 sc for every 4 rows up right front neck and 1 sc in every st to center back. Fasten off.

ARMHOLE EDGINGS

With RS facing and crochet hook, join yarn at center of underarm, work 1 rnd of sc around armhole edge as foll: 1 sc in every st for each CO st, 3 sc for every 4 rows up to shoulder line and down to underarm and 1 sc for each CO st. Fasten off.

Weave in ends. Block to measurements.

glass palace tee

Allison Jane

Finished Size

Bust circumference: 38 (42, 45, 49½, 53, 57½, 62, 66)".

Tee shown measures 42" bust circumference, modeled with 7" of positive ease.

Yarn

DK weight (#3 light).

Shown here: Juniper Moon Farm Findley DK (50% wool, 50% silk; 131 yd [119 m]/50 g): #04 graphite (gray, MC), 6 (6, 7, 8, 9, 10, 11, 12) skeins; #15 hyacinth (purple, CC), 2 skeins.

Needles

Size U.S. 6 (4 mm): straight needles.

Size U.S. 5 (3.75 mm): 16" and 32" circular (cir) needles.

Adjust needle size if necessary to obtain the correct gauge.

Notions

Markers (m); removable m; stitch holders or waste yarn; tapestry needle.

Gauge

22 sts and 31 rows = 4" in St st on larger needles.

Notes

▪ This tee is worked back and forth in separate pieces and seamed. Stitches for the sleeves are picked up along the armhole and the sleeves are worked from the top down. Stitches for the lower ribbed band are picked up along the lower edge after the tee is complete.

▪ The colorwork pattern is worked using the intarsia method. Use a separate length of yarn for each color area. On every row at each color change, twist yarns to avoid a hole by laying the strand just worked over the strand to be worked. To wind bobbins, measure out about ½ yard of a color for small bobbins (each small square in the intersecting grid), and about 10 yards of a color for large bobbins (a horizontal or vertical MC or CC stripe). Refill large bobbins if necessary. Bobbin size is stated as new bobbins are added. For very large sections of color, a new ball is added.

Back

With MC and larger needles, CO 104 (116, 124, 136, 146, 158, 170, 182) sts.

Work in St st for ¾", ending with a WS row.

COLORWORK PATT

Row 1: (RS) With MC, k4 (8, 8, 10, 10, 10, 12, 12), with large bobbin of CC (see Notes), knit to end.

Row 2: (WS) With CC, purl to last 4 (8, 8, 10, 10, 10, 12, 12) sts, with MC, purl to end.

Rows 3 and 4: Rep Rows 1 and 2.

Row 5: With MC, k4 (8, 8, 10, 10, 10, 12, 12), with CC, k3, [with small bobbin of MC, k3, with small bobbin of CC, k3] 3 times, with large bobbin of MC, knit to end.

Row 6: With MC, p79 (87, 95, 105, 115, 127, 137, 149), [with CC, p3, with MC, p3] 3 times, with CC, p3, with MC, purl to end.

Rows 7 and 8: Rep Rows 5 and 6.

Break all yarns except MC ball and CC bobbin at right-hand edge.

Rows 9–24: Rep Rows 1–8 two times.

Rows 25–28: Rep Rows 1–4.

Next row: (RS) With MC, k4 (8, 8, 10, 10, 10, 12, 12), with CC, k3, [with large of bobbin MC, k3, with large bobbin of CC, k3] 3 times, with ball of MC, knit to end.

Next row: (WS) With MC, p79 (87, 95, 105, 115, 127, 137, 149), [with CC, p3, with MC, p3] 3 times, with CC, p3, with MC, purl to end. Rep last 2 rows until piece measures 18 (18, 19, 19, 20, 20, 21, 22)" from CO, ending with a RS row.

Shape shoulders using short-rows as foll (maintaining colorwork patt):

Short-row 1: (WS) Purl to last 6 (7, 7, 9, 9, 12, 11, 14) sts, wrap next st, turn.

Short-row 2: (RS) Knit to last 6 (7, 7, 9, 9, 12, 11, 14) sts, wrap next st, turn.

Short-row 3: Purl to 6 (6, 6, 9, 9, 9, 12, 12) sts before wrapped st, wrap next st, turn.

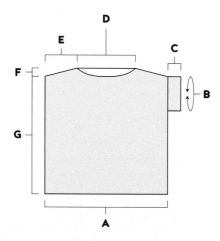

A: 19 (21, 22½, 24¾, 26½, 28¾, 31, 33)"

B: 10¼ (11¼, 12¼, 13¾, 15, 16¼, 17½, 18½)"

C: 2"

D: 9 (9½, 9½, 9½, 10½, 10½, 10½, 10½)"

E: 5 (5¾, 6½, 7¾, 8, 9¼, 10¼, 11¼)"

F: 1¼"

G: 18 (18, 19, 19, 20, 20, 21, 22)"

Short-row 4: Knit to 6 (6, 6, 9, 9, 9, 12, 12) sts before wrapped st, wrap next st, turn.

Rep Short-rows 3 and 4 two more times.

Next row: (WS) Purl to end, working wraps tog with wrapped sts.

SHAPE NECK

Next row: (RS) K27 (32, 36, 42, 44, 50, 56, 62) and place these sts on holder, BO 50 (52, 52, 52, 58, 58, 58, 58) sts, knit to end, working wraps tog with wrapped sts, and place these sts on holder—27 (32, 36, 42, 44, 50, 56, 62) sts rem each side.

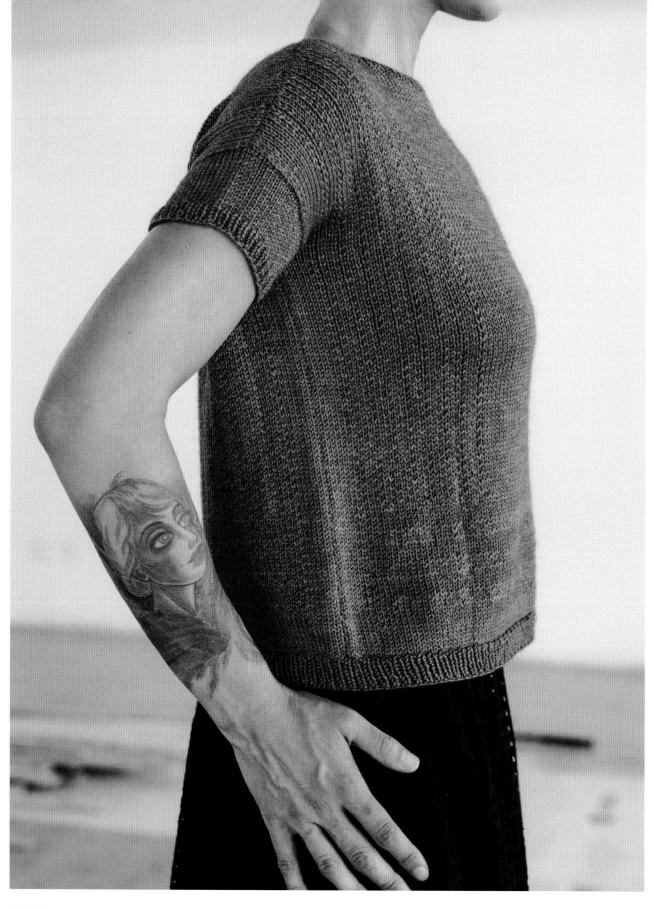

Front

With MC and larger needles, CO 104 (116, 124, 136, 146, 158, 170, 182) sts.

Work in St st for ¾", ending with a WS row (drop MC ball yarn but do not break, carry MC and large bobbin of CC up the side when not in use for the following 28 rows).

COLORWORK PATT

Row 1: (RS) With large bobbin of CC, knit to last 4 (8, 8, 10, 10, 10, 12, 12) sts, with large bobbin of MC, knit to end.

Row 2: (WS) With MC, p4 (8, 8, 10, 10, 10, 12, 12), with CC, purl to end.

Rows 3 and 4: Rep Rows 1 and 2.

Row 5: With MC, k79 (87, 95, 105, 115, 127, 137, 149), [with small bobbin of CC, k3, with small bobbin of MC, k3] 3 times, with small bobbin of CC, k3, with MC, knit to end.

Row 6: With MC, p4 (8, 8, 10, 10, 10, 12, 12), [with CC, p3, with MC, p3] 3 times, with CC, p3, with MC, purl to end.

Rows 7 and 8: Rep Rows 5 and 6.

Break all small bobbins.

Rows 9–24: Rep Rows 1–8 two times.

Rows 25–28: Rep Rows 1–4.

Next row: (RS) With MC, k79 (87, 95, 105, 115, 127, 137, 149), [with large bobbin of CC, k3, with large bobbin of MC, k3] 3 times, with large bobbin of CC, k3, with MC, knit to end.

Next row: (WS) With MC, p4 (8, 8, 10, 10, 10, 12, 12), [with CC, p3, with MC, p3] 3 times, with CC, p3, with MC, purl to end.

Rep last 2 rows until piece measures 18 (18, 19, 19, 20, 20, 21, 22)" from CO, ending with a WS row.

Shape neck and shoulders using short-rows as foll (maintaining colorwork patt):

Short-row 1: (RS) K47 (52, 56, 62, 66, 72, 78, 84) and place these sts on holder for left shoulder, BO 10 (12, 12, 12, 14, 14, 14, 14) sts, knit to last 6 (7, 7, 9, 9, 12, 11, 14) sts, wrap next st, turn—47 (52, 56, 62, 66, 72, 78, 84) sts rem for right shoulder.

Short-row 2: (WS) Purl to end.

Short-row 3: BO 8 sts, knit to 6 (6, 6, 9, 9, 9, 12, 12) sts before wrapped st, wrap next st, turn—39 (44, 48, 54, 58, 64, 70, 76) sts rem.

Short-row 4: Purl to end.

Short-row 5: BO 6 sts, knit to 6 (6, 6, 9, 9, 9, 12, 12) sts before wrapped st, wrap next st, turn—33 (38, 42, 48, 52, 58, 64, 70) sts rem.

Short-row 6: Purl to end.

Short-row 7: BO 3 (3, 3, 4, 4, 4, 4, 4) sts, knit to 6 (6, 6, 9, 9, 9, 12, 12) sts before wrapped st, wrap next st, turn—30 (35, 39, 45, 48, 54, 60, 66) sts rem.

Short-row 8: Purl to end.

Next row: BO 3 (3, 3, 3, 4, 4, 4, 4) sts, knit to end, working wraps tog with wrapped sts—27 (32, 36, 42, 44, 50, 56, 62) sts rem.

Break yarn, leaving a 12" tail. Do not break CC. Place sts on holder.

LEFT SHOULDER

Return 47 (52, 56, 62, 66, 72, 78, 84) left shoulder sts to needle and, with WS facing, rejoin MC.

Shape shoulder using short-rows as foll:

Short-row 1: (WS) BO 8 sts, purl to last 6 (7, 7, 9, 9, 12, 11, 14) sts, wrap next st, turn—39 (44, 48, 54, 58, 64, 70, 76) sts rem.

Short-row 2: (RS) Knit to end.

Short-row 3: BO 6 sts, purl to 6 (6, 6, 9, 9, 9, 12, 12) sts before wrapped st, wrap next st, turn—33 (38, 42, 48, 52, 58, 64, 70) sts rem.

Short-row 4: Knit to end.

Short-row 5: BO 3 (3, 3, 3, 4, 4, 4, 4) sts, purl to 6 (6, 6, 9, 9, 9, 12, 12) sts before wrapped st, wrap next st, turn—30 (35, 39, 45, 48, 54, 60, 66) sts rem.

Short-rows 6 and 7: Rep Short-rows 4 and 5—27 (32, 36, 42, 44, 50, 56, 62) sts rem.

Short-row 8: Knit to end.

Next row: (WS) Purl to end, working wraps tog with wrapped sts.

Break yarn, leaving a 36" tail. Place sts on holder.

Join shoulders using three-needle BO, using MC tail on left shoulder and tails appropriate to colorwork patt on right shoulder.

Place removable m on front and back 5 (5¾, 6¼, 7, 7½, 8¼, 8¾, 9¼)" below shoulder for armholes.

Sleeves

With MC, larger needles, and RS facing, pick up and knit 56 (62, 68, 76, 82, 90, 96, 102) sts evenly along armhole edge between m. Work in St st until piece measures 1½" from pick-up row, ending with a WS row.

Change to smaller needle and work in k1, p1 rib for ½".

BO all sts in patt.

Finishing

Sew side and sleeve seams.

Block to measurements.

NECKBAND

With MC, 16" cir needle, and RS facing, beg at shoulder seam and pick up and knit 108 (112, 112, 112, 124, 124, 124, 124) sts evenly around neck edge. Pm and join in the rnd.

Work in k1, p1 rib for ½". BO all sts in patt.

BOTTOM HEM

With MC, 32" cir needle, and RS facing, beg at side seam and pick up and knit 204 (228, 244, 268, 288, 312, 336, 360) sts evenly around entire lower edge. Pm and join in the rnd.

Work in k1, p1 rib for 1". BO all sts in patt.

Weave in ends

one way tee

Debbie O'Neill

Finished Size

Bust circumference: 30½ (34½ , 38, 41½ , 45, 49)".

Pullover shown measures 34½", modeled with ½" of negative ease.

Yarn

DK weight (#3 light).

Shown here: Madelinetosh Tosh DK (100% superwash Merino wool; 225 yd [206 m]/3½ oz [100g]): grasshopper, 3 (4, 4, 5, 5, 6) skeins.

Needles

Size U.S. 4 (3.5 mm): straight and 20" circular (cir).

Adjust needle size if necessary to obtain the correct gauge.

Notions

Markers (m); stitch holders or waste yarn; tapestry needle.

Gauge

22 sts and 26 rows = 4" in St st.

Notes

▪ This pullover is worked in separate pieces and seamed.

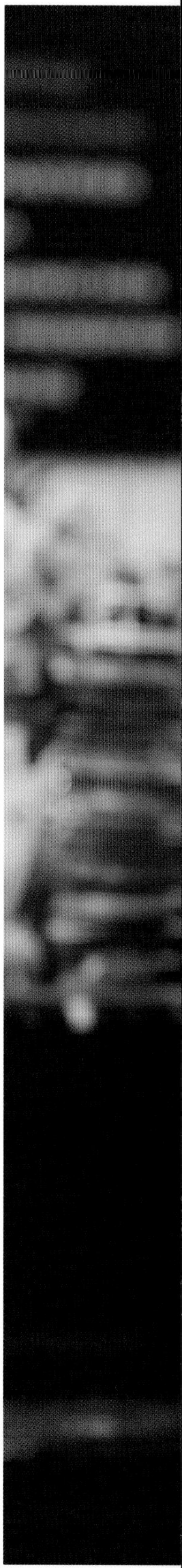

Back

With straight needles, CO 83 (93, 103, 113, 123, 133)sts.

Set-up row: (WS) K36 (41, 46, 51, 56, 61), place marker (pm), p11, pm, k36 (41, 46, 51, 56, 61).

Next row: (RS) Knit to m, sl m, work Arrowhead Lace chart over 11sts, sl m, knit to end.

Rep last row 4 more times, ending with a RS row.

Next row: (WS) Purl to m, sl m, work in patt to m, sl m, purl to end.

Keeping 11sts between m in chart patt as est and remsts in Stst, work until piece measures 4 (4, 5, 5, 6, 6)" from CO, ending with a WS row.

Dec row: (RS) K2, ssk, work to last 4sts, k2tog, k2—2 sts dec'd.

Rep Dec row every 6th row 2 more times— 77 (87, 97, 107, 117, 127) sts rem.

Work 9 rows even.

Inc row: (RS) K2, M1, work to last 2sts, M1, k2—2 sts inc'd.

Rep Inc row every 6th row 2 more times— 83 (93, 103, 113, 123, 133) sts. Work even until piece measures 14½ (15, 15½, 16, 16½, 17)" from CO, ending with a WS row.

SHAPE ARMHOLES

BO 6 (6, 8, 8, 10, 10) sts at beg of next 2 rows—71 (81, 87, 97, 103, 113) sts rem.

Dec row: (RS) K2, ssk, work to last 4sts, k2tog, k2—2 sts dec'd.

Rep Dec row every RS row 5 (5, 5, 7, 7, 7) more times—59 (69, 75, 81, 87, 97) sts rem.

Work even until armhole measures 5 (5, 5½, 6, 6½, 7)".

BO all sts.

Front

Work as for back until armhole measures 3½ (3½, 4, 4½, 5, 5½)", ending with a WS row—59 (69, 75, 81, 87, 97) sts rem.

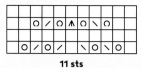

ARROWHEAD LACE

11 sts

	k on RS; p on WS
A	sl 2 as if to k2tog, k1, p2sso
/	k2tog
\	ssk
o	yo

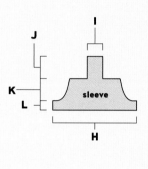

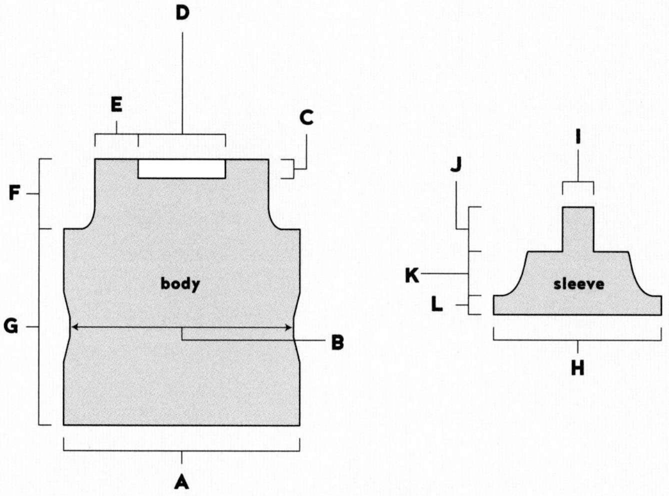

BODY

A: 15¼ (17¼, 19, 20¾, 22½, 24½)"

B: 14¼ (16, 18, 19¾, 21½, 23¼)"

C: 1½"

D: 5½ (6¼, 7, 7¾, 8½, 9¼)"

E: 2¾ (3¼, 3½, 3¾, 3¾, 4¼)"

F: 5 (5, 5½, 6, 6½, 7)"

G: 14½ (15, 15½, 16, 16½, 17)"

SLEEVE

H: 12½ (12½, 13¼, 14, 14½, 15¼)"

I: 2½"

J: 2¾ (3¼, 3½, 3¾, 3¾, 4¼)"

K: 3 (3, 3½, 4, 4¼, 4¼)"

L: 1½"

SHAPE NECK

Next row: (RS) K15 (18, 19, 20, 21, 24), join 2nd ball of yarn and BO 29 (33, 37, 41, 45, 49)sts, knit to end—15 (18, 19, 20, 21, 24) sts rem each side.

Working each side separately, work even until armhole measures 5 (5, 5½, 6, 6½, 7)".

BO all sts.

Sleeves

With straight needles, CO 67 (67, 71, 75, 79, 83) sts.

Set-up row: (WS) K28 (28, 30, 32, 34, 36), pm, p11, pm, k28 (28, 30, 32, 34, 36).

Next row: (RS) Knit to m, sl m, work Arrowhead Lace chart over 11sts, sl m, knit to end.

Rep last row 4 more times, ending with a RS row.

Next row: (WS) Purl to m, sl m, work in patt to m, sl m, purl to end. Keeping 11sts between m in chart patt as est and rem sts in St st, work until piece measures 1½" from CO, ending with a WS row.

SHAPE CAP

BO 3 (3, 4, 4, 5, 5)sts at beg of next 2 rows—61 (61, 63, 67, 69, 73) sts rem.

Dec row: (RS) K2, ssk, work to last 4sts, k2tog, k2—2 sts dec'd.

Rep Dec row every RS row 8 (8, 9, 11, 12, 12) more times—43 (43, 43, 43, 43, 47) sts rem.

Work 1 WS row even.

BO 15 (15, 15, 15, 15, 17) sts at beg of next 2 rows—13 sts rem for saddle shoulder.

Work even until saddle shoulder measures 2¾ (3¼, 3½, 3¾, 3¾, 4¼)".

BO all sts.

Finishing

Weave in ends.

Block pieces to measurements.

Sew saddle shoulder to front and back shoulders.

Sew in sleeves, working from saddle to underarm.

Sew side seams.

Sew sleeve seams.

NECKBAND

With cir needle and RS facing, beg at right front saddle shoulder, pick up and knit 96 (106, 116, 126, 136, 146) sts evenly around neck edge. Pm and join in the rnd.

Knit 1 rnd.

second story tee

Debbie O'Neill

Finished Size

Bust circumference: 34 (38, 42½ , 47, 51½ , 55½)".

Pullover shown measures 38", modeled with 3" of positive ease.

Yarn

DK weight (#3 light).

Shown here: Filatura Di Crosa Zara (100% Merino wool; 137 yd [125 m]/1¾ oz [50g]): #1490 dark denim heather, 7 (8, 10, 11, 12, 14) balls.

Needles

Size U.S. 4 (3.5 mm):straight and 16" circular (cir).

Adjust needle size if necessary to obtain the correct gauge.

Notions

Markers (m); removable m; stitch holders or waste yarn; tapestry needle.

Gauge

21sts and 28 rows = 4" in St st.

22sts and 28 rows = 4" in Diagonal Rib patt.

Notes

▪ This pullover is worked in separate pieces and seamed.

Back

With straight needles, CO 93 (105, 117, 129, 141, 153) sts.

Next row: (WS) *P3, k3; rep from * to last 3 sts, p3.

Next row: (RS) *K3, p3; rep from * to last 3 sts, k3.

Cont in rib until piece measures 1½ " from CO, ending with a WS row.

Work Rows 1–12 of Right Diagonal Rib chart 2 times, then work Rows 1 and 2 once more.

> **Note:** *At this point, transition the Diagonal Rib to St st by changing the last purl st of every RS row to a knit st as foll:* ——

Next row: (RS) *K2, p3, k1; rep from * to last 3 sts, k3.

Next row: (WS) Knit the knits, purl the purls.

Next row: (RS) *K1, p3, k2; rep from * to last 3 sts, k3. Cont in patt as est, working 1 more st at end of each RS row in St st, until piece measures 23 (24, 25, 26, 27, 28)" from CO, ending with a WS row.

SHAPE NECK

Next row: (RS) Work 22 (25, 28, 34, 40, 46) sts in patt, BO 49 (55, 61, 61, 61, 61) sts, work to end—22 (25, 28, 34, 40, 46) sts rem each side. Place sts on holders.

Front

With straight needles, CO 93 (105, 117, 129, 141, 153) sts.

Next row: (WS) *K3, p3; rep from * to last 3 sts, k3.

Next row: (RS) *P3, k3; rep from * to last 3 sts, p3.

Cont in rib until piece measures 1½ " from CO, ending with a WS row.

Work Rows 1–12 of Left Diagonal Rib chart 2 times, then work Rows 1–8 once more.

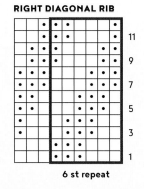

LEFT DIAGONAL RIB

6 st repeat

RIGHT DIAGONAL RIB

6 st repeat

☐ k on RS; p on WS

• p on RS; k on WS

☐ pattern repeat

Note: *At this point, transition the diagonal rib to St st by changing first purl st of every RS row to a knit st as foll:*

Next row: (RS) K4, *p3, k3; rep from * to last 5 sts, p3, k2.

Next row: (WS) Knit the knits, purl the purls.

Next row: (RS) K5, *p3, k3; rep from * to last 4 sts, p3, k1.

Cont in patt as est, working 1 more st at beg of each RS row in St st, until piece measures 21½ (22½ , 23½ , 24½ , 25½ , 26½)" from CO, ending with a WS row.

SHAPE NECK

Next row: (RS) Work 22 (25, 28, 34, 40, 46) sts in patt and place these sts on holder for left front, BO 49 (55, 61, 61, 61, 61) sts, work to end—22 (25, 28, 34, 40, 46) sts rem for right front.

RIGHT FRONT

Work even until piece measures same length as back to shoulders. Place sts on holder.

LEFT FRONT

Return held left front sts to needle and, with WS facing, rejoin yarn.

Work even until piece measures same length as back to shoulders. Place sts on holder.

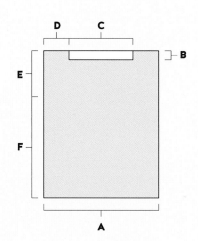

A: 17 (19, 21¼ , 23½ , 25¾ , 27¾)"

B: 1½ "

C: 9¼ (10½ , 11½ , 11½ , 11½ , 11½)"

D: 4 (4½ , 5, 6¼ , 7¼ , 8¼)"

E: 7 (7½ , 8, 8½ , 9, 9½)"

F: 16 (16½ , 17, 17½ , 18, 18½)"

Finishing

With RS tog, join shoulders using three needle BO.

Place removable m 7 (7½, 8, 8½ , 9, 9½)" down from shoulder on front and back for armhole.

Sew side seams from lower edge to armhole m.

ARMHOLE EDGING

With cir needle and RS facing, pick up and knit 66 (72, 78, 84, 90, 96) sts evenly spaced around armhole opening.

Pm and join in the rnd.

Next rnd: *K3, p3; rep from * to end.

Work 9 more rnds in rib.

Dec rnd: K2tog, work in patt to last 2 sts, p2tog—64 (70, 76, 82, 88, 94) sts rem.

Work 1 rnd even.

BO all sts in patt.

NECKBAND

With cir needle and RS facing, pick up and knit 114 (126, 138, 138, 138, 138) sts evenly spaced around neck edge. Pm and join in the rnd.

Work in k3, p3 rib for 4 rnds.

BO all sts in patt.

Weave in ends.

Block to measurements.

driftwood tee

Mercedes Tarasovich-Clark

Finished Size

Bust circumference: 36½ (39, 42, 45, 48½, 52)".

Tee shown measures 36½", modeled with 4½" of positive ease.

Yarn

DK weight (#3 light).

Shown here: Manos del Uruguay Serena (60% alpaca, 40% cotton; 170 yd [155 m]/1¾ oz [50 g]): #2680 sea urchin, 4 (5, 5, 6, 6, 7) skeins.

Needles

Body: size U.S. 3 (3.25 mm) and 5 (3.75 mm): straight.

Neckband: size U.S. 3 (3.25 mm): 24" circular (cir).

Adjust needle size if necessary to obtain the correct gauge.

Notions

Markers (m); stitch holders or waste yarn; tapestry needle.

Gauge

25 sts and 33 rows = 4" in St st on larger needle.

Notes

▪ This tee is worked in separate pieces and seamed.

Back

With smaller straight needles and using the cable method, CO 114 (122, 131, 140, 151, 162) sts.

Work in garter st for 5 rows.

Next row: (WS) K71 (79, 88, 97, 108, 119), place marker (pm), k43.

Change to larger needles.

BEG RIGHT-SLANTING LACE PATT

Row 1: (RS) K1, *k1, k2tog, yo; rep from * to m, sl m, knit to end.

Rows 2 and 4: Purl to m, remove m, p1, pm, purl to end.

Row 3: K3, *k1, k2tog, yo; rep from * to m, sl m, knit to end.

Row 5: K2, *k1, k2tog, yo; rep from * to m, sl m, knit to end.

Row 6: Rep Row 2.

Rep Rows 1-6 twelve more times.

Next row: (RS) K2, k2tog, yo, remove m, knit to end.

Work in St st until piece measures 11" from CO, ending with a WS row.

SHAPE SLEEVES

Inc row: (RS) K2, M1L, knit to last 2 sts, M1R, k2—2 sts inc'd.

Rep Inc row every RS row 2 more times—120 (128, 137, 146, 157, 168) sts.

Next row: (WS) Purl.

Using the cable method, CO 3 sts at beg of next 2 rows—126 (134, 143, 152, 163, 174) sts.

Next row: (RS) Knit.

Next row: (WS) K3, purl to last 3 sts, k3.

Inc row: (RS) K4, M1L, knit to last 4 sts, M1R, k4—2 sts inc'd.

Keeping 3 sts at each armhole edge in garter st (knit every row), rep Inc row every 10 (10, 10, 10, 12, 12)th row 5 more times—138 (146, 155, 164, 175, 186) sts.

Work even until sleeve measures 7 (7½, 8, 8½, 9, 9½)" from last sleeve CO, ending with a WS row.

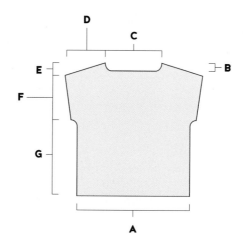

A: 18¼ (19½, 21, 22½, 24¼, 26)"

B: 1¼ "

C: 9¼ (9½, 9½, 10, 10, 11)"

D: 6½ (7, 7¾, 8¼, 9, 9½)"

E: 2"

F: 7 (7½, 8, 8½, 9, 9½)"

G: 11¾"

SHAPE SHOULDERS AND NECK

BO 5 (6, 6, 7, 7, 8) sts at beg of next 6 rows—108 (110, 119, 122, 133, 138) sts rem.

Next row: (RS) BO 5 (5, 6, 6, 7, 7) sts, k26 (26, 30, 30, 34, 34), join 2nd ball of yarn, BO center 46 (48, 47, 50, 51, 56) sts, knit to end—26 (26, 30, 30, 34, 34) sts rem for right shoulder and 31 (31, 36, 36, 41, 41) sts rem for left shoulder.

Left shoulder

At beg of WS rows, BO 5 (5, 6, 6, 7, 7) sts 5 times, **_at the same time_**, BO 3 sts at neck edge 2 times—no sts rem.

Right shoulder

At beg of RS rows, BO 5 (5, 6, 6, 7, 7) sts 4 times, **_at the same time_**, BO 3 sts at neck edge 2 times—no sts rem.

Front

With smaller straight needles and using the cable method, CO 114 (122, 131, 140, 151, 162) sts.

Work in Garter st for 5 rows.

Next row: (WS) K43, pm, knit to end.

Change to larger needles.

BEG LEFT-SLANTING LACE PATT

Row 1: (RS) Knit to m, sl m, *yo, ssk, k1; rep from * to last st, k1.

Row 2 and all WS rows: Purl.

Row 3: Knit to m, sl m, k1, *yo, ssk, k1; rep from * to last 3 sts, k3.

Row 5: Knit to m, sl m, k2, *yo, ssk, k1; rep from * to last 2 sts, k2.

Row 7: Knit to m, remove m, k3, pm, *yo, ssk, k1; rep from * to last st, k1.

Row 9: Knit to m, sl m, k1, *yo, ssk, k1; rep from * to last 3 sts, k3.

Row 11: Knit to m, sl m, k2, *yo, ssk, k1; rep from * to last 2 sts, k2.

Row 12: Purl.

Rep Rows 7–12 eleven more times.

Next row: (RS) Knit to m, remove m, k3, yo, ssk, k2.

Work in St st until piece measures 11" from CO, ending with a WS row.

Complete as for back.

Finishing

Block pieces.

Sew shoulder and side seams.

With smaller cir needle and RS facing, beg at shoulder seam and pick up and knit 136 (140, 138, 144, 146, 156) sts evenly around neck edge.

Purl 1 rnd.

Knit 1 rnd.

Purl 1 rnd.

BO all sts.

Weave in ends.

tinctoria tee

Sachiko Burgin

Finished Size

Bust circumference: 44½ (49½, 55½, 61, 66)".

Tee shown measures 44½" bust circumference, modeled with 12½" of positive ease.

Yarn

Worsted weight (#4 medium).

Shown here: Mirasol Pima Kuri (100% cotton; 208 yd [190 m]/100 g): #02 Greenwood Lake, 4 (5, 5, 6, 6) skeins.

Needles

Size U.S. 9 (5.5 mm).

Size U.S. 8 (5 mm): 16" circular (cir.).

Adjust needle size if necessary to obtain the correct gauge.

Notions

Markers (m); stitch holders or waste yarn; tapestry needle.

Gauge

16½ sts and 22 rows = 4" in St st on larger needles.

Notes

■ This top is worked back and forth in two separate pieces from the bottom up and seamed.

■ During shoulder shaping, when there are not enough stitches to complete both a yarnover and its paired decrease, work these stitches in stockinette stitch instead.

Back

With larger needles, CO 92 (102, 114, 126, 136) sts.

Next row: (WS) P2, k1, p1, knit to last 4 sts, p1, k1, p2.

Next row: (RS) K2, p1, knit to last 3 sts, p1, k2.

Next row: (WS) P2, k1, p1, place marker (pm), k24, pm, k36 (46, 58, 70, 80), pm, k24, pm, p1, k1, p2.

Next row: (RS) K2, p1, k1, sl m, work Chart A over 24 sts, sl m, knit to m, sl m, work Chart A over 24 sts, sl m, k1, p1, k2.

Cont in patt as est until Rows 1–8 of chart have been worked 5 (5, 5, 6, 6) times, then substitute Chart B for Chart A and work Rows 1–28 of chart 3 times, then change back to Chart A and work until piece measures 28 (28, 28, 29½, 29½)" from CO, ending with a WS row.

SHAPE SHOULDERS

BO 10 (11, 13, 14, 16) sts at beg of next 4 rows, then BO 10 (12, 13, 15, 15) sts at beg of next 2 rows—32 (34, 36, 40, 42) sts rem.

BO all sts.

Front

Work as for back until Rows 1–8 of Chart A have been worked 2 (2, 2, 3, 3) times, then substitute Chart B for Chart A and work Rows 1–28 of chart 3 times, then change back to Chart A and work until piece measures 21 (21, 21, 22½, 22½)" from CO, ending with a WS row.

SHAPE NECK

Next row: (RS) Work 34 (38, 43, 47, 51) sts in patt and place these sts on holder for left shoulder, BO 24 (26, 28, 32, 34) sts, work to end—34 (38, 43, 47, 51) sts rem for right shoulder.

RIGHT SHOULDER

Work 1 WS row.

Dec row: (RS) K1, ssk, work to end—1 st dec'd.

Rep Dec row every RS row 3 more times—30 (34, 39, 43, 47) sts rem.

Work even until piece measures 24 (24, 24, 25½, 25½)" from CO, ending with a RS row.

SHAPE SHOULDER

At beg of WS rows, BO 10 (11, 13, 14, 16) sts 2 times, then BO 10 (12, 13, 15, 15) sts once—no sts rem.

LEFT SHOULDER

Return 34 (38, 43, 47, 51) sts to needle and, with WS facing, rejoin yarn.

Work 1 WS row.

Dec row: (RS) Work to last 3 sts, k2tog, k1—1 st dec'd.

Rep Dec row every RS row 3 more times—30 (34, 39, 43, 47) sts rem.

Work even until piece measures 24 (24, 24, 25½, 25½)" from CO, ending with a WS row.

SHAPE SHOULDER

At beg of RS rows, BO 10 (11, 13, 14, 16) sts 2 times, then BO 10 (12, 13, 15, 15) sts once—no sts rem.

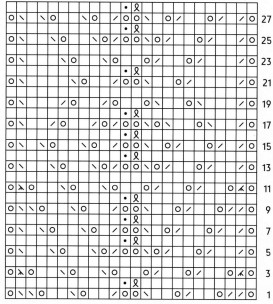

CHART A

24 sts

CHART B

24 sts

□ k on RS; p on WS		∕ k2tog
• k on WS		＼ ssk
ℛ p1tbl on WS		⋏ k3tog
○ yo		⋌ sl 1 kwise, k2tog, psso

Finishing

Sew shoulder seams.

NECKBAND

With RS facing and cir needle, beg at left shoulder seam, pick up and knit 18 sts evenly along left front neck edge, 24 (26, 28, 32, 34) sts along center front BO sts, 18 sts along right front neck edge, and 32 (34, 36, 40, 42) sts along back neck—92 (96, 100, 108, 112) sts. Pm and join in the rnd.

Work in k2, p2 rib for 1½".

BO all sts in patt.

Beg 7 (7½, 8, 8½, 9)" down from shoulder seam, sew sides of back and front tog for 7½ (7, 6½, 7½, 7)", ending 9½" above CO edge of front and 13½" above CO edge of back.

Weave in ends and block to measurements.

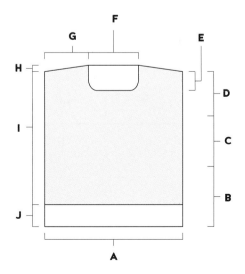

A: 22¼ (24¾, 27¾, 30½, 33)"

B: 13½"

C: 7½ (7, 6½, 7½, 7)"

D: 7 (7½, 8, 8½, 9)"

E: 3"

F: 7¾ (8¼, 8¾, 9¾, 10¼)"

G: 7¼ (8¼, 9½, 10½, 11½)"

H: 1"

I: 24 (24, 24, 25½, 25½)"

J: 4"

kricka top

Sherrie Kibler

Finished Size

Width: 29¾ (31, 32¼)".

Height: 15½ (16¼, 18¾)" tall.

Top shown measures 31".

Yarn

Fingering weight (#2 fine).

Shown here: Blue Moon Fiber Arts Woobu (60% Merino wool, 40% bamboo; 620 yd [567 m]/8 oz [226 g]): neptune, 2 skeins.

Needles

Size U.S. 6 (4 mm): 32" circular (cir).

Adjust needle size if necessary to obtain the correct gauge.

Notions

Markers (m); tapestry needle.

Gauge

19 sts and 19 rows = 4" in Indian Cross st.

Notes

■ This top is worked in two identical pieces, then the shoulder and side seams are sewn.

■ The crosses in the stitch pattern are worked by pulling three stitches through the center of three adjacent stitches. Because the crosses happen on wrong-side rows, the Left Cross will slant to the right on the right side and the Right Cross will slant to the left on the right side.

■ Work the three border stitches on each side of the front and back loosely to ease edge tension and aid in blocking.

■ A circular needle is used to accommodate the large number of stitches.

Seed Stitch: (even number of sts)

Row 1: (RS) *K1, p1; rep from * to end

Row 2: (WS) *P1, k1; rep from * to end.

Rep Rows 1 and 2 for patt.

Left Cross: Sl 6 sts pwise, dropping extra wraps.

Insert left needle from left to right into 4th, 5th, and 6th sts on right needle and pull these sts over first 3 sts on right needle and onto left needle. Transfer 3 sts from right needle to left needle. P6, being careful to keep sts in new order.

Right Cross: Sl 6 sts pwise, dropping extra wraps.

Transfer 6 sts to left needle. Insert right needle from right to left into 4th, 5th, and 6th sts on left needle and pull these sts over first 3 sts on left needle and onto right needle. Transfer 3 sts from right needle to left needle. P6, being careful to keep sts in new order.

Indian Cross Stitch: (multiple of 6 sts + 4)

Row 1: (RS) Knit.

Row 2: (WS) Purl.

Row 3: K2, *k1, wrapping yarn 3 times around needle; rep from * to last 2 sts, k2.

Row 4: P2, *Left Cross; rep from * to last 2 sts, p2.

Rows 5-7: Rep Rows 1-3.

Row 8: P2, *Right Cross; rep from * to last 2 sts, p2.

Rep Rows 1-8 for patt.

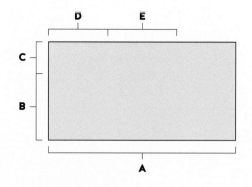

A: 29¾ (31, 32¼)"

B: 10½ (10¼, 10¾)"

C: 5 (6, 8)"

D: 9½ (9½, 9¾)"

E: 11 (12, 13)"

Back

Using the long-tail method, CO 142 (148, 154) sts. Do not join.

Work 6 rows in Seed st (see Stitch Guide).

Next row: (RS) K1, p1, k1 (see Notes), place marker (pm), work Indian Cross st (see Stitch Guide) to last 3 sts, pm, p1, k1, p1.

Next row: P1, k1, p1, sl m, work in patt to m, sl m, k1, p1, k1.

Cont in patt until Rows 1–8 of patt have been worked 8 (8, 10) times, then work Rows 1–2 (1–6, 1–2) once more—piece measures about 14¾ (15½, 18)" from CO.

Work 6 rows in Seed st.

Using Jeny's surprisingly stretchy method, BO all sts.

Front

Work as for back.

Finishing

Weave in ends.

Block pieces to measurements.

Sew 9½ (9½, 9¾)" shoulder seams on each side, leaving center 11 (12, 13)" unsewn for neck opening.

Sew side seams for 10½ (10¼, 10¾)" from lower edge, leaving 5 (6, 8)" unsewn for armholes.

puck's tunic

Susanna IC

Finished Size

Bust circumference: 32½ (36, 40½, 44, 48½, 52, 56½)".

Tunic shown measures 36", modeled with 4" of positive ease.

Yarn

DK weight (#3 light).

Shown here: Juniper Moon Farm Zooey (60% cotton, 40% linen; 248 yd [260 m]/3½ oz [100 g]): #06 sel gris, 3 (3, 3, 3, 4, 4, 4) balls.

Needles

Size U.S. 6 (4 mm).

Adjust needle size if necessary to obtain the correct gauge.

Notions

Markers (m); tapestry needle.

Gauge

18 sts and 26 rows = 4" in St st; Lace chart = 5½" wide.

Notes

▪ This tunic is worked back and forth in separate pieces and seamed.

▪ Slip stitches purlwise with yarn in back.

STITCH GUIDE

Border Pattern:

Row 1: (RS) Sl 1 (see Notes), k2tog, yo, knit to last 3 sts, yo, ssk, k1.

Row 2: (WS) Sl 1, knit to end.

Rep Rows 1 and 2 for patt.

Front

CO 71 (79, 89, 97, 107, 115, 125) sts.

Work Border patt (see Stitch Guide) for 6 rows, ending with a WS row.

Next row: (RS) Sl 1, k2tog, yo, k21 (25, 30, 34, 39, 43, 48), place marker (pm), work Lace chart over 23 sts, pm, k21 (25, 30, 34, 39, 43, 48), yo, ssk, k1.

Next row: (WS) Sl 1, k6, purl to last 7 sts, k7.

Cont in patt as est until piece measures 23½ (23½, 24, 24, 24½, 24½, 25)" from CO, ending with a WS row.

Work Border patt for 4 rows.

BO all sts.

Back

Work as for front.

Finishing

Weave in ends.

Block pieces to measurements.

Sew 3 (3½, 4½, 5, 6, 6½, 7½)" shoulder seams.

Sew side seams starting 8 (8, 8½, 8½, 9, 9, 9½)" from shoulder seam, leaving 5" vents at bottom.

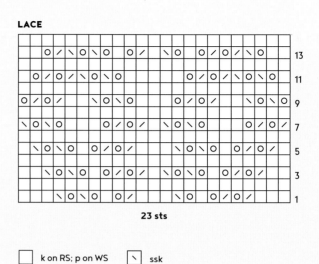

LACE

23 sts

| | k on RS; p on WS | | ssk |
| | k2tog | | yo |

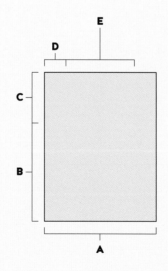

A: 16¼ (18, 20¼, 22, 24¼, 26, 28¼)"

B: 15½"

C: 8 (8, 8½, 8½, 9, 9, 9½)"

D: 3 (3½, 4½, 5, 6, 6½, 7½)"

E: 10¼ (11, 11¼, 12, 12¼, 13, 13¼)"

about the designers

In addition to her design career, **GRACE AKHREM** teaches locally and nationally. You can find her blog, patterns, and teaching schedule at www.graceakhrem.com.

MEGHAN BABIN is an enthusiastic knitter, reader, hiker, pretend cook, lover of New York–style pizza, Wyoming-raised buffalo steak, Hot Kitchen chicken, spicy cumin lamb noodles, Shamrock buffalo wings, Colorado craft beer, bourbon, PBR, and the friendships that led her to these discoveries. She is also the editor of *Interweave Knits*.

HANNAH BAKER is the editor of *knitscene* magazine. Along with knitting, she enjoys reading, singing, friendship, and time spent with her black lab named Girlfriend.

AMANDA BELL is trying to master the art of knitting with her feet to leave her hands free for infant/toddler wrangling. Or maybe vice versa.

REBECCA BLAIR lives in Alberta, Canada, and has always drawn inspiration from stranded colorwork mittens from the Baltic countries.

KIYOMI BURGIN is a knitter and fiber craft enthusiast from Toronto, Canada. See her work at www.kiyomiburgin.com.

SACHIKO BURGIN lives in Toronto, Canada, and works part-time at Romni Wools. Despite having a degree in jewelry and metalsmithing, these days she prefers to work with yarn.

CASSIE CASTILLO lives in North Carolina with her husband and dog. When she isn't knitting, you can find her sewing, gardening, or baking bread. You can visit her website at www.azaleaandrosebudknits.com.

MARI CHIBA relearned to knit as a Peace Corps Volunteer in Armenia. Her passion for design flourished while she was teaching English in China, and now she knits from her home in Raleigh, North Carolina. Learn more about Mari and her designs at www.mariknits.com or on Ravelry as MariChiba.

CHERYL CHOW admits to being a crafting addict. She can be found knitting, crocheting, spinning, sewing, and quilting near Seattle, Washington. In her spare time, she enjoys the outdoors, where she looks for inspiration and takes in the beautiful Northwest scenery with her family.

AMY CHRISTOFFERS is the author of *New American Knits: Classic Sportswear Patterns* and is savoryknitting on Ravelry. She blogs at www.savoryknitting.com.

EVELYN A. CLARK lives in the Northwest, where she loves to knit lace shawls.

THEA COLMAN is babycocktails on Ravelry and can be found at www.babycocktails. blogspot.com.

JENN EMERSON is a knitwear designer living in Pittsburgh, Pennsylvania. Her designs focus on classic silhouettes with a modern twist. She can be found on Ravelry as JennEmerson.

MOIRA ENGEL lives and designs on the magnificent West Coast of Canada. She has knitted since the age of nine. Over time, knitting and designing have been hobby, business, obsession, and therapy! Being the wife of a tugboat captain for thirty-three years and mom to two delightful children has helped to inspire serviceable, snuggly knits for soggy, foggy west-coast weather.

VANESSA EWING has recently been appointed Design Director at Plymouth Yarn Company. Find her on Ravelry as vanessaewing.

A native of the Pacific Northwest, **JARED FLOOD** is an artist, a photographer, and a knitwear designer living in Brooklyn. He has published designs in both books and magazines and is the creator of Brooklyn Tweed, at www.brooklyntweed.com.

NORAH GAUGHAN was born in New York City, raised in the Hudson Valley, schooled in Rhode Island and has wandered about New England, knitting, ever since. Her duties as design director at Berroco take her to northern Rhode Island for most of the week, while the call of husband, home, and cats keeps her in New Hampshire for the remainder.

KATE GAGNON OSBORN is the co-owner of Kelbourne Woolens. She designs regularly for *Interweave Knits*, *knitscene* and *knit.wear*, as a contribution designer to many books and as part of the Kelbourne Woolens design team. She lives and knits in Flourtown, Pennsylvania.

GENERAL HOGBUFFER'S professional background is in fashion design. His grandmother taught him the basics of knitting as a child, but he didn't take it up seriously until 2007. Almost immediately, he became fascinated by sock knitting. Discovering how various design elements work with the specific shape of the foot and finding alternative ways to construct the classic sock shape have been the two main goals of his designs so far.

MARIE GODSEY is an avid knitter who learned to knit in high school. She specializes in socks and accessories. Look for her other work published at www. normallyabnormalknits.com.

TANIS GRAY lives in Alexandria, Virginia, with her mechanical engineer husband, her son, her daughter, and her lazy pug. She is currently writing her eighth knitting book, photographing knitting books for others, and sewing project bags for her Etsy shop. Find out more at www.tanisknits.com.

ALISON GREEN is part of the Berroco design team. She has been working in the knitting industry since 2002 as a designer, teacher, and technical editor.

LAURA GRUTZECK lives and knits in Philadelphia, Pennsylvania. Find her on Ravelry as Laara.

By day, **AMY GUNDERSON** works as creative director for Universal Yarn. By night, she knits like crazy and hangs out with her husband and their two insane dogs. Red wine and lots of TV may also be involved.

Some of the elements that **ANGELA HAHN** enjoys including in her designs are texture and lace worked in unexpected directions, unusual methods of shaping, and decreases and increases worked into stitch patterns. You can find more of her patterns on her website, www.knititude.com.

HUNTER HAMMERSEN didn't really like knitting the first time she tried it. She didn't much care for it the second time either. It wasn't till the third time, and the discovery of knitted socks, that she was properly smitten. Once she realized she could make up her own patterns, her fate was sealed. She's been busy designing ever since. You can find her work at ViolentlyDomestic.com.

ANNE HANSON, Knitspot owner and designer, is a lifelong knitter with a background in fashion and graphic design. She teaches and writes about knitting, spinning, and designing on her blog at www.knitspot.com. Anne lives and works in Ohio with David, who loves wool, too. Together, they are the owners and creators of the Ensemble Designer collection, the renowned Knitspot yarn clubs, and the Bare Naked Wools yarn collection.

AMY HERZOG is the author of *Knit to Flatter* (STC Craft, 2013), and you can find more about how to make sweaters you will love to wear at www.amyherzogdesigns.com.

ROSEMARY (ROMI) HILL learned to knit lace in 2005, and that kindled her true passion for fiber and needles! Romi is the author of *Elements of Style* and *New Lace Knitting*, and her work has appeared in numerous publications, among them *Knitty*, *knitscene*, *Interweave Knits*, and *Twist Collective*. Find out more at designsbyromi.com.

MEGHAN HUBER lives in Salem, Massachusetts, and is pursuing a doctoral degree in bioengineering. She loves colorwork and textures, and she is constantly experimenting with ways to combine the two in her knitting. Find her on Ravelry or at www.newenglandknitting.com.

SUSANNA IC has an extensive collection of studio arts and art history degrees as well as a rather large yarn stash. Her projects and designs can be found on Ravelry as zuzusus, and at www.artqualia.com.

BRISTOL IVY is a knitting designer and teacher from Portland, Maine. Her work focuses on the intersection of classic tailoring and innovative technique. You can find out more about her and her work at www.bristolivy.com.

ALLISON JANE can be found on Ravelry as vexcon, or under the designer name Allison Jane.

YOKO JOHNSTON is a Japanese knitter living in Australia with her husband and two children. Besides knitting, she teaches Japanese and plays table tennis.

SARAH JORDAN is a recovering sock addict living in Pittsburgh, Pennsylvania. She blogs at www.paknitwit.blogspot.com and can be found on Ravelry as PAKnitWit.

COURTNEY KELLEY is part owner of Woolens. See more of her work at www.kelbournewoolens.com.

SHERRIE KIBLER comes from a family of knitters inspired by Morticia, the prolific knitter of the original *Addams Family* television show. A trained engineer and high school pre-engineering teacher, she enjoys using her knitting skills to create designs that focus on simple, clear solutions to knitting challenges.

ISABELL KRAEMER writes at owlsisters.blogspot.com and can be found on Ravelry at www.ravelry.com/designers/isabell-kraemer

Designer **KYLE KUNNECKE** has a not-so-secret passion for color work. Tirelessly creative, he puts himself to sleep at night dreaming of new design concepts, collaborations, and outreach projects. Through his fiber workshops, he provides inspiration to his students, exploring the skills necessary to continue their personal knitting journeys. His patterns are published in numerous knitting books and magazines, by yarn companies, and under his label, Kyle William. Learn more about Kyle and his work at www.kylewilliam.com.

MELISSA LABARRE is a freelance knitwear designer and work-at-home mama. She is co-author of the books *Weekend Hats*, *New England Knits*, and *Weekend Wraps*, all from Interweave. Her designs have been published in *knitscene* and *Vogue Knitting* as well as in design collections for Quince & Co, Classic Elite, Valley Yarns, Blue Sky Alpacas, Brooklyn Tweed, and other yarn companies. She lives in Massachusetts with her husband and two children. knittingschooldropout.com

ADRIENNE LARSEN works as a knitting instructor and yarn guru at Prairie Yarns in Fargo, North Dakota. She lives with her loving husband and industrious ferret. She published her first book, *Welts & Waves*, in 2015; her second book, *Flutter & Flow*, featuring lace designs was published in 2017.

QUENNA LEE is a freelance knitwear designer based in Northern California. Her work has appeared in *knitscene*, *Interweave Knits*, *Twist Collective*, and Knit Picks. Read more about her crafting endeavors at www.blissfulbyquenna.com.

RACHEL LEGGETT is an avid knitter and crafter of things. She dabbles in sewing and spinning, has recently become obsessed with cross-stitch, and is the one-woman show behind the Arbor Twist line of yarns and knitting patterns.

HEATHER LODINSKY has designed for many yarn companies and magazines for almost 20 years. She is the author of *150 Knit and Crochet Motifs* (Interweave) which has been published in 5 languages. She is also the designer of the popular "Central Park Hoodie" cardigan. Heather lives in Buffalo, New York with her family and teaches 3 times a week at the Elmwood Yarn Shop in Buffalo.

JEN LUCAS has been designing just about as long as she has been knitting. She is the author of the book *Sock—Yarn Shawls* (Martingale, 2013). Visit her website at www.jenlucasdesigns.com.

JESSIE MCKITRICK is a knitwear designer living in Edmonton, Alberta, Canada, with her husband, two daughters, and lots of wool. She loves reading design schematics for fun, and writes about knitting, crochet, spinning, and other things she likes at www.grammargrouse.blogspot.ca.

AMY MILLER is a stay-at-home mom with two little kids. When she's not busy with her family, she's designing sweaters and renovating her nearly one-hundred-year-old house. See more of her designs on Ravelry as amymiller.

LISA R. MYERS lives in Philadelphia, Pennsylvania, where she works with the cooperatives of Manos del Uruguay as their United States distributor.

MEGAN NODECKER is a knitwear designer who has been creating and publishing patterns for the past seven years. She lives in the cloudy and wet Pacific Northwest, and the temperamental climate has fueled her love for all things cozy.

DEBBIE O'NEILL is a software engineer by day and designer by night. She lives in Boulder, Colorado, where she enjoys raising a family and pursuing all sorts of crafty endeavors.

JESIE OSTERMILLER has been knitting nonstop since the day in high school she found a family friend to teach her. She tells stories of her many mistakes made in the years since, such as sorting out the yarnovers she accidentally made every other stitch when she knit her first ribbed hat and how gauge finally clicked (after years of just knitting with any yarn at hand) when she wrote out the many sizes for her first published sweater. Such moments are instructive, for they are reminders of how far you can travel in mastering the craft when you take little setbacks as encouragement to improve.

SHIRLEY PADEN is the author of *Knitwear Design Workshop* (Interweave). She lives in New York City.

BEATRICE PERRON DAHLEN lives in Southern Maine with her family. She studied fibers, photography, and sculpture at Massachusetts College of Art in Boston, where she received her BFA. Find her on Ravelry as beatrice2009 and at www.threadandladle.com.

ANNE PODLESAK knits, spins, and designs in the mountains of northern New Mexico. She is the author of several self-published collections as well as *Free Spirit Knits* from Interweave. She is also the indie dyer behind Wooly Wonka Fiber. Woolywonkafiber.com

KEPHREN PRITCHETT has been knitting nonstop for ten years and making her own designs for almost as long. Because she enjoys the challenge of finding a seamless solution to every design idea, she specializes in seamless construction.

ASHLEY RAO is an architect and avid knitter in Boston, Massachusetts. See more of her work at www.ashleyraoknits. wix.com/knits.

ANDREA RANGEL is a knitwear designer and teacher. She's the author of *Rugged Knits* and *AlterKnits Stitch Dictionary* (Interweave), and her patterns have been published in *Interweave Knits*, *knitscene*, Brooklyn Tweed's *Wool People*, *Twist Collective*, and other publications, as well as independently. She lives on Vancouver Island in British Columbia.

LAURA REINBACH is a native Floridian who now resides in a small town in Maine with her husband and four boys. Although she may complain of the cold from time to time, she is very grateful to wear her knitted items most of the year, and she really enjoys the creative outlet designing knitwear provides. Find her at www. LauraReinbach.com.

Originally from the Midwest, **AMANDA SCHEUZGER** now lives in beautiful Maine. She is a freelance designer, architect, and mother to two active boys. Find her online at www.handmaineknits.com.

BONNIE SENNOTT is an artist and knitwear designer based in western Massachusetts. Find her online at www. bluepeninsula knits.com and on Ravelry as bluepeninsula.

LISA SHROYER is a lifelong knitter who works in media as a writer and director.

SARAH SOLOMON lives in New York City, where she designs and teaches knitting. You can find her designs on Ravelry as Sarah Solomon Designs and on her blog at www.intothewool.wordpress.com.

COURTNEY SPAINHOWER is a stay-at-home mom, knitting instructor, and the lady behind Pink Brutus Knits. She recently authored her first book, *Family-Friendly Knits* with Interweave. Pinkbrutus.com

Visit **CARINA SPENCER** at www.carinaspencer.com

KATHLEEN SPERLING'S obsessive love of knitting led her to designing, where she constantly finds inspiration.

KRISTEN TENDYKE designs classic sweaters with unique construction and easy-to-follow, enjoyable patterns. She specializes in seamless knitting and always keeps Mother Nature in mind when making yarn choices. See more of her patterns and read her blog at www.kristentendyke.com.

MERCEDES TERESOVICH-CLARK is a designer and writer living in Birmingham, Alabama. Visit her website at www.mercedesknits.com.

ELA TORRENTE lives and works with her family in northern Italy. She is a mom, an independent knitwear designer, a yarn maniac, and an amateur chef. She has published her designs on Ravelry since 2010. Meet her on the Modish People Group on Ravelry or follow her on www.modishknits.com.

ANNIE WATTS lives, plays, and daydreams for Wattsolak Designs in Lafayette, Colorado. She spends most of her days making things up as she goes.

HOLLI YEOH is a Vancouver knitwear designer who has been self-publishing knitting patterns and teaching knitting techniques for well over a decade. In 2014, Holli collaborated with SweetGeorgia Yarns to publish *Tempest*, a sophisticated collection of knitting patterns for women. Her designs appear regularly in books and magazines including *Vogue Knitting, Noro* Magazine, and several of the *60 Quick* series of books (Sixth&Spring Books) as well as the online magazines *Knitty* and *Twist Collective*. Holliyeoh.com.

HEATHER ZOPPETTI, author of *Unexpected Cables* and *Everyday Lace*, both from Interweave, lives and works in Lancaster, Pennsylvania, with her husband and yarn collection. She is the owner of Stitch Sprouts. Stitchsprouts.com and hzoppettidesigns.com.

abbreviations

The following are the most common abbreviations that appear in this book. For other terms be sure to check individual pattern stitch guides. For more advanced techniques or terms you don't know, please visit the glossary at Interweave for more information. **www.interweave.com/interweave-knitting-glossary/**

beg(s) begin(s); beginning

BO bind off

CC contrast color

cir circular

cm centimeter(s)

cn cable needle

CO cast on

cont continue(s); continuing

dec(s)('d) decrease(s); decreasing; decreased

dpn double-pointed needles

foll follow(s); following

g gram(s)

inc(s)('d) increase(s); increasing; increase(d)

k knit

k1f&b knit into the front and back of the same

stitch (increase)

k2tog knit two stitches together (decrease)

kwise knitwise; as if to knit

m marker

mm millimeter(s)

M1 make one (increase)

M1L make one with left slant (increase)

M1P make one purlwise (increase)

M1R make one with right slant (increase)

oz ounce

p purl

p1f&b purl into the front and back of the same stitch (increase)

p2tog purl two stitches together (decrease)

patt(s) pattern(s)

pm place marker

psso pass slipped stitch over

pwise purlwise; as if to purl

rem remain(s); remaining

rep repeat(s); repeating

Rev St st reverse stockinette stitch

rnd(s) round(s)

RS right side

sl slip

st(s) stitch(es)

St st stockinette stitch

tbl through back loop

tog together

w&t wrap and turn

WS wrong side

wyb with yarn in back

wyf with yarn in front

yd yard(s)

yo yarnover

* repeat starting point

* * repeat all instructions between asterisks

( ) alternate measurements and/or instructions

[ ] work instructions as a group a specified number of times

Expand your knitting library with must-have resources!

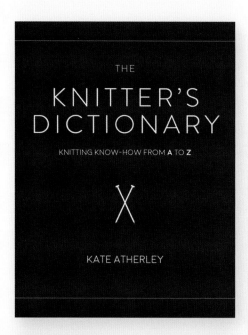

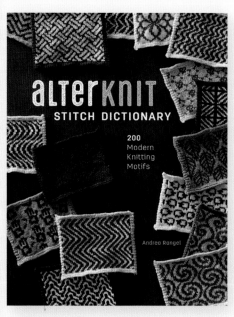

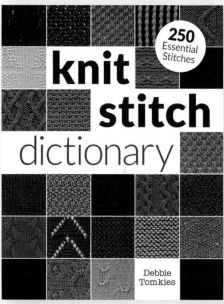